# Russia

## modern architectures in history

This international series examines the forms and consequences of modern architecture. Modernist visions and revisions are explored in their national context against a backdrop of aesthetic currents, economic developments, political trends and social movements. Written by experts in the architectures of the respective countries, the series provides a fresh, critical reassessment of Modernism's positive and negative effects, as well as the place of architectural design in twentieth-century history and culture.

Series editor: Vivian Constantinopoulos

Already published:

*Brazil*
Richard J. Williams

*Britain*
Alan Powers

*Finland*
Roger Connah

*France*
Jean-Louis Cohen

*Greece*
Alexander Tzonis and Alcestis P. Rodi

*India*
Peter Scriver and Amit Srivastava

*Italy*
Diane Ghirardo

*Russia*
Richard Anderson

*Turkey*
Sibel Bozdoğan and Esra Akcan

*USA*
Gwendolyn Wright

# Russia

modern architectures in history

Richard Anderson

REAKTION BOOKS

*For Tara, with love*

Published by Reaktion Books Ltd
Unit 32, Waterside
44–48 Wharf Road
London N1 7UX, UK

www.reaktionbooks.co.uk

First published 2015


Printed and bound in Great Britain by Bell & Bain, Glasgow

A catalogue record for this book is available from the British Library

ISBN 978 1 78023 503 5

# Contents

М
МЕТРО

# Introduction

Russia's relationship to modern architecture is complicated. The country was an undisputed epicentre of architectural creativity during the 1920s, its leaders later enforced explicitly anti-modernist tendencies and the urban landscape of Soviet socialism has, in the popular imagination, become synonymous with the bankruptcy of modern architecture's aspirations. The Italian periodical *Casabella-continuità* conveyed the complexity of this relationship on the cover of its April 1962 issue, which showed Vladimir Tatlin's strikingly original *Monument to the Third International* superimposed on an image of Lev Rudnev's monumental Moscow State University. Today one finds a heterogeneous mix of attitudes among Russia's architects: some aspire to the quality and sophistication of the modernist vernacular of the international scene; others to the quality and sophistication of ancient Rome and Renaissance Florence. All of this indicates that the story of Russia's relationship to modern architecture cannot be told as the evolutionary development of a unitary idea. Instead, it is a story marked by rapid change, nearly inexplicable reversals of opinion and long periods, such as the allegedly 'stagnant' 1970s, when it may appear that nothing happens at all. The particular shape of this story derives from the tumultuous transformations in politics, culture, society and economy that Russia experienced in the 150 years covered by this book. The complexity of this story has confounded many observers of Russian architecture. I think it makes the story more interesting.

This book takes the symbolic year 1861, which marked the beginning of Russia's era of Great Reforms, as its starting point and traces the transformations in Russian architecture up to the present. Such a time frame is unusual in writing about architecture in Russia, which tends to be divided into a rigid set of periods. Historians, particularly those trained in the Soviet Union, commonly treated nineteenth-century architecture, early twentieth-century architecture and architecture of the Soviet era as separate fields of inquiry. We do not yet have a historiography of post-Soviet Russian architecture, but the writing that exists tends to emphasize the novelty and importance of new market conditions as key elements of a new period for Russian architecture. While respecting and describing

Arbat Square, Moscow, mid-1930s.

*Casabella-continuità*, no. 262 (1962); issue dedicated to the USSR.

the radical breaks and turning points in Russia's history – the revolution of October 1917 or the death of Joseph Stalin in 1953, for instance – this book also highlights continuities across successive phases of Russian architectural culture. In order to do this effectively, it reaches back into the second half of the nineteenth century, to the era when Russian architects first established the professional organizations and platforms for the dissemination of architectural knowledge that would have definitive consequences for later architectural production. Similarly, it extends beyond the collapse of the USSR in 1991 and explores some of the ways in which the architectural culture of the Soviet Union survives today. This book thus provides a comprehensive, though not exhaustive, account of Russian architecture from the first stages of its modernization to the present.

The constitution of Russian architecture in this time span is not self-evident. Between the late nineteenth century and today, Russia transformed from one of the largest empires in world history to the largest and most dominant republic of the Soviet Union and ultimately into the Russian Federation as we know it. Each of these changes gave Russia a new territorial definition, requiring us to be sensitive to the shifting geography of the national field in which Russian architectural practice unfolded. Political borders were at times less stable than buildings, and structures built in one country might endure in another. This happened to the Russian-Baltic Shipbuilding Factory, designed by the Russian architect Aleksandr Dmitriev, built in Riga from 1911 to 1914. After four years of wartime operation, it suddenly found itself in a Latvian republic that was fighting for independence. And after 1940, when the Latvian Soviet Socialist Republic was established, its location became part of the USSR. I have sought to be as inclusive as possible in the selection of buildings and projects for discussion, and I count Dmitriev's factory and many other buildings in similar predicaments as part of the story of Russian architecture.

The interpretive challenge posed by shifting national borders is compounded by the ideology of internationalism that underpinned the self-image of the USSR throughout much of its existence. The desire to lend primacy to the international context of culture and economy was inspired in part by the tradition of socialist organization – a position encapsulated in the memorable phrase from the *Communist Manifesto*, 'Workers of the world, unite!' Internationalism also allowed the Soviet Union to consciously represent itself as a new kind of state – one composed of many nations and peoples; one which might expand along with the projected success of the socialist experiment. Dziga Vertov captured the internationalist patriotism of the Soviet project in his film of 1926, *One Sixth of the World*, which offered a monumental and poetic vision of the USSR from the Baltic to the Caucasus and from the Black Sea to the Pacific Ocean.[1] Other cultural projects, such as the illustrated magazine *USSR in Construction*, reinforced the image of the Soviet Union as a unitary multinational state. An exemplary manifestation of these ambitions was the use of internationalist architectural forms for Soviet administrative buildings in republican capitals such as Kharkov (Ukranian: Kharkiv) and Baku.

A related, though more complex, problem emerges when we consider the work of Russian architects beyond imperial and national borders. Like other empires, Russia sponsored building projects in a variety of foreign territories. This includes the Orthodox churches of Mikhail Preobrazhenskii in Florence (1886–1903), Buenos Aires (1898–1901), Nice (1903–12) and other cities. Likewise, Russian architects were responsible for the design and development of the cities of Dalian and Kharbin, both in present-day China. In the Soviet period Russian architects worked both in the 'internal periphery' of the Union republics and in foreign nation states. Aleksei Shchusev, for example, designed the Marx-Engels-Lenin Institute in Tbilisi (1933–8), incorporating Georgian motifs into its decoration. In the 1950s, Soviet architects would design buildings in China, Poland and a number of other countries within the socialist camp. Later still, Moscow-based architects and design organizations created projects for cities in East Asia, the Middle East and on the African continent. A history of Russia's modern architecture must account for the many ways that it engaged with sites and cultures beyond its borders. Recent scholars have emphasized the international genealogy of the country's architecture by focusing on its long-standing relationship to 'the West'.[2] I take a broader view by attending to the relationship of Russian architecture to 'the world'. To do this, I acknowledge that the agency of Russian institutions – architectural offices, design institutes, government ministries and other organizations – was not confined within political borders but rather traversed them in myriad and complex ways. The incorporation of this broad range of architectural territories into this story tests the category of the nation as a matrix for understanding modern architecture's development. This book is thus an international history of a national architecture, albeit one that often aspired to project a new image of internationalism.

The term 'modern architecture' rarely appears in Russian architectural discourse. The major exception to this was the stylistic explosion of the late nineteenth and early twentieth centuries that is known in other countries as Art Nouveau, Jugendstil or *stile floreale* but as *stil modern* in Russia. *Stil modern* – literally 'modern style' – was a name that accurately conveyed the self-confident formal innovations of Russian architects, becoming a banner of pride for many. But after the exhaustion of this relatively short-lived fashion for whiplash lines and organic forms, the term *modern* acquired a negative connotation that would be diluted only when the style became fashionable in Russia once again in the 1980s and '90s. In Russia, the preferred label for what many outside observers would call 'modern architecture' was the rather neutral *sovremennaia arkhitektura* – translatable as either modern or, more directly, contemporary architecture. This was the name that the constructivists adopted for their journal in the 1920s, and this was how architects and critics classified their work throughout much of the Soviet period.[3] When, for example, the Congrès internationaux d'architecture moderne (CIAM), which provided a degree of coherence to what is commonly referred to as the 'modern movement', was unsuccessful at integrating Russian architects into the organization in the 1920s and early '30s, Russia was left without an analogous body able to promote the virtues of modern architecture. Russian critics would not directly address the modern movement or modernism as such until the late 1970s and early '80s, when it became necessary to contextualize postmodernism in relation to modernist practices.[4] These semantics are important because they manifest the specificity of Russian and Soviet architectural discourse. They also convey the unique experience of socialist modernity that was both the object and context for several generations of architectural work.

The particular relationship between architecture and socialism in Russia has generated wildly divergent interpretations. In the popular press, this relationship has been approached with scepticism. One reads, for example, that the Soviets had transformed Moscow into 'a stinking slum' in Hergé's comic novel *Tintin in the Land of the Soviets*, first published in 1930.[5] In historical writing both of and about the 1920s and early '30s, the experiment of state socialism and contemporary experiments in architecture are seen to go hand in hand. At this time, the Soviet Union appeared as the place where the dreams of modern architects – new industrial cities built by a planned economy, the rationalization of everyday life, state support for a new aesthetic – could be realized. This quasi-utopian view of the heroic 1920s has inspired generations of architects around the world, and it continues to be a primary lens through which twentieth-century architecture in Russia is viewed.

The decades after the 1920s are vexing for architects and architectural historians alike. The era of High Stalinism, roughly 1932–53, was disastrous for all of Soviet society, architects included. In addition to the policies that cost the Soviet Union millions of lives, the Communist Party, under Stalin's leadership, sought to dictate the norms of Soviet cultural

Aleksandr Dmitriev, Russian-Baltic Shipbuilding Factory, Riga, 1911–14.

life and creative practice. In the early 1930s Party officials took an active interest in architectural affairs, proscribing the radical innovations of the 1920s and demanding an approach to architecture that would 'critically assimilate the architectural heritage of the past'. This intervention into architectural culture irrevocably altered the course of twentieth-century architecture in the Soviet Union, directing it away from the path followed by modernist architects in the capitalist world. For many outside observers, this shift signalled the end of modern architecture in the Soviet Union. As a consequence, writing on Soviet architecture – particularly in the Anglophone world – has focused almost exclusively on the 1920s and early '30s. Typically only monuments from this period make it into histories of modern architecture, although there are signs that this is changing.[6] For a long time, when architecture of the Stalin era was discussed, it would be summarily dismissed as fundamentally anti-modern, considered simply irrelevant or met with incomprehension. Thankfully scholars have recently come to appreciate the complexity of architectural culture both under Stalin and in the following years.[7]

The world of Soviet architecture certainly was different from the capitalist worlds – first or third; developed or developing; north or south – in which 'modern architecture', with all its internal complexity and nuance, flourished. The relations among professional organizations, the building industry, the state and the population in the USSR produced concerns, habits, conventions, preoccupations and systems of values for Soviet architects that were specific to the milieu in which they emerged. In the relation to building types one can sense some of the differences between the world of Soviet architecture and that of the advanced capitalist world. The architect-designed single-family house, for example, has been a measure of architectural developments throughout the twentieth century in many countries. In the Soviet Union, however, this building type was – with certain extraordinary exceptions – virtually non-existent. Conversely Soviet architects were likely to spend much more of their time designing typified apartment buildings, workers' clubs and cinemas than their counterparts in the capitalist world. Soviet architects also worked within a specific system of client and patronage relationships. Private individuals, including architects themselves, almost never commissioned projects in the Soviet Union – the overwhelming majority of architectural work was funded by state, municipal, industrial or cooperative bodies. And in a most general sense, architecture was self-consciously invested with great ideological significance; it was often seen as the most visible manifestation of the 'construction of socialism'. The differences between architecture in the USSR and the capitalist worlds were by no means absolute, and this book highlights moments when the concerns of Soviet architects converged or, indeed, competed with the concerns of the international architectural community. This is thus not a story about what Soviet architectural culture prevented, though that is part of it, but rather about what it produced: a complex and contradictory system that made up the architecture of the second, or socialist, world.

The architecture of Soviet Russia is the focus of this book. Seven of its nine chapters are devoted to the Soviet decades. Arranged chronologically, each chapter begins with a discussion of the political, cultural and social events that shaped the context in which architects worked and to which architects responded. Each chapter then offers a set of thematic cross sections. Major themes such as housing and urban planning recur, but each chapter is organized according to the issues that are of most import to the period in question. The periodization adopted here departs slightly from the milestones in the political history of modern Russia. Chapter Seven, on architecture and de-Stalinization, concludes not with the removal of Nikita Khrushchev from office in 1964, but with the invasion of Prague in 1968 under Leonid Brezhnev. Likewise, the final chapter addresses Mikhail Gorbachev's *perestroika* (reconstruction) and the first decades of post-Soviet architecture as fundamentally related phenomena. The at times glacial pace of construction on major buildings in the Soviet Union poses some problems for periodization: the construction time of some buildings, such as Iurii Platonov's Presidium of the Academy of Sciences of the USSR in Moscow (1973–90), spans almost two chapters of the present volume. In these cases I have placed buildings in the chapter in which the issues they raise are most relevant. Effort has been made to include a range of buildings beyond the capitals of St Petersburg and Moscow; it is nevertheless true that the extreme centralization of architectural culture in the Soviet period meant that most architects worked in these cities and much of the most important architecture was built in them. The vast expanse of Russia's territory and its broad sphere of architectural influence have produced many significant buildings, projects and architects that could not be addressed. I hope this story raises questions for future work at the same time that it provides a framework for the further study of Russia's tremendous architectural legacy.

chapter one

# National Forms, Rational Techniques, 1861–95

The abolition of serfdom in 1861 initiated the era of Great Reforms that fundamentally transformed the nature of social, economic and administrative relations in the Russian Empire.[1] Although tsarist autocracy remained constant throughout the nineteenth century, Russia's modernization begins in the post-reform era. Newly created banks and railway networks supported rapid industrialization and an expansion of commerce. The populations of St Petersburg and Moscow bloomed as peasants became city dwellers and members of the gentry became businessmen. The reforms gave the provinces institutions of limited self-government, while the turbulent processes of economic growth and urbanization reinforced the centralized nature of Russia's social, economic and cultural life.

Russia's large cities experienced unprecedented physical and social transformations in the second half of the nineteenth century. Linked by newly constructed railways, urban centres and rural hinterlands became increasingly integrated units. The concentration of trade and manufacturing in St Petersburg and Moscow caused a building boom that was as powerful as it was unregulated. Speculative developers – a new feature of urban life in post-reform Russia – profited from the extensive construction of a new building type: the *dokhodnyi dom*, or investment property. Agglomerations of wooden apartment houses soon defined the urban periphery, while multi-storey dwellings came to dominate urban centres. The architecture of these new buildings and districts was marked by stylistic pluralism and a lack of formal coherence. In 1873 Feodor Dostoyevsky described the architecture of his day as 'some sort of total disorder, one which nevertheless corresponds to the disorder of the present moment'.[2]

Architecture responded to the demands of post-reform Russia by giving form and representation to new building programmes, serving a new class of clients and embodying new national myths. In urban centres, architects built factories and private houses for an emerging bourgeoisie. The *zemstva*, the institutions of provincial government created in the 1860s, built schools and hospitals for the rural population. Russian cities did not develop European-style department stores until the early

Vladimir Shervud, Historical Museum, Moscow, 1875–83.

twentieth century, but commercial structures such as trading rows, covered markets and arcades made use of progressive structural techniques, rationalizing trade and consumption. New theatres and music halls expanded the repertoire of urban entertainments. While the scale of construction and the character of building technologies in Russia lagged behind the achievements of Western Europe, the combined effects of late nineteenth-century urbanization transformed the Russian way of life.

The most complex task architecture was called upon to perform involved the representation of Russia's national character. The era of Great Reforms witnessed the integration of the empire through new social and economic policies, but it also propelled Russia onto an international stage. Social thinkers debated the relative value of Western models and native traditions for the future of Russian culture and society. Architecture became a central arena in which these debates unfolded. In their search for a national style, architects excavated the history of Russian building. They relied on contemporary archaeological surveys of ancient monuments and anthropological investigations of peasant artefacts to supply a vocabulary of forms suitable for the present. Although many Russian architects sought to create a synthetic national style based on historical forms, the most astute observers recognized that this historicist approach to architecture participated in a European world of ideas. 'If we can celebrate the promise of the Russian style to acquire predominant significance', wrote the historian Lev Dal, 'we should nevertheless not forget that even this new direction in architecture has been called forth in part by the habit of imitating the West.'[3] Participating in an international project that aspired to represent the singularity of national cultures in built form, Russian architects proposed a variety of formal and structural solutions to the problem of style. Despite the retrospective nature of this search, historical forms were, for many architects, crucial elements in the definition of Russia's progressive architecture.

In post-reform Russia, architects sought to marry national forms to rational techniques. Buildings were not only to express the uniqueness of national culture; they had also to correspond to the material and economic conditions of modern life. Expediency of construction, it was thought, could become an architectural ideal. According to Apollinari Krasovskii, Russia's father of rationalist architecture, this was to be achieved through 'the transformation of the functional into the beautiful'.[4] That structures might achieve beauty through the frank expression of their material qualities became a guiding proposition for many architects. Russian rationalism, like historicism, participated in an international field of architectural ideas. Paris and Berlin offered examples of how public and utilitarian buildings could achieve both economy and beauty. By the

1890s engineers such as Viktor Evald would look to the United States for lessons on the use of new materials in large buildings.[5] While many Russian architects sought to reconcile national form and rational construction, some produced works that transcended historicist design practices by affirming the reality of the present.

The Russian architectural profession was modernized in the post-reform era. The establishment of the Moscow Architectural Society in 1867 created the first professional forum for the concerns of architects. Through the sponsorship of lectures, publications and competitions, the Society advanced research into the history of Russian architecture and promoted progressive building technologies. According to Mikhail Bykovskii, the Society's founder, the organization's outlook was forward-looking: 'Freed, where possible, from the prejudices left to us by tradition, our activities permit us to work toward the achievement of the utility that architecture can offer through the construction of buildings that correspond to contemporary necessities of life and fulfil local and climatic conditions of durability, hygiene and economy.'[6] The St Petersburg Society of Architects was founded in 1870, and two years later it began publishing the professional journal *Zodchii* (Architect). This publication, which survived until the outbreak of civil war in 1918, sustained architectural culture as a platform for documentation and debate. Architectural education was reformed as the profession acquired a modern structure. From the 1860s to the 1880s new schools of architecture and engineering emerged to challenge the authority of St Petersburg's venerable Academy of Fine Arts. Soon the generation of architects that had matured in the era of reform began to question the relevance of historical models for contemporary practice. By the end of the nineteenth century these modernizing tendencies came into conflict with established conventions in what one commentator called 'a battle between old architectural traditions and new attitudes'.[7]

## Classicism, Eclecticism and the Academic Tradition

Although Russia's Academy of Fine Arts was founded in the mid-eighteenth century, it retained enormous influence throughout the nineteenth century and into the first years of the Soviet Union's existence. From the time of its inception, the Academy dictated the canons of architectural design throughout the empire. As one of the principal cultural achievements of Russia's Enlightenment, the foundation of the Academy brought Russia ever closer to European, and particularly to French, architectural culture. Under Empress Catherine the Great the classical language of architecture acquired near universal significance. The building that

Jean-Baptiste Vallin de la Mothe, Academy of Fine Arts, St Petersburg, 1764–88.

housed the Academy was itself a model of the classical tradition that the school promoted. Constructed to the design of the French architect Jean-Baptiste Vallin de la Mothe between 1764 and 1788, the Academy of Fine Arts building demonstrated a restrained classicism of geometrical rigour and monumental scale. It was both a monument to the arts and a model for the students in the school's architectural section. Vallin de la Mothe's building was also emblematic of an approach to architecture in which universal architectural values outweighed the specificity of climatic, historical and national characteristics.

The academic tradition of classical design remained virtually unchallenged in Russia until the 1830s, when a change of generations brought new ideals into focus. Architects now sought to qualify the importance of classicism by historicizing its cultural and formal origins. Once classicism was reconceived as a historically and culturally determined phenomenon, it seemed logical that a new architecture could be fashioned for and by the present. Under the leadership of Mikhail Bykovskii, the Moscow Court School of Architecture became a centre for this progressive approach to architecture, which constituted a significant challenge to the authority of the Academy of Fine Arts. In his 'Discourse on the groundlessness of the opinion that Greek or Greco-Roman architecture can be universal and that the beauty of architecture is based on the five known orders' of 1834, Bykovskii argued that architecture's development had always been intimately related to the history of its creators. Architecture, he claimed, is 'dependent on its aims, its time and its place'.[8] This historicist view unseated classicism as the dominant style of Russian architecture, which in turn stimulated experiments in a variety of stylistic languages.

Symptoms of a general decline of classicism's dominance within Russian architectural culture were evident in the Academy of Fine Arts as well. The promotion of the architects Aleksandr Briullov and Konstantin Ton to leading professors of the Academy's architectural class in 1831 has been called Russia's 'farewell to classicism'.[9] Briullov had experimented with pointed arches and Gothic forms since the beginning of the decade. In his Lutheran Church of St Paul on Nevskii Prospect in St Petersburg (1832–8) he abandoned explicit references to classical architecture, using instead a vocabulary of forms derived from the round arches of Romanesque buildings. Ton departed from the classical tradition in his early attempts to develop a Russian national style. His Church of St Catherine the Martyr in St Petersburg (1830–38) bore many of the stylistic traits of the architecture of early Muscovy: five onion domes raised on drums, bands of arches called *kokoshniki* supporting them, a four-pillared interior and three apses. Although the church maintained the geometrical rigour characteristic of classicism, Ton was clearly moving Russian architecture into new territory.

During the reign of Tsar Nicholas I (1825–55) Russian architecture was charged with the task of representing national myths, and Ton was the architect of the greatest national monument of the nineteenth century: the Cathedral of Christ the Saviour. The project was initially conceived as a shrine to Russia's victory over the French in the Napoleonic Wars, and the architect Aleksandr Vitberg's design of 1817 sought to commemorate this event in a classical idiom. Ton's project of 1832, however, was designed not to demonstrate Russia's participation in the shared European culture of classicism, but to proclaim the nation's historical affiliations with Byzantine culture. The church, according to Ton, was designed in 'the Byzantine style, which long ago united with the elements of our nationality'.[10] Both the size of the monument and its extended period of construction (1839–83) made it Russia's most ambitious architectural endeavour to date. Among the novelties introduced by the Cathedral of Christ the Saviour was the programmatic integration of spaces of worship with spaces of exhibition. The interiors, designed by the architect Viktor

Aleksandr Briullov, Lutheran Church of St Paul, St Petersburg, 1832–8.

Rezanov, fused neo-Byzantine formal devices with a sculptural programme that recounted episodes from Russian history. Within the peripheral gallery of the Greek-cross plan, visitors were presented with panels describing the Russian victory in the War of 1812. National history thus circumscribed the religious heart of the largest monument to orthodoxy in the empire. The synthesis of values achieved in the Cathedral of Christ the Saviour embodied the three foundations of Russian culture proclaimed by Sergei Uvarov, the minister of public education under Nicholas I: orthodoxy, autocracy and nationality. Indeed, Ton's neo-Byzantine church architecture would be officially recognized as representative of this triumvirate when his designs were recommended by the Tsar for use throughout the empire in 1841.

In the half-century between the initial design and the completion of the Cathedral of Christ the Saviour the coordinates of architectural practice shifted from a reliance on the classical tradition to a search for new methods of design. Architects in both Western Europe and the Russian

Empire began working in multiple architectural styles, sometimes incorporating elements derived from several formal traditions into a single building. This approach came to be called eclecticism. Architects across the world have long maligned this term, but at its inception eclecticism was seen as a positive advance in architecture and culture. As early as 1837 the writer, poet and critic Nestor Kukolnik declared that 'Our age is eclectic; in everything it has a characteristic feature: intelligent choice.'[11] This unprecedented freedom of choice had mixed results. Certain architects experimented with non-classical styles to great effect. Mikhail Bykovskii's Gothic-inspired ensemble at Marfino near Moscow is a prime example of the potential of stylistic pluralism. Yet the downside of eclecticism was soon recognized in Russia's capital cities. As new construction accelerated, the stylistic choices of architects and their clients, while harmonious in themselves, produced a visual cacophony at the scale of a city. Dostoyevsky called this mess 'the negative substance of the Petersburg period'. 'In terms of architecture', he wrote, 'the city is a reflection of all architectures in the world, of all periods and fashions: everything has been gradually borrowed and distorted in its own way.'[12] Thus eclecticism was Janus-faced: although it brought the entire history of architecture into the realm of contemporary practice, this expansion of means was achieved by abandoning the category of a universal style.

The dual nature of eclecticism was clearly expressed in the Palace of Grand Duke Vladimir Aleksandrovich Romanov (1867–72) in St Petersburg.

Konstantin Ton, Cathedral of Christ the Saviour, Moscow, 1839–83.

Aleksandr Rezanov, Palace of Grand Duke Vladimir Aleksandrovich, St Petersburg, 1867–72.

In this urban residence for a member of the imperial family, the stylistic pluralism described by Dostoyevsky was exacerbated. Built on a long, narrow site overlooking the Neva River in the heart of the city, the design of the palace was constrained by the same density of urban development that reduced the architecture of apartment houses to a single street facade. Aleksandr Rezanov, who had worked with Ton on the Cathedral of Christ the Saviour, placed the quarters of the Grand Duke in the U-shaped block facing the river. A service block occupies the opposite end of the site and stables stand in its centre. A volumetric solution to the palace's design was impeded by the proximity of adjacent structures, leaving only the flat Neva facade available for Rezanov's heavily rusticated neo-Renaissance design. Inside, Rezanov sought to impart a unique stylistic mode to each of the principal rooms. A tour through the Palace revealed a parade of styles from the neo-Renaissance of the facade and vestibule to the neo-Venetian of the guest-rooms and ultimately to the bathroom's neo-Russian decor.

In the Palace of the Grand Duke stylistic variety usurped the ideal of stylistic unity. This marked the emergence of a new model for Russian architecture – one founded not on the timeless values of classicism, but on the notion that style is a question of choice. Architects soon recognized the danger presented by this eclectic condition: once the universality of classical hierarchy was abandoned, stylistic choice was potentially arbitrary. Thus although eclecticism was productive, it brought architecture to a difficult impasse. If, as Bykovskii had claimed, architecture was dependent on its aims, its time and its place, then how could the seemingly capricious architectures of eclecticism be justified? Was it possible to create an architecture unique to the present by using historical styles? Could stylistic unity be obtained after the breakdown of the classical system? Struggling with questions such as these, architects sought stable

Dining room, Palace of Grand Duke Vladimir Aleksandrovich.

foundations in two related endeavours: in the search for a Russian national style and in the parallel development of architectural rationalism.

## Populism and the Styles of Nationalism

The transformation of Russian society entailed by the Great Reforms directed the intelligentsia's attention inwards. Whereas Russia's leaders had, at least from the time of Peter the Great, looked to the cultural achievements of the West as models for domestic appropriation, the 1870s witnessed a broad movement to celebrate the distinctiveness of Russian culture. This was achieved, in part, by a shift in the geography of cultural production, and the direction of this shift was almost always away from St Petersburg, the city designed as Russia's window to the West. The formation of the Association of Travelling Art Exhibits – also known as the *Peredvizhniki*, or the Wanderers – in 1870 weakened the Academy of Fine Arts' monopoly on the form and content of art and brought a distinctly Russian realist school of painting to the provinces. There were political stakes to this inward turn as well. Populism – the belief that the peasantry's way of life represented an organic model of social and cultural organization – became influential among the intelligentsia. In both art and politics, the central concern of the first decades of the post-reform era was the *narod* – a word meaning both 'people' and 'nation'.

For architecture, this geographic shift brought the most important projects to Moscow. It had long been considered the more distinctly Russian of the empire's two largest cities, and in the 1870s the significance of this distinction was redoubled. Architecture played a crucial role in sustaining the myth of St Petersburg as Russia's most European city, and now architecture would become the agent and instrument of a project to affirm the national character of Moscow – and, by extension, of Russia as a whole – as distinct from the northern metropolis. In order for this project to succeed, Russia needed to demonstrate that it possessed a *sui generis* architecture; an architecture developed for and by Russian architects. In this decade historians, anthropologists and architects rediscovered the grandeur of ancient monuments scattered around the empire and the supposed authentic dignity of Russian peasant traditions. These endeavours led many scholars to postulate the existence of a uniquely Russian antiquity that could reinvigorate contemporary culture without recourse to foreign models.

Russian architects had worked with a plurality of styles since the 1830s; they now sought to define a single, universal style through the study of indigenous architectural traditions. Prior to the 1870s forms derived from Byzantine and Russian architecture were used primarily in religious structures. The ambitions of the search for a Russian national style were great: this was an attempt to define an architecture that would be equally suitable for religious, civic and private construction. Although this search was designed to yield uniquely Russian results, the endeavour was framed by the pan-European movement of architectural revivalism. Indeed, many parallels between the Russian experiment and the Gothic revival movement in France, England and Germany can be found. Architects in each of these European countries asserted the primacy of their respective nations in the development of Gothic architecture and claimed that these forms were suitable for development in the present. Russian architects adopted a similar position, but turned instead to their own architectural traditions for inspiration.

Although this general aim was shared by most architects in the search for a Russian national style, there was never a unified movement or a codified set of stylistic principles. Some architects sought to incorporate the material and spatial qualities of ancient structures into contemporary practice. These architects recognized that the lessons of the past could inspire thoroughly modern solutions. For others, the accumulation of formal motifs from Russia's past provided a vocabulary that could be applied to modern structures. These two interpretations of the Russian style could be called the populist and the pictorial, respectively. Yet architects had no monopoly on the search for a Russian style. A unique and prescient treatment of the volumetric qualities of ancient Russian architecture was developed by a very special group of artists. This was a plastic approach to the problem of style, and its results had broad implications for the future of Russian architecture.

A distinguishing feature of the populist approach to the Russian style was the privileged place given to wooden construction and the crafts of the peasantry. Historians and critics were the first to highlight the architectural significance of these structures and artefacts, which had traditionally escaped the attention of high culture. Ivan Zabelin, who would later become director of the Historical Museum in Moscow, found in the daily life of the pre-Petrine period a national, peasant culture that seemed to develop independently and more powerfully than that of the state.[13] 'The community of the people', he wrote, 'is the principal and chief agent of national consciousness.'[14] Zabelin located the original and independent quality – the *samobytnost* – of Russian architecture in the tradition of wooden peasant dwellings. The 'beautiful disorder' found in the free distribution of volumes according to functional needs in the traditional peasant *izba* (hut) and the noble houses of the pre-Petrine period represented the originality and uniqueness of Russian architectural traditions.

Viktor Hartmann pioneered the use of wood and vernacular techniques to create a new architecture for Russia. Having studied at the Academy of Fine Arts in the 1860s, Hartmann's major contribution to the search for a national style for Russia was made in the design of several pavilions for the All-Russian Polytechnic Exposition of 1872 in Moscow.[15] More than any other, this was the event that brought the carved and textured wooden forms of peasant construction into an urban context. Hartmann's design for the Military Museum was lauded by critics as the most significant architectural achievement of the exposition. Situated inside the Kremlin walls, the museum consisted of a semicircular gallery and a vertical entry pavilion. Rising more than 35 m, the *shatyor*, or elongated tent roof, of the entry pavilion was clothed in multi-coloured shingles and studded by finely carved dormer windows. The walls of the surrounding galleries seemed to dissolve into an intricate pattern of glass panes and wooden mullions. The critic Vladimir Stasov recognized in the Military Museum a synthesis of the traditions of Russian wooden architecture and an evident familiarity with contemporary European buildings. In Hartmann's pavilion, he wrote, 'nothing remains of the former Russian

Viktor Hartmann, Military Museum, All-Russian Polytechnic Exposition, Moscow, 1872.

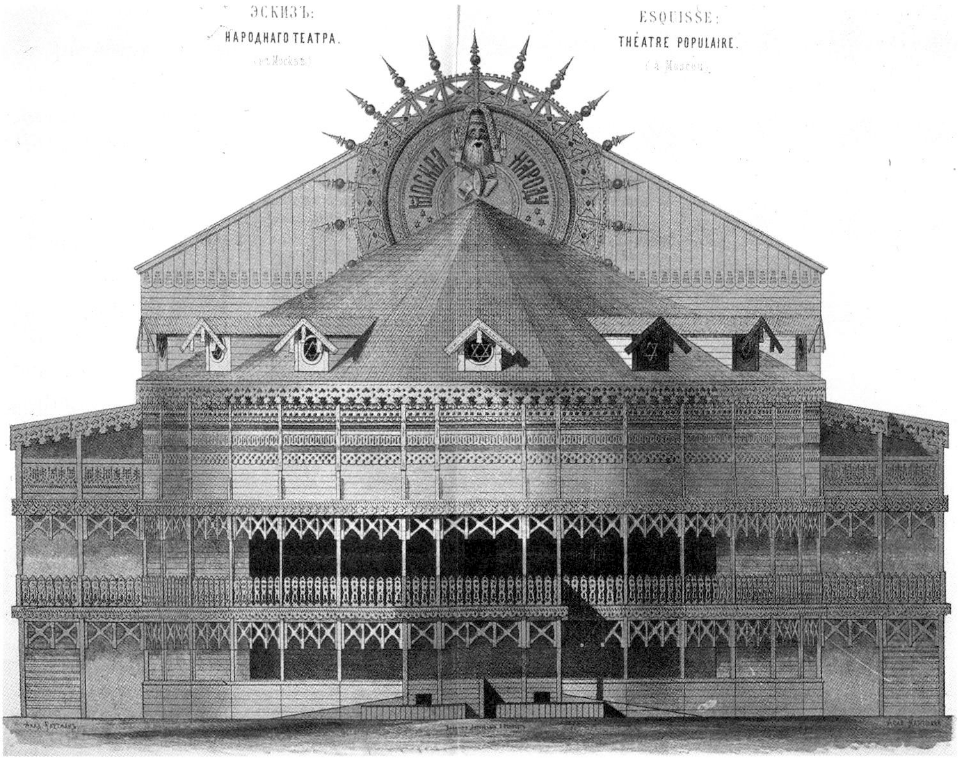


Viktor Hartmann, People's Theatre, Moscow, 1872.

compression and narrowness in dimensions and disposition; there is no more of the former gloomy darkness and stuffiness: everywhere there is spaciousness, breadth, air, light.'[16]

Hartmann's activity was not confined to exposition pavilions. His design for a People's Theatre combined rational construction techniques, national ornament and a democratic programme. The theatre was built to be fully demountable. Hartmann hoped that once the Polytechnic Exposition had closed the theatre could be disassembled and reconstructed elsewhere. All of the principal spaces of the theatre – the hall, stage and circulation – were clearly expressed as distinct volumes in the wooden structure. Loggias were avoided in the theatre, and the semicircular shape of the audience hall ensured an equality of sightlines during performances. Hartmann derived his decorative scheme from peasant weaving and woodcarving, which scholars and critics promoted as vital sources of national forms.[17] Horizontal bands of polychrome shingles unified the theatre's masses at cornice level, while details in carved wood enlivened the facades. Hartmann's achievement at the Polytechnic Exposition was to show that traditional materials and design motifs could be reinvigorated by combining them with new programmes and techniques. His influence would spread throughout the architectural profession and beyond. Indeed, it was a posthumous exhibition of Hartmann's work that inspired Modest Mussorgsky's composition *Pictures at an Exhibition* of 1874.

Hartmann's success reflected the unprecedented popularity of the Russian style among an emerging class of merchants and industrialists. These new patrons commissioned dachas and suburban homes in which architects experimented with the spatial qualities of ancient Russian building. Flexible planning and asymmetrical compositions came to define this genre of residential design. Architects presented these ideas in built work and in the pages of new publications. The remarkable journal *Motivy russkoi arkhitektury* (Motifs of Russian Architecture), which was published from 1873 to 1881, documented the work of Hartmann and others in this direction. Ivan Ropet's designs for suburban houses demonstrate the richness of decoration and spatial variation characteristic of this populist approach to the Russian style.[18] His project for a suburban wooden house of 1876 exemplified what Ivan Zabelin described as the defining traits of old-Russian architecture: 'along horizontal and vertical lines, the facade of the ancient dwelling was dissolved into quite distinct and independent parts, which could in no way be given any sort of symmetry.'[19] Ropet imparted similar qualities to the building of the Russian embassy in Japan of 1875 and Russian Imperial pavilion at the International Exposition of 1878 in Paris, where he represented the empire's architectural originality by drawing on ancient residential design. Although Hartmann and Ropet sought to combine spatial flexibility and decorative richness in their search for a Russian national style, the latter often trumped the former when this approach was in vogue. The habit of applying abundant peasant forms to the inert masses of dachas and suburban homes came to be known pejoratively as 'Ropetism'.

It was not Ropet's assimilation of peasant forms into contemporary practice that dismayed architects, but the fact that only the pictorial nature of his work seemed to acquire general popularity. In cities and villages across the empire, to build in the Russian style often amounted to little more than the application of a few decorative carvings to a building's facade. For many architects the Russian style was not defined by an organic relationship between interior spaces and their external expression, the proposition advanced by Hartmann and Ropet, but rather by the external, pictorial expression of national character.

With the construction of civic monuments that followed the Polytechnic Exposition of 1872, the centre of Moscow was reinvented in the Russian style. The Polytechnic Museum (Nikolai Shokhin and Ippolit

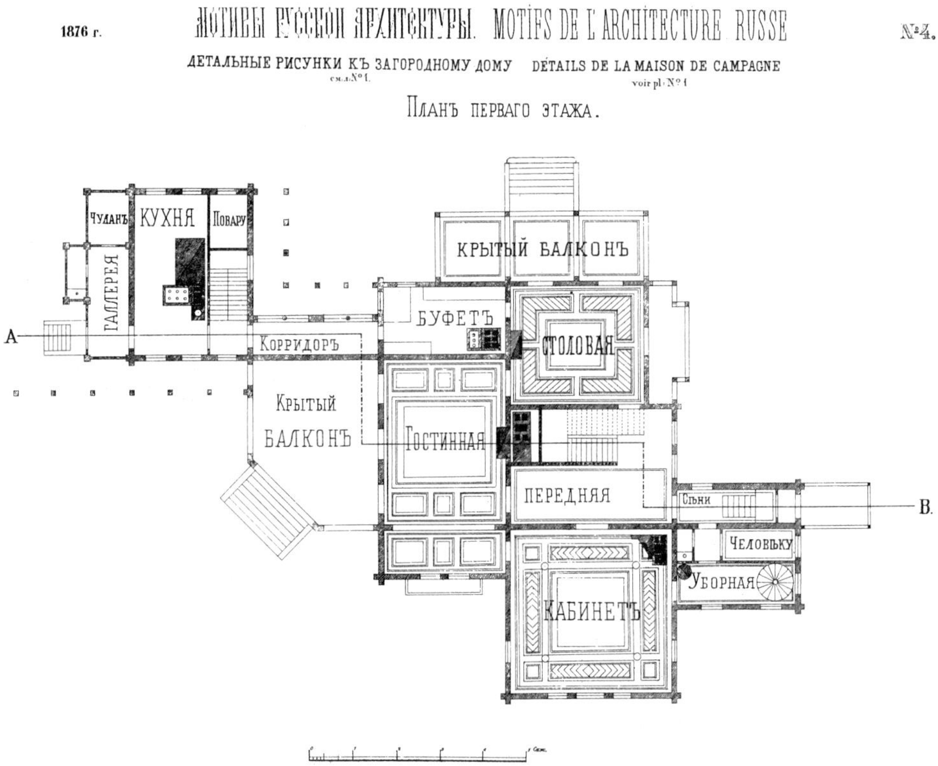


Ivan Ropet, project for a wooden house, 1876.

Monigetti, 1873–7) and the Historical Museum (A. A. Semenov and Vladimir Shervud, 1875–83) were built to accommodate the vast array of historical and technical objects collected for the exposition. Each of these buildings was the product of an increasingly common division of labour between an architect or engineer responsible for structure and layout and an architect responsible for the facade. This evident separation of internal and external design would later be criticized on the grounds that it could not produce the structural and artistic unity that characterized truly great architecture. Nevertheless, this approach to the Russian style was widely adopted by architects, and it largely determined the character of civic monuments throughout the empire.

The architectural ambitions of Moscow's Historical Museum were high. Sited next to the Kremlin walls and opposite St Basil's Cathedral, the Historical Museum's architectural mission was, according to its founders, to serve as a 'visual history of the principal epochs of the Russian state'.[20] In 1873 an advisory commission was formed to guide the

Museum's construction. Led by the archaeologist Aleksei Uvarov and Ivan Zabelin, this commission awarded Vladimir Shervud and A. A. Semenov's joint design first place in a competition of 1875. Shervud, whose primary interest was painting and sculpture, was responsible for the facade and interiors, while Semenov, who had an engineering background, designed the Museum's structure.

In his design for the museum's facade, Shervud synthesized the principles of Russian architecture that Zabelin had deduced from his studies of ancient monuments. Zabelin recommended that the museum be built 'in such a Russian style that would express to everyone the familiar and, so to speak, native characteristics Russian buildings'.[21] It was thus an abstract Russian character that Zabelin hoped to see embodied in the historical museum. For Shervud this character was not to be found through the study of a single period of Russian architecture, or in a single class of buildings. The general laws of the Russian style would only be revealed in the accumulated characteristics of all Russian building. In dialogue with Zabelin, Shervud determined that the museum should have strong contours, many distinct, but unified volumes, a variety of lines and a tower-like verticality. Completed in 1883 after an extended design and construction process, the Historical Museum's towers harmonize with the irregular masses of St Basil's Cathedral, its pendant building across Red Square, while its red brick exterior echoes the materiality of the adjacent Kremlin walls. Although the museum's lively silhouette may not entirely correspond to the internal disposition of gallery spaces, the fluency of Shervud's facade set a new benchmark for quality in urban construction.

The Russian style found a compelling plastic expression in the work of the circle of artists gathered at Abramtsevo, the estate of the railway tycoon Savva Mamontov. Abramtsevo occupies a special place in the history of Russian art.[22] It was a creative experiment that sought to renew Russian art by studying native traditions. Many of the country's leading artists, including Ilia Repin, Viktor Vasnetsov, Vasilii Polenov, Elena Polenova and Mikhail Nesterov, among others, contributed to the collective work at the estate. Architecture had framed the activities at Abramtsevo since it was purchased by Mamontov in 1870. He commissioned Hartmann to design a studio for visiting artists in 1873, and five years later he had Ropet build a *bania* (bathhouse) in the form of a *teremok*, or miniature castle. The decorations of these buildings echoed the forms of peasant artefacts that the artists at Abramtsevo collected from the surrounding villages, but the architecture of Hartmann and Ropet had only a distant relationship to the work of Mamontov's circle.

The artists at Abramtsevo developed a unique approach to architecture, albeit largely without the help of professional architects. Viktor Vasnetsov

V. M. Vasnetsov and V. Polenov, church, Abramtsevo, 1881–2.

and Vasilii Polenov, both of whom were primarily painters, together designed a modest church for Mamontov's estate in 1881–2 that synthesized painterly and structural themes into an architecture of pure masses and plastic forms. Inspiration for their design came from two primary sources: the medieval architecture of Novgorod and Pskov, which lacked the polychromatic richness of later Muscovite churches, and representations of architecture found in traditional icon paintings.[23] The lesson of the icon painters was that veracity of detail in rendering architectural forms was less important than the creation of a synthetic image. Although the general features of their church can be traced back to ancient models, Vasnetsov and Polenov avoided direct quotations. As early sketches for the project demonstrate, they arrived at their design not by accumulating archaeological details, but by combining all of the elements of the church – the walls, windows, doors, roof, drum and dome – in a series of informal perspectival views. This painterly approach produced highly plastic effects. The church's compact volume obtains a monumentality incommensurate with its scale. Its white surfaces seem to be modelled out of a single mass, and its external volumes appear to grow out of the church's internal organization. This organic unity of structure, form and space was a singular achievement in the search for the Russian style, and it would remain an ideal towards which Russian architects aspired in the ensuing years.

The Russian style proliferated in the final decades of the nineteenth century. In apartment buildings, theatres, markets, city halls and a variety of other building types across the empire, architects sought to lend national character to modern structures. The pictorial approach to Russian design predominated, while the populist experiments of Hartmann and the plastic synthesis seen at Abramtsevo remained exceptions. But not all architects were satisfied with the widespread application of Russian national forms. At the First Congress of Russian Architects in 1892, the problem of the Russian style was hotly debated, and some argued that this approach to architecture could hardly be justified for modern buildings. 'How', asked the architect Ieronim Kitner, 'are we to subordinate our contemporary life and the organization of our dwellings to these forms, or even to the dimensions of earlier epochs?'[24] The scale of new construction, it was argued, outstripped anything that ancient Russian architects had ever seen. What could the Russian style offer to designers of multi-storey apartment buildings, factories and warehouses? According to Kitner, the application of historical forms to contemporary tasks could only produce 'a most unwelcome disharmony'.

## Varieties of Rationalism

Many architects shared Kitner's sceptical view of the problem of style. Moreover, the notion that style was the central concern of the architectural profession had become a proposition with diminishing authority in some circles. St Petersburg's College of Building, which would later become the Institute of Civil Engineers, was the epicentre of a movement that sought to subordinate the problem of style to the ideal of structural rationality.[25] The rationalist position described by Apollinari Krasovskii, a professor at the college from 1842 to 1863, in *Grazhdanskaia arkhitektura* (Civil Architecture), his book of 1851, presented a persuasive challenge to the tenets of stylistic revivalism.[26] Architects, Krasovskii claimed, had long defined their work as the art of abstract forms, an idea that led them to disregard structural design and to focus only on the external appearance of buildings. Engineers, on the other hand, sought to create purely functional structures that were free of any aesthetic conceptions other than economy. For Krasovskii neither position was valid. A rational architecture could only emerge from a synthesis of the two, from 'the transformation of the functional into the beautiful'.[27]

Whereas architects working in the Russian style founded their work on the study of indigenous architectural forms, Krasovskii countered revivalist aims with a theory of architecture that was based on the very process of construction. 'Technology and construction', he wrote, 'are the principal sources of architectural forms. The role of art in the composition of these forms consists only in the conveyance of artistic completeness to the crude forms of technology.'[28] Architects working in the classical tradition and those who sought to revive national forms ultimately arrived at the same impasse: both schools could only imitate, with varying degrees of success, ready-made forms. They 'either adhere strictly to these forms; that is, copy them, or they modify these forms; that is, distort (barbarize) them'.[29] Rationalists, on the other hand, claimed that 'art is to be the mirror of the present.' According to Krasovskii, rationalists adopted a flexible approach to architectural design that was firmly rooted in the building process:

> Forms and details are formed of themselves from construction. In the composition of a project one should not arbitrarily determine form in advance – neither the form of the whole building, nor of its parts. The whole should be a consequence of the building's function, and the parts should follow from the qualities of materials and their use.[30]

This was a theory of architecture that sought to transcend the problem of style by making functional and material considerations the basis of form.

Krasovskii's teaching would influence several generations of Russian architects and engineers, and his rationalism would play a significant role in the debates on national style of the 1870s. In a variation on the search for the Russian national style, some architects argued that Russia's historical architecture embodied rational principles that could be applied to contemporary practice. The most remarkable proposal in this direction came not from a Russian architect, but from Eugène-Emmanuel Viollet-le-Duc, the French architect, conservationist and historian. In his book *L'Art russe: ses origines, ses éléments constitutifs, son apogée, son avenir* (Russian Art: Its Origins, Its Constitutive Elements, Its Apogee, Its Future) of 1877, he argued that the structural forms of the brick architecture of the fifteenth century could be combined into a rational, national style of architecture for Russia.[31] As a demonstration of his argument, he designed a large twelve-sided hall using a distinctly Russian tectonic system. Its roof of masonry arches, descendants of ancient Russian *kokoshniki*, is fully supported by inclined metal supports, creating a distinction between supporting and enclosing elements. 'The walls', he wrote, 'are no more than simple enclosures that have nothing to carry except their own weight.'[32] Despite his attempts at national specificity, however, Viollet-le-Duc's Russian hall bears a striking resemblance to his earlier project for a concert hall (*c.* 1866). Viollet-le-Duc nevertheless argued that Russian architecture was more susceptible to the use of new materials and structural techniques than Western architecture because it was unhindered by a reliance on the Greco-Roman orders. Thus, he claimed, there was every reason to believe that Russian architecture could obtain great effects with an economy of means through a synthesis of historical forms and contemporary techniques.

Eugène-Emmanuel Viollet-le-Duc, project for a large hall, from *L'Art russe*, 1877.

When St Petersburg's College of Building was reorganized as the Institute of Civil Engineers in 1882, Nikolai Sultanov attempted to make Viollet-le-Duc's combination of national forms and rational techniques the institution's programmatic aim. As a student of Krasovskii and the translator of *L'Art russe* into Russian, Sultanov was in a unique position to bridge the gap between rationalism and the Russian style. On the one hand he claimed that 'the builder has only to ensure that a building fully satisfies its functional purpose'.[33] Yet he felt that this aim could best be achieved through a revival of Russia's historical architectural forms. 'The new national movement does not contradict our guiding principle – that of rationalism; the two are fully congruent', he wrote.[34] Sultanov's position, however, was met with significant resistance from civil engineers. One commentator claimed that 'the science of styles, which has no exact foundation . . . is conventional to the highest degree'.[35] Style, in all its variations, remained in the realm of subjective choice, while the proponents of rationalism made function and construction the foundations of architecture.

For some architects, the rational use of building materials became an objective

V. A. Shreter and I. S. Kitner, Straus apartment building, St Petersburg, 1872.

basis for design, and, in Russia's harsh northern climate, this meant working in brick. This material became for Ieronim Kitner and Viktor Shreter the foundation for a rational architecture that abandoned the use of historical forms. 'The brick cladding of a facade', Kitner wrote, 'is immeasurably more rational than plaster decorations . . . There is no logical reason not to profit from the advantages of the material of which the building is made and to hide it under a layer of plaster.'[36] Prussia's architecture of the 1830s, the work of Karl Friedrich Schinkel above all, became a model for Kitner and others. The economy of structure, the frank use of brick and the lack of stylistic precedents in Schinkel's Building Academy in Berlin, erected between 1832 and 1836, demonstrated the 'convenience of this type of construction, both in relation to material strength and richness of form'.[37] In their apartment building for V. F. Straus in St Petersburg of 1872, Kitner and Shreter eschewed historical forms, creating instead a design based on the tectonic qualities of brick, its primary building material. As if recalling Krasovskii's teaching, in this and many other buildings, Kitner and Shreter made technology and construction the generators of form.

Brick was not the only material used by rationalist architects. Across Western Europe the increasingly popular use of metal construction in civic buildings led to bold structural experiments. The same was true in Russia. Although iron had long been used in Russian building, it remained an obscure, concealed material until the building boom of the post-reform era propelled industrial construction forward.[38] In factory buildings architects and engineers typically spanned masonry wall construction with roofs made of iron trusses to create large enclosed spaces.[39] Towards the end of the nineteenth century the lightness and expanse of these metal structures would penetrate the hearts of cities in the forms of covered markets and train sheds at railway stations. In the market on Sennaia Square (Haymarket) in St Petersburg the architecture of iron found its first expression in a civic monument. Ieronim Kitner presented his winning design at a competition held in 1883 under the motto 'Stone, Iron and Glass'.[40] During his travels abroad in the 1860s Kitner had worked with Victor Baltard, the builder of Paris's famous Les Halles market, and he applied the multi-pavilion layout of this Parisian model to his project for Russia's capital.[41] With the help of the engineers G. E. Pauker and O. E. Krel, Kitner created four pavilions of iron and glass,

I. S. Kitner, G. E. Pauker and O. E. Krel, Haymarket, St Petersburg, 1883–6.

Aleksandr Pomerantsev, Vladimir Shukhov and Artur Loleit, Upper Trading Rows, Moscow, 1889–93.

each of which spanned more than 23 m. The structural bravado and spatial clarity of the market on Sennaia Square seemed to announce the rational architecture of the future as early as its completion in 1886.

As the use of new building materials such as steel and reinforced concrete became routine, the role of the engineer in the design and construction of buildings acquired greater importance. One could often distinguish the respective contributions of engineers and architects within a single project, and progressive structures commonly supported retrospective architectural design. Moscow's Upper Trading Rows, the enormous commercial complex abutting Red Square built between 1889 and 1893, illustrates the divergent aims of the two professions. The architect Aleksandr Pomerantsev designed both the exterior and interior facades in the Russian style. Vladimir Shukhov and Artur Loleit, two of Russia's leading engineers, designed the building's structure. Loleit was a specialist in reinforced concrete, and he was responsible for the design and construction of the wafer-thin footbridges that connect each pavilion at multiple levels. Shukhov, whose towering influence would shape Russian architecture for decades to come, designed the glazed roof, which was the product of one of his many structural innovations. Its barrel vaults consist of many steel arches, or ribs, each of which was stabilized by multiple oblique transverse steel cables.[42] This remarkably economical solution reduced the thickness of each rib, dematerializing the roof and creating the illusion that the building communicates directly with the sky. In the design of the Upper Trading Rows, the intentions of the architect and those of the engineers seem to be at odds. Pomerantsev's facades are

Upper Trading Rows, Moscow; interior.

solid and weighty; they recall ancient Russian architectural traditions. Loleit's bridges and Shukhov's roof foreshadow the spatial effects of modern tectonic minimalism. Lodged somewhere between Russia's past and its future, the Upper Trading Rows were both architecturally *passé* and on the cutting edge of structural innovation.

Russian architects recognized that the art of architecture and the science of structure had slipped out of joint. In 1895, at the Second Congress of Russian Architects, Konstantin Bykovskii, the son of Mikhail, discussed the profession's failings in his programmatic speech on 'the tasks of architecture in the nineteenth century'. 'In what other time', he asked in defence of his waning age, 'have such hospitals and schools been built for the good of humanity, when else have such palaces of iron and glass been created for international communication in the interest of industry, art and science?'[43] Architecture had indeed contributed to the modernization of Russia's urban environment. Industry and commerce acquired new factories and exchanges, while expositions, theatres and museums offered enlightenment and entertainment. But, Bykovskii continued, 'despite the great undertakings of this age, before us still prevails an architectural masquerade; buildings are disguised in the garments of diverse styles'.[44] This masquerade began with the slavish imitation of the forms of classical antiquity and found its climax in the stylistic multiplicity characteristic of the common, eclectic approach to architecture. 'The idea that a building can obtain beauty principally through its decoration has taken root; an artificial division of architecture into artistic and technical spheres has occurred.'[45] Russian architects developed national forms and rational techniques in parallel, and each search yielded lasting architectural results. But, Bykovskii implied, until the formal and the rational intersected, architecture would remain an art of disguise. The position that he and other like-minded architects represented was clear: unless architects could bridge the gap between art and technology, the masquerade would continue.

chapter two

# Style, Innovation and Tradition, 1896–1916

'We need new forms. New forms are needed, and if we can't have them, then we had better have nothing at all.'[1] Thus spoke Konstantin Treplev, the youthful hero of Anton Chekhov's play *The Seagull*, which premiered in 1896, to the theatrical conventions of his day. Treplev's animosity towards the 'routine' and 'prejudice' of contemporary theatre, his passion for formal innovation and his willingness to jettison historical precedents conveyed an attitude shared by a broad spectrum of artists and intellectuals at the turn of the twentieth century. A desire for the new propelled Russia's 'Silver Age' forwards, lending this *fin de siècle* revival of the arts a dynamism matched only by the grandeur of the early nineteenth-century 'Golden Age' of Pushkin.

New forms of artistic collaboration supported the search for a new style. Led by Sergei Diaghilev and Alexandre Benois, the 'World of Art' group sponsored exhibitions, staged theatrical performances and published its eponymous journal, which presented the newest trends in painting, poetry, literature and the decorative arts to an eager public. The 'World of Art' was a loose confederation of individuals with a shared interest in cultural renewal. Dmitrii Filosofov, a founding member of the 'World of Art', recalled the words of Chekhov's Treplev in a programmatic statement from 1902: 'For the new, future-oriented style, the past should not exist. One must embody eternal laws in forms that correspond to a contemporary worldview.'[2] This was a classic formulation of the promise and paradox of modernism. While rejecting direct references to the past, the new style would nevertheless be marked by a delicate tension between eternal values and an innovative creative impulse. Filosofov's characterization of the new style of art as a union of timelessness and novelty captured the intentions of Russia's leading artists, writers and architects.

Between the coronation of Nicholas II in 1896 and his abdication in 1917, Russian society witnessed both the consecration of eternal social hierarchies and technological upheaval. The Tsar's elaborate coronation reinforced the divine source of autocratic authority within the Russian empire. Having taken the throne after Aleksandr III's untimely death, Nicholas was formally crowned in a ceremony that drew thousands of

G. V. Baranovskii, apartment building, St Petersburg, 1897.

peasants to the city and showcased such modern inventions as light bulbs, which illuminated the Kremlin during the course of the event. The central spectacle of the ceremony, however, took place under the gilded domes of the fifteenth-century Cathedral of the Dormition, emphasizing, as Richard Wortman has observed, that the monarch himself represented the chosen of the Lord.[3]

A tension between autocracy and innovation characterized the political and economic features of Nicholas II's reign. Seeking to bring ethnic and religious minorities into imperial administrative structures, the Tsar attacked the *zemstva*, weakening the power of these institutions of local self-government. He also handed down a policy of Russification that exerted greater influence on Finland, the Baltic territories and Ukraine. In a bid for territorial expansion, Nicholas also sought to establish a Russian presence in the Far East. The completion of the Trans-Siberian Railway in 1904 and a southern branch through Manchuria brought the Russian Empire to Port Arthur, a valuable ice-free port. This venture established several Russian cities in the Far East, notably Dalnyi and Kharbin (both in present-day China), but it led to the Tsar's humiliating defeat in the Russo–Japanese War of 1904–5. This failure in foreign relations was met with massive unrest throughout the country as broad sectors of the population, led by the liberal intelligentsia, initiated the Revolution of 1905. In a push for democratic reforms, the population demanded the creation of a constituent assembly that would check the Tsar's autocratic power. Nicholas ultimately created the Duma, a council of ministers, but severely limited its power. The Tsar and this elected body remained in a constant struggle for political power until the outbreak of the First World War, the beginning of a cataclysmic series of events that precipitated the fall of the House of Romanov and the end of the Russian Empire.

Nicholas II's coronation coincided with an imperial show of innovation: the All-Russian Industrial and Artistic Exposition. Held in Nizhniy Novgorod, a manufacturing city east of Moscow, the Exposition presented new technologies such as electric streetcars, the cinema of the Lumière brothers and the first Russian-made automobile. To Maksim Gorky, the prolific writer and Nizhniy Novgorod native, the exposition's effect was epochal. 'The age of mercantilism and materialism proclaims itself in everything', he wrote, 'and the exposition is and will be a clear illustration of the power and influence of the age on the spirit of human creation.'[4] Among the most exhilarating features of the Exposition were the structures conceived by the pioneering engineer Vladimir Shukhov. Assembled from thin steel members, his hyperboloid water tower and steel mesh enclosures created vertiginous visual effects. Shukhov's constructions suggested a world of dematerialized geometric forms, illustrating the

Villa of supervisors of the Russian Railway, Kharbin, *c.* 1904.

Nizhniy Novgorod Exposition, 1896; Vladimir Shukhov's water tower at centre.

Moscow of the Future, postcard, 1914.

potential of engineering to create radically new spatial experiences. His structures manifested the accelerating industrialization of Russian society.

The territorial expansion and rapid industrial growth achieved under Nicholas II were enabled by the shrewd economic policies of Sergei Witte, one of the Tsar's most talented civil servants. Witte understood that the empire could not afford to remain dependent on the West for critical materials such as coal, metal and oil. In developing the empire's natural resources – coal in the Don basin, oil in the fields of Baku, metal in the Ural Mountains – Witte used state intervention to make Russia's rate of industrial growth higher than any other country.

Intense urban development accompanied Russia's industrialization. Between 1897 and 1916 the population of St Petersburg doubled to 2.4 million inhabitants.[5] Over the same period Moscow's population grew from 1 million to 1.8 million inhabitants. Although the vast majority of Russian subjects lived in rural conditions, the swelling urban centres became the sites for the creation of a new way of life. As 'coal becomes a diamond, Russia becomes a new America', wrote the poet Aleksandr Blok.[6] Streetcars and electric lights gave the city new rhythms and nocturnal dimensions. Apartment buildings of enormous scale populated newly fashionable districts. Industrial complexes, department stores and office buildings displayed great formal and typological invention. In Moscow, engineers lobbied for the construction of a quintessentially metropolitan mode of transportation: a subway. The poet Velimir Khlebnikov captured the fantastical quality of Russia's urban growth in his poem of 1914–15, 'We and Houses', in which he imagined a future city made up of buildings on great legs, towers in the forms of trees and settlements elevated on flowing ribbons.[7]

Russian architects, like their colleagues in Western Europe and North America, responded to the pervasive sense of cultural transformation by developing a new approach to style. To many, the previous century now appeared, in the words of the critic Pavel Makarov, as an age of 'lifeless eclecticism'.[8] He derided the previous generation, noting that 'the primary task of their artistic creativity is nothing more than an attempt to approximate as closely as possible old forms, which they all worship.'[9] Others complained that the formal imagination of the previous decades was out of sync with the present – that 'buildings and objects intended for contemporary people were dressed in forms developed in entirely different conditions, conditions radically different from those of today.'[10] Convinced that their age required its own architectural expression, critics defined the principles of a 'new style': the foundation of architecture would be constructive truth; a building's function would determine its composition; form would become a symbolic expression of structure.[11]

Supporters of this position drew on the rationalist doctrine of Apollinari Krasovskii from the mid-nineteenth century as well as the work of leading Western European architects, whose impact on the Russian scene reached a peak at the turn of the century. Russian professionals knew well the writings of John Ruskin and William Morris, who called for an ethical unity between art and labour.[12] In the cottages built by Charles Voysey and other English architects, Russians found a free approach to domestic planning, one unhindered by conventions of symmetry and monumentality. The Art Nouveau of France and Belgium, the Jugendstil of Germany and the style of the Viennese Secession showed that vegetal forms, vernacular traditions and dynamic lines could enliven architectural design. Otto Wagner, the innovative Austrian architect and professor, exerted a particularly strong influence on Russian designers with his book *Modern Architecture*, first published in 1896.[13] According to Vladimir Apyshkov, Russia's most ardent promoter of rationalism, the importance of Wagner's ideas lay in his insistence that 'the sole departure point for our artistic work can only be modern life.'[14] Architects were also receptive to the formal qualities of Wagner's mature work. The flat surfaces and formal simplicity of Gavril Baranovskii's apartment house in St Petersburg of 1897 attests to the resonance of Wagner's principles in Russia.[15] Finding further inspiration in the work of Joseph Maria Olbrich, one of Wagner's star pupils, Russian architects responded to the international movement for renewal by developing an all-encompassing approach to design, one that would generate rational models for chairs, train stations and everything in between. Russia's *stil modern* – modern style – arose from this variety of sources and gained widespread currency after the turn of the century. A remarkably flexible approach to design,

Aleksei Shchusev, Church of the Intercession, Martha and Mary Cloister, Moscow, 1908–12.

Russia's *stil modern* encompassed both projects that rejected the use of historical forms and buildings, such as Aleksei Shchusev's Martha and Mary Cloister in Moscow (1908–12), that offered thoroughly modern interpretations of ancient Russian forms.

Although the transformations entailed by rapid industrial growth and explosive urbanization inspired many architects to seek a new style, some looked deeper into the past for a suitable architectural response. This 'retrospective' position obtained its greatest popularity around 1910, but it emerged at the same time as the *stil modern*.[16] Alexandre Benois was among the first to call for a revival of the severe and noble simplicity of St Petersburg's early architecture in protest at the cacophony of styles that accompanied the city's building boom.[17] Like the proponents of the new rationalism, Benois sought to return to architecture an allegedly lost stylistic unity. The architect Ivan Fomin and the critic Georgii Lukomskii gave this position further definition, arguing that the so-called Empire Style of the early nineteenth century represented the final age of architecture's authentic vitality.[18] To Lukomskii, the severe classicism of this age represented an epoch, in contrast to his own, when 'people wanted and were able to build everything that they had to build beautifully.'[19] Like contemporary trends in Western Europe – notably the argument presented by the German architect Paul Mebes in his book *Um 1800* (Around 1800) – this turn to a vernacular classicism was both an antidote to the alleged hyper-individualism of the *stil modern* and an attempt to connect with what many considered to be a living tradition in architecture.[20]

Most architects arrived at a modernized classicism by the time the First World War began, tempering the radical plasticity of the rationalist approach with an austere and inventive interpretation of classical design. Ivan Zholtovskii's Tarasov House in Moscow (1909–12) and Vladimir Shchuko's Makarov Apartment Houses in St Petersburg (1908–11) were symptomatic of this shift. While the *stil modern* and the 'retrospective' positions appear to be antagonistic – the former based on the principle of the new, the latter on a love of the past – they share a hostility to the 'lifeless eclecticism' of the previous generation and they both sought to develop an all-encompassing approach to design. Opposing the previous generation's stylistic plurality, both the *stil modern* and the 'retrospective' position made stylistic unity an architectural ideal. This new form of unity implied both an organic relationship between the forms and functions of buildings and a unity of conception across multiple scales. Russian architects now sought to integrate the decorative arts, domestic interiors, civic and commercial structures and entire urban ensembles. This was a desire to fashion the entire built environment anew – a key element of Russian architectural culture that would survive the collapse of the Russian Empire.

## Domestic Revolutions

The renewal of Russian design and decorative art began in rural workshops established by wealthy patrons. The revival of folk crafts at Savva Mamontov's Abramtsevo estate exerted a powerful influence on artistic taste and inspired others to establish similar institutions.[21] At Talashkino, an artists' estate near Smolensk founded by Princess Maria Tenisheva, artists and architects trained local artisans to produce furniture, household tools, fabric and other decorative arts with stylistic unity and decorative integrity. Pavel Makovskii described the output of Talashkino's workshops as an antidote to the 'architectural anachronism' of the contemporary middle-class interior.[22] Drawing on sources such as pseudo-Doric ornamentation, faux-marble finishes and furniture in the style of Louis XIV, the average bourgeois dwelling possessed 'the pretence of luxury

Sergei Maliutin, *teremok*, Talashkino, 1901.

without a concept of artistic unity'.[23] Harmony and honesty reigned at Talashkino. In the *teremok* – a cottage in the form of a small castle – Sergei Maliutin designed for the estate in 1901 whimsical carved ornamentation enhances the building's simple wooden construction. Inside, rough-hewn tables, chairs, doors and other furnishings obtain a unified appearance through shared design motifs.[24] Talashkino presented models of coherent design and made the workshop's folk-inspired objects available at a retail outlet in Moscow, where the reform of the domestic interior was becoming a popular concern.

In late 1902 the 'Exhibition of Architecture and Arts Industries in the New Style' presented the unified interior as an artistic ideal. The show was organized by Ivan Fomin, an active young architect with significant international connections.[25] He sought to introduce the work of leading European architects and designers to the Russian scene and ultimately invited, as he wrote, 'the entire Viennese Secession' as well as Charles Rennie Mackintosh from Glasgow. Olbrich, the designer of the Vienna Secession building (1898) and artistic director of the Darmstadt Artists' Colony (1901), and Mackintosh obliged, sending furniture and other household objects to be exhibited with Russian pieces. Although the show was small by international standards – a rented apartment in the centre of Moscow constituted the exhibition space – its impact was great. For the first time, Russian architects, designers and the interested public could immerse themselves in an environment designed completely in the new style.

Ivan Fomin, dining room, Moscow Exhibition of Architecture and Arts Industries in the New Style, 1902; detail of hearth.

Although many designers participated in the show, Fomin was the star. He designed and furnished the dining room and two living rooms

Feodor Shekhtel, Riabushinskii House, Moscow, 1900–1902.

within the apartment. Using a range of materials – oak, maple, metal, ceramic – Fomin's pieces are related by shared forms and textures. In the dining room, a long wooden table defined a central axis that terminated in a deep niche containing a decorative water basin. Low benches extended from a large hearth in one corner of the room, adding asymmetrical volumes to the rectilinear space. Two triangular chandeliers hung above the rectangular table, evoking a contrast between parallel and intersecting lines. Bands of gridded reliefs adorn the flat planes of objects, tying the variety of furnishings into a cohesive whole. Although some observers recognized remnants of Russian folk forms in Fomin's designs, their novelty separated them from direct precedents. Writing of the difference between European work and Fomin's objects, one critic noted with pride that in the latter 'all of the ribbon-like, curved and snake-like lines have yielded to calm rectilinear forms'.[26]

The first permanent displays of this new ideal of design coherence appeared in the building type favoured by the growing merchant class: the *osobniak*. A descendant of the French *hôtel particulier*, the *osobniak* is a detached urban mansion. Typically situated on large plots of land, an *osobniak* often included a private garden as a respite from the otherwise dense urban fabric of Moscow and St Petersburg. The number of these structures built before the First World War transformed the character of entire districts, giving them a new semi-urban appeal.

Feodor Shekhtel was Moscow's most celebrated builder of urban villas. A prolific architect, he had close ties to several of the city's influential merchant families. Although he designed some of the most important buildings of the *stil modern*, Shekhtel began his career with projects inspired by a range of historical styles. For Zinaida Morozova – the wife of an industrialist and patron of the arts – Shekhtel created a large mansion

Riabushinskii House, main staircase.

in the Gothic style (1893–6). The Riabushinskii House (1900–1902) was a true breakthrough, both for Shekhtel and for Russian architecture as a whole. The building's young patron, Stepan, was a member of a progressive merchant family. Situated on a large, corner parcel, the building's asymmetrical mass is clearly visible from the street. Its irregular volumes clearly express the internal disposition of spaces, while glazed bricks and a broad frieze tie the entire structure together. The building's ornament

Vasilii Schöne, Schöne House, St Petersburg, 1903–4.

lacks direct historical references, drawing instead on the world of organic forms to enliven its lines and profiles. The vegetal theme of the frieze softens the geometric rigour of the structure's intersecting volumes. Both rectilinear and curved windows pierce the thick masonry walls, emphasizing Shekhtel's belief that 'the principal task of every architectural construction is the enclosure of spaces with walls'.[27] The undulating curves of the porch suggest the organic lines of the interior. Cast in a shimmering blend of concrete and pulverized marble, the central stair is the pivot of Shekhtel's entire design. Its undulating banister draws visitors upwards, while large skylights bathe this vertical axis in soft light. Most rooms connect to the central stair, and wave-like forms in the floors, ceilings and walls draw the space together. A small chapel occupies the uppermost level of the house, reflecting the owner's piety and the architect's ability to modernize traditional Russian forms. Both inside and outside, Shekhtel achieved a fundamental unity of form and structure in the Riabushinskii House.

In St Petersburg, new interpretations of the *osobniak* appeared outside the city centre, primarily on the Petrograd and Stone islands. These areas were removed from both the tumult of Nevskii Prospect, the city's primary artery, and the grit of the growing manufacturing sector on the city's periphery. Amid the forests of Stone Island, Vasilii Schöne designed and built a house for himself (1903–4) with compact massing, clear geometric forms and a high mansard roof. Its overall conception recalls the work of

Aleksandr von Gogen, Kshesinskaia House, St Petersburg, 1904–6.

Kshesinskaia House, plan of main floor.

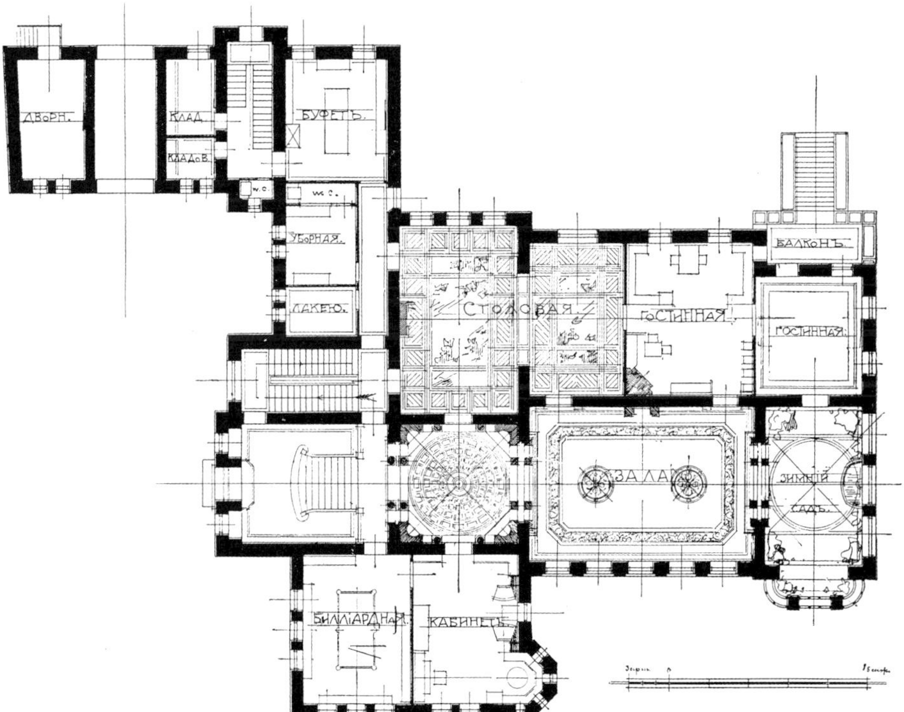
ДВОРН.
КЛАД.
КЛАДОВ.
БУФЕТЪ.
W.C.
W.C.
УБОРНАЯ.
ЛАКЕЮ.
СТОЛОВАЯ.
ГОСТИННАЯ.
БАЛКОНЪ
ГОСТИННАЯ.
ЗАЛА
ЗИМНIЙ САДЪ.
БИЛЛIАРДНАЯ.
КАБИНЕТЪ.

Olbrich at the Darmstadt Artists' Colony, testament to the powerful influence the Viennese architect exerted on the Russian scene. On Petrograd Island, Aleksandr von Gogen designed a grand and sprawling house (1904–6) for Mathilda Kshesinskaia, the prima ballerina of the Mariinskii Theatre. Like Shekhtel's Riabushinskii House, the Kshesinskaia House displays the internal distribution of spaces in its exterior volumes. Large windows open the building's main axis, which runs from the vestibule through a large hall and into a winter garden, creating a reciprocal relationship between inside and outside. The interest of the house's external forms arises from the contrast of glazed brick, extensive glazing and exposed metalwork. At the patron's request, von Gogen designed the large hall in the reduced classical language characteristic of the Empire Style. Kshesinskaia used this space to receive guests and to dance; after the February Revolution of 1917, the owner was driven from the building and its hall became the meeting place of the Bolshevik Party. In the Soviet period the building became a museum of the October Revolution; today it is the home of the State Museum of Political History.

Von Gogen's project for the Kshesinskaia House influenced Vladimir Apyshkov's design for the home of S. N. Chaev (1906–7), a prominent engineer of transportation.[28] The logic and clarity of Apyshkov's design, however, distinguished it from the projects of his colleagues. An engineer and architect, Apyshkov was a staunch supporter of architectural rationalism. In his book of 1905, *Ratsionalnoe v noveishei arkhitekture* (The Rational in Recent Architecture), he defended the tradition established by Apollinari Krasovskii and continued by figures such as Otto Wagner. Apyshkov's rationalism sought to achieve 'constructive forms and architectural truth'.[29] The Chaev House was a demonstration of his theory of architecture.

Vladimir Apyshkov, Chaev House, St Petersburg, 1906–7.

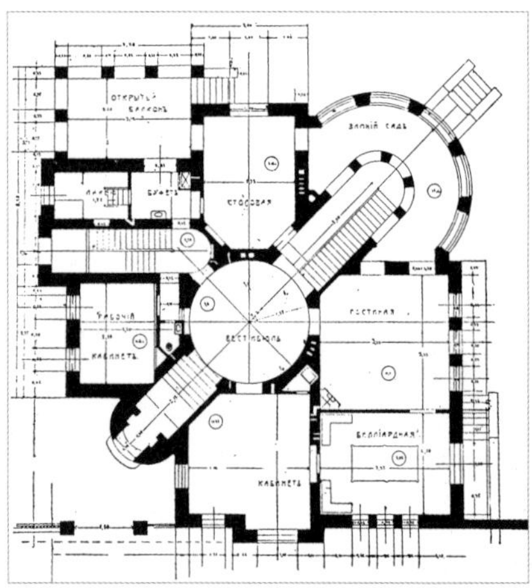

Chaev House, ground-floor plan.

Although compact, the Chaev House is a highly sculptural mass. Its complex geometry is composed of intersecting cubes and cylinders, solids that correspond to the elementary shapes of the plan. Three cylinders constitute the house's principal axis: a small vestibule leads to a large central hall, which opens onto the grand curve of the conservatory. The primary stair lies on this axis and projects into the glazed double-height space of the conservatory, giving the visitor a dramatic spatial experience ascending to the second floor of the hall, which serves as a picture gallery. This level contains bedrooms, boudoirs and bathrooms. All rooms are accessible from the central hall, which is illuminated by skylights above. The hall's top two floors are separated by a large plane of glass that allows light in but keeps the odour of the third-floor staff kitchen and laundry out. Apyshkov's distribution of rooms and paths of circulation fully complied with the patron's request 'to avoid dark or scantily lit corridors'.[30] Outside, the building's surfaces are covered in granite, glazed brick and several figural reliefs. Its asymmetrical distribution of masses lends the entire composition a tense dynamism. Seen from the garden, the bold cylinder of the conservatory and a low, covered terrace provide informal counterpoints to the three-storey central block. Apyshkov's masterful use of geometric solids made a lasting impression on Russian architects. In the post-Revolutionary era architects such as Ilia Golosov and Konstantin Melnikov would appropriate and reinterpret Apyshkov's glazed, drum-like volumes.

Like Kshesinskaia, Chaev demanded the use of historical styles in certain rooms of his new home: Empire Style for the bedroom and Louis XVI style for the guest rooms and boudoir. Their preferences reflected a broader awareness of neo-classicism and the historical character of St Petersburg. Alexandre Benois led this revival of interest in Peter the Great's city with his call for a new appreciation of 'picturesque St Petersburg'. New journals such as *Starye gody* (Bygone Days), which chronicled the buildings and artefacts of the Petrine legacy, and new cultural societies, such as the Commission for the Study of Old Petersburg, which established a museum of the city in 1909, supported this trend.[31] The event that had the greatest impact on architectural design, however, was the 'Historical Exhibition of Architecture' that opened at the museum in 1911. Organized by a large team of architects and historians, and directed by Ivan Fomin, the exhibition was a coordinated display of architectural graphics and period furniture from the eighteenth to the early nineteenth centuries. In the sumptuous catalogue, Benois described the event as an opportunity to study the work of past architects that remained relevant in the early twentieth century, to learn from their 'monumental forms, fully worthy of the external magnificence of our grandiose fatherland'.[32] The exhibition responded to a widespread sentiment that the radical individualism of the *stil modern* was exhausted. Whiplash lines and vegetal ornament, which had once represented a general antipathy to historical forms, now seemed to be mere novelty. While the 'retrospective' tendency behind the exhibition of 1911 rejected the formal language of the *stil modern*, it maintained that the sober tradition of Russian classicism offered a model of all-encompassing design and rational principles.

While most Russian architects, including Shekhtel and Apyshkov, turned to classicism in the years around 1910, Ivan Fomin's transformation was most dramatic. After his earlier experiments in the *stil modern*, he returned to the Academy of Fine Arts to complete his education. Under the tutelage of Leontii Benois, Alexandre's brother, Fomin discovered Russian classicism and became a leading ideologue of the classical revival. In an impassioned appreciation of the work of A. D. Zakharov, the designer of the Admiralty in St Petersburg (1805–23), Fomin argued that the reign of Tsar Aleksandr I (1801–25) witnessed the 'period of the greatest flourishing and maturity of Russian architecture'.[33] Taking a nationalist stance, Fomin claimed that the Empire Style should rightly be called the style of Aleksandr I, for at this time Russian architecture surpassed Western European models in both its breadth and refinement. For Fomin, this was the last era in which Russian architecture, decorative arts and even clothing attained a living unity.

This desire to restore integrity and coherence to Russian architecture was at the centre of Fomin's design for the Polovtsev House (1911–13) on Stone Island in St Petersburg. Composed of a large central block and projecting lateral wings, the building strongly recalls the Razumovskii Palace in Moscow designed by N. A. Lvov (1799–1806).[34] Paired Ionic columns lend the portico a forest-like density. Straight axes and regular geometric forms characterize the entire design. Screened by columns, the central portal steps back from the portico, creating a semicircle that rises to form a coffered half-dome. Inside, the visitor passes through a compressed vestibule into a circular hall. The centre of the building is the 'Tapestry Hall', named for the tapestries by Peter Paul Rubens that originally hung in the room. The hall's coffered barrel vault and the Greek key pattern of the marble floors form a harmonious counterpoint. A grand oval staircase opens up one side of the hall, offering screened views of the upper floor. The central enfilade continues into the hall of white columns. The paired Ionic columns in this room recall the portico and support a richly painted barrel vault. At the far end of the hall, the central axis terminates in a large glazed conservatory. Fomin's design achieved grandiosity by way of what he called a 'monotony of form'. Repeated details and archi-

Ivan Fomin, Polovtsev House, St Petersburg, 1911–13.

Polovtsev House, ground-floor plan.

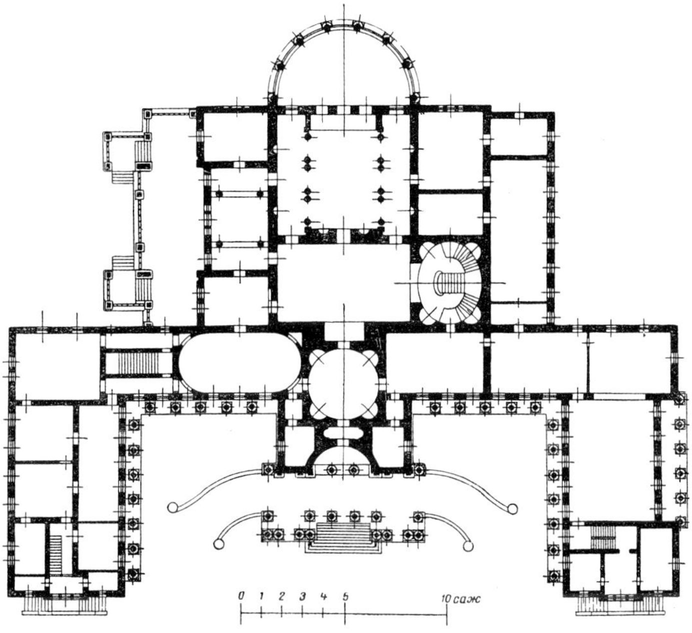


tectural forms gave the Polovtsev House the noble simplicity that he admired in the work of past architects. While explicitly tied to the past, Fomin's design lacks the inconsistencies, stylistic anachronisms and faux patinas characteristic of an earlier, 'eclectic' age. As if in response to the demands of domestic reformers, Fomin's space elevated stylistic unity to the pinnacle of architectural ambition.

## Typological Inventions

While the domestic scale of the *osobniak* allowed architects to test new stylistic principles, parallel experiments undertaken in other building types attest to the vitality of Russian architectural life and the public it served. The burgeoning middle class required new office buildings as well as new homes. Composed primarily of repetitive units, these structures made rhythmic repetition a key feature of business districts in Russian cities. Department stores grew to unprecedented dimensions and demonstrated the spatial potential of new building materials such as reinforced concrete. Commerce and the pageantry of shopping merged in the great light-filled interiors of the era's vast palaces of consumption. The age that witnessed the completion of the Trans-Siberian Railway produced monuments to travel in grandiose train stations. New values found architectural expression in the people's house, a new building type that combined theatrical and pedagogical programmes with socially progressive aims. While people's houses served factory workers, new immigrants from the country and village communities, the explosive growth of the urban populations precipitated a radical reconceptualization of the large apartment house, the fundamental building block of urban centres. Together, these new building types gave spatial expression to the rapid transformation of the Russian economy, population and political life.

Moscow's architects produced striking designs for commercial enterprises. In a series of projects for the Riabushinskii brothers, a bank of 1903 and a printing house of 1907, Shekhtel stripped his architectural language of the decorative flourishes that saturated his landmark house for Stepan Riabushinskii. But Shekhtel's most innovative commercial project was a large office building for the venerable Moscow Merchants' Society that he completed in 1909. Occupying a prominent corner in the city centre, Shekhtel's structure radiates clarity and rationalism. Spandrel panels and large, plate glass windows span each of the evenly spaced piers. Extensive glazing allows ample light to penetrate the interior, where the building's concrete frame is frankly expressed. Eschewing classical ornamentation, Shekhtel nevertheless gave the building a column-like tripartite division: each pier stands on a low base and is crowned by an attic that supports a thin, abstract cornice. The building's structure is as clear as its glazed brick exterior is bright. Shekhtel's pier and infill solution would also inspire Viktor Vesnin's experimental designs for office buildings, key projects in the early career of a founder of Constructivism.[35]

Traces of the Merchants' Society building appear in the nearby Northern Insurance Company headquarters, designed by Ivan Rerberg and Marian Peretiatkovich in 1909. Better described as a complex than a single building, Rerberg and Peretiatkovich's design is composed of two

Feodor Shekhtel, Moscow Merchants' Society building, Moscow, 1909.

structures that enclose a large, irregular private street. The reinforced concrete frame and restrained classical details of the pavilions lend the ensemble regularity and unity. The innovative approach to volume, massing and urban circulation adopted by the architects would be further developed by Ivan Kuznetsov in his design for Moscow's Delovoi Dvor (1912–13), an expansive complex of commercial and manufacturing spaces in the heart of the city. In order to accommodate increased demand for office space, Russian architects worked with large sites, expanding horizontally and creating large, unified ensembles. In so doing they began to renegotiate the relationship between the building and the street – between the block and the perimeter – suggesting that the one might open onto the other in a new type of fluid transition.

In the design of department stores, architects set interior and exterior spaces into new dynamic relationships. Shopping had traditionally taken place in large markets or trading rows, in which small vendors offered specialized goods. Moscow's Upper Trading Rows (1889–93), while grand and technically innovative, was a monument to the small-scale commerce characteristic of the late nineteenth century. The rapid expansion of industry and economic prosperity of the early twentieth century entailed a concentration of commodity distribution. The modern department store was both an expression and facilitator of this shift in consumption.

Originating in France in the second half of the nineteenth century, the department store was given paradigmatic form in designs such as Paul Sédille's Magasins du Printemps in Paris (1881–9): stacked sales floors surround a grand atrium that allows daylight to permeate the building. The designers of the Guards' Economic Society (1908–9), St Petersburg's most advanced department store, studied Sédille's model and innovative German designs like Alfred Messel's Wertheim store on Leipziger Platz in Berlin (1896–1904) as they refined their project.[36] Ernest Virrikh and

Ernest Virrikh and Stepan Krichinskii, Guards' Economic Society, St Petersburg, 1908–9.

Stepan Krichinskii, the building's designers, used a reinforced concrete frame to produce a remarkably light-filled interior. Large plate glass windows span the intervals between the paired piers that provide the structure's primary support. A simple pediment indicates the main entrance, and a decorative spire gives the acute corner of the building a formal accent. The interior is unified by a grand atrium. Four storeys high and enclosed by a glass dome, it appears to open onto the sky. Sales floors encircle this central court, creating an open and fluid sense of spatial interpenetration along both horizontal and vertical axes. Although only the officers of the Imperial Guards and Navy could shop there, the store's architecture set a new standard for the architectural treatment of commercial space in Russia. Sergei Zalesskii designed a similar department store for officers in Moscow – popularly known as Voentorg (1910–13) – soon after the completion of Virrikh and Krichinskii's building.[37] The central atrium of Zalesskii's design was one of the most grandiose commercial spaces constructed in Moscow before the October Revolution. It survived in the centre of the city until Moscow's mayor ratified its destruction in 2003 in the face of vehement public protest.

Like Russia's new department stores, a new generation of train stations displayed the potential of advanced building techniques to articulate ambitious spatial programmes. In the decades before the First World War both Moscow and St Petersburg witnessed the construction of grand new stations. In Moscow, Shekhtel's design for the Yaroslavl Station (1902) and Aleksei Shchusev's project for the Kazan Station (begun in 1911) reinterpreted traditional Russian forms for the railway age. In St Petersburg, S. A. Brzhozovskii and S. I. Minash's reconstruction of Tsaroselskii Station (1902–4), known today as Vitebsk Station, produced a remarkably complex response to the spatial requirements of the modern passenger station.[38] The building's location near the city's Obvodny Canal required the elevation of the platforms to the level of the first storey, complicating the building's pattern of vertical circulation. The grand foyer – a large hall decorated in the curvilinear forms of the *stil modern* – dramatizes this change of grade with a sweeping staircase that draws passengers upwards. The foyer, ticket hall, waiting room and restaurant seem to flow into one another, forming a complex spatial organism. Beyond the waiting room a shallow gallery forms a transition to the platforms. In both the gallery and the vast train shed, the solid walls and linear motifs of the interior transform into naked metalwork, revealing the structural skeleton of the station.

The competition for the reconstruction of Nikolaevskii Station, today's Moscow Station in St Petersburg, was a landmark event in pre-Revolutionary Russian architecture.[39] After several preliminary stages,

S. A. Brzhozovskii and S. I. Minash, Vitebsk Station, St Petersburg, 1902–4.

the final competition was announced in 1912. Vladimir Shchuko, a prominent classicist, prevailed with an expansive structure composed of three barrel vaults. Colossal columns run across the facade and support a heavy Doric frieze. Large semicircular windows terminate the vaults and illuminate the interior, while a lateral clock tower provides a vertical accent to the entire building. Although he did not win, Ivan Fomin presented a more prescient design. His combination of arches, heavy rustication, Doric columns, austere pediments and vast interior spaces gave his design a sense of scale that can only be compared to the fantastical engravings of the eighteenth-century architect Giovanni Battista Piranesi. Fomin pushed the combinatory possibilities of classicism further than any of his contemporaries, illuminating the path Russian architects would follow in the wake of the October Revolution.

In the decades before the First World War architects and social reformers established the basic programme of a new type of institution: the people's house, the progenitor of the Soviet workers' club. The people's

Vladimir Shchuko, Nikolaevskii Railway Station, St Petersburg, 1912 (project).

house emerged in Western Europe as an alternative site for working-class entertainment and education.[40] Supported by socialist or social democratic parties, these buildings had complex programmes that would often include a cafeteria, study halls, libraries, gymnasiums, meeting halls and spaces for amateur scientific experiments. The theatre, however, was the heart of these institutions. Projects such as Victor Horta's Maison du Peuple (1895–9), built in Brussels for the Belgian Workers' Party, demonstrated that this diverse programme might inspire architectural innovation. In Russia, factory owners and wealthy citizens provided more support for these institutions than working-class political parties. Nevertheless, by 1915 the leftist cooperative movement would lay claim to the people's house, calling it, in the words of L. M. Armand, 'the monument of our time'.[41] In St Petersburg Liudvig Nobel, the director of a successful mechanical factory, commissioned a people's house from Roman Meltser (1897–1901) in a settlement for the employees of the Nobel factory.[42] Moscow's municipal government supported the construction of the Vvedenskii People's House, designed by Illarion Ivanov-Shits (1903–5). Hundreds of people's houses were built in the years before the First World War. The cooperative movement helped these institutions flourish by publishing standardized designs that were distributed to urban and rural communities across the empire.[43]

The people's house became a vital centre of cultural innovation. St Petersburg's Ligovskii People's House (1901–4) led the way and helped foster the development of a new genre of theatre: the itinerant mass theatre. The institution was founded by Sophia Panina, a wealthy heiress who devoted her life to philanthropic activities. Designed by Iulii Benois, the building occupies a prominent corner in a working-class neighbourhood.

Panina's interest in children's education informed the project's pedagogical character. A large cafeteria, a gymnasium and a reading room for children occupied the lower floor. A small museum and a public observatory, where astronomers offered popular courses for patrons, were integral parts of the institution's programme. But the theatre was the building's most important space. Pavel Gaideburov and N. F. Skarskaia directed theatrical events, creating a democratic counterpoint to the elite theatres of the capital. Theirs was a 'mass theatre' accessible to all. Aleksandr Tairov, the director whose collaborations with constructivist architects in the 1920s transformed Soviet theatre, began his career at the Ligovskii People's House. Gaideburov and Skarskaia eventually turned their mass theatre into an itinerant ensemble that visited working-class neighbourhoods and agricultural communities throughout the country. Theatre at the people's house was more than just entertainment; it was also a forum for political enlightenment. In the words of one organizer, the theatre was valuable 'because it unifies and educates people'.[44] Gaideburov continued his work after the October Revolution, but Panina would be forced into exile.[45] Her legacy, however, was great. Before the Revolution she supported educational institutions and the growing movement for the construction of people's houses, laying the foundation for the network of workers' clubs that would spread throughout the Soviet Union in the 1920s.

## Urban Dimensions

Architects responded to the rapid growth of industry, commerce and population at the scale of both the individual building and the city as a whole. The building boom of the early twentieth century brought urban issues into public view like never before.[46] The concerned public recognized that unregulated construction was an impediment to rational urban growth. New investment in large infrastructural systems – water, gas, electricity – likewise demanded some municipal oversight of new construction. New, larger apartment houses increased population density in city centres, and greater density produced greater demands on sanitation. Speculative construction put the control of standards in the hands of developers, whose primary interest was profit, not quality living space. On the periphery of Russian cities, where industry settled, workers' housing was a pressing concern. As the pioneering urban planner Vladimir Semenov noted, broad expanses of the country were being resettled as workers followed industry and the railway east of the Urals.[47] In small towns and on the outskirts of large cities growing populations posed new social and spatial questions for architects and planners. They sought to

Fedor Lidval, Lidval apartment house, St Petersburg, 1899–1904.

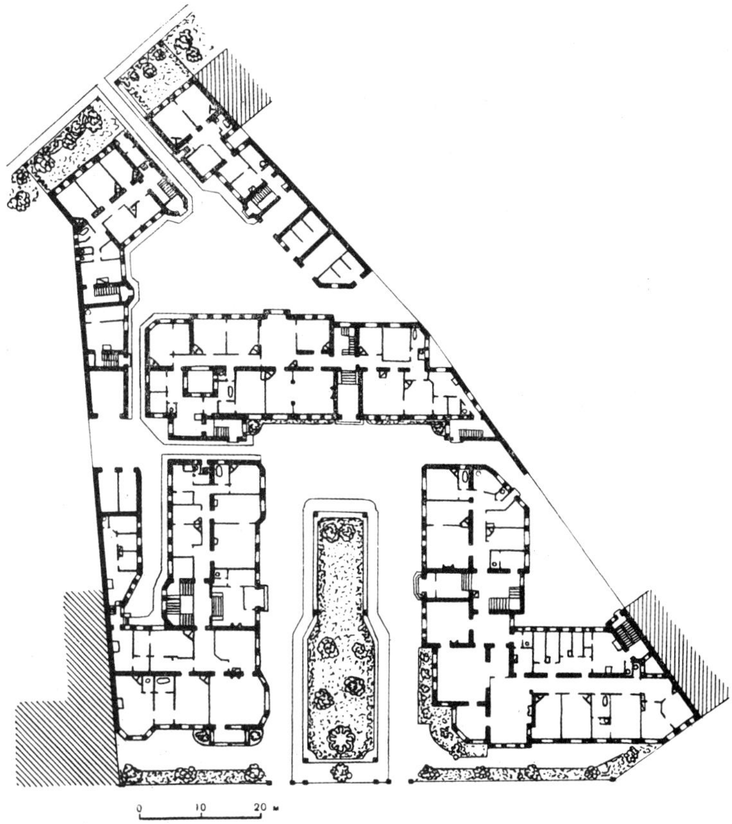


ameliorate living conditions by following the garden city model that was first articulated by the British planner Ebenezer Howard. In projects for city centres and urban satellites, architects sought to exert a new kind of control over space that might channel urban growth into rational, socially responsible and beautiful forms.

As the basic building block of urban fabric, the large apartment house was a primary candidate for reform. Like large commercial structures, architects gave the apartment house a new relationship to the street. They replaced the perimeter block with more plastic plans, placing courtyards on the street side of a parcel or allowing streets to pass through a complex. These changes depended on a new scale of construction and new methods of finance.[48] The residential complex designed by Fedor Lidval in St Petersburg between 1899 and 1904 is composed of four coordinated pavilions that are grouped around a large courtyard.[49] Lidval's building is a celebrated monument of the *stil modern*, but its spatial composition is its most striking feature. He designed the project not as an isolated object but as an ensemble that would integrate public streets and a semi-private network of open courts, lending the urban fabric a permeable character. Similar housing complexes were built in Moscow and other parts of St Petersburg. In Moscow, Leontii Benois and A. I. Gunst designed a large complex for the First Russian Insurance Society (1905–6), whose complex configuration reconstructed an entire block along Bolshaia Lubianka Street. Supported by corporate finance, this building and similar projects were able to attain ever larger scales.

The residential complex built by the Basseinaia Street Cooperative Housing Association (1912–14) was both an ambitious spatial project and an innovative experiment in finance. Designed by E. F. Virrikh, A. I. Zazerskii and others, the complex was an attempt to offset the pressure of the housing market through collective organization. According to Zazerskii, 'the construction of apartment houses lies in the hands of capitalists, not in the hands of those who need apartments', and the

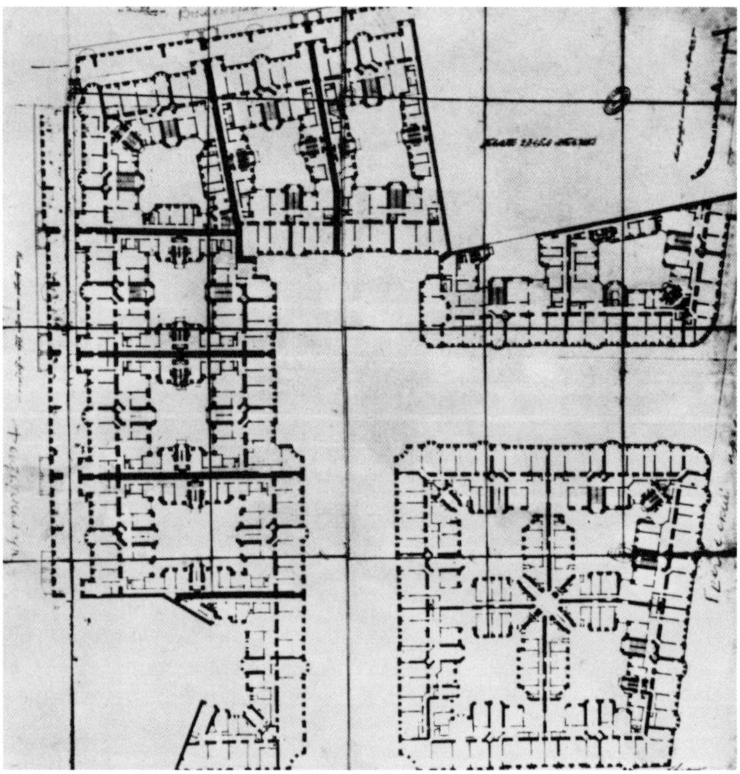

Residential complex of the Basseinaia Street Cooperative Housing Association, St Petersburg, 1912–14.

housing cooperative was an organizational form intended to compensate for this imbalance.[50] By pooling the resources of many individual stakeholders, the association was able to build and maintain this complex as a cooperative property. The scale of the complex is immense. An L-shaped street runs through the territory, uniting seven-storey-tall apartment blocks. Elevators serve apartments of three to six rooms. The complex occupies an entire city block; it is itself an urban ensemble with a unified appearance and a rational disposition of functions. As a large, coordinated development, the Basseinaia Street complex was an important precedent for Soviet Era mass housing construction.

The housing problem was more severe for the working class. Many of the factory workers who followed Russia's industrial growth into large cities lived in miserable conditions. Like other rapidly growing metropolises, the working-class districts of Moscow and St Petersburg were poorly developed and unsanitary. Poor or polluted water supplies, overcrowding and unregulated disposal of rubbish made these parts of the city dangerous places to live; according to Timothy Colton, Moscow was the unhealthiest big city in Europe.[51] Efforts to combat the social ill of poor housing led to the implementation of new urban and architectural programmes. Social advocacy groups in St Petersburg led the way. Founded by D. A. Dril in 1903, the Association Against Housing Need sponsored the construction of the Gavanskii Settlement (1904–6) on the outskirts of the city.[52] Nikolai Dmitriev, the designer of the complex, travelled to Western Europe to study recent trends in low-income housing in preparation for the project. The settlement is composed of five five-storey buildings: there are 200 apartments for families and 110 suites for singles, a school for 300 children, a nursery, a cafeteria, a library and a meeting hall. The suites for singles lack kitchens; their inhabitants were to eat in communal facilities. Occupying a large landscaped site, all of the structures receive ample sunlight. Although the settlement was not the only effort to improve low-income housing in Russia, it was praised by housing reformers as the most progressive project undertaken before the war.[53] The integration of social functions in the Gavanskii Settlement would influence Soviet experiments in communal housing.

Russian architects and planners conflated territorial ambitions and rational city planning as the empire expanded to the east. The Trans-Siberian Railway, officially completed in 1904, was part of a transportation network that the Russian state and entrepreneurs sought to turn into a profitable commercial enterprise in the East. The Chinese Eastern Railway was an important part of this network. A southern spur of the Trans-Siberian line, this route traversed Manchuria in present-day China, descending towards the city of Port Arthur and its ice-free port on the

N. V. Dmitriev, V. A. Fedorov, Gavanskii Workers' Settlement, St Petersburg, 1904–6.

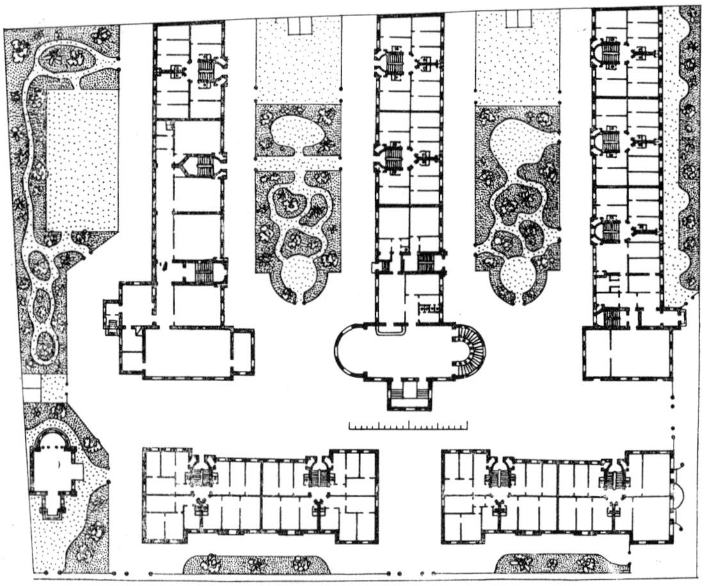

Gavanskii Workers' Settlement, plan of complex.

Yellow Sea.[54] Russian planners created multiple cities along this railway network, bringing imperial policy and architectural ideals to the edge of the Pacific Ocean. Dalian – today a city with more than six million inhabitants in China's Liaoning Province – was established during this period of expansion under a different name: Dalnyi, the Russian word for 'distant'. K. Skolimovskii designed its general plan between 1899 and 1903. The railway commissioned him to 'build a first class commercial port that will attract Russian and foreign capital' and to use 'cheap and compliant Chinese labour to create a large industrial city'.[55] Skolimovskii integrated this frankly racist commercial ambition into the plan, creating separate 'Chinese' and 'European' zones. He further divided the city into commercial, residential and suburban areas. A circular public square forms the heart of a road system composed of radial axes and rectilinear grids. The public square was a conscious reference to the Place de l'Etoile in Paris, while the picturesque subdivision of the 'European' sector was, Skolimovskii noted, informed by his reading of Josef Stübben's influential textbook *Der Städtebau* (The Building of Cities).[56] The 'Chinese' sector was designed in what Skolimovskii called 'an American grid', a very dense gridiron adjacent to a 'central bazaar'. Despite the colonialist elements of Dalnyi's plan, its design was based on the principle of functional zoning, a key concept in the development of modern urbanism. Located at an important railway junction north of Dalnyi, Kharbin became a major economic centre of the region. The city was also an outpost of the *stil modern* – its train station and several villas for railway officials made formal innovation a symbol of Russia's expansionist policy.[57]

While the Far East was a laboratory for *ex nihilo* urban planning, Russia's existing cities presented architects and engineers with more

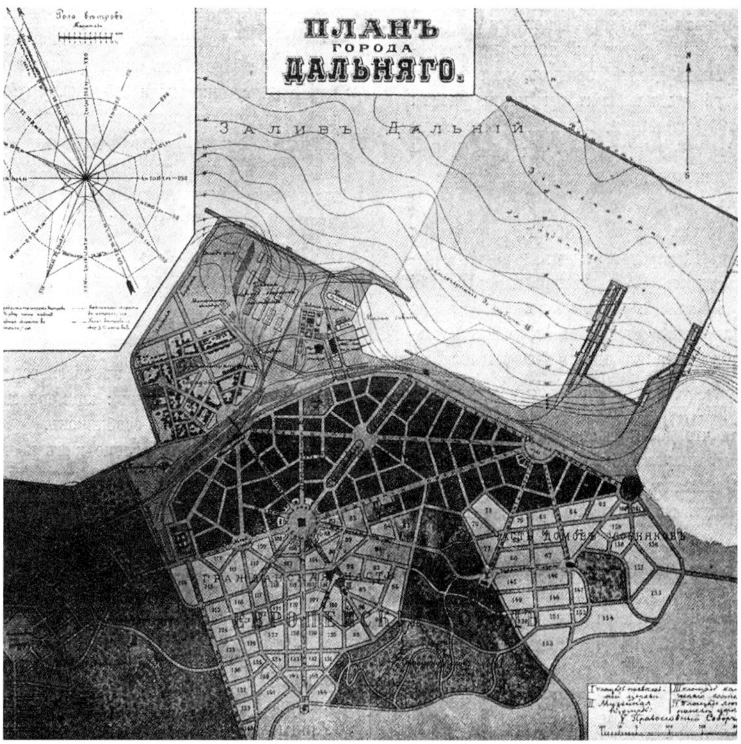


K. Skolimovskii, general plan for Dalnyi, 1899–1903.

complex problems. Urban growth was chief among them. In St Petersburg several ministries were formally charged with the verification and approval of construction documents, but their practical oversight was minimal and lacked a coherent programme for urban development. Leontii Benois was among the first architects to challenge this situation and propose the creation of a 'complete project for urban facilities in light of the pressing needs for its growth'.[58] The Academy of Fine Arts and the chairman of the Council of Ministers, Petr Stolypin, approved Benois' initiative, but the city council rejected it, citing its potential to diminish private initiative. Nevertheless, Benois worked with the transportation engineer Fedor Enakiev on a development proposal for the city between 1908 and 1910. Their project sought to reconcile aesthetic and technical considerations.[59] A monumental prospect named after Tsar Nicholas II was to become a new axis of circulation. They collected the western train stations into a single terminal, which occupied one end of the new corridor. This street was to extend north, past the Mariinskii Theatre, to a new bridge over the Neva to Vasilievskii Island. It would cut through dense urban fabric, but it would create a major traffic artery through rapidly developing districts. The Benois/Enakiev plan also proposed the development of the Vyborg side, an expanding industrial zone in the north.

Although private initiative was often seen as an impediment to coherent urban development, some speculators turned architectural unity into a marketing strategy. Ivan Fomin's project for 'New Petersburg', a real estate venture on St Petersburg's Golodai Island, was the most ambitious undertaking of the era. 'New Petersburg' was the vision of Riccardo Gualino, an Italian financier. He saw this as an opportunity to 'create a city . . . to create life where there had been silence'.[60] In order to finance this project Gualino founded the St Petersburg Land and Mortgage Company in 1911 and sold bonds on the London and Paris Markets. The aim of the company, however, was not to construct buildings. Gualino sought to provide a network of streets, public amenities and design regulations in order to entice investors to lease his plots of land. Fomin created a monumental architectural language for the projected ensemble. Facades composed of heavy rustication and colossal orders surround the territory's central square. The immensity of the plan was bolstered by grand porticos that traverse radial streets. Fomin's design recalls the austere unity of eighteenth-century Petersburg. But despite Gualino's international financial assets, 'New Petersburg' could not survive the outbreak of the First World War, when the city was renamed Petrograd in an assertion of the distinctly Russian nature of the capital. The network of streets that Fomin designed survives, but only one structure, designed by Fedor Lidval,

Ivan Fomin, project for 'New Petersburg', Golodai Island, St Petersburg, 1912.

was built before the war. Tied as he was to private finance, Gualino depended too heavily on the same market forces that had created the urban environment he was trying to reform.

Many planners thought the true path of urban reform led away from the large city. The price of land encouraged speculators to increase housing density. Cramped, unhygienic conditions seemed to be an endemic ill of the large metropolis. Russian reformers participated in an international movement to find an alternative to what many saw as the misery of the urban poor. Ebenezer Howard's theory of the garden city exerted an enormous influence on planners outside his native Britain. In *To-morrow: A Peaceful Path to Real Reform*, Howard promoted small, satellite communities set amid verdant agricultural land as the ideal settlement of the future.[61] These communities were to have no more than 32,000 inhabitants. Canals and railways would traverse the broad green belts between each locality and a larger central city. Municipal ownership of land and revenue from light industry would make it possible for the single family home to become the basic unit of development. The cottage was seen as both an antidote to the unsanitary tenement and a tool to uplift the working classes. Howard's vision of this 'social city' led to the creation of the Garden City Movement, which swept across Europe in the early twentieth century. The Movement came to Russia with the help of Mikhail Dikanskii, A. K. Ensh, Aleksandr Blokh and Dmitri Protopopov.[62] Dikanskii, an advocate of housing reform, translated extracts of Howard's book and published Russian versions of Howard's key diagrams of the garden city model in his book *Kvartirnyi vopros* (The Housing Question) of 1908, which was first published in serialized form in *Zodchii* the preceding year.[63] In 1913 the Russian Garden City Society was founded. This new type of community was desirable to advocates for its rationality and potential to diffuse growing social tensions. According

Vladimir Semenov, housing for Prozorovskaia Settlement, 1913.

to one reformer, the garden city was a way to achieve 'socialism without politics' – to appease disenfranchised citizens and avoid revolutionary struggle.[64]

In the design of garden cities, reformers countered the mono-functional gridiron plans found in the dacha settlements that surrounded large Russian cities. These traditional suburban retreats provided an escape from the heat and misery of the city, but they lacked the rational planning and communal facilities valued by garden city advocates.[65] The garden city was imagined as a complete social system: it was to include a school, a market, a bathhouse, a theatre, a church, a library and a hospital, as well as commercial enterprises, public parks and hygienic dwellings. Architects and planners designed garden city settlements across the empire, but the most ambitious and detailed undertaking was Vladimir Semenov's design for a settlement for railway workers on Moscow's periphery.[66] Commissioned by the Moscow–Ryazan Railway Company in 1912, the Prozorovskaia Settlement (it was named after the local station) radiated away from the track in gently curving bands of residential streets. A system of internal parks connected the settlement to agricultural land. Most of the territory was reserved for residential construction. Semenov foresaw the construction of nearly 1,000 four- to five-room houses. The simple forms, broad roofs and lack of ostentation of Semenov's houses recall British precedents. Large plots would keep the population density extremely low. Preliminary construction began in 1912: trees were cleared, roads were laid and subdivisions were plotted. The outbreak of the First World War, however, interrupted the development of the Prozorovskaia Settlement. Its street pattern survives, but its greatest legacy was the experience that Semenov gained from devising its plan. He codified this theory in his influential book *Blagoustroistvo gorodov* (The Improvement of Cities, 1912), and would apply his knowledge to solving some of the Soviet Union's greatest urban problems.

The war of 1914 interrupted much of the country's non-military construction. Aleksandr Blokh recognized that the time of hostilities might serve as a preparatory phase for post-war reconstruction. 'The greatest evil Russian cities suffered . . . was the lack of a plan', he wrote. He called upon his colleagues to 'use this period to prepare for the future growth of construction, to ensure that the new will be better than the old'.[67] Although Blokh could not foresee the revolutionary events of 1917, the garden city model that he promoted would become a key element of urban policy in the early years of the Soviet government.

When Tsar Nicholas II abdicated in February 1917 and the Provisional Government was established, architects greeted the new de facto social democracy. Amid the disastrous campaigns of the war, *Zodchii* published celebrations of the country's 'new life'. 'We are now citizens of free Russia', proclaimed the architect G. Kosmachevskii. 'We will heal our cities and towns, give our people comfortable and beautiful dwellings; we will create grand parliamentary buildings; we will build cathedrals of justice, science and art.'[68] Russian architects experienced the February Revolution as the liberation of their profession. They established an All-Russian Union of Architects, which was to 'ensure and reinforce recently won freedoms', reform building law, architectural education and professional ethics.[69] The Union's chairperson was Aleksei Shchusev, who used his talent for political compromise to enlist Russia's leading architects and institutions in the project. Under Shchusev's leadership, the Union made the construction of garden cities and monuments to fallen Russian soldiers a priority. He also helped negotiate the organizational integration of the All-Russian Union of Architects into the regime that emerged after the second, Bolshevik, revolution of 1917. But the hiatus in construction brought about by the First World War did not end with the conclusion of a peace treaty between Russia and Germany at Brest-Litovsk in 1918. It would extend through Russia's long and bitter civil war, which left the country in ruins, devastated by years of conflict, and with scarce economic means. When architecture emerged from this laboratory period, it did so with radical new concepts for a fundamentally new society.

электрификация всей страны

chapter three

# Laboratories of Soviet Architecture, 1917–23

After visiting Moscow and Petrograd in 1920, the writer H. G. Wells described a society on the verge of collapse. 'Our dominant impression of things Russian is an impression of a vast irreparable breakdown', he wrote.[1] Shops had been closed down, streets were in disrepair, inhabitants lived in a state of privation, food prices soared on the black market and wooden houses were used for firewood. Chaos, profiteering and starvation reigned. 'About the only things that seem to be fairly well supplied are tea, cigarettes and matches.'[2] The devastating losses of the First World War, the tumult of the October Revolution and the ongoing Civil War left Russia weak, poor and grasping for survival. But this material poverty was fertile ground for utopian aspirations. Wells ended his journey with an interview with 'the dreamer in the Kremlin', Vladimir Lenin. The leader of the Bolsheviks was not the orthodox Marxist Wells had expected. The two agreed that the eradication of private industry virtually required the 'the scrapping of the existing towns and their replacement'. The objective of Bolshevik industrial policy matched the boldness of this proposition. 'For Lenin', Wells wrote, 'has succumbed at last to a Utopia, the Utopia of the electricians.'[3] Lenin declared that 'Communism is Soviet power plus the electrification of the entire country' as he initiated his plan for the transformation of a largely peasant society into a modern industrial state.[4] Amid the ruins of Russia's old regime, Lenin, the Bolshevik Party, and countless economists, artists, architects and other visionaries imagined the shape of a new society and the forms of a new culture.

As novel as they might seem, the utopias that Wells found in Lenin's plans for the country had been developing for decades. Indeed, the influence of pre-Revolutionary radical thought on early Soviet leaders cannot be underestimated. Nikolai Chernyshevsky's novel *What is to be Done?* (1863) was an indispensable reference for Lenin and others. Chernyshevsky offered a vision of a utopian community of the future for which the city and state had ceased to exist and which organized itself around collective labour and communal values. Other radical thinkers such as Peter Kropotkin proposed alternative, anarchist models of social organization.

Gustav Klutsis, *Electrification of the Entire Country*, 1920.

By the early twentieth century, writers such as Aleksandr Bogdanov were offering hypothetical future scenarios for the socialist organization of society in science fiction novels. His *Red Star* (1908) and *Engineer Menni* (1913), which chronicled the life of a communist society on Mars, contributed to the utopian aspirations that Lenin sought to realize after rising to power.[5]

The Bolsheviks seized control of the state in a *coup d'état* in October 1917. The Provisional Government that emerged after the abdication of the Tsar in February proved to be unstable, in part because it found a fierce competitor for legitimacy in the Petrograd Soviet.[6] The Petrograd Soviet was established at the same time as the Provisional Government, and its organizational structure was based on the workers' councils – the soviets – that socialist activists created during the Revolution of 1905. The Petrograd Soviet called for the democratization of the armed forces and demanded Soviet authority over military policy. When the Soviet was established, most leading Bolsheviks, including Lenin, were in exile, either abroad or in Siberia. This left control of the Soviet's Executive Committee in the hands of the less radical Menshevik faction of the Russian socialist movement. The two factions had split in 1903 following a dispute over party membership and organization: Lenin led the *bolsheviki*, the majority, while the *mensheviki*, the minority, encompassed a broader range of positions. Lenin articulated the programme of the Bolsheviks and recalled the social mission of Chernyshevsky in *What is to be Done?* (1902), calling for a committee of professional revolutionaries, a militant Marxism, a centralization of party authority and violent revolutionary tactics. When Lenin returned to Petrograd's Finland Station in April 1917, he adopted the slogan 'all power to the soviets'. Massive casualties of the continued war effort and a failed counter-revolutionary coup led by General Lavr Kornilov created a wave of popular unrest that Lenin saw as an opportune revolutionary moment. Heeding Lenin's orders, the Petrograd Soviet launched an insurrection on 24 October. Governmental buildings, public works and railway stations were seized. On the following day, the Winter Palace, where the Provisional Government was in session, was besieged and occupied by the military committee of the Soviet. The October Revolution had begun and state control formally passed to the workers' councils that had been established throughout the country. Lenin and the Bolsheviks took leadership of the country in the new, centralized institution of the Council of People's Commissars.

As many historians have noted, the victory in Petrograd was not the end but the beginning of the Bolshevik Revolution.[7] Soon after the October coup, Lenin ended Russia's involvement in the First World War with the treaty of Brest-Litovsk. Moscow was quickly taken by the Bolsheviks, becoming the new capital in early 1918. Multiple campaigns from counter-revolutionary forces plunged the country into civil war. Battles between the 'Red' Bolshevik Army and the 'White' insurgency lasted for years, tapering off only in 1920–21. The Bolsheviks eliminated counter-revolutionary threats only at great cost. The landowning class virtually disappeared, its members either killed or forced into emigration.[8] The populations of Petrograd and Moscow dropped to less than half their pre-war size. The war and the events following the October Revolution displaced nearly 17.5 million people, and some 3 million soldiers were killed in combat. Famine and epidemics killed some 13 million civilians in 1921 and 1922. The years of the Civil War also coincide with the foundation and expansion of the Cheka, the 'Extraordinary Commission to Fight the Counter-revolution and Sabotage' – a ruthless secret police force and precursor to the KGB. The Cheka instituted 'concentration camps' for political prisoners and so-called 'class enemies'. Such camps were created across Russia; by the end of the Civil War seven camps in Moscow and three in its surrounding districts held more than 4,000 prisoners.[9] Industry was at a standstill, and food and fuel crises were pervasive. Such were the causes of the breakdown that Wells had recognized during his visit of 1920.

The Civil War gave the Bolshevik leadership its first opportunity to rule. During the conflict, 'planning' became a central concern of economists and politicians as they established a system of 'War Communism'. Intrigued by the work of the industrialist Walther Rathenau on the regulation of the German wartime economy, Bolshevik leaders made centralization and nationalization key elements of Soviet economic policy.[10] Planning was an antidote to what Bolshevik leaders saw as the chaos and disorder of the capitalist market. Although central planning generated black markets, redundancy and waste – that is, its own form of chaos – it offered a utopian image of totality, of a society and economy with purposeful direction.[11] These ideas were at the heart of the *ABC of Communism* (1919), a condensation of the Party Programme written by Nikolai Bukharin and Evgenii Preobrazhenskii. They predicted that the communist future would be 'one vast people's workshop' where 'everything must be precisely calculated'.[12]

The ideals of organization, precision and control influenced many Soviet endeavours, both social and cultural. The State Commission for the Electrification of Russia (GOELRO), formed in 1920, articulated a plan for national industrial development. Enthusiasts such as Bogdanov advocated a new, organized form of proletarian culture, or *Proletkult*. He hoped for the realization of the social vision he had presented in his pre-Revolutionary novel *Red Star*: 'When the social order is like a well-oiled machine, all will work in accordance with the indications of [the] statistical bureau.'[13] Aleksei Gastev, a poet and labour theorist, used Frederick Winslow Taylor's principles of scientific management to promote the 'scientific organization of labour'.[14] For others, such as the writer Evgenii Zamiatin, the prospect of total organization was a dystopian nightmare. His novel *We* (written in 1919 and banned in 1921) described a shimmering glass city in which transparency and omnipresent surveillance enabled the ubiquitous 'One-state' to manage every aspect of a citizen's daily life.

The Bolshevik government instituted sweeping reforms of urban policy soon after taking power. Private ownership of land and natural resources was abolished with a decree of February 1918. Later that year, private ownership of real estate in cities was eliminated.[15] The Council of People's Commissars decreed the demolition of monuments to Tsars, igniting an iconoclastic campaign of destruction and a creative search for symbols for the Revolution. Some enthusiasts sought to create a museum of 'bad taste' for demounted sculptures and memorials.[16] Streets in Moscow and Petrograd were renamed in honour of Marxist theorists and revolutionary heroes. New state and municipal institutions took control of urban planning and construction. Ivan Fomin directed the planning and architectural workshops in Petrograd, while Ivan Zholtovskii led Moscow's architectural department. Although very little was built in Russian cities before the end of the Civil War, these agencies were incubators of architectural ideas.

Among the most palpable urban reforms was the policy of 'housing repartition' that the Bolsheviks instituted in 1917.[17] Under this policy, persons considered 'bourgeois elements' were either evicted from their apartments or forced to share quarters with working-class families. This movement of people created a persistent feature of the Socialist city: the *dom-kommuna*, or communal house. Although these were often pre-Revolutionary apartment buildings in which each unit was shared by multiple families, their promoters saw great social and ideological potential in their creation. 'The *dom-kommuna* is a residence whose economic structure and way of life were intended to foster the development of collectivist principles in the inhabitants of the building', one commentator wrote.[18] By 1921 there were more than 550 communal houses in Moscow alone, and such practices can still be found in St Petersburg. Yet the policy was also a pragmatic measure: the overcrowding of apartment buildings represented a stopgap solution to the severe housing crises faced by large cities. Nevertheless, the ideal of collective living and the abolition of private ownership of land gave architects unprecedented conditions for social and spatial experimentation.

Exposure to avant-garde artistic projects transformed architectural conventions. Before and during the First World War, architects remained relatively aloof to the flourishing of Russian artistic culture. Neo-Primitivism, Futurism, Cubo-Futurism, Rayonism and a variety of other '-isms' changed the basic premises of artistic practice before the Revolution.[19] The '0.10 Exhibition', held in Petrograd in 1915, was a watershed event in Russian artistic culture. Billed as 'the last Futurist painting exhibition', this was the public debut of Kazimir Malevich's Suprematist paintings and Vladimir Tatlin's 'counter-reliefs'. Malevich had explored a variety of styles prior to the exhibition, but he claimed to have arrived at the ultimate stage of painting with Suprematism.[20] 'Objects have vanished like smoke, for the sake of the new culture of art', he declared.[21] His *Black Square* of 1915 proclaimed the task of non-objective painting to be not the reproduction of nature but an act of creation. Malevich's commitment to the creative power of the artist and the geometric world of floating and sliding forms would exert a powerful influence on artists and architects for years to come. Tatlin's 'counter-reliefs' pushed his exploration of artistic material into the third dimension: they were sculptures composed of found materials and suspended in gallery corners. According to Nikolai Punin, these works transferred the field of artistic activity from the space of representation into 'real spatial relationships'.[22] Tatlin's interest was in the analysis of materiality, volume and construction as such. His study of objective qualities set the stage for post-Revolutionary artistic practice.

The painter Wassily Kandinsky had a unique relationship to the Russian avant-garde before the revolution. He spent the first decade of the twentieth century in Germany, where he participated in the circle of artists known as the Blue Rider, and he undertook early experiments in painterly abstraction. In his book *Concerning the Spiritual in Art* (1912) he sought to categorize the psychic and emotional responses elicited by pure colour and form.[23] Drawing on Richard Wagner's theory of the *Gesamtkunstwerk*, the total work of art, Kandinsky called for the creation of a 'monumental art' that would be 'the combination of every art in one single work, whereby each art, while remaining exclusively within the bounds of its given form, becomes a joint begetter of the work'.[24] With the outbreak of the First World War, Kandinsky was forced to return to Russia, where he pursued both painterly abstraction and the ideal of 'monumental art'.

In the first years of Soviet power, artists attained powerful positions within new cultural institutions. Led by the People's Commissariat of Enlightenment (Narkompros) and its chairman, Anatolii Lunacharskii, a dense and overlapping group of organizations elevated the analysis and advancement of artistic conventions to a national concern.[25] Narkompros was the highest state agency for culture and education. Its Fine Arts Department (Otdel izobrazitelnykh iskusstv, known by its abbreviation IZO) was created in 1918.[26] The painter David Shterenberg led the IZO board in Petrograd and Vladimir Tatlin was the Moscow section's deputy chair. In the autumn of 1919 Kazimir Malevich moved to Vitebsk and assumed leadership of a collective of young artists known as the 'Affirmers of New Art', or UNOVIS. Kandinsky developed the founding programme of the Institute of Artistic Culture (INKhUK), a new section of IZO established in 1920.

Within the alphabet soup of Soviet cultural institutions, new, ideologically charged groups emerged. SINSKULPTARKh, a union dedicated to the synthesis of painting, sculpture and architecture, was founded in 1919. It became a platform for the development of a new type of 'rationalist' architecture. The 'First Working Group of Constructivists', whose members believed that the artist should be a creator of new economical objects, was founded within INKhUK in 1921. Constructivist principles produced the ideology of productivism – the idea that the future of artistic labour lay in the creation of mass-produced industrial products.[27] Supported by the journal *LEF* (Left Front of the Arts), which Vladimir Mayakovsky edited from 1923 to 1925, Constructivism and productivism achieved widespread currency among radical artists, designers and architects.

The theoretical paradigms worked out in research institutes formed the basis for new methods of teaching. Established in Moscow in 1920, VKhUTEMAS, the Higher State Artistic and Technical Workshops, was the leading school of design and architecture.[28] Its major achievement was its basic course in which students analysed the fundamental artistic categories of colour, plane, volume and space. Seven faculties offered specialized training. The architecture faculty sought to combine 'contemporary scientific truths and artistic truths with the culture of human living space'.[29] Virtually all of Moscow's leading architects taught at the school in the early 1920s; it was the epicentre of Soviet architectural creativity.

In 1921 the Bolshevik leadership recognized that the state's total control of the economy during War Communism had become unsustainable. Lenin devised and instituted a 'New Economic Policy', NEP, in that year in order to boost the production of agriculture and manufactured goods. A private sector was allowed to emerge, while the state retained control over the 'commanding heights' of the economy: industry and banking.[30] International investors were invited to Russian markets, and a variety of consumer cooperatives were established. The NEP fostered transnational relationships between cultural producers as well. The Berlin-based, tri-lingual journal *Veshch/Objet/Gegenstand* proclaimed in 1922 that 'the blockade of Russia is coming to an end'.[31] El Lissitzky and

Ilia Ehrenburg, the journal's editors, wrote of a new internationalism in the arts, noting that all of Europe and America had entered a new 'creative period'. Through growing networks of communication – journals, exhibitions, conferences, personal contacts – Russian architects and institutions participated in the international world of modernism. These were mutual exchanges: both Russia and the West sought to create new forms and new practices for a 'new, collective, international style'.[32]

## Art of the Commune

The Soviet state took possession of cities symbolically. Vladimir Mayakovsky called for a new order of urban iconography in his poem 'An Order to the Army of Art' (1918):

> The streets – our brushes
> the squares – our palettes
> the revolution's days
> are not yet praised in the millennial book of time
> to the streets, futurists,
> drummers and poets![33]

Aleksandr and Viktor Vesnin, decorations for the Kremlin, 1 May 1918.

Artists and architects collaborated on elaborate street festivals and demonstrations to celebrate the victory of the October Revolution. For May Day 1918, Aleksandr and Viktor Vesnin – two of the three brothers who would soon revolutionize Soviet architecture – took charge of scenography for an elaborate spectacle. They transformed the Kremlin and its gates into a billowing mass of red banners and victory slogans. Petrograd staged a dramatic re-enactment of the storming of the Winter Palace on the third anniversary of the Revolution. Buildings were bathed in electric lights and the Navy stationed ships in the Neva, recalling the participation of the mutinied battleship *Aurora* in 1917. As rockets were fired into the air, a new mythology of the Revolution was thrust into place.[34]

Bolshevik leaders edified the new state with monumental sculptural programmes. Lenin initiated a 'Plan for Monumental Propaganda' in 1918. Informed by his reading of Tommaso Campanella's utopian dialogue *The City of the Sun* (1623), Lenin planned to erect monuments to a number of revolutionary figures and Russian cultural leaders. His list included Marx, Engels, Robespierre, Bakunin, Dostoevsky, Scriabin and many others. Lenin's aim was pedagogical, not commemorative. Each statue was to include biographical panels, and the unveiling of each was to be accompanied by a small festival in which accounts of the deeds and significance of each figure would be read. Throughout 1918 and 1919 monuments appeared in Petrograd and Moscow. They replaced the monuments of the Tsarist era, which the Bolsheviks had slated for destruction, but most of the figural sculptures erected by the Soviet regime remained well within conventional realist conventions.[35]

D. M. Osipov and N. Andreev, Obelisk of the Soviet Constitution, Moscow, 1918.

The first monumental complexes constructed after the Revolution exposed the conservative artistic taste of the Bolshevik leadership. On Lenin's personal initiative, a competition for a monument to the new Soviet constitution was held in 1918. Dmitrii Osipov's winning proposal was composed of historical architectural forms and figurative sculpture. Standing directly opposite the headquarters of the Moscow Soviet on Soviet Square, his design set a towering obelisk atop a massive stone pedestal. N. A. Andreev's sculpture of victory stood in front of the obelisk, its arms extending skywards. The text of the constitution was cast in bronze and attached to

Lev Rudnev, monument to the victims of the Revolution, Field of Mars, Petrograd, 1917.

the monument's pedestal. The obelisk of the constitution reflected Lenin's commitment to figural, literal and pedagogical artistic traditions. He believed that Marxism had 'assimilated and refashioned everything of value in the more than two thousand years of the development of human thought and culture', and that Soviet artists were to do the same.[36] Some architects, however, approached commemorative structures with innovative forms. In 1917, the young architect Lev Rudnev devised a laconic tomb for the 'Victims of the Revolution' on the Field of Mars in Petrograd. He used large granite blocks from a dismantled granary, which had been designed by Jean-François Thomas de Thomon (1805–7), to create a severe memorial complex. The monument consists of four low walls that separate an interior court from the surrounding park. Each of the L-shaped sections is composed of four tiers of granite blocks. Large slabs bear commemorative texts composed by Lunacharskii. Rudnev's forms are coarse, bold and sombre. He combined simple geometric solids to create powerful and complex shapes.[37]

The first large-scale projects conceived after the October Revolution made dynamic use of historical forms. Architects maintained the interest in classicism that had dominated the profession before 1917. But they now exaggerated, stretched, simplified and otherwise transformed classical elements, generating an approach to design that is often described as 'Symbolic' or 'Revolutionary' Romanticism.[38] In his winning project for

Ivan Fomin, Palace of Workers, Petrograd, 1919.

Ilia Golosov, crematorium, competition project, Moscow, 1919.

a 'palace of workers' in Petrograd (1919), Ivan Fomin developed what he called 'proletarian classicism'. The 'palace of workers' is more severe and muscular than any of Fomin's earlier designs, save perhaps his project for Nikolaevskii Station in St Petersburg of 1912. Colossal Doric columns surround the building, lending its projecting wings and broad courtyard grandiose dimensions. The building's principal volume contains a large amphitheatre that is crowned by a multi-tiered dome, which recalls the Roman Pantheon. Although many of Fomin's forms were derived from historical models, their combination and treatment was unprecedented.[39]

Later in 1919, competitions for municipal crematoria in both Petrograd and Moscow solicited innovative reinterpretations of classical forms.[40] Few crematoria existed in Russia prior to the Revolution, for the Russian Orthodox Church condemned the practice of cremation. This gave architects relative freedom of design. Fomin prevailed in the Petrograd competition with a project composed of a slender tower and compact forecourt. Ilia Golosov was victorious in Moscow. Golosov had built little

Vladimir Tatlin with assistant in front of model for the Monument to the Third International, 1920.

before the Revolution, but he would soon become an influential teacher and leading architect in Moscow. His project for the Moscow crematorium presented the major themes of his later work: large volumes, intersecting forms and dynamic relationships between circular and rectangular geometries. His design recalls the work of visionary architects of the eighteenth century such as Boullée, Ledoux and Piranesi. A squat Doric portico leads to a large rectangular base. The principal space is a multi-storey drum that is crowned by a semicircular dome. A spiral staircase encircles the central shaft of the chimney and provides access to the circular galleries of the columbarium. Filled with niches, crossed by bridges and drowned by shadows, this complex space evokes the labyrinthine interiors of Piranesi's *Carceri* series. The building's geometric mass dwarfed Golosov's classical orders. In the dynamic combination of geometrical solids, Golosov found a productive technique for the generation of what he would later call 'architectural organisms'.[41]

Vladimir Tatlin cast Soviet ideology in new symbolic forms with his *Monument to the Third International* of 1919–20. Tatlin, chair of the Moscow section of IZO, objected to the conservative direction of the Plan for Monumental Propaganda, and issued a memorandum that declared that the 'state, as it is now, cannot and must not be the initiator of bad taste'.[42] Initially conceived as a monument to the October Revolution, Tatlin rededicated his monument to the Third Communist International (formed in 1919) when it was completed and presented at the Eighth All-Russian Congress of Soviets in 1920. The final design was revolutionary in both conception and form. Four hundred metres tall (almost 80 m taller than the Eiffel Tower), its system of girders formed an ascending spiral and recalled his earlier experiments with 'counter-reliefs'. The tower combined the symbolic and the utilitarian. Its structural frame supported four glazed, rotating halls that served administrative functions: a large cube housed legislative assemblies and rotated once per year; a pyramid served executive bodies and turned once per month; the cylinder and, presumably, the uppermost hemisphere were reserved for information services and rotated once per day. Tatlin envisioned his monument as a synthesis of art and the technologies of everyday life.[43] Although he insisted upon the technical feasibility of the Monument, it functioned primarily as a symbol of artistic innovation. Mayakovsky called it 'the first monument without a beard' and the 'first object of October'; Berlin Dadaists proclaimed the victory of 'Tatlin's machine-art' over conventional artistic practice; Ilia Ehrenburg declared that 'a new architecture begins' with Tatlin's

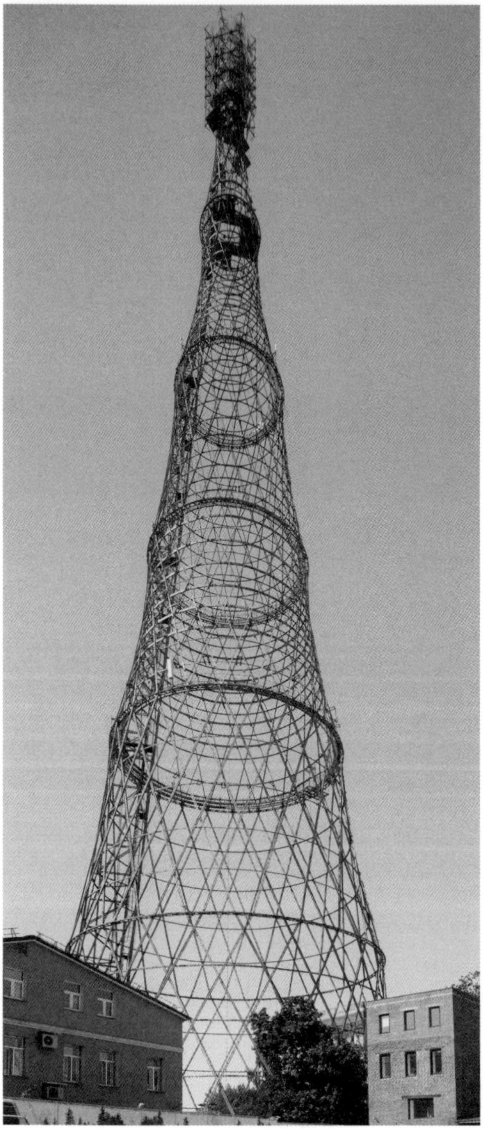

Vladimir Shukhov, Shabolovka Radio Tower, Moscow, 1919–22.

Monument.[44] His vision of a dynamic, new monument spurred sculptors, painters and architects on to ambitious undertakings.[45] It was, nevertheless, impossible to construct Tatlin's tower in the economic climate of the early 1920s.

As Tatlin developed his ambitious project, the engineer Vladimir Shukhov was at work on a tower with similar vertical aspirations. Shukhov's Shabolovka Radio Tower in Moscow (1919–22) was initially intended to be 300 m tall. In his project, Shukhov refined the structural system of hyperboloids assembled from thin steel members that he had deployed at the Nizhniy Novgorod Exposition of 1896 and in countless water towers across Russia. But the Shabolovka tower had far greater ambitions than his earlier structures. A decree signed by Lenin himself authorized the construction of the tower in July 1919, indicating that a radio connection to the western regions of Soviet territory was vital for the ongoing Civil War. As the primary broadcast centre of the Comintern, Shukhov's tower fulfilled some of the functions Tatlin had proposed. Although the height of the realized tower was reduced by half of Shukhov's initial projections, it became a revered landmark in Moscow's cityscape, manifesting the importance of new media to early Soviet culture.[46]

## The City and Soviet Power

The first attempts to relieve Russia's urban crisis drew on the garden city model. In theory, the Bolshevik government's policies created ideal conditions for the construction of new, rational settlements. Private ownership of land – the scourge of pre-war urban development – disappeared with the success of the October Revolution. New departments of planning and construction were established in municipalities across the country. They projected garden suburbs for Moscow, Petrograd, Yaroslavl, Perm, Novosibirsk and many other cities. These institutes continued the work undertaken by the Garden City Movement before and during the First World War, and the Russian branch of the Movement was re-established in 1922.[47] In addition to the alleged healthful effects of this model of urban development, its importance in the early years of Soviet power was also a pragmatic response to the economic conditions of the time. 'We are not in a position to provide our settlements with the engineering works required for a large city', Vladimir Semenov wrote in 1922. 'We should consider only the simplest methods of improvement . . . In other words, we can only build small cities.'[48] Leonid Vesnin's general plan for a settlement in Podolsk, a city south of Moscow, supplemented the garden-city tradition with a new social ideal. A people's house and an athletic field occupy the centre of the plan. Terraced houses surround broad green

Leonid Vesnin, workers' settlement of the Podolsk locomotive repair factory, 1922; general plan.

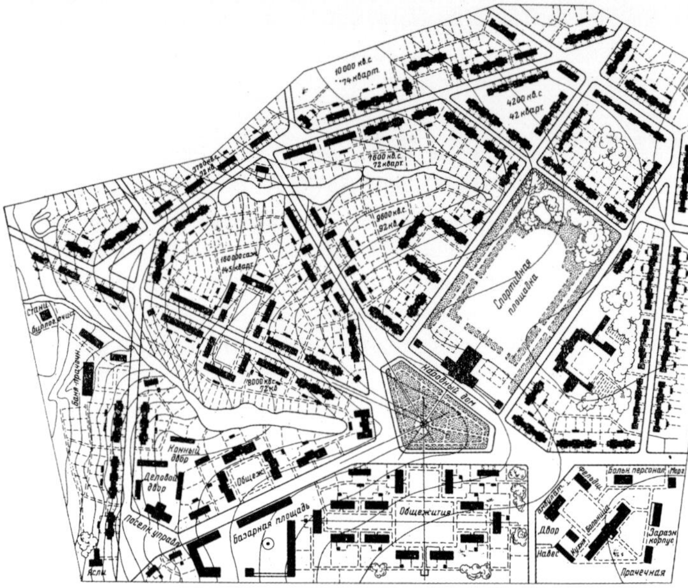


courts, while blocks of dormitories face the principal square. A school, a hospital and a market served the workers of the city's locomotive factory and maintenance shop.

The adoption of the New Economic Policy in 1921 enabled housing cooperatives to establish small suburban settlements. These groups, like their pre-revolutionary antecedents, facilitated the collective leasing of land and construction of housing. Tsentrosoiuz, the Central Union of Consumer Cooperatives, outlined regulations for the administration of housing cooperatives and provided model plans for dwellings, libraries, people's houses and a variety of other services.[49] Rural communities in Chelyabinsk province, Smolensk province and other parts of the country established new settlements based on Tsentrosoiuz's guidelines. In 1921 a group of employees from Tsentrosoiuz and other organizations established the Sokol housing cooperative in Moscow.[50] Among the first model settlements in the capital, Sokol was planned in consultation with Aleksei Shchusev and populated with cottages designed by Nikolai Markovnikov. This low-density suburban idyll still stands today. Markovnikov's modest, two-storey houses have strong pitched roofs, prominent gables and generous gardens. Recalling the pre-war designs of Semenov and their English precedents, the Sokol houses reflected the importance of the single family home to civil servants in the era of the NEP.

The GOELRO plan for the electrification of Russia stimulated great enthusiasm for the creation of new industrial settlements.[51] In 1920 the engineer and economist Gleb Krzhizhanovskii, chairman of the plan's commission, declared that 'regional electricity stations are to become oases and centres which will produce new industrial and cultural values – they will build a completely new map of industrial and economic geography'.[52] The artist Gustav Klutsis turned such statements into utopian visions of future cities. In Klutsis's photomontage *Electrification of the Entire Country* of 1920, Lenin, wielding an electrical tower, strides into an axonometric cityscape, conflating Soviet power and electrical current.[53] The industrial settlements of the GOELRO plan, however, were quite mundane. The settlement of the Kizelovskaia Electrical Station, located east of the Ural Mountains in Gubakha, Perm Province, was typical. The town had four categories of housing: barracks, dormitories, multi-family dwellings and a limited number of semi-detached cottages. The settlement included a stadium, a school, a people's house and a hospital. Designed by a number of Moscow architects, including Dmitrii Osipov, Leonid Vesnin and Boris Korshunov, the town's buildings retained the forms of traditional wooden construction.

During the years of Civil War, architects in Moscow and Petrograd developed plans for the reconstruction of their respective cities. Ivan Zholtovskii and Aleksei Shchusev organized municipal design ateliers for the Moscow Soviet in 1918. In these workshops architects devised a

Nikolai Markovnikov, cottage in Sokol Garden Settlement, Moscow, 1923.

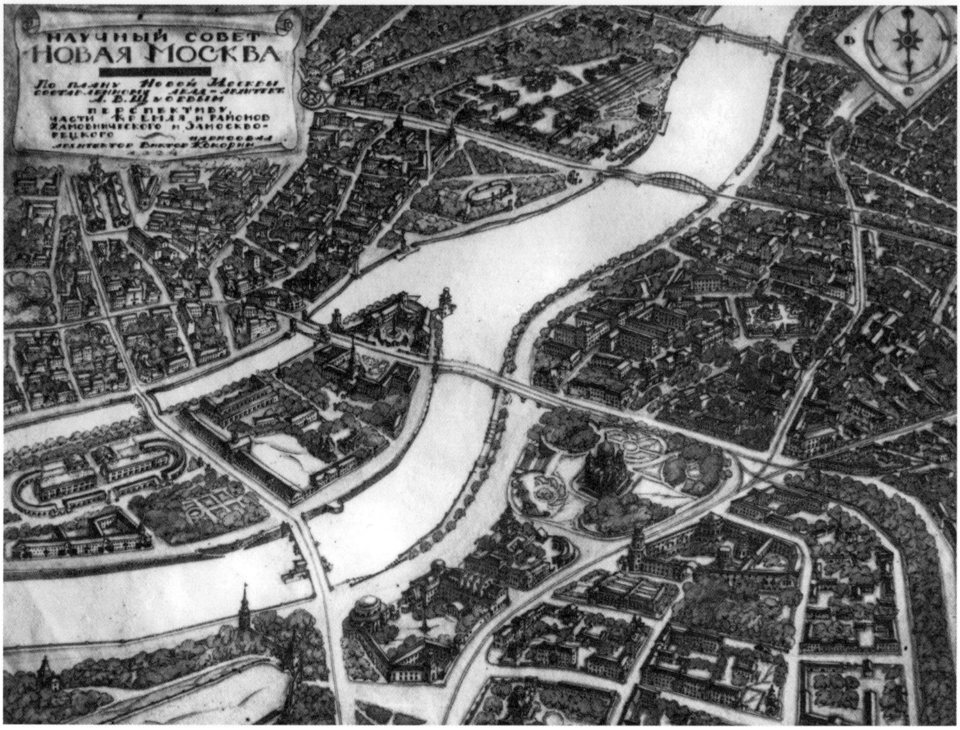


Aleksei Shchusev, New Moscow, project, 1922.

project for 'New Moscow'. Shchusev sought to maintain Moscow's historical radial-concentric street network. He specified a broad ring of parks and garden suburbs beyond the historic centre. Recalling the concepts of the German planners Bruno Möhring and Rudolf Eberstadt, Shchusev devised great green wedges of parkland that would connect the city centre and the periphery. The Kremlin was to remain the city's cultural centre; the city's railways were to be collected in a large northern station; and a new ring of light rail was to serve the suburbs. Along with the economic development plans devised by Boris Sakulin (1918) and Sergei Shestakov's plan for 'Greater Moscow' (completed in 1925), 'New Moscow' was a first attempt to create a comprehensive approach to urban development.[54] The approach to planning undertaken in Petrograd had a piecemeal character. The city's municipal planning office was established under Ivan Fomin's leadership in 1918. The following year he sought to rationalize traffic along Nevskii Prospect, the city's primary artery, by expanding parallel streets. His design had the same goal as Leontii Benois and Fedor Enakiev's plan of 1910–11: to relieve the city centre of heavy traffic. Fomin foresaw the creation of new communal spaces: public bath houses, stadiums and new public squares. He hoped to oversee the 'restoration of the city's ancient beauty' and create a general plan for Petrograd. Although Fomin and his colleagues were able to beautify the city with projects such as the regulation of the Field of Mars, a general plan for Leningrad would not be ratified until 1936.[55]

Competitions for workers' housing produced innovative visions of urban development. While the planning of garden suburbs for the periphery had concentrated on the single family home, these events made mass housing a critical concern. Architects placed public and private space into a new relationship as they created a new image of the collective city. The basic unit of this form of urban development was the *kvartal*, what we would today call a superblock. Konstantin Melnikov submitted a radical and influential project to a competition for workers' housing sponsored by the Moscow Soviet in 1922.[56] Taking the 'saw' as a competition motto, Melnikov's project for a block on Bolshaia Serpukhovskaia Street organized a complex array of functions on an irregular site. Eschewing the traditional perimeter block, his design establishes numerous connections with the surrounding city via footpaths, green space and courtyards. The brief specified two types of dwelling units: apartments for families and economy apartments for singles. Melnikov arranged these units in distinct, interlocking zones. Six rows of family units occupy much of the site. Their staggered juxtaposition helped isolate views and

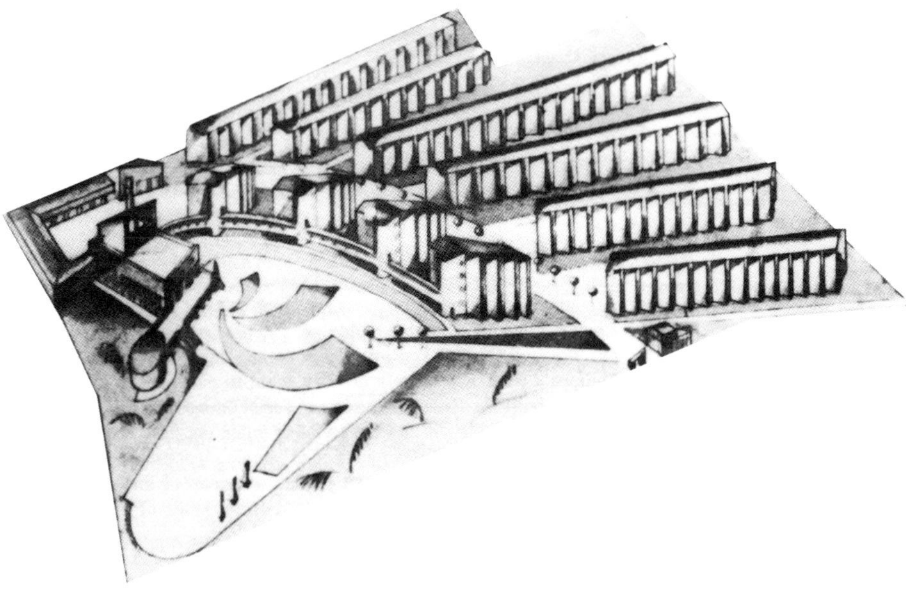

Konstantin Melnikov, project for a residential complex on Bolshaia Serpukhovskaia Street, Moscow, 1922–3.

reduce the incidence of party walls; this arrangement also created the appearance of a saw-blade in plan. Four, four-storey towers housed units for singles. Melnikov linked these structures with an elevated, climate-controlled passage. This passage led to the social centre of the complex: a club and communal-services building. The passage itself was a bridge between private and public space – an intermediate zone that symbolized a new concept of dwelling. Dramatizing the interdependence of the individual and the collective, Melnikov's complex evoked the communal utopia of Charles Fourier's *phalanstère*.[57] Although his design only received second prize in the competition, the image of communal dwelling Melnikov created would be reinterpreted many times in years to come.

## Great Utopias

Synthesis was a guiding principle for Russia's young avant-garde artists and architects. Like their colleagues in the West, they sought to place painting, sculpture, music, drama and architecture into a new unity. Rigorous analysis, they believed, would lay the foundation for unification. An explosion of trans-disciplinary projects emerged from this experiment in the science of art. In Moscow, study groups reformulated architectural principles in theoretical designs for temples to internationalism. IZO Narkompros systematized the collaboration of the arts in a new organization: INKhUK, the Institute of Artistic Culture. In Vitebsk, a city on Russia's western border, Malevich encouraged the synthetic experiments of an innovative group of young Suprematists. The experiments undertaken between 1919 and 1921 would transform the course of the arts in Russia and abroad for the next decade. Architectural rationalism was born from the analysis of space. Constructivism grew out of research into the structure of works of art. Vanguard artists ceased reflecting nature and radical architects stopped decorating structure – they both now sought to transform life.

Boris Korolev founded SINSKULPTARKh, a commission of sculptors and architects, in 1919 in order to investigate the synthesis of these arts. Korolev occupied a high administrative position within the Moscow branch of IZO, and his sculptural work – characterized by semi-Cubist fragmentation of planes – exerted significant influence over his colleagues. Many of the union's architects – Nikolai Ladovskii, Nikolai Istselenov, Vladimir Krinskii and others – worked in the municipal atelier of Ivan Zholtovskii, whose classical erudition was admired but considered outmoded by this younger generation of architects. Recalling the ideas of the German architects Bruno Taut and Walter Gropius, the founder of the Bauhaus, members of SINSKULPTARKh elevated the Gothic cathedral to

Nikolai Istselenov, Temple of the Communication among Peoples, 1919.

a new ideal, admiring not its forms but the collaborative nature of its creation. They imagined that by working in concert, artists and architects of the Middle Ages had created total works of art. Istselenov delivered the first statement of SINSKULPTARKh's principles in a lecture on 'the rebirth of the pure meaning of the architectural structure – as the temple of a new cult'. Istselenov argued that 'utilitarianism was foreign' to the temples of the past, but in the modern age 'the pure meaning of the architectural art had been lost'. He echoed Taut's concept of the *Stadtkrone*, or city-crown, calling for the construction of a new, non-utilitarian building that would be a collaborative work of painters, sculptors and architects.[58] This structure was to be a work of architectural art which would loom over the city as a new cult building.[59] Members of SINSKULPTARKh tested this proposal in theoretical projects for a 'temple of the communication

Nikolai Ladovskii, project for a communal house, 1920.

among peoples' – the first of many 'paper projects' in which radical new ideas would be articulated. Istselenov's temple resembled a mountain of crystalline forms. Its fractured geometric planes towered above a broad, variegated base, evoking a dynamic, non-utilitarian monumentality.

SINSKULPTARKh's synthetic mission was soon displaced by the analysis and definition of medium specificity. Although the group changed its name to ZHIVSKULPTARKh (Painting, Sculpture and Architecture) in late 1919 to reflect the new membership of painters, including Aleksandr Rodchenko, architecture remained its primary concern. Ladovskii became the group's leading theorist, and he urged his colleagues to explore the expression of abstract qualities such as rhythm, dynamism, equilibrium and tension. He sought to find a correspondence between architectural form and human perception – to discover the laws of formal expression. He believed their discovery depended on the analysis of each art's distinct field of activity. 'Space, not stone, is the material of architecture', he declared.[60] Eschewing historical forms and material constraints, Ladovskii placed spatial dynamism at the heart of his design for a communal house (1920). The building rises in an upward spiral of intersecting, fragmented volumes from a large central hall. Roofs rise to a central, crane-like tower. Supported by a system of concealed trusses, the tower terminates the building's twisted spatial axis with an audacious cantilever.

When it was exhibited in 1920, Ladovskii's communal house impressed his colleagues and confirmed his leading role in the search for a theoretical basis for architecture.

The analytical method practised by Ladovskii and his colleagues was institutionalized with the foundation of INKhUK in May 1920. Kandinsky, the Institute's founding director, outlined a programme devoted to the study of the 'reverberation of artistic means on the emotional experience of the viewer; i.e. on his psyche'.[61] Artistic disciplines were to be studied in relation to their essential means of communication: painting in its colourful and volumetric form; sculpture in its spatial and volumetric form; architecture in its volumetric and spatial form; music in its phonic and temporal form; and dance in its temporal and spatial form. Such analyses were to disclose fundamental laws of 'construction and composition in monumental art'. Kandinsky viewed the programme of INKhUK in an international context; he saw it as preparation for 'the building of an international house of art' that would become 'for all nations the house of utopia', a project he called 'the Great Utopia'.[62]

INKhUK's members applauded the analytical foundation of Kandinsky's programme, but his investment in individual psychological response aroused widespread scepticism. The 'General Working Group for Objective Analysis' was formed in response to what it saw as Kandinsky's arbitrary psychologism. Opposition to his principles culminated in Kandinsky's departure from the institute in 1921 and his ultimate emigration to Germany, where he took up a post at the Bauhaus. Led by the sculptor Aleksei Babichev, the new working group divided its activities into two categories: theoretical analysis of artworks and 'laboratory' work on practical themes.[63] In an attempt to elucidate the laws of organization of works of art, the group initiated a series of debates on the nature of construction and composition in the spring of 1921. To the artists and architects taking part in the discussion, construction and composition implied fundamentally different modes of practice and the debate over their distinctions led to the radicalization of artistic positions.

Rodchenko argued that 'the real construction is utilitarian necessity', expressing the sentiments of a nascent group of artists who sought to make useful objects the ultimate aim of artistic practice.[64] Adherents to this position – including Rodchenko, Varvara Stepanova and Aleksei Gan – formed the 'First Working Group of Constructivists' in the spring of 1921. The Constructivists conflated the organizing principles of 'Scientific Communism' with the organization of utilitarian objects, seeking to 'synthesize the ideological part with the formal part for the real transfer of laboratory work to the rails of practical activity'.[65] Gan, an organizer of 'mass demonstrations' and critic, described the group's aims and methods in his landmark book *Konstruktivizm* (Constructivism, 1922).[66] 'Death to art!' he declared. Constructivism's aim was to establish a scientific basis for building structures and services for a Communist culture. Expediency, utility and economy shaped the work of the Constructivists, many of whom sought to apply their skills to industry. Rodchenko teamed up with Mayakovsky to create advertising for state-run industries; Varvara Stepanova designed sports attire and dresses; Gan designed kiosks and folding sales stands for state ventures.[67] Aleksandr Vesnin, who joined the group of Constructivists soon after its formation, created some of the first architectural interpretations of Constructivism in stage design. His 'stage device' for Aleksandr Tairov's production of *The Man Who was Thursday* (1922–3) was a three-dimensional mobile structure. Composed of shifting ramps, elevators, moving sidewalks and a descending stage floor, Vesnin's stage device evoked a mechanized world of movement. Its open network of wooden trusses revealed the inner workings of the device, laying bare its material components and their organization. The project embodied Vesnin's 'credo' of 1922: 'Objects created by the contemporary artist should be pure constructions – without the ballast of artistry, constructed according to the straight line and the geometric curve and based on the principle of economy with maximum effect.'[68]

After participating in the construction–composition debate of 1921, Ladovskii founded the 'Working Group of Architects', which pursued a distinct approach for design. Unlike the Constructivists, who generally rejected Kandinsky's interest in the psychology of form, Ladovskii and his colleagues – Vladimir Krinskii, Nikolai Dokuchaev and others – sought to place the 'psychological perception' of architectural form on a firm scientific foundation.[69] The group took space, form and construction to be architecture's primary elements, but they insisted that their primary aim was the analysis of the 'means of acting on the perception of man'. Ladovskii would later call this position 'ratio-architecture', a combination of the economy of labour and material in the creation of a structure with 'the economy of psychic energy in the perception of the spatial and functional properties of a building'.[70] Distinct from earlier rationalisms, Ladovskii's understanding of architecture rejected the primacy of function and structure. In 1923 he founded the Association of New Architects (ASNOVA) as a platform for the development of rationalist principles.

Changes in the conception of artistic labour and architectural theory were reflected in the pedagogy of VKHUTEMAS. In the school's early years, Constructivists remained outside of the architectural faculty, which was divided into an 'academic section' led by Zholtovskii and Shchusev and a semi-autonomous section dominated by Ladovskii and his colleagues.[71]

Aleksandr Vesnin, set for Tairov's *The Man who was Thursday*, Moscow, 1922–3.

ЧЕЛОВЕК
КОТОРЫЙ
БЫЛ
ЧЕТВЕРГОМ
Г. К.
ЧЕСТЕРТОН
CAFE
BOX
PROGRAMME
FOX TROT

Mikhail Turkus, demonstration of dynamism, rhythm, correlation and proportion on a surface; student work from VKhUTEMAS, Ladovskii Studio, 1923.

The latter introduced a 'psychoanalytical method' of teaching in the 1920/21 school year, offering a series of assignments that were to help students understand the qualities of architectural form. Students in lower courses received abstract projects, while second- and third-year students were given concrete building types to study. Working primarily with models and perspectival renderings, students explored the expression of mass and weight, mass and equilibrium, dynamism and rhythm, among a variety of other architectural qualities. In Mikhail Turkus's study of dynamism, rhythm and surface, curved lines intersect, dividing a plane into unequal quadrants. A torqued grid supports a set of rectangular prisms placed diagonally across the plane. Staggered in a staccato sequence, these white forms appear to be sliding across the model's surface, suggesting movement with static materials. Ladovskii's architectural pedagogy was so influential that it served as the foundation for the 'spatial' section of VKhUTEMAS's basic course when its curriculum was restructured in 1923.

UNOVIS, an association of artists led by Malevich from 1919 in the Art Institute of Vitebsk, fostered similar experiments in form. Meaning 'Affirmers of the New Art', UNOVIS was a laboratory for the development of Malevich's concept of Suprematism. After his white-on-white paintings of 1918, Malevich abandoned the medium for several years and focused instead on writing and teaching. His followers sought to bring the flat planes of early Suprematist paintings into the third dimension. Ilia Chashnik created 'Suprematist reliefs' by adding thin layers of material to his canvases. Malevich experimented with perspectival renderings of rectilinear solids, evoking a sensation of hovering motion similar to his earlier paintings. He later produced a series of 'arkhitektons' that rendered Suprematist geometry in sculptural form. El Lissitzky radically transformed Malevich's visual language with the invention of the 'Proun' – an abbreviation for 'Project for the Affirmation of the New'. Lissitzky arrived

El Lissitzky, Proun 1 E, *Town*, 1921.

in Vitebsk after receiving an architectural degree from the Technical University of Darmstadt. The Proun, he said, was the 'interchange station between painting and architecture'.[72] Lissitzky's *Town* of 1921, a work of oil and sand on plywood, combines fields of muted colour – a circle, a black square, grey negative space – and axonometric projections. Treating 'canvas and wooden board as a building site', Lissitzky created a new world of rectilinear prisms. He conflated communist politics with his vision of the new world: 'Thanks to the Prouns', he wrote, 'monolithic communist towns will be built.'[73] Although Lissitzky's Proun grew out of Malevich's Suprematism and promoted a communist ideology, its greatest impact was made in the capitalist West. When Lissitzky moved to Berlin in 1921, he transmitted his rich knowledge of new Russian trends to an eager, international art world. Through the multilingual journal *Veshch/Objet/Gegenstand* that he edited with Ehrenburg in 1922 and his participation in a number of pan-European artistic events, such as the Great Berlin Art Exhibition of 1923, where he installed his Proun Room, Lissitzky contributed to the foundation of 'international Constructivism'.[74] This trend found a voice in the little magazines of the avant-garde – *De Stijl*, *L'Esprit nouveau*, *G: Material zur elementaren Gestaltung*. Constructivism's international variant exposed Europeans to new artistic ideas – clarity, economy, geometric abstraction – but it remained fundamentally committed to the category of art. Aleksei Gan dismissed the Constructivism of Lissitzky and Ehrenburg as the work of 'fellow travellers', promoting instead the 'irreconcilable war on art' that he and his colleagues who remained in the USSR had declared.[75]

## Competing Visions

As the hostilities of the Civil War came to an end and the New Economic Policy's modest recovery set in, the Bolshevik leadership sought to express the viability of the new state in monumental projects. Although reforms came too late to help Russian farmers prevent the famine of 1921/2, agriculture benefited most from the NEP. Peasants cultivated more land, produce could again be found in urban markets, and rural unrest appeared to be on the decline. The conclusion of the Civil War altered the Bolshevik regime's political and economic geography. In 1922, the Soviets of Ukraine, Belarus, the Caucasus and Central Asia merged with Russia to form the Union of Soviet Socialist Republics. The prospect of economic recovery and the establishment of the USSR found architectural expression in the First All-Union Agricultural and Domestic

Ivan Zholtovskii, main gates, All-Union Agricultural Exposition, Moscow, 1923.

Konstantin Melnikov, Makhorka Pavilion, All-Union Agricultural Exposition, Moscow, 1923.

Industry Exposition and the competition for the Palace of Labour in Moscow. These architectural events unfolded in parallel from late 1922 and through 1923. They revealed the diversity of positions within Soviet architectural culture and exacerbated tensions between conservative tastes and radical modernism.

The Agricultural Exposition was a spectacle for both domestic and foreign consumption. Pavilions devoted to grains, poultry, livestock and the 'old and new village' demonstrated the importance of rural industry to the NEP. A large foreign section housed agricultural implements and industrial goods from abroad. A group of 'national' pavilions displayed crafts and produce from the Ukraine SSR, the 'Far East', Turkestan and a number of other regions representing the USSR's new territorial borders. But, according to Shchusev, this was 'not only an agricultural exposition but also an exhibition of architecture'.[76] It took place in a large wooded area along the Moscow River, the site of today's Gorky Park. Shchusev designed the Exposition's general plan, making the newly developed amusement space part of his project for 'New Moscow'.[77] As architect of most of the Exposition's major pavilions, Ivan Zholtovskii made the greatest impact on the ensemble. Zholtovskii developed a festive classical language for the semi-permanent structures. He designed the main gate as a triumphal arch. Its skeletal timber construction conflicted with its ponderous classical forms. Zholtovskii experimented with geometric form in other pavilions: a large hexagon for the main pavilion; a great wooden cylinder for the auditorium; a ring of six monumental porticos for the machine building court. Innovative pavilions by younger architects supplemented Zholtovskii's classicist conservatism. The *Izvestiia* Newspaper pavilion by Alexandra Exter and Boris Gladkov was a towering open assemblage of curves, geometric planes and publicity slogans. Vladimir Shchuko collaborated with Exter on structures in the foreign section, creating dynamic, forward-looking designs. The bold masses and intersecting volumes of Konstanin Melnikov's Makhorka tobacco pavilion recalled his 'saw-tooth' designs for residential structures. Fedor Shekhtel and Ilia Golosov designed pavilions for Turkestan and the

'Far East', respectively. Combining kitsch and a naive language of national forms, they could not escape the pull of exoticism. The one common denominator among the Exposition's stylistic plurality was the exclusive use of timber construction. This both promoted the Soviet timber industry and highlighted the continued scarcity of industrial building materials.

As preparations for the Agricultural Exposition were under way, the Moscow Soviet announced a competition for the Palace of Labour. At the first Congress of the Soviets of the USSR in December 1922, Sergei Kirov described the building as a 'monument in which the representatives of labour could meet'. It was to be an 'emblem of the coming power, of the victory of communism not only at home but also abroad, in the West'.[78] The brief called for a grand structure: halls for 8,000 and 2,500 spectators; a cafeteria for 1,400 workers; an array of offices; a 'museum of social knowledge'; a radio transmission studio; and a variety of secondary spaces. The brief noted that 'the Palace of Labour should have a luxurious visage that corresponds to its basic idea; this should be expressed in simple contemporary forms, beyond a specific style of a past epoch'.[79] A large block in the centre of Moscow was the competition site. Situated on Okhotnyi Riad, a stone's throw from the Kremlin, the Palace of Labour was to occupy the symbolic heart of the USSR. The composition of the jury caused significant controversy. Lev Kamenev, chairman of the Moscow Soviet, led the jury and Ivan Zholtovskii, Fedor Shekhtel, Igor Grabar and several other architects were voting members. Nikolai Ladovskii, Vladimir Krinskii and others protested the membership, claiming that it was a 'conspicuously reactionary competition jury' composed of officials and architects who appreciated and practised only historical architecture.[80] The competition went forward despite their accusations; in retaliation Ladovskii and his rationalist colleagues refused to participate.

Among the 47 entries submitted in March 1923, the project labelled 'Antenna' received the greatest acclaim. The design came from Aleksandr, Viktor and Leonid Vesnin, the three brothers who brought Constructivism to architecture. Their project balanced an office tower and elliptical hall in dynamic opposition. A rhythmic grid of vertical piers and horizontal members establish points of emphasis. The authors claimed that 'all of the building's forms follow from the most rational disposition of the required spaces – from consideration of their utilization, their scale in three dimensions and the most constructive use of the selected building materials: iron, reinforced concrete and glass'.[81] They had distilled the building's programme into its elemental form and united a diversity of functions in a coherent structure. The play among open structural frames, taut infill panels and high-tension radio masts recalls Aleksandr's

Vesnin brothers, project for the Palace of Labour, Moscow, 1923.

earlier designs for theatrical productions, but the application of these elements to a large-scale project was unprecedented. The architect and critic Moisei Ginzburg would later call this 'the first milestone of authentic Constructivism'.[82] With their insistence on constructive logic, utility, rationality and economy, the Vesnin brothers crystallized Constructivism's basic elements and laid the foundation for one of the leading architectural ideas of the 1920s.

Vladimir Krinskii, skyscraper on Lubianka Square, Moscow, 1923.

While it was not submitted to the Palace of Labour competition, Vladimir Krinskii's design for a skyscraper in Moscow (1922–3) provided a conceptual counterpoint to the Vesnins' Constructivism. Krinskii selected a concrete location for his design – Lubianka Square – but not a specific programme. Although he dedicated it to the Soviet of Ministers, there is no indication that he considered the variety of facilities required by a top-level governmental organization. Krinskii's skyscraper was a study in what he called 'abstract form'. He had declared that 'there is no such thing as pure utilitarian form'. Only a 'general theory of form' could help architects develop an authentic new style.[83] Like a theoretical assignment from Ladovskii's course at VKhUTEMAS, Krinskii's skyscraper was an essay in experimental composition. Grids of various densities articulate the facade. Some of the pillars are tilted out of plumb, while others rise unimpeded to the top of the building. The step-back massing of the upper register reflects a burgeoning interest in American skyscraper design in Russia. Unlike the Vesnins, who made utilitarian considerations paramount, Krinskii rejected the utilitarian basis of form, advocating formal research instead. The Vesnins' Palace of Labour and Krinskii's skyscraper instantiated a nascent tension between the Constructivist belief in the primacy of utility and the rationalist commitment to the power of abstract form.

Although the Vesnins' project was highly praised, it was awarded only a third-place prize. Noi Trotskii won the grand prize with a monumental, neo-Byzantine design. To many, his centrally planned complex symbolized not a forward-looking Soviet state, but the glory of the ancient world. 'We are threatened by a new, gigantic, stone hulking Soviet Cheops', the critic Kornelii Zelinskii wrote. 'It is a broad-rumped, ponderous domino that will bear down upon us from Teatralnyi square.'[84] Shchusev claimed that some members of the jury had been 'frightened by innovation', suggesting that conservative taste had defeated superior proposals.[85] Be that as it may, the competition thrust Constructivism into the centre of architectural debate at a critical moment, for by the time the controversy cooled, the Soviet building industry had begun to get off the ground.

ПРОЛЕТАРИИ ВСЕХ СТРАН, СОЕДИНЯЙТЕСЬ!

# СССР на стройке

№ 3 • МАРТ • 1934

chapter four

# Socialist Construction, 1924–31

The new Russia recognizes the law of the new world. Technology is its idol. America is its desire. The hereafter is worth nothing; the present – everything.[1]

With this telegraphic description of Russia's drive for industrialization, the German architect Erich Mendelsohn conveyed the urgency and tempo of the country's social and economic development. By the end of the 1920s production figures had become popular obsessions. Steel mills, tractor factories and hydroelectric dams had become outposts in a new civilizing mission. Mechanization had taken command, and a new industrial society was being born. Mendelsohn's book, *Russia, Europe, America: An Architectural Cross-section* (1929), articulated a new triad of modern culture. Russia promoted a new social order; America produced a new order of technology; and Europe mediated the radical innovations that emerged from these poles. This triangular relationship supported the unprecedented volume of construction undertaken in the USSR in the second half of the 1920s. Foreign capital and private initiative stimulated commercial growth, reaching a peak around 1927, when the Soviet government began to take control of the Union's entire economic apparatus. The First Five-year Plan (1928–32) set the Union on a course of rapid industrial development. At stake in this project, as Mendelsohn understood, was nothing less than an acceleration of time: the USSR sought to pull itself out of 'economic backwardness' to become a leading industrial nation in the span of a few years. Enthusiasts worked at great speed, suffered incredible losses and fulfilled quotas ahead of schedule. The individual was sacrificed to the collective in the name of the socialist construction of the future.

The construction of socialism, however, was fraught with catastrophe. In 1924, as the New Economic Policy showed its first signs of success, Lenin died. (In his honour Petrograd was renamed Leningrad later that year.) His demise prompted a struggle for leadership within the Communist Party – a struggle that Joseph Stalin would win. Lenin had recognized Stalin's 'coarseness' in a final testament and had suggested that someone with 'greater courtesy' and 'less capriciousness' be named general secretary of

The Dnepr Hydro-Electric Station, Zaporozhe, from *USSR in Construction* (1934).

the Party.[2] But Stalin, in a series of opportunistic political manoeuvres, wrested control of the bureaucracy away from so-called 'oppositionists' on the left and right. By 1927 Stalin had expelled many of the most powerful Bolshevik leaders – Leon Trotsky, Lev Kamenev and Grigorii Zinoviev among them – from the Party and taken possession of the machinery of state. Stalin assumed the role of *vozhd*, leader, which he would occupy until his death in 1953. During his nearly 30-year reign, Soviet society suffered enormously. Stalin expanded the secret police, authorized the summary execution of millions and knowingly ratified policies that would starve the countryside.

But as Stalin consolidated his control of the Party, a diverse and vibrant cultural life unfolded. After spending the winter of 1926–7 in Moscow, the critic and theorist Walter Benjamin wrote that 'each thought, each day, each life lies here as on a laboratory table'.[3] Everything, it seemed, was subject to reinvention. Artists like Aleksandr Rodchenko turned to mechanical means of reproduction, declaring 'a file of photographs' to be immeasurably superior to the art of 'synthetic portraiture'.[4] The writer Sergei Tretiakov rejected narrative literature in favour of a 'literature of facts'.[5] Sergei Eisenstein explored the potential of montage in internationally renowned films such as *The Battleship Potemkin* (1925), *October* (1927) and *The Old and The New (The General Line)* (1929). Jazz bands flourished in nightclubs, while agit-prop groups like the 'Blue Blouses' proselytized in workers' clubs and villages. *Nepmen*, a class of small-scale entrepreneurs, profited in the USSR's roaring twenties and provided comic relief to readers of satirical books, plays and films. In the architectural laboratories of VKhUTEMAS, students imagined flying cities, towering skyscrapers and restaurants suspended from cliffs. An experimental impulse saturated Soviet culture.

Commerce gave cities new life. *Nepmen* scrambled to rent buildings, shops and market stalls. By 1924 Muscovites could choose among roughly 5,000 private shops, 600 cooperatives or 800 state stores.[6] Benjamin witnessed bustling markets during his visit, but noted a familiar – and persistent – aspect of Soviet consumption: at state stores 'one stands in line for butter and other important staples'.[7] In Moscow the state took possession of the city's largest commercial spaces. The Upper Trading Rows became GUM, the State Department Store. Mosselprom, the Moscow State Agricultural Trust, advertised its success in its new headquarters, a renovated apartment building covered in Rodchenko-designed slogans. Konstantin Melnikov gave small vendors a new architectural stage with his design for Sukharevskii Market (1924). Its saw-toothed arrangement of stalls created a dynamic visual experience while maximizing shelf and display space. By 1927 industrial production, textile manufacturing and

Strastnaia (Pushkinskaia) Square, Moscow, 1929 with Grigorii Barkhin's *Izvestiia* Building (1925–9) in background.

ИЗВЕСТИЯ
БОРЖОМ

rail transport had regained 1913 levels. Cities began to grow. The first census of the USSR (1926) reported two million inhabitants in Moscow, double the number of inhabitants under War Communism. Nearly 150 million people lived in the Soviet Union in 1926, 18 per cent of whom lived in urban areas.

The First Five-year Plan fundamentally transformed the Soviet economy. A ruthless campaign of creative destruction, its tumult and rapidity have been compared to 'the birth pangs of a world'.[8] It began with large-scale construction sites: the Dnepr (Ukranian: Dnieper) Dam complex in Zaporozhe (Zaporizhya), the blast furnaces of Magnitogorsk and the tractor factories at Stalingrad. Margaret Bourke-White, an American photojournalist, explored these industrial giants for *Fortune* magazine and captured 'the Five-year Plan as a great drama being unrolled before the eyes of the world'.[9] Millions of uprooted peasants flocked to these projects, becoming 'shock-workers' in the process. Agricultural production was reorganized into a state-led network of collective farms in order to support the burgeoning cities-in-construction. The Plan obliterated traditional ways of life and cost millions of lives. Cities grew at unprecedented rates as peasants fled collective farms. Inhabitants of Novosibirsk christened their city *Sib-Chik* – Siberian Chicago – for its rapid expansion during the years of the plan.[10] Moscow integrated and directed the economic life of the Union republics. The oil fields of Baku and the Ukraine's coal-producing Donets Basin became tributaries of the Five-year Plan. The 'Turksib' railway, opened in 1930, connected Central Asia and Siberia, assimilating far-flung economic centres.

The Plan radicalized cultural positions as well. In the name of Cultural Revolution, organizations claimed the support of the proletariat and initiated campaigns against the 'old intelligentsia'.[11] Engineers became targets of scorn when industrial quotas were not met. In 1928 engineers in the Shakhty region of the Donets Basin were tried for sabotage of the mining industry. Their conviction fuelled suspicions that 'bourgeois experts' remained class enemies. Activists declared that the class war within the Soviet Union continued. The Russian Association of Proletarian Writers, RAPP, led campaigns against alleged 'fellow travellers' and promoted the work of working-class authors. The group's ideological campaign set a coarse and violent tone for cultural debate: 'brigades' of writers were said to be locked in a 'militant struggle' for 'proletarian hegemony' in the arts. Social theorists made the redefinition of social relations a centrepiece of Cultural Revolution. The social theorist Iurii Larin advanced a programme for the 'collectivization of everyday life', which sought to put communitarian ideals into practice.[12] Other theorists promoted 'children's homes', institutions where professionals, not parents, would manage child care.

Konstantin Melnikov, Soviet Pavilion, Paris Exposition, 1925.

Architecture responded to and accelerated the transformation of Soviet society. Architects articulated the centralization of government and industry in a new and pervasive building type: the house of the Soviets. Trade unions commissioned housing, clubs, offices and sanatoria. The modernization of cities required new structures: garages, post offices, telephone exchanges. 'Physical culture' demanded new stadiums, pools and athletics facilities. Such tasks entailed a redefinition of the relationship between the architect and society. Moisei Ginzburg argued that architects had to do more than synthesize client demands, building technologies and artistic concepts. The Soviet architect needed to recognize his or her capacity to give form to new social relations, to play a role 'in the construction of a new life, to create a new organism – the social condenser of our epoch'.[13] To this end architects devised new residential configurations that might stimulate socialist consciousness. They presented comprehensive visions of the socialist city in which all aspects of life – production, consumption, dwelling and leisure – were integrated into an organized totality.

Between the NEP and the First Five-year Plan, the architecture of the Soviet Union appeared on the world stage, demonstrating that the USSR had become an active participant in the international world of modernism. The Exposition internationale des arts décoratifs et industriels modernes, held in Paris in 1925, was Soviet architecture's international debut. Most of the exposition's structures were conservative, but the USSR Pavilion by Konstantin Melnikov and the *L'Esprit nouveau* pavilion by Le Corbusier and Pierre Jeanneret offered a breath of fresh air. Parisian newspapers and European architects praised Melnikov's ability to create strikingly original forms with modest materials. The Russian critic Iakov Tugendkhold compared the USSR's building to Le Corbusier's theory of architecture, noting that 'our pavilion is a "machine for agitation"'.[14] Russian architects followed the work of their Western colleagues closely. Le Corbusier's theories and projects were hotly debated in the Soviet architectural press.[15] Key texts, such as Adolf Behne's *The Modern Functional Building* and Richard Neutra's *Wie baut Amerika?* (How does America Build?), appeared in Russian translation.[16] The *New York Times* praised the Soviet architectural projects exhibited at New York's 'Machine Age Exhibition' of 1927, noting that Russia was building 'industrial civilization on the basis of new forms'.[17] In 1928 a group of students from Moscow visited the Bauhaus Dessau, an epicentre of modern architecture and design. Soviet architects had become members in what Ginzburg called the 'international front of modern architecture'.[18]

The foundation of VOKS, the All-Union Organization of Cultural Ties Abroad, in 1925 facilitated the travel of foreign architects and critics to the USSR.[19] Erich Mendelsohn, Bruno Taut, Adolf Behne, Karel Teige, Le Corbusier and many others visited the USSR during the twenties. Some foreigners received commissions; others popularized Soviet ideas at home. Moscow, in Le Corbusier's opinion, had become 'the focus of architecture and city planning in the world'.[20] The financial crash of 1929 shook the economic foundations of the United States and Western Europe and lent credibility to his claim. As building industries faltered, foreign architects flocked to the USSR in search of work.[21] In 1930 Hannes Meyer, after his dismissal from directorship of the Bauhaus for alleged 'communist activity', settled in Moscow with a 'Red Brigade' of former students. Ernst May, director of urban planning for Frankfurt am Main, accepted a contract from the Soviet government to assist in the design of cities.[22] The Congrès internationaux d'architecture moderne (CIAM) selected Moscow as the initial site for its conference on the 'functional city' in 1931–2.[23] During the financial crisis, ideas advanced by Soviet architects resonated with Western observers. Teige declared in 1930 that 'the architectural avant-garde, led by Constructivism', had a duty to 'further the struggle of the proletariat actively, and not through utopian-political treaties'.[24] A group of communist students organized a 'Collective for Socialist Building' in Berlin in 1931, declaring that 'architecture must become a weapon in class war'.[25] In response to the 'Great German Building Exhibition' of that year, they organized a 'Proletarian Building Exhibition', which displayed recent advances in Soviet city planning.[26] The Swiss publicist Alexander von Senger decried these undertakings in his incendiary book *Die Brandfackel Moskaus* (Moscow's Torch), which painted the entire modern movement in architecture as *Baubolschewismus* – Bolshevist building.[27] The spirit of Soviet architecture haunted Europe. As the economic crisis set in and ideological battles intensified, the Soviet Union looked like a haven for unemployed architects and the place where the future, for better or worse, was under construction.

## Ideological Superstructures

'Modern architecture in Russia? There isn't any. There is a struggle for modern architecture.'[28] El Lissitzky's characterization of the Russian architectural scene conveys the agonistic nature of architectural debate in the second half of the 1920s. Liberal organizations like the Moscow Architectural Society (MAO) and its sister organization in Leningrad (LAO) organized competitions, regulated education and promoted public interest in the discipline. Smaller groups like the Association of New Architects (ASNOVA) and the Union of Contemporary Architects (OSA) clashed in charged disputes over the nature of architectural practice. As partisan architectural societies sought to place architecture on new conceptual foundations, their contest of ideas would become a competition between what Lissitzky called 'ideological superstructures'.[29]

Nikolai Ladovskii founded ASNOVA, the 'rationalist' group, in 1923. ASNOVA's members built little but made many contributions to architectural theory. Ladovskii propagated the group's position from his post as an instructor at VKhUTEMAS, where he created a 'psycho-technical laboratory' for formal research. Drawing on the work of Hugo Münsterberg, a pioneer of psycho-physiology, Ladovskii sought to integrate architectural design and the systematic study of perception.[30] ASNOVA members called this a 'rationalist' approach. In the words of Nikolai Dokuchaev, 'The "rationalists" consider it necessary for the architect to study the biological and physiological sides of our perception in relation to our emotional and aesthetic sensations.'[31] Affective form, according to ASNOVA, could be derived neither from functional necessities nor material qualities. For ASNOVA, the perception of form represented a semi-autonomous field of investigation. This approach to design would yield such innovative projects as Lissitzky's Wolkenbügel, or Cloud-Iron (1924), which was intended to organize the experience of moving through Moscow by creating a series of abstract, Proun-like visual markers.[32] OSA was larger than ASNOVA and had a greater presence on building sites around the USSR. It was founded in 1925 by Moisei Ginzburg, Aleksandr Vesnin, Viktor Vesnin and several others. Although Ginzburg had not taken part in the early debates on Constructivism at INKhUK, he quickly became the principal theorist of Constructivist architecture. His book *Style and Epoch* (1924) presented Constructivism as the logical outcome of a Wölfflinian cycle of stylistic change.[33] Aleksei Gan's declaration of an 'uncompromising war on art' was in Ginzburg's view a symptom of the 'primordial conditions for a new style' based on the logic of the 'machine and the mechanized life associated with it'.[34] Like Walter Gropius and Le Corbusier, Ginzburg found in the American grain elevator a symbol of

El Lissitzky, Wolkenbügel project, 1924.

the machine's organic unity – a quality lacking in contemporary work.[35] In 1926 OSA launched the journal *Sovremennaia arkhitektura* (Contemporary Architecture, SA), establishing a stable platform for architectural agitation. Gan designed many of the journal's issues, creating a serialized Constructivist object from the open structure of print media.[36] In SA's pages, OSA argued for a 'functional method' of design, claiming that 'the fundamental task of architecture consists in the organization, according to clearly defined prescriptions of productive-everyday processes, of the spaces in which these processes flow.'[37] Programme took precedence over formal research as Constructivist architects sought to make the correlation of concrete requirements and material economy the foundation of design. The group consolidated its claim to leadership of the Soviet architectural scene with the 'First Exhibition of Modern Architecture' of 1927, which showcased the work of OSA members from Moscow and Leningrad in relation to international trends.[38] By 1928 OSA had members throughout the Soviet Union. They left indelible marks on cities from Kharkov to Baku.

In the cultural and economic climate of the NEP, talented individuals flourished. Konstantin Melnikov, the most famous Soviet architect of the day, remained generally aloof to the ideological bickering of ASNOVA and OSA. 'Theoretical institutes', he wrote, 'cannot explain architecture.'[39] His private house and his designs for workers' clubs demonstrated his commitment to bold geometries and poetic forms. Ilia Golosov identified at times with OSA but devoted more energy to the creation of dynamic forms than the articulation of a theoretical paradigm. Aleksei Shchusev, who had risen to authority as a founder of the short-lived Union of Russian Architects after the February Revolution in 1917, maintained an authoritative position within Soviet architectural culture. His political skill and chameleon-like ability to modulate his formal approach won him major commissions, including Lenin's Mausoleum.

The foundation of the All-Union Association of Proletarian Architects (VOPRA) in 1929 changed the political stakes of Soviet architectural culture. Composed primarily of Communist Party members, VOPRA brought class war to architecture. The group opposed both rationalism, which they decried as 'formalism', and Constructivism. Led by Karo Alabian and Arkadii Mordvinov, VOPRA initiated polemics that exaggerated the antipathies between ASNOVA and OSA and lowered the intellectual rigour of theoretical discourse. VOPRA rode a wave of 'proletarian' enthusiasm that engulfed Soviet cultural organizations at the outset of the Five-year Plan.[40] Just as they hoped that the Plan would wipe out the remains of capitalist enterprise, VOPRA and other militant groups hoped to eradicate so-called remnants of capitalist culture. 'We believe that in the age of the dictatorship of the proletariat and the fight for the socialist reconstruction of the world, architecture must have class-form and class-content', they declared.[41] They sought to take control of architectural discourse not by advocating a concrete approach to design but by turning aggressive political rhetoric into a weapon of architectural debate.

Despite the differences that divided Soviet architectural societies, they shared an antipathy to architectural conservatism. The competition for the design of the Lenin Library of 1928–9 brought this united front into focus.[42] A first stage of competition produced overwhelmingly modernist results. The team of D. S. Markov, Danil Fridman and V. I. Fridman won first place, indicating that the jury disliked the 'relapse into old styles' seen in projects submitted by Shchusev and Vladimir Shchuko. But the tables turned in the competition's second stage, when the jury – to the surprise of many – awarded the commission to Shchuko.[43] Shchuko's design, executed between 1929 and 1941, included a grand portico, a rich sculptural programme and monumental proportions. OSA called it a 'reactionary project'; VOPRA labelled Shchuko an 'historical recidivist'. Together with Moscow's

Protest against results of the Lenin Library Competition; from bottom to top: Shchuko's classical and modernist project and Shchusev's classical and modernist project, inscribed 'whatever you like, we are not proud people', from *Sovremennaia arkhitektura*, no. 3 (1929).

other organizations, they lobbied the Moscow Soviet to reconsider the competition results. Their protest registered a binding commitment to the new shared by most Soviet architects. It also exacerbated oppositions between modernist groups and generally conservative individuals like Shchuko, Ivan Fomin and Ivan Zholtovskii.

In the wake of the Lenin Library competition, Soviet architects sought to transcend factional differences by creating an inclusive architectural organization. The aims of the Five-year Plan, they thought, could be better fulfilled by a unified architectural front. The All-Union Architectural Scientific Society (VANO), created in 1930, declared that 'all strengths must be unified and directed to the definitive victory of the proletariat. Whoever is not with the working class is against them.'[44] The group absorbed all existing architectural societies except VOPRA, which maintained its organizational independence. Swept up by the Cultural Revolution, Constructivists and rationalists alike enlisted in the state-led drive for socialist construction. VOPRA continued to assail its opponents, charging them with conceptual sabotage, 'subservience to the West' and a variety of other slanderous charges. The group's ability to remain independent was an index of the growing importance of Communist Party affiliations within architectural culture. In 1932 the Communist Party would consolidate all architectural factions into a single union.

## Administration, Industry and the State

International trade, commercial recovery and state-run industry – these slogans of the NEP ushered in a compelling new architectural imaginary. Economic reconstruction entailed institution building and architects gave new form to the spaces of exchange, governance and production. The first years of economic recovery were marked by widespread optimism. Architects envisioned new structures in high-profile competitions for factories, industrial headquarters and department stores. Andrei Burov, a young member of OSA, brought this new vision to Soviet cinema with his design for a factory farm complex for Sergei Eisenstein and Grigorii Aleksandrov's film *The General Line* (set design, 1926, film release, 1929).[45] The white walls, ribbon windows and production-line efficiency of Burov's set cast the collective farm as a modern industrial enterprise. It obscured the bitter reality of collectivization but conveyed the image of industry that architects sought to achieve. Iakov Chernikhov converted industry into architectural fantasies in his sustained investigation of the compositional possibilities of 'machine forms'.[46] In projects across the USSR, industry and its image came to symbolize the Soviet state's effort to place the Union on a new economic foundation.

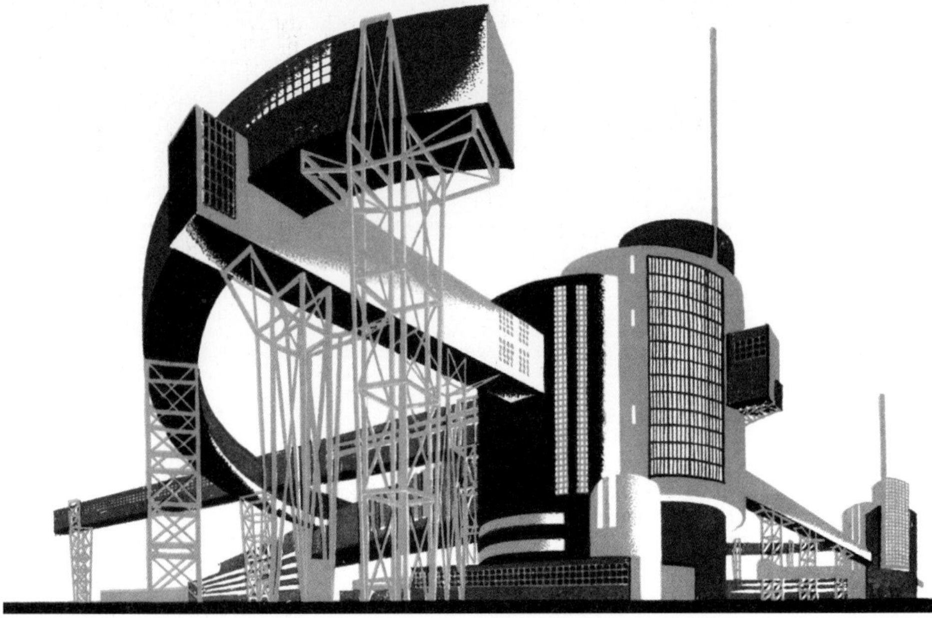

Iakov Chernikhov, industrial vignette, from *Architectural Fantasies* (1933).

During the NEP the state expressed its control of the 'commanding heights' of industry in monumental form. Centralization achieved its greatest effects not in the centre, but on the periphery. An unprecedented campaign of construction made Kharkov, the capital of the Ukrainian SSR until 1934, an epicentre in this process. The centrepiece was the House of State Industry, or Gosprom building (1925–8). Designed by Sergei Serafimov, Mark Felger and Samuil Kravets, Gosprom's mammoth scale edified the functions of bureaucracy. The building embraces Kharkov's central square; its three primary pavilions are linked by elevated passages, recalling the conveyors characteristic of industrial complexes. Gosprom's eleven storeys could accommodate between 6,000 and 8,000 employees. To the French journalist Henri Barbusse, who visited the city in 1929, it was a 'maison montagne'.[47] Containing a library, a radio station, a cafeteria, as well as a bank and a post office, Gosprom was – and remains – a city within a single building. The project became the anchor of an entirely new urban district, which arose along the axes of Gosprom's radial internal streets. Echoes of Gosprom's monumentality can be found in Shchusev's design for the headquarters of the National Commissariat of Agriculture (Narkomzem) in Moscow (1929–33) and in other administrative buildings throughout the USSR. Despite the modernism of these buildings, certain institutions remained tied to conservative forms. The

Sergei Serafimov, Mark Felger and Samuil Kravets, Gosprom building, Kharkov, Ukraine, 1925–8.

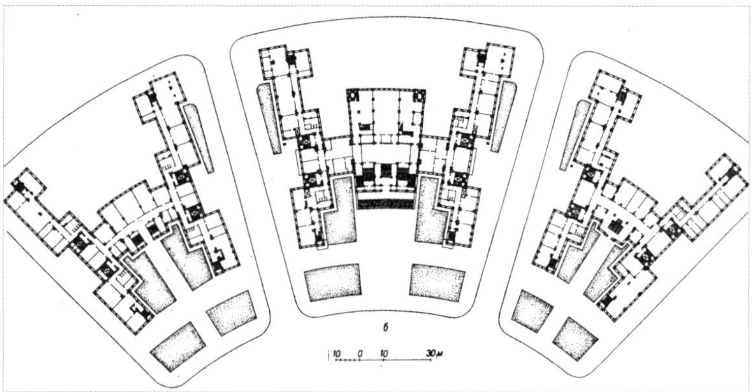

Gosprom building, ground-floor plan.

State Bank commissioned Zholtovskii's Renaissance-inspired extension to its Moscow headquarters in 1927, provoking considerable protest in vanguard architectural circles.

The Soviet government consolidated its claims to political authority with the construction of 'houses of the Soviets' – the regional headquarters of the Communist Party and state administrations. Ginzburg's design for the house of the Soviets in Alma-Ata (1927–31) – the newly appointed capital of the Kazakh ASSR, now known as Almaty – stood in

Moisei Ginzburg, project for the Government House of the Kazakh ASSR, Alma-Ata, 1927–31.

stark contrast to the region's monumental traditions.[48] Rejecting the region's religious institutions, Ginzburg argued that 'the brilliant mosques are the dead material of history, while the homely dwelling of the poor Muslim is a starting point for the development of a new culture.'[49] Ginzburg valued vernacular traditions more than religious forms. His building's courtyard contains pools of water and shade-creating trellises. A speaker's rostrum at the centre of the principal volume announces the building's civic function. Tucked beneath the large, elevated hall, the main entrance leads to a mezzanine foyer. Ginzburg opened this space to the elements with broad sliding doors, allowing cross-ventilation during summer months. Traces of Le Corbusier's influence appear in his combination of curved and rectilinear surfaces, his ample use of ribbon windows, systematic use of colour and generous roof terraces. A symbol of Soviet rule, the building conflated modern forms and bureaucratic administration.

Although houses of the Soviets were built in cities across the USSR, the institution was conspicuously absent at the centre. The failure of the Palace of Labour competition of 1923 left Moscow without an architectural statement of Soviet power. The passing of the first Bolshevik leader in 1924, however, gave the Soviet Union a symbolic heart: Lenin's mausoleum. Between Lenin's death and 1929, Shchusev designed three successive projects for the tomb. The first two wooden structures resembled stepped pyramids, recalling ancient traditions of funerary architecture.[50] The final iteration, which stands in Red Square today, is clad in red granite and bears Lenin's name above the central portal. The tomb is located underground, where Lenin lies in state. While delivering speeches or viewing parades, Soviet leaders – from Stalin to Gorbachev – stood atop the structure, drawing on Lenin's mythic status for support. More symbolic form than functional building, Lenin's Mausoleum was nevertheless the mythological centre of the Soviet regime.

The growth of Soviet commerce and industry depended on foreign relations. Organizations such as the All-Russian Cooperative Society

Aleksei Shchusev, Lenin's mausoleum, Moscow, 1930.

(Arcos), which managed trade with Great Britain, and the Russo-German Trade Association (Rusgertorg) injected consumer goods into the Soviet economy and established institutional recognition through a series of high-profile architectural competitions. These events produced innovative designs, such as the Vesnin brothers' winning project for Arcos (1924), but failed to yield built work. Erich Mendelsohn's design for a knitwear factory in Leningrad was the first of many architectural manifestations of international collaboration. Impressed by his hat factory at Luckenwalde near Berlin (1923), the Leningrad Textile Trust awarded Mendelsohn the commission in 1925.[51] His 'Red Banner' factory consisted of a dynamic power station, an L-shaped multi-storey building and three large workshops. The power station's semicircular prow projects into a prominent intersection and serves as the fulcrum of the entire design. Mendelsohn's commission caused a stir in the Soviet press. Some architects objected to the Textile Trust's failure to hold a competition; others to the dependence on foreign architectural ideals. Nevertheless, the leaders of industry recognized that foreign capital and machinery were sorely needed in the USSR.[52]

Throughout the 1920s the Soviet network of cooperative enterprises expanded rapidly. The 1928 competition for a new headquarters of Tsentrosoiuz, the organization that managed the cooperative movement, produced one of the landmarks of international modern architecture. After several initial stages, Moscow's Constructivists lobbied in support of Le Corbusier's proposal, noting that 'the Tsentrosoiuz building, if executed to [his] designs, will not only make a magnificent contribution to the new Moscow, but also constitute a powerful incentive to reconsider buildings under construction that are out of phase with contemporary life-styles.'[53] OSA's request was granted. His largest commission to date, the Tsentrosoiuz was in part a vindication of Le Corbusier's controversial

Erich Mendelsohn, power-house of the 'Red Banner' textile factory, St Petersburg, 1925–7.

Le Corbusier, Pierre Jeanneret and Nikolai Kolli, Tsentrosoiuz building, Moscow, 1928–36.

Miron Merzhanov, Voroshilov Sanatorium, Sochi, 1930–34.

disqualification from the League of Nations competition the previous year. As in the League of Nations project, he raised the building on a forest of pilotis, creating covered parking spaces and minimizing foundation work. A system of ramps turned vertical circulation into what Le Corbusier elsewhere called an 'architectural promenade'. The building's curtain walls were composed of red Crimean tuff and extensive glazing. Four principal volumes contained offices for 2,500 workers, a restaurant and a large auditorium. The play of the rectilinear office blocks against the curved volumes of the ramp enclosures and auditorium created a dynamic sculptural object. Le Corbusier visited Moscow three times before 1930. Nikolai Kolli assisted him during his stay and oversaw construction. Material deficits interrupted work in 1931 as industrial enterprises assumed priority during the First Five-year Plan. Completed in 1936, Le Corbusier's poetic forms and exploration of 'architecture as circulation' left lasting impressions on the Soviet architectural scene.[54]

Like the cooperative movement, trade unions, industrial trusts and government agencies became major architectural patrons during the Five-year Plan. These institutions sponsored the development of a new system of sanatoria and rest homes. Although similar institutions existed before the October Revolution, they became key elements of the incentive system within Soviet society as State- or union-funded vacations became valued rewards. Sanatoria took many forms, ranging from spartan seaside accommodations to elaborate leisure complexes. Miron Merzhanov's

Voroshilov Sanatorium in Sochi (1930–34) was the largest resort in the Soviet Union.[55] The Red Army, the project's patron, spared no expense in this luxurious multi-building compound. A large central pavilion and symmetrical sleeping quarters overlook the Black Sea from terraces built into a steep hill. A funicular connects guest-rooms to a landscaped esplanade. Accommodation for 700 guests, a large theatre, medical facilities and a large cafeteria make up this miniature city of leisure. Constructed in reinforced concrete, Merzhanov's buildings have broad balconies, large windows and light-filled interiors; they were – and remain – ideal spaces for healthful relaxation.

The primary building sites of the First Five-year Plan, however, were devoted to heavy industry. Architects like Ivan Nikolaev, who designed a series of spinning mills in Ivanovo-Voznesensk, contributed to the Soviet Union's industrial base, but the Plan's 'great leap forward' was accomplished with American technical assistance. Through the American –Russian Trade Association (Amtorg), the Soviet government purchased cars, trucks, tractors and the equipment to manufacture such vehicles from the Ford Motor Company.[56] Albert Kahn Assoc., the designer of Ford's River Rouge plant, produced designs for the expansion of automobile factories in Nizhniy Novgorod – at the time known as 'Soviet Detroit' – that the Cleveland-based Austin Company executed.[57] Kahn's firm provided designs for plants at sites across the USSR: tractor factories in Stalingrad, Chelyabinsk and Kharkov; steel works in Nizhniy Tagil; aircraft factories

Albert Kahn Assoc., Dzerzhinskii tractor plant, Stalingrad, 1929–30.

in Kramatorsk and Tomsk; and many others.[58] American know-how helped complete the metallurgical complex at Magnitogorsk at the foot of the Ural Mountains and the hydroelectric station on the Dnepr River.

Part of a vast technical ensemble, Dneprostroi was one of the most celebrated projects of the Five-year Plan.[59] Constructed with the help of the American engineer Colonel Hugh L. Cooper, it was both a technological marvel and a symbol of Soviet industrialization. The creation of this power station entailed the creation of an entire urban ensemble, complete with new collectivist typologies such as factory kitchens. Viktor Vesnin, with help from his brother Aleksandr, Nikolai Kolli, Georgii Orlov and others, won the commission for the power plant in 1929. They worked at a geological scale, integrating nature and industry in sublime form. Vesnin's turbine hall is a long, solid volume, and acts as a counterpoint to the powerful rhythm of the dam's vertical piers. A projecting band of windows extends nearly the entire length of the structure, which was more than 200 m long. Inside, the power plant's steel skeleton was exposed and unadorned. The vast hall is a unified space in which spinning turbines converted flowing water into electrical current. Bringing the interior into dialogue with the surrounding landscape through a wall of windows, Vesnin combined natural power and industrial force in thoroughly modern form.

## A New Way of Life

Collectivity captured the Soviet architectural imagination. New municipal bathhouses, bread factories and cafeterias – known as 'factory kitchens' – served growing urban populations. The garden-city model and the single family home gave way, with few exceptions, to the 'residential complex' – an integrated group of apartment buildings, often with shared laundries and other services. Housing, always in short supply, was aggregated into larger and larger units. Driven by the persistent housing crisis and an enthusiasm for the socialization of daily life, architects made *byt*, 'lifestyle' or 'way of life', a field of architectural intervention.[60] Everyday life was the arena where Bolshevik cultural aspirations and spatial programmes intersected. A *novyi byt*, or 'new way of life', depended on the liberation of women from 'domestic slavery' through the socialization of cooking, cleaning and child rearing.[61] Such a project required a spatial fix that architects were eager to supply. El Lissitzky saw 'the forms of the dwelling' as a 'material expression of the essence of the new way of life', arguing that residential design was the most important field of architectural investigation.[62] The search for new habitats produced a variety of experiments: monumental apartment blocks, essays in formal

A. I. Gegello, A. S. Nikolskii and G. A. Simonov, residential complex on Traktornaia Street, St Petersburg, 1925–7.

individualism, expressions of elite privilege and manifestos of radical social transformation.

The housing crisis motivated the first large urban developments of the NEP. In Moscow and Leningrad construction in traditionally working-class districts provided new dwellings to previously under-served populations. Replacing the dark, unhygienic wooden houses characteristic of the urban periphery, new apartment complexes presented a new morphology of uniformity, austerity and cohesion. The Traktornaia Street housing development (1925–7) in Leningrad was the centrepiece of the reconstructed Narva – now Kirov – district. Designed by A. I. Gegello, A. S. Nikolskii and G. A. Simonov, the complex has a strong axial emphasis. Staggered rows of three-storey buildings line the street. Stepping back from the building line as they approach the main thoroughfare, the complex expands to embrace Nikolskii's adjacent state school (1925–7). A latent monumentality suffuses the development. Large semi-arches link each apartment building, creating an image of cohesion. Nikolai Travin, an ASNOVA member, exploited municipal ownership of land to great spatial effect. His design for a residential district in Moscow's Shabolovka district (1927–8) subverted traditional relationships between building and street. Twenty-four apartment buildings form four zigzag lines at the heart of the complex. Perpendicular intersections and broad courtyards create alternating impressions of compression and expansion throughout

Konstantin Melnikov,
Melnikov House,
Moscow, 1927–9.

Melnikov House, studio.

the development. Travin's innovative application of colour to the building's surfaces heightened this effect. Abandoning the perimeter block in favour of spatial buffers and intermediate zones, developments like Travin's contributed to the increased permeability of Moscow's urban fabric.

Konstantin Melnikov's private house and studio (1927–9) was without precedent or progeny. Having acquired both fame and relative wealth from his commissions for workers' clubs and other municipal structures, Melnikov defied the communitarian impulses of his contemporaries and built a modern *osobniak*, or urban villa. An essay in unconventional forms, it embodied the architect's individualistic approach to design. Composed of two intersecting cylinders, the building's walls are load-bearing and pierced by a grid of hexagonal windows. Melnikov devised a system of deep, interlocking wooden beams to span the interior space without intermediary supports. The facade is glazed on the ground and first floors. A low, centrally placed door provides access to the interior, while a double-height window puts the building's complex section on display. Inside, the house-studio is composed of a combination of single- and double-height spaces. The low-ceilinged ground floor, which contains the dining room, bathroom and kitchen, is divided by partition walls. A small staircase leads to the grand living room on the first floor. The bedroom, which has built-in beds, is accessible from this room. The studio space, the largest room in the house, lies above the bedroom and looks onto the yard. Rows of hexagonal windows bathe the space in light, creating an ethereal workshop for Melnikov's architectural dreams. Although Moscow's architectural community praised Melnikov's bold forms and innovative structural techniques, some questioned the value of the private house as a basis for Soviet society.[63]

The luxury of Melnikov's private space was multiplied 500-fold in Moscow's Residential Complex for the Central Executive Committee of the Communist Party (1927–31). This colossal structure, known alternately as the 'Government House' or, following Iurii Trifonov, the 'House on the Embankment', was designed by Boris Iofan.[64] Standing just across the Moscow River from the Kremlin, the building was the largest and most technologically advanced apartment building in Moscow of its day. It was a stronghold for the families of the political elite. The building's wings sprawl across an irregular site, integrating 500 apartments, a department store, a club and a large movie theatre. The largest apartments have five bedrooms, many times larger than the living space then available to the average Soviet family. Iofan's building became an infamous site of political repression during the 'Great Purges' of the 1930s, when the sudden disappearance of its residents became a terrifyingly regular occurrence. Similar projects for the political elite were constructed in other Soviet cities. Yekaterinburg's 'Checkist Village', designed by Ivan Antonov and Veniamin Sokolov (1929–36), housed members of the Secret Police.

Boris Iofan, Government House, Moscow, 1927–31.

E. A. Levinson and I. I. Fomin, first apartment building of Lensovet, St Petersburg, 1931–5.

Evgenii Levinson and Igor Fomin – Ivan's son – created an elegant apartment house for the members of the Leningrad Soviet (1931–5). Some of the building's units include servants' quarters, reflecting a growing inequality between the political and working classes.

The architectural vanguard sought to transform the lives of the working population. Both ASNOVA and OSA lobbied for new forms of dwelling, but only OSA won official support for its work. In 1928 the Building Commission of the Economic Council of the RSFSR, better known as Stroikom, commissioned Ginzburg and his colleagues to explore the rationalization and standardization of residential units. The economization of the dwelling, they felt, was a key step in the movement 'toward new, higher social forms of everyday life'.[65] Stroikom's most innovative work responded to the overcrowding typical of multi-family communal apartments. In such 'communal houses', as Benjamin observed, 'through the hall door one steps into a little town' where as many as eight families shared facilities designed for one.[66] The solution, Ginzburg and his colleagues argued, was a reduction of private space and an expansion of collective space. In their 'Type F' residential unit, private kitchens were reduced to 'kitchen nooks' and bedrooms became 'sleeping niches'. Its split-level design gave living space a floor to ceiling height of about 3.6 m, while the height of sleeping and cooking areas, where one spends little time, was reduced. The economy of vertical space allowed one broad corridor to serve F-units over three levels. When the units were combined in an apartment building, shared kitchens, laundries, nurseries and clubs would compensate for the reduction of private space and stimulate a new, collective way of life. The chairman of Stroikom ratified Ginzburg's propositions and recommended his designs for use in experimental constructions.

The Stroikom discussions mark the emergence of the *dom-kommuna*, or communal house, as a new architectural ideal. Part utopian projection

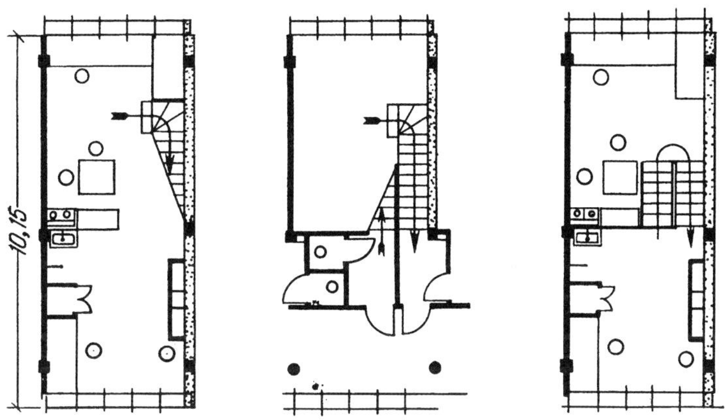


Narkomfin Building, 'Type F' split-level units.

Moisei Ginzburg and Ignatii Milinis, Narkomfin apartment building, Moscow, 1928–30.

into the future of life in the Soviet Union, part response to the dismal reality of communal apartments, this building type encapsulated Soviet architects' claims to social agency. The *dom-kommuna* conflated architectural design with social programming, allowing architects to view their work as the creation of a new way of life. These projects did not just remain on paper. Communal houses were constructed in cities throughout the Soviet Union. From 1928 to 1930, six buildings based on Stroikom's units were built in Moscow, Yekaterinburg and Saratov. Designed by Ginzburg and Ignatii Milinis, the Narkomfin House (1928–30) for the workers of the Ministry of Finance was the most celebrated communal project of the day.[67] The reinforced concrete building is divided into residential and communal sections. Raised on pilotis and striated by ribbon windows, the residential section bears the mark of Le Corbusier's influence. The communal block is a glazed four-storey cubic volume. This sector was designed to house a gym on the ground floor and a cafeteria above, but much of the lower section was eventually used as a kindergarten. The building's two sections are linked by an elevated walkway. Ginzburg and Milinis used the Stroikom F-units in the fourth to sixth floors and larger two-bedroom apartments in the second and third floors. They considered the Narkomfin building a 'transitional' project, giving residents the option to cook and dine privately while encouraging use of the communal sector. The Narkomfin building's innovative layout influenced housing projects in both the USSR and abroad. Its economical use of space impressed European architects as they searched for a 'minimum dwelling' for a time of economic crisis.[68] Le Corbusier brought blueprints of the Narkomfin building back to Paris on a return trip from Moscow, eventually using them as a prototype for his Unité d'Habitation.[69]

Ivan Nikolaev's communal housing complex for the Moscow Textile Institute (1929–32) offered a more radical social vision. Much larger than the Narkomfin building, Nikolaev's structure housed 2,000 students in 'sleeping cabins'. A 'sanitary sector' connects night-time and daytime blocks. Showering and dressing as they moved through this sanitary 'sluice-box', students descended to the daytime sector along a multistorey, ferro-concrete ramp. The saw-toothed roof of the daytime block both recalls Nikolaev's earlier work in the field of industrial architecture and provides diffuse sunlight for 2,000 square metres of study and recreational space. The ground floor of the daytime block contained a cafeteria and spaces for group activities. With distinct, yet seamlessly integrated functional zones, Nikolaev's communal house was not only a machine for living; it was a factory for a new, collective way of life.

The communal house was but a microcosm of the world that architects sought to create. While foreign specialists like Ernst May applied urban

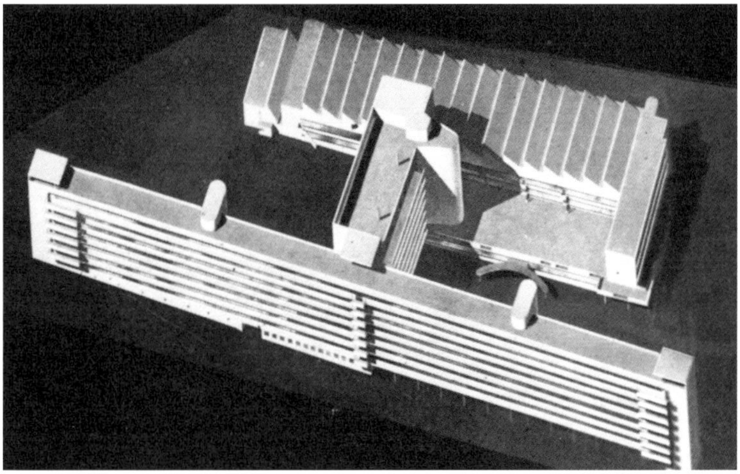

Ivan Nikolaev, communal house for students of the Textile Institute, Moscow, 1929–32.

models developed in Western Europe to Russia's new industrial cities, Soviet architects, economists and social theorists envisioned radically new forms of urbanism. May's Russian bureau supplied plans for cities based on the *Zeilenbau* principle he had used in Frankfurt am Main – the arrangement of housing blocks in parallel rows in order to enable assembly-line construction and capture advantageous sun exposures.[70] May managed the design of at least twenty cities and settlements between 1930 and 1933.[71] These included Magnitogorsk – where May's so-called 'first district' still stands as an embodiment of the *Zeilenbau* principle – Karaganda, Kuznetsk and many others.

Nikolai Miliutin, the chairman of Narkomfin and patron of its communal house, applied the assembly-line principle to the city as a whole, imagining 'linear' cities composed of ribbons of housing, industry and recreational zones.[72] The Constructivists offered alternative programmes for urban concentration and urban dispersal. Led by the economist Leonid Sabsovich, Aleksandr and Leonid Vesnin created model projects for 'residential combines'.[73] These so-called 'urbanist' designs were to accommodate 1,100 persons each. They were to become cells of a large, collectivist city. Ginzburg and the economist-architect Mikhail Okhitovich, who argued that 'the city should die in the ruins of the capitalist mode of production', proposed the dispersal of the population throughout the territory of the USSR.[74] Their 'disurbanist' model foresaw the construction of millions of lightweight, prefabricated houses – for both individuals and small groups – from local materials. Their decentralized urban programme sought to realize a goal inscribed in the *Communist Manifesto*: the abolition of the distinction between town and country. Unlike the

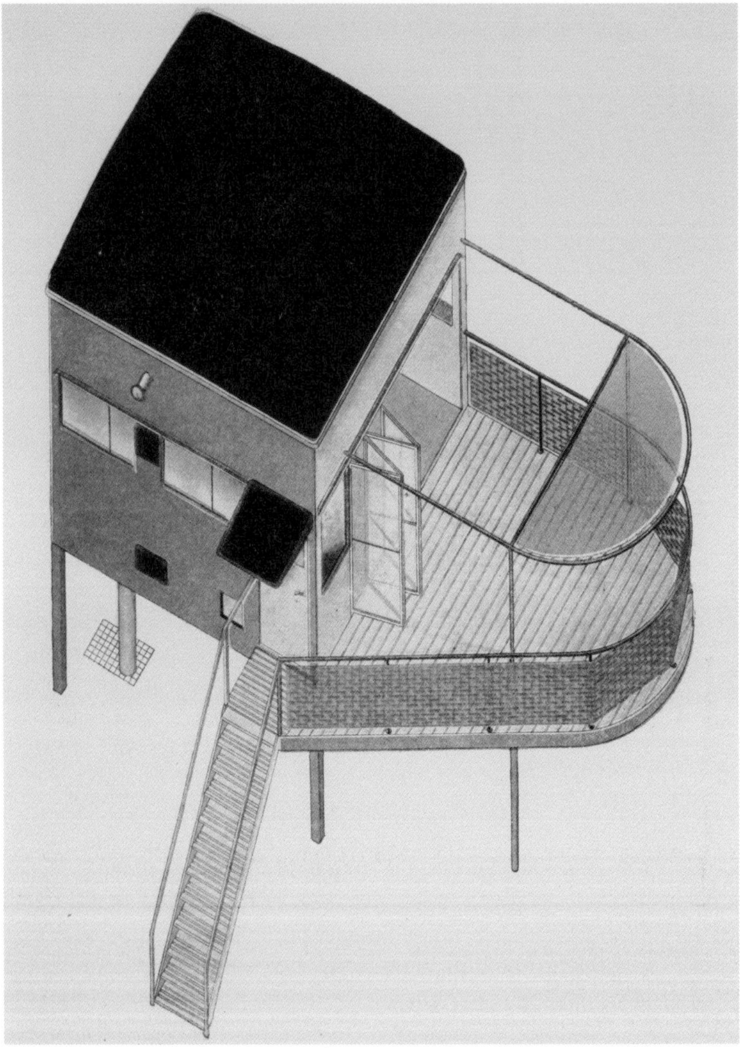

Moisei Ginzburg and the Section for Socialist Settlement of the State Planning Agency, dwelling unit, 1929–30.

communal houses constructed during the First Five-year Plan, these urban proposals would not be implemented. In 1930 the Communist Party issued a decree on the 'reconstruction of everyday life', censuring the 'half-fantastic' plans for the great leap to communism.[75] A symptom of the further concentration of the Party's authority, this decree maintained that the Plan, not the architectural vanguard, dictated the course of socialist construction.

## Spaces of the Cultural Front

Culture was an instrument and object of Soviet social and economic aspirations. Campaigns for literacy and numeracy sought to produce a better educated, and thus more productive, labour force. Educational policy underlined the importance of technical training for a society intent on economic modernization. 'Physical culture' – athletics – encouraged a relationship to the body that would produce healthy workers. Scientific investigation was both a motor of development and a form of popular entertainment. The construction of workers' clubs in cities throughout the Soviet Union made books, theatre and cinema available to an unprecedented number of people. The spaces of this civilizing mission were designed with the aim, in the words of education reformer Beatrice King, of 'changing man'.[76]

Bolshevik educators sought to transform the school 'from the weapon of bourgeois class domination into a weapon for the total destruction of class divisions within society'.[77] Under the leadership of Anatolii Lunacharskii, the Commissar of Enlightenment, and Nadezhda Krupskaya, Lenin's wife and Minister of Education, Soviet schools abandoned the rigid hierarchies, scholastic curriculum and religious emphasis of the Tsarist educational system. Entrance to institutions of primary education was drastically expanded, and the nature of the curriculum transformed. Seeking to find a unity of educational and productive work, traditional subjects were complemented by vocational training. This curricular programme was designed to produce students equally at home in the library and the workshop. Architects articulated these policy changes in new

G. A. Simonov, school on Tkachei Street, St Petersburg, 1927–9.

forms. The compact monumentality of Tsarist urban schools gave way to expansive pavilion systems. Grigorii Simonov set his primary school on Tkachei Street in Leningrad (1927–9) amid a broad landscaped site. Two parallel blocks contain classrooms for students of a range of ages. An elevated gallery links the two principal volumes, evoking Walter Gropius's design for the Bauhaus building in Dessau (1925–6). The gallery contains a library, a cafeteria and the entrance to a large, enclosed gymnasium. The school's polytechnic mission is expressed in its taller northern wing where the small dome of the observatory's enclosure crowns the structure, becoming a symbol of scientific education.

Scientific institutes and technical colleges provided expertise for a rapidly developing society and gave architects opportunities to envision new civic structures. Aleksandr Kuznetsov used brick, glass and steel to create an innovative plastic form for Moscow's Central Institute of Aerodynamics and Hydrodynamics (1924–8). Moscow's All-Union Electrotechnical Institute and the related Electro-technical Trust transformed the Lefortovo neighbourhood into a modern scientific city. Lev Meilman, Gennadi and Vladimir Movchan and Rotislav Chuenko deployed Corbusian ramps and a dramatic curtain wall in their design for the Trust's headquarters (1929–32). A sign of Le Corbusier's shifting reception on the Russian scene, the building led critics to question the appropriateness of *korbiuzianstvo* (Corbusianism) for Soviet architecture.[78] Ivan Leonidov's diploma project for the Lenin Institute of Library Sciences was the most inspired educational project of the day (1927). Designed for a site on Moscow's Sparrow Hills, the project is composed of elementary geometric forms. A glazed sphere houses an auditorium for 4,000 people, a slender tower contains library stacks and a long horizontal pavilion holds a museum and classrooms. An 'aerial tram' would integrate the building and the city, while 'a powerful radio station' would connect it to the world. Soon after its completion, Leonidov's project received

Ivan Leonidov, Lenin Institute of Library Sciences, Diploma Project, 1927.

M. O. Barshch and M. I. Siniavskii, planetarium, Moscow, 1927–9.

wide exposure in the international architectural press, becoming a symbol of the radical inventiveness of Soviet architecture.

Science was both an architectural inspiration and a form of popular entertainment. The 'scientific theatre' of the planetarium came to rival traditional theatrical venues. Moscow's Planetarium (1927–9), designed by Mikhail Barshch and M.I. Siniavskii, was sponsored by the ministry of education and used optical and structural technologies developed by the Carl Zeiss Company in Germany. The architects drew upon earlier models – in particular the planetarium constructed in Jena – in their design, filtering precedents through the principles of Constructivism. Essentially an enclosure for a Zeiss projector, the building's principal space is a circular auditorium 27 m in diameter. Ribbon windows, curved walls and a circular staircase echo the arc of the Planetarium's great dome. Reinforced concrete columns support the auditorium's floor, lifting it off the ground and relieving the ground-floor walls of their load-bearing function. The cupola was constructed with a densely woven steel frame and sprayed concrete. With a thickness of 12 cm at its base and 8 cm at its apex, the concrete structure of the dome was remarkably light and economical. Inside, a hemispherical projection screen hangs from the roof, creating an open, centralized space. The building's ground floor originally housed an astrological museum. A recent renovation has altered the building's appearance dramatically.

Mental exercise and 'physical culture' went hand in hand. 'The new society wants a healthy generation because strength is a sign of optimism and well-being', Lissitzky wrote.[79] Trade unions sponsored sporting leagues and supported the construction of athletic fields in cities across the USSR. Sport was both a healthy form of proletarian leisure and a pervasive form of mass-spectacle. Moscow became the centre of an international network of workers' sports leagues with the Spartakiada of 1928. Like the Olympic Games, the Spartakiada encompassed a wide variety of competitions; the competitors, however, were members of workers' sports delegations from the republics of the USSR and abroad. The Dinamo Stadium in Moscow (1927–8) was the centre of the event. Designed by Arkadii Langman and Lazar Cherikover, the arena had an initial capacity of 20,000. The architects avoided classical references in their design, choosing instead to let its

L. Z. Cherikover, A. Ia. Langman, Dinamo Stadium, Moscow, 1927–8.

A. I. Gegello and D. L. Krichevskii, A. M. Gorky Palace of Culture, St Petersburg, 1925–7.

muscular reinforced concrete frame serve as the image of Soviet sport. But physical culture entailed more than mass spectacle; personal hygiene and care of the body were also important parts of social life. In municipal bathhouses personal cleanliness was turned into a public good. Aleksandr Nikolskii's circular bathhouse, or *bania*, in Leningrad (1927–30) gave this ancient institution a modern, economical form. Its circular geometry reduced the amount of surface area exposed to the elements, thereby reducing heat transference, while its location at a prominent site in a residential district emphasized the social value of personal hygiene.

Workers' clubs were the true powerhouses of Soviet culture. During the NEP and the First Five-year Plan these institutions were built in cities, towns and villages across the USSR. Developing the programme of the pre-revolutionary peoples' house, the workers' club became a centre of entertainment and political education. The spaces of the club varied, but a theatre or audience hall was commonly the core of the institution. Clubs provided libraries, classrooms, meeting halls, sports equipment and a variety of other services. The innovative chess set in Rodchenko's model workers' club, which was presented at the international exhibition in Paris of 1925, emphasized that play was also part of club life. Aleksandr Gegello's Gorky Palace of Culture in Leningrad (1925–7) established an influential morphology for the building type: its theatre formed a central, conical volume to which ancillary spaces were attached, clearly expressing the building's internal logic on its exterior. Following the Seventh Trade Union Conference of the USSR in 1926, unions assumed leadership in

Ilia Golosov, Zuev Club, Moscow, 1927–9.

club construction. The largest unions held competitions for standardized club plans that might be reproduced as needed. Other unions commissioned leading architects to create distinctive structures.

Moscow's Union of Municipal Workers initiated an unprecedented campaign of construction in 1927. Ilia Golosov's and Konstantin Melnikov's designs for the Union became some of the most famous experiments in modern architecture. Golosov's Zuev Club (1927–9) stands on a narrow rectangular site in the city centre. Seeking to integrate places of work and recreation, the Union decided to build the Zuev Club across the street from a garage for trams. Constructed in brick and reinforced concrete, the building seems to be composed of a series of intersecting geometrical solids. The variety created by this interplay of forms visually tempers the building mass, lending the structure a human scale. A glazed cylinder, which contains the club's primary staircase, resolves the facade's vertical and horizontal movements, creating a balanced asymmetry. Inside, a double-height foyer occupies much of the ground floor. The club's central feature, an auditorium for 950 viewers, lies above this space. Expressed on the exterior as a pure cylindrical form, the glazed stairwell springs to life as visitors ascend to the auditorium.

Melnikov's Rusakov Club (1927–30) is located in the heart of Moscow's Sokolniki district. Based on the complex intersection of geometrical forms, the structure represents Melnikov's belief that workers' clubs were to be unique buildings that would stand out from their surroundings. He approached the complex programme of the workers' club through the

Konstantin Melnikov, Rusakov Workers' Club, Moscow, 1927–30.

interpenetration of spaces both in plan and in section. A wedge-shaped auditorium is the functional and programmatic core of the building. The projecting volumes on the main facade contain the upper rows of seating. Glazed stairwells provide internal circulation and access to an open terrace that is connected to the street by two symmetrical staircases. The terrace rests on a foyer that leads down to the gymnasium and up to the auditorium. Melnikov conceived of the club as a system of spaces that could be connected at will by 'living walls'. He intended to mount retractable partitions between the general auditorium and five semi-isolated ranges of seats, but technical difficulties prevented their installation. The acoustics of the auditorium, which also functions as a cinema, are enhanced by the triangular geometry of the building, calling to mind its popular designation as the 'megaphone on Stromynka Street'.

At the end of the 1920s the 'palace of culture' acquired greater social significance. Larger than clubs, such palaces were designed to serve large urban populations. The competition for the palace of culture in Moscow's Proletarian district of 1930–31 became a turning point within Soviet

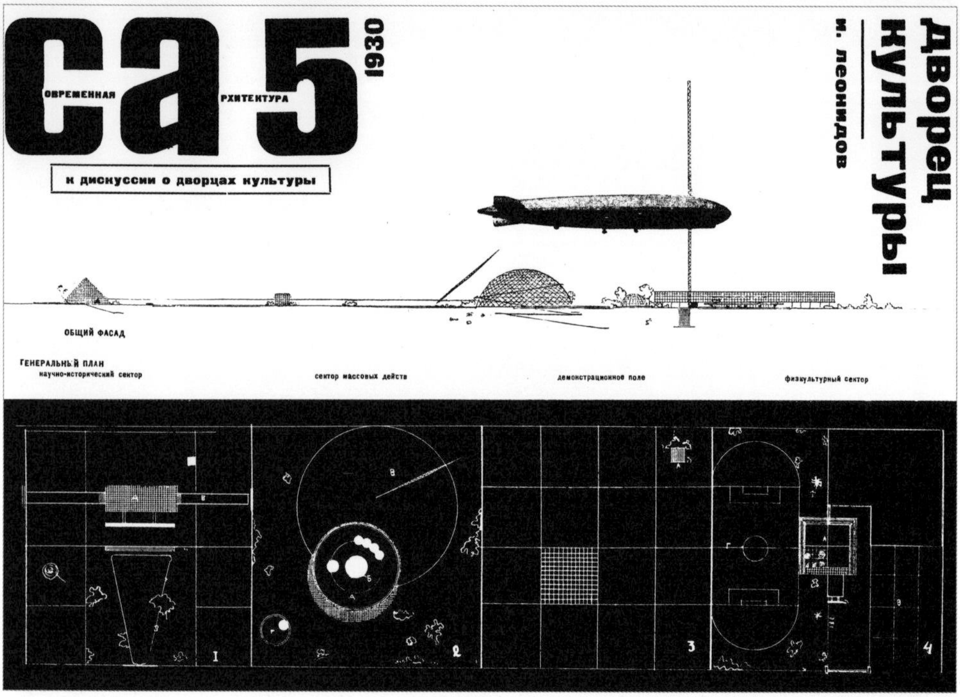


Ivan Leonidov, Palace of Culture, Proletarian District, Moscow, project, 1930; from *Sovremennaia arkhitektura*.

architectural life. The event was hailed as a 'cultural Dneprostroi', counting it among the major building sites of the First Five-year Plan.[80] Ivan Leonidov's project provoked widespread controversy. Developing an earlier theoretical design for a 'club of the new social type', he divided the palace into sectors for physical culture, demonstrations, mass spectacles and science and history. Large glazed volumes serve each sector; an athletics pyramid, a hemispherical mass theatre, a rectangular museum of science and a cubic rostrum create a vast cultural landscape. Leonidov imagined this as a centre of Union-wide cultural significance. Radio communications would connect it to the world, and a large dirigible mast – the project's principal vertical feature – would allow airships from across the USSR to dock at what Leonidov called the 'headquarters of the cultural revolution'.[81] Critics called the project 'the fantasy of an individualist', accusing Leonidov of formal self-indulgence.[82] The editors of SA, where the project first appeared, questioned its technical feasibility but defended its experimental character. Arkadii Mordvinov, an outspoken VOPRA member, turned the competition into an opportunity to attack the Constructivists and argue for 'proletarian hegemony' in architecture. He rejected so-called *leonidovshchina* – a pejorative designation for

'Leonidovism' – in an incendiary article, alleging that Leonidov and his followers represented a 'formalistic wing of Constructivism'. According to Mordvinov, they had introduced a 'foreign ideology' into Soviet architectural life, one that true Communists needed to purge in the 'fight for a proletarian architecture'.[83] Characteristic of the violent rhetoric of class war that activist groups turned against the old intelligentsia, Mordvinov's campaign led the Communist Academy to declare 'Leonidovism' 'harmful to proletarian construction' and a manifestation of the 'class enemies of the proletariat'.[84] The campaign indicated that the Communist Party and its architect members sought greater control over architectural life. Socialist construction, they believed, required the subordination of architectural politics to Party directives.

Following the scandal of 'Leonidovism' and a second round of competitions, the Vesnin brothers were awarded the commission for the Palace of Culture of the Proletarian District. Constructed in two phases between 1931 and 1937, it was the largest and most sophisticated structure built by the pioneers of Constructivism in Moscow. The building partially replaced the remains of the Simonov Monastery in the city's largest industrial district. Turning away from the street, it embraces a green landscape. A convex field of glass expresses the foyer of the theatre

Aleksandr, Viktor and Leonid Vesnin, Palace of Culture of the Proletarian District, Moscow, 1931–7.

N. A. Trotskii and S. N. Kazak, Kirov Palace of Culture, St Petersburg, 1931–7.

block, and a varied fenestration pattern indicates the building's programme, which includes a library, a gym, a winter garden and an observatory. The interior of the Palace of Culture is spatially complex and refined in its details. The primary axis leads from the semicircular winter garden, in which lush planting and water elements bring nature inside, through an elongated lobby to the theatre. A café leads to the theatre's grand foyer. Illuminated by a double-height window, this space is defined by sculptural stairwells and a loft that serves the balcony of the theatre. The smooth volume of the foyer establishes a reciprocal relationship between interior and exterior, creating an abstract unity of structure and landscape.

The fidelity of the Vesnin brothers' executed building to its initial conception was exceptional, for during its construction Soviet architectural culture would undergo radical transformations. Designed and built in parallel with the Moscow Palace of Culture, Noi Trotskii's project for a Palace of Culture on Vasilevskii Island in Leningrad (1931–7) registered the changes taking place in these pivotal years. Between design and execution, glazed curtain walls gave way to pilaster fronts and figural relief panels; its smooth plaster exterior was scored to resemble masonry construction; its formal language was 'enriched' with allusions to the tradition of classical architecture. It represented the new significance accorded to historical models – a revolution ushered in by the growing influence of the Communist Party in Soviet architectural life.

chapter five

# Architecture and Stalin's Revolution, 1932–41

In antiquity there were seven wonders of the world. The Palace of the Soviets will be the eighth.[1]

With these words Aleksei Tolstoi, a writer of fantastical novels, conveyed the world-historical significance ascribed to the Palace of the Soviets, the building that was intended to symbolize the alleged success of Stalin's revolution. An international competition of 1931, at the nadir of economic depression in the capitalist world, thrust the Palace and the USSR into the global architectural spotlight; the demolition of the Cathedral of Christ the Saviour to make way for the Palace heightened the drama of the spectacle. One hundred and sixty competition entries offered a cross section of contemporary approaches to the large, administrative building. Le Corbusier, one of several invited participants, offered a poetic landscape of reinforced concrete; Nikolai Ladovskii made a hemispherical theatre the centrepiece of his entry; other competitors imagined vast spaces that might turn the building into a theatre for mass demonstrations. Many thought the competition would lead to the triumph of modern architecture. It did not. Against international expectations, in February 1932 the jury awarded first prizes to Boris Iofan, Ivan Zholtovskii and the little-known American architect Hector Hamilton, each of whom rejected the symbolic values of lightness, transparency and abstract form. 'The Palace of the Soviets', wrote the jury's chair, 'is not a machine.'[2] Its form was to arise from the 'critical assimilation of architectural heritage'. To become the eighth wonder of the world, the Palace of the Soviets would have to draw upon ancient precedents.

To Western observers, the outcome of the competition represented a betrayal of the Soviet Union's architectural revolution. Hans Schmidt, a Swiss architect employed in the USSR, noted that 'the result of the competition for the Palace of the Soviets has put the radical architects of the West in a state of indignation.'[3] The idea of Zholtovskii building the Palace in an 'Italian Renaissance style' scandalized Le Corbusier. 'We were expecting from the USSR an example of authority, edification and leadership, since such an example expresses the noblest and purest judgment', he

Boris Iofan, Vladimir Shchuko and Vladimir Gelfreikh, Palace of the Soviets: initial project, 1932; model, 1947.

Le Corbusier, project for the Palace of the Soviets, Moscow, 1931; axonometric.

wrote to the cultural commissar Anatolii Lunacharskii. 'And if this is not to be? Then there is no more USSR, no doctrine, no mystique, or anything else!!!'[4] The outcome seemed inexplicable to Western and Soviet architects alike. Why would the jury emphasize the relevance of 'architectural heritage' to the design of the Palace of the Soviets? What might this mean for modern architecture in the USSR?

A symbol and symptom of its epoch, the Palace expressed the confluence of authoritarian despotism and utopian dreaming that characterized Stalin's 1930s. The entire competition had been a bureaucratically orchestrated event. Communist Party leaders had named Iofan chief architect of the Palace before the competition was publicly announced.[5] His task was to create a working project based on the best features of other competitors' work. Stalin personally intervened in the design of the Palace of the Soviets, recalling the image contained in Osip Mandelstam's infamous *Epigram against Stalin*: 'Forging decree after decree, like horseshoes, he pitches one to the belly, another to the forehead, a third to the eyebrow, a fourth in the eye.'[6] Tossing off a letter from his summer residence on the Black Sea, Stalin asked Iofan to 'give the top of the "Palace" a shape by extending it upward in the form of a tall column' and 'to make it as tall as the Eiffel Tower, or a little taller'.[7] Perpetually in construction but never built, the Palace was to be a soaring monument to Soviet power. By 1939, it had a projected height, including an immense statue of Lenin at the building's summit, of 516 m – more than 70 m taller than the Empire State Building. One booster predicted that it would be visible on the horizon from 70 km outside of Moscow, roughly the distance between London and Brighton.[8] Its vertical extension expressed the impulse conveyed in the popular aviators' song 'Ever Higher': 'We were born to make fairy tales come true. To conquer the vastness of space reason gave us steel wings for arms.'[9] The Palace of the Soviets, a dream image called forth by decree, gave utopian form to the centralized, hierarchical and bureaucratic apparatus of Soviet socialism.

The Palace was the architectural analogue of Stalin's revolution, a brutal set of policies and events that both devastated the Soviet population and created new social forms.[10] To Leon Trotsky, exiled from the USSR in 1929, Stalin's revolution represented a betrayal of the basic principles of the Bolshevik project. The 'Soviet Thermidor', he claimed, was a 'triumph of the bureaucracy over the masses'.[11] The 'new Soviet intelligentsia' was composed of engineers, managers, trade union representatives and other professionals who had benefited from preferential educational policies.[12] Fiercely loyal to the regime, they were an elite class of citizens who benefited from higher wages, better housing and easier access to consumer goods. The upper tier of this class was composed of members of the Communist Party. An omnipresent element of Soviet life, the Party was neither a governmental body nor a political party in the traditional sense. It was a closed organization to which admittance was gained through extended candidacy and from which one might be expelled at any time. Nevertheless, the Soviet Constitution of 1936 defined the Party as 'the guiding nucleus of all organizations, both social and governmental'. The Party had 'cells' in every enterprise. Its members were expected to enforce ideological vigilance on matters ranging from grain requisitions to architectural design. The Communist Party constituted a mammoth, authoritarian bureaucracy that forged policies on social, economic and cultural development.

The focus of the Party's First Five-year Plan on heavy industry and the collectivization of agriculture produced disastrous results for the rural population. Millions died of hunger as the famine of 1932–3 hit Ukraine, Kazakhstan and other provinces.[13] The suppressed 1937 census revealed that the USSR had a population of 162 million people, eight million fewer than demographers had predicted.[14] Collectivization also spurred the rapid growth of urban centres. Between 1928 and 1939, Moscow's population grew from 2.1 million to 4.1 million people.[15] Leningrad's population grew almost as fast. Sverdlovsk (Yekaterinburg), a Siberian industrial city, grew from 150,000 inhabitants to nearly half a million in the same period.[16] But standards of living could not keep up with urban growth, and housing, services and food supplies suffered. According to the writer André Gide, who visited the Soviet Union in 1936, housing was grossly inadequate: 'Many of the recent buildings erected for workers' dwellings have been so hastily, or rather, so carelessly built, and with such shoddy materials that there is every prospect of their soon being uninhabitable.'[17] The Second and Third Five-year Plans, projected for 1933–7 and 1938–42, sought to raise living standards by providing more housing and increasing the production of consumer goods, but the constant spectre of 'capitalist encirclement' and the looming possibility of war made defence spending a priority throughout the decade.[18]

Material privation was compounded by a growing atmosphere of fear. In late 1934, Sergei Kirov, the Leningrad Party boss, was assassinated. An elaborate show trial of August 1936 convicted Leon Trotsky (in absentia), Lev Kamenev, Grigorii Zinoviev and Ivan Smirnov – all former rivals of Stalin – of conspiring to overthrow the Soviet government.[19] The trial was the first event in a wave of terror directed against so-called 'enemies of the people'. Nobody was left untouched by the maelstrom of violence that ensued. A second show trial of 1937 accused industrial leaders of sabotage and wrecking; in 1938 Nikolai Bukharin, one of the most gifted Bolshevik intellectuals, was tried, convicted and sentenced to death. The Bolshevik Party 'purged' its ranks, sending former Party members to the GULAG or the execution chamber. The populations of prison camps and labour colonies grew throughout the decade.[20] The 'Great Terror' transformed the nature of public and private life. Neighbours 'denounced' neighbours and, as in the mysterious apartment Number 50 in Mikhail Bulgakov's *Master and Margarita*, 'people disappeared without a trace.'[21] Party activists disposed of rivals with charges of 'Trotskyism', and a generally combative and violent tendency spread throughout political and cultural institutions. International observers recognized the brutality and groundlessness of the repressive campaigns unfolding in the USSR. Many Communist sympathizers felt that the light from the East had been extinguished – that Moscow had become a centre of socialist disenchantment.

Cultural production was centralized and bureaucratized. The diversity of artistic societies characteristic of the NEP and the First Five-year Plan gave way to institutional uniformity. In 1932 the Communist Party issued a decree on the 'reconstruction of literary-artistic organizations' that liquidated independent groups and called for the creation of a single union for each type of artistic activity.[22] The unions, which would remain key cultural institutions throughout the Soviet period, held conferences, published journals and managed the living conditions of members. Like other Soviet enterprises, they contained Communist Party cells that monitored ideological vigilance and established complex feedback loops and patronage networks among cultural producers and political elites. Although it was highly centralized, Soviet cultural policy was never stable. As Stalin forged decrees like horseshoes, the Party unleashed a stream of cultural directives. The unions interpreted, debated and managed ideological change.

But Stalin's revolution produced both social devastation and utopian aspirations – the two often went hand in hand. In 1932 the magazine *Nashi dostizheniia* (Our Achievements), which Maksim Gorky founded, proclaimed that 'the time has come to construct our fatherland anew with the hands of machines . . . to dress the whole country, from Arkhangelsk to Tashkent and from Leningrad to Vladivostok in the iron armour of industrial giants . . . to weave the whole country into a network of electrical power lines.'[23] The conquest of space was a major preoccupation of the decade. Soviet scientists and engineers harnessed state resources and coercive techniques to construct new waterways and explore the arctic. As the centre of a new Soviet imperium, Moscow supported national self-determination for peripheral republics.[24] Paradoxically, distinct 'national cultural traditions' flourished under a centralized policy of ethnic particularism.[25] The General Plan for the Reconstruction of Moscow of 1935 and the opening of the first line of the Metropolitan in that year made the capital an emblem of spatial transformation. 'It was both possible and necessary to alter everything: the streets, the houses, the cities, the social order, human souls', wrote Raisa Orlova of her youth in Moscow during the 1930s.[26] The old succumbed to the new in countless campaigns of creative destruction.

## Creative Reconstruction

The twin events of 1932 – the Palace of the Soviets competition and the consolidation of artistic and literary organizations – raised more questions than they answered. When the committee for the construction of the Palace of the Soviets asked competitors to use 'both new techniques and the best techniques of classical architecture', it initiated a major transformation in the theory and practice of Soviet architecture. The Union of Soviet Architects (Soiuz sovetskikh arkhitektorov, SSA) gave organizational form to the centralization of architectural life. Founded in 1933, the structure of the Union enabled Communist architects, who represented only a small fraction of the profession, to exert greater influence over the politics of architectural affairs.[27] Generally younger and less experienced than their colleagues, Party-member architects remained dependent on non-Communists for leadership in the fields of design, planning and architectural theory. Through its publications, *Arkhitektura SSSR*

(Architecture of the USSR) and *Arkhitekturnaia gazeta* (Architectural Newspaper), and a dense programme of research, lectures and debates, the Union reinforced Moscow's position as the capital of Soviet architectural culture.

The SSA's first resolution questioned the authority of modernist principles. David Arkin, historian and the SSA's 'scientific secretary', criticized what he considered to be 'the complete and unconditional subjugation of architecture to technology' in the work of Le Corbusier, Moisei Ginzburg and others.[28] Constructivists and rationalists alike were criticized for allegedly turning technical forms into 'ready-made aesthetic values'. The SSA did not, however, reject architectural innovation outright. Concluding the Union's first major theoretical debate, Arkin noted that 'the process that we refer to as the "critical assimilation of architectural heritage", is a source for the internal enrichment of Soviet architecture's movement forward, not backward; for the creation of authentically new (not simply novel) architectural forms; for the creation of a new architectural culture.'[29]

Architecture schools and research institutes became centres of this new architectural culture. At the end of 1933, the Central Committee of the Communist Party initiated a sweeping reform of architectural education and established the All-Union Academy of Architecture.[30] The Academy's design curriculum supplemented the offerings of architectural schools with advanced training for practising architects and a three-year postgraduate programme. It sponsored tours of classical and contemporary architecture in Western Europe. Opportunities of this type had generally been unavailable to young architects in the years since the Revolution. The Academy's publication programme brought new translations of classics of architectural theory – including the works of Vitruvius, Alberti, Palladio and Viollet-le-Duc – to the Russian scene. It sponsored research on contemporary architecture of the West with its journals *Akademiia arkhitektury* (Academy of Architecture) and *Arkhitektura za rubezhom* (Architecture Abroad), as well as with translations of contemporary Western authors. Architectural history was put on display in 1934 with the creation of the world's first museum devoted entirely to architecture within the Donskoi Monastery. These developments represented a widespread belief that a multifaceted understanding of architecture's traditions and intellectual culture would help transform Soviet architectural practice.

In preparation for the 'reconstruction' of Moscow, the chair of the Moscow Soviet, Lazar Kaganovich, established municipal design and planning ateliers in 1933. An authoritative Party leader, Kaganovich coordinated some of the largest modernization campaigns of the 1930s: the

Moscow Metropolitan and the Moscow–Volga Canal. The client–architect relationship characteristic of liberal economies had disappeared in Russia with end of the NEP. Arkhplan, as the new ateliers were called, liquidated previous municipal architectural organizations and established a new patronage system. Paradoxically, it gave architects greater control over design while subordinating their work to the oversight of Kaganovich and his advisors. Leading architects – Ivan Zholtovskii, Aleksei Shchusev, Konstantin Melnikov and others – directed design and planning studios. Together, the ateliers were responsible for the design of individual buildings and entire urban ensembles. These were large operations: by 1934 Arkhplan had a staff of more than 1,000 people.[31] Through selective administrative appointments, Arkhplan directed Moscow's architectural development and expanded Communist Party influence. Typically, Kaganovich asked experienced, non-Communist architects to lead the ateliers but named young Communists as their deputies. In design atelier No. 8, for example, Viktor Vesnin was assisted by the inexperienced, Party-card-carrying architect Nikolai Kostochkin. Kaganovich frequently briefed Communist architects in closed meetings. They then transmitted Party directives to the ateliers and informed Kaganovich of the political atmosphere of architectural life. Because atelier leaders retained the 'rights and responsibilities of authorship' for all the products carried out under their direction, many saw Arkhplan as an anti-bureaucratic measure.[32] Kaganovich, however, retained his seat at the top of the organizational pyramid. Throughout the 1930s the system of ateliers was replicated throughout the Soviet Union, making Party bosses primary architectural patrons. The design ateliers also established a paradigm for the organization of architectural labour that would have a lasting impact on Soviet and, indeed, post-Soviet architecture.

Architectural experiment flourished in this new architectural environment. Seeking to bring the 'lessons of architectural heritage' to contemporary design, Soviet architects pursued a course of *obogashchenie*, or 'enrichment'. Ginzburg and the Vesnin brothers felt the economic conditions that fostered the development of Constructivism had passed: 'We have become richer; we have more possibilities; we can now allow ourselves a broader scope of activity and a break from asceticism.'[33] The 1934 competition for the headquarters of Narkomtiazhprom, the Commissariat of Heavy Industry, showcased the enrichment of architectural design. Though never realized, the building was to replace the Upper Trading Rows on Red Square. Many competitors used the skyscraper to engage the verticality of the Kremlin's towers, the Historical Museum and St Basil's Cathedral. In Ivan Leonidov's proposal, a broad tribune acts as a plinth to a set of three soaring towers. Poetic meditations on the forms

Ivan Leonidov, Commissariat of Heavy Industry (Narkomtiazhprom), competition project, Moscow, 1934.

of industry, they resemble inhabited smokestacks. Behind the towers, a colonnade supports a horizontal office slab. A grand arch connects the heart of the complex to a workers' club. Murals composed of abstract, archaic forms enclose the club's primary volume – an immense hyperboloid. Recalling Vladimir Shukhov's applications of the form, Leonidov's project sought to reconcile advanced techniques with a historical context. Other competitors, notably Konstantin Melnikov, explored the combination of monumental forms and heroic sculptural programmes as they searched for a new, historically informed architectural language.

This search, however, was difficult. In its course, architects became both agents and victims in the social atrocities of the 1930s. They participated in the Communist Party's attempt to 'purge' its membership of 'undesirable elements'. Party-led campaigns against individuals could lead to expulsion from the SSA or, as in the case of Mikhail Okhitovich, to denunciation, arrest and execution.[34] The show trial of August 1936 accelerated Communist 'vigilance' on the architectural front. The ensuing search for 'Trotskyists' and 'enemies of the people' led to the expulsion of a number of architects – both Communists and unaffiliated architects – from the Union. Many of these architects, including Ginzburg's former collaborator Solomon Lisagor, were transferred to the GULAG. Foreign architects also suffered during the campaign. The brigades of Ernst May and Hannes Meyer were accused of espionage and either arrested or deported. The hysteria of the 'Great Terror' made fear, repression and political opportunism central aspects of Soviet architectural culture.

The language of architectural life acquired new political functions as the Communist Party launched a campaign against 'formalism' in the arts. Following the premiere of Dmitrii Shostakovich's opera *Lady Macbeth of the Mtsensk District* in early 1936, *Pravda*, the Party's primary newspaper, called the work a 'petty-bourgeois formalist essay' that sacrificed originality to 'cheap attempts at novelty'.[35] Cries of 'formalism' appeared in newspapers, journals and debates as writers, artists and architects tried to interpret the Party's vague line on culture. The architectural press decried an alleged 'cacophony in architecture'.[36] Melnikov and Leonidov were accused of producing nothing but 'formalist stunts' and asked to recognize the 'mistakes' they had made. Led by Karo Alabian, the Party members of the Union initiated a campaign for *tvorcheskaia perestroika* – creative reconstruction – that aimed to bring architecture into conformity with other cultural spheres. The SSA demanded that its members reject 'formalist mistakes' categorically. Virtually everyone complied, but without necessarily adopting new design methods. The ambiguity of the term allowed a wide range of architectural positions to persist behind the new 'anti-formalist' rhetoric. Architects like Melnikov, who refused to denounce 'formalism', were pushed further and further from the centre of Soviet architectural life.

The politics of architectural language reached a dramatic climax at the First Congress of Soviet Architects in 1937. The event's resolution declared socialist realism the basic creative method of Soviet architecture. Socialist realism had been recognized as the official path of Soviet literature at the Writers' Congress of 1934; now architects sought to join a unified cultural front. But like that of 'formalism', socialist realism's meaning for architecture remained highly ambiguous. According to Arkin, the Congress 'wasted neither time nor words trying to find subtle and rhetorical interpretations of the meaning of socialist realism in architecture. Yet still this meaning prevailed in all the work of the Congress, in every multi-day discussion of the creative questions of Soviet architecture.'[37] Such circular logic expressed socialist realism's function as a symbol of architecture's uniform adherence to the Party's erratic cultural policy. From the presidium of the Congress, architect-bureaucrats turned political directives into ideological imperatives. Nevertheless, the architectural expression of socialist realism differed from architect to architect and changed in response to the Party's developing social and economic policies. As a rhetorical device, it was flexible enough to be applied both to the monumental Palace of the Soviets and the industrialization campaign of the Third Five-year Plan that sought to eliminate 'gigantomania' from socialist construction.

## Radiant Cities

As the sky clears overhead, a woman sits behind the wheel of an automobile on a central Moscow boulevard. The glimmer of reflections turns the windshield and the street into a continuous luminous surface. Pedestrians, cars and buses form an indistinct, metropolitan crowd. The avenue recedes deep into the background, where towering structures are engulfed in a shimmering haze. Surrounding buildings appear squat next to these new behemoths – their height matched only by the breadth of

Iurii Pimenov, *New Moscow*, 1937.

the mirror-like asphalt surface. This urban vision was the subject of Iurii Pimenov's monumental canvas *New Moscow* of 1937. A hopeful image of the capital's development, Pimenov's painting represented the urban transformation unfolding in the mid-1930s. The demolition of the Kitai-gorod walls in 1934 opened up broad vistas around the city's central district, creating the perspectives that Pimenov admired. New structures like the Hotel Moscow (1936) and the Council for Labour and Defence (1935) – the buildings in the background of Pimenov's image – established a monumental scale for the new city. *New Moscow* resembles a still from an imaginary film about the 1935 General Plan for the Reconstruction of Moscow.

The General Plan was in part a reaction to the radical urban proposals that emerged during the First Five-year Plan. In 1930 Le Corbusier proposed the complete reorganization of the Soviet capital in his famous 'response to Moscow'.[38] Arguing that Moscow was 'in reality a provisional city', he called for the demolition of all but the most significant historical structures – the Kremlin, the Bolshoi Theatre, St Basil's Cathedral – and the creation of a new city based on a grid of functional zones, a field of expansive *redent* blocks and diagonal connecting streets. His schema was flexible; it could expand in any direction. Although the Soviet audience gave the 'response to Moscow' a mixed reception, Le Corbusier would make it the basis for his major urban statement of the 1930s: the *ville radieuse*.[39] Le Corbusier's proposal was part of an intense debate on Moscow's urban form. In late 1931 the Moscow Soviet sponsored a planning competition that produced projects for the dispersal of the city's population in garden suburbs (Ernst May); for the endless expansion of the city's boundaries in the form of a large, urban parabola (Nikolai Ladovskii); for its transformation into a 'city of satellites' (Hannes Meyer); for the expansion and renovation of the compact urban centre (Kurt Meyer); and many other schemes.[40] As the debate unfolded, Kaganovich offered a new set of directives for urban development in the Soviet Union. First, in a landmark speech of June 1931, he rejected radical proposals that predicted the withering away of the large city. He maintained that cities had become socialist with the success of the October Revolution; to speak of their dissolution or radical reconstruction amounted to dangerous utopian thinking.[41] Second, in a speech to the Moscow Party Committee in early 1932, he argued that the planning of Moscow needed to take the historical city as its basis: it would have to develop the city's radial-concentric street network and 'beautify and give architectural form to the entire city'.[42]

Following Kaganovich's recommendations, Vladimir Semenov outlined a schematic approach to the reconstruction of the city. He made the

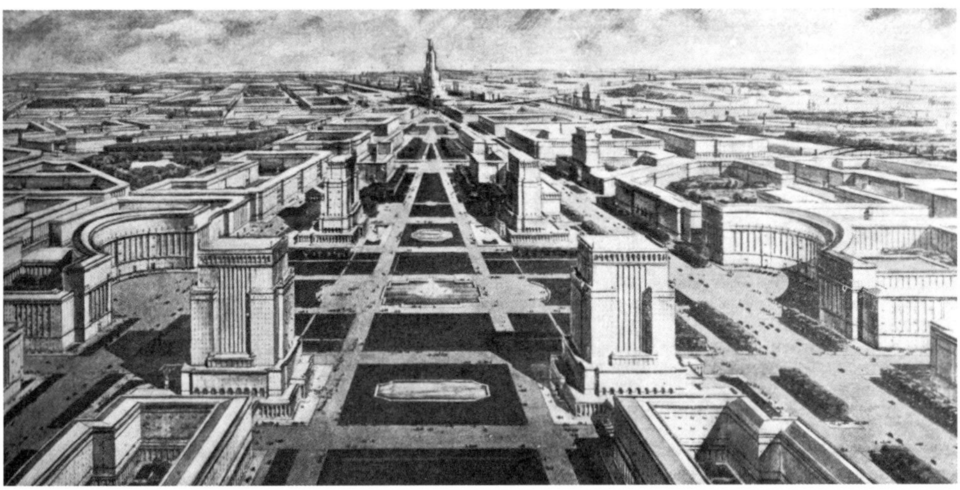

Project for the Avenue of the Palace of the Soviets, Second Planning Studio of Moscow Soviet, 1936.

city's *magistrali* – arterial streets – the primary sites of intervention. The planning and architectural workshops of Arkhplan set to work on a detailed project for the development of the city. In the ateliers, architects and planners articulated the future of Moscow in relation to both historical urban forms and contemporary planning projects. They looked for precedents in the urban ensembles of the Italian Renaissance, the French city of the *ancien régime*, contemporary planning in Fascist Italy and even the architectural fantasies of the American draughtsman Hugh Ferriss.[43] These models offered images of the city as a cohesive system, but Soviet planners believed they could surpass previous plans in both coherence and grandeur, for Moscow, the capital of the world's first socialist economy, was free from the impediments of private land ownership. But despite the Moscow Soviet's political efficacy – its ability to expropriate land, fund new construction and enlist a large workforce – it was constrained by the city's history of underdevelopment. Although municipal construction had improved in the years since the revolution, urban infrastructure lagged far behind growth. Basic services such as running water, waste disposal, electric power, telephones and urban transport had improved little since the revolution, and Moscow was far behind other European cities in these areas. The new plan was designed to transform a decrepit urban centre into a metropolis; to restart the process of modernization that had stalled with the fall of the Tsarist empire.[44]

The territorial ambitions of the General Plan for the Reconstruction of Moscow were vast. By 1945, the end of the decade covered by the plan's provisions, the city would double in area. Its target population was five million inhabitants. Moscow was to obtain unimpeded access to the Baltic, Black and Caspian seas through the construction of the Moscow–Volga Canal and the Volga–Don Canal, making the Soviet capital a 'port of five seas'. The Moscow Metropolitan and the extension of tram and bus services would improve urban circulation. A ring of municipal canals would link the city's reservoirs. The Moscow River was to be shored up with granite embankments – in emulation of Leningrad's urban waterways – and lined with parks and housing. The primary axis of growth was to be to the southwest, beyond the Sparrow Hills. Streets were to be widened; population density was to be redistributed; and a new social and technical infrastructure was to be created. The *magistral*, the *kvartal* (block) and the monument were the primary elements of the plan. Along radial and concentric boulevards, buildings of no fewer than six storeys were to be constructed. The density of residential districts would be reduced through the demolition of low structures and the construction of new apartment houses, schools and other facilities. Monumental buildings at large squares and intersections would define urban districts. When the German writer Lion Feuchtwanger visited Moscow in 1937, he viewed an electrified model of the plan's projected outcome and was astounded at its totality. 'Never before has a city of millions been rebuilt from the ground up according to the laws of functionality and beauty like this new Moscow.'[45]

The reconstruction of Gorky Street dramatized Moscow's transformation. Renamed in honour of the Soviet writer in 1933, this primary radius runs from Okhotnyi Riad in the city centre to Leningrad Chausee in the northwest. The Plan foresaw new dimensions for the street: its breadth was to expand from 19–21 m to 40 m. Many buildings were demolished to make way – including the Strastnoi Monastery on Pushkin Square. The most spectacular aspect of the campaign, however, involved the movement of historic structures. In a comic scene from Aleksandr Medvedkin's film *New Moscow* (1938), a startled woman shrieks with surprise as the cityscape outside her window appears to jump into motion. She reaches for a telephone, demands to know 'where her Moscow is going', only to find out that it is not Moscow, but her apartment building that is on the move. Medvedkin captured the shocking sense of change that accompanied the engineering feat of lifting, moving and replanting entire structures along Gorky Street. More than 50 buildings were shifted to accommodate its new breadth, notably I. Kuznetsov's

Arkadii Mordvinov, Blocks A and B, Gorky Street, 1937–9.

townhouse for the Savvo-Storozhevskii Monastery (1905–7) and the headquarters of the Moscow Soviet.[46] Arkadii Mordvinov designed a massive mixed-use apartment building to take the place of fourteen structures at the base of Gorky Street (1937–9). Its form elevated dwelling to a monumental scale: two seven-storey wings flank a triumphal arch. Plate-glass windows of shops and commercial spaces line the first and second floors. The upper storeys appear as a continuous surface: ceramic tiles, shallow balconies and vegetal reliefs establish coherence across the facade. Sculptural groups enliven its silhouette. Classically inspired details – mouldings, pilasters and cornices – enrich its surface while prefabricated wall and floor sections rationalize the 300 apartments in the block. Given to members of the Soviet elite, these apartments were – and remain – some of the city's most desirable. Mordvinov designed several other houses along Gorky Street before the Second World War; together, they were prototypes of grandiose urban gestures that would be built in socialist cities in the USSR and abroad.

Moscow's plan became a model for other Soviet cities. Architects and planners in Leningrad developed a general plan for their city between 1935 and 1939, first under the leadership of Lev Ilin, and later, Nikolai Baranov.[47] As in Moscow, Leningrad architects sought to create a new axis of urban growth. The city's 'second centre' was located to the south along the newly constructed Moskovskii Prospect. In a residential district along Ivanovskaia Street (1937–8), a major cross axis in Leningrad's general plan, Evgenii Levinson and Igor Fomin – Ivan's son – articulated the formal and spatial dimensions of the new planning paradigm. Whereas housing developments of the 1920s generally enabled open communication between streets and courtyards, the residential *kvartal* of the 1930s established a hierarchical relationship between them. Six-storey buildings line Ivanovskaia Street, creating what Levinson called the 'magnificence of the *magistral*'.[48] On the facades, pillars composed of concave and convex forms recall classical orders without reproducing them. Gaps between the monumental structures provide access to broad courtyards in which other apartment buildings and service structures stand. The interiors of the blocks have an intimate scale. The rhythmic repetition of windows, pillars, loggias and cornices along the length of Ivanovskaia Street lend the complex a sublime grandeur.

E. Levinson and Igor Fomin, residential district on Ivanovskaia Street, St Petersburg, 1937–8.

Andrei Burov and Boris Blokhin, large-block building on Leningradskii Prospect, Moscow, 1940–41.

According to one commentator, Levinson and Fomin's project represented an 'entirely new conception' while remaining true to the 'great Leningrad style that one finds in the broad, clear lines of its streets'. It was a 'compelling example of the proper combination of innovation and tradition'.[49]

The Third Five-year Plan emphasized the importance of economy and mass production in the construction industry. At the First Congress of Soviet Architects the chairman of the State Planning Commission, Gennadii Smirnov, who would be arrested during the 'Great Terror' of 1937, called upon architects to work with engineers to curb the 'gigantomania' characteristic of recent construction. Industrialization, standardization and economy were to become guiding principles for architects and the building industry alike.[50] Moisei Ginzburg applauded Smirnov's directive in a speech on the industrialization of residential construction. Ginzburg praised the efficiency of building sites in the USA and urged his colleagues to adopt the organizational accuracy of American construction schedules.[51] Modernization was the primary concern of a campaign for 'rapid construction' that hit Moscow's building sites in the aftermath of the Congress. Most of Moscow's apartment buildings were made with brick and manual labour, and construction was often disorganized and chaotic. Work was now to be improved by applying the principles of the production line to the building industry. In Moscow, Leningrad, Kharkov and other large cities, prefabricated concrete blocks offered the greatest potential for mass production. Andrei Burov and Boris Blokhin were leaders in the use of these materials in the race to accelerate construction. The team designed and oversaw the construction of four apartment buildings between 1938 and 1940. Working with engineers at local concrete plants, they devised a system of blocks that integrated structural dimensions and architectural forms. Burov and Blokhin made pillar and spandrel components the primary architectural theme of their building on Leningradskii Prospect (1940–41). Its skeletal frame is clearly legible; every seam and joint is crisply articulated. The building reflected their interest in the structural rationalism of Viollet-le-Duc whose *Lectures on Architecture* had recently been published by the Academy of Architecture: his dictum that 'every architecture is derived from structure' was at the heart of Burov and Blokhin's project.[52] When it was completed, the building was hailed as a truly innovative synthesis of contemporary technology and historical principles. 'There is not a single classical element, not one classical form, but it is entirely classical', one commentator wrote.[53] Architects viewed Burov and Blokhin's building as a symptom of a 'great break' within Soviet architecture on the eve of the Second World War: its unity of form and structure forged what they saw as a productive synthesis of modern techniques and the spirit of classical design.

## Infrastructure, Art and Labour

Moscow's modernization was an intensive and extensive process. The Moscow Metro's dense network of tunnels created a new, subterranean world; the Moscow–Volga Canal changed the course of a river. Infrastructure transformed the spatial dimensions of the Soviet capital, establishing connections between disparate neighbourhoods and integrating Moscow's waterways into a territorial network that extended from the White Sea in the north to the Caspian Sea in the south. This transformation was dramatized with great art and human sacrifice: each of the Metro's stations was to be an underground palace; each kilometre of the Moscow–Volga Canal was built by the dying hands of a workforce of prisoners. The art of infrastructure articulated the utopian and dystopian aspects of Stalin's Revolution. It created a new world of dense, frictionless, geographical relationships and their doubles: the unregulated workers' settlements on Moscow's periphery and the labour colonies of the GULAG. These complementary spaces were symptoms of a paradoxical attempt to build a modern metropolis on the basis of arduous, unskilled and often forced labour.

Nikolai Ladovskii, vestibule of the Krasnye vorota Metro Station, Moscow; opened in 1935.

The first line of the Moscow Metro opened with great ceremony on 15 May 1935. After four years of design and construction, the Metro encompassed thirteen stations and nearly 12 km of track. Named after Lazar Kaganovich, the Metro's development was directed by Pavel Rotert, who had previously managed the construction of the Gosprom building in Kharkov and at Dneprostroi. The engineers of Metrostroi – as the Metro's construction firm was known – created three types of station. Shallow stations had either trabeated or vaulted construction; in deep stations great pylons divided platforms into broad central halls and side aisles. Escalators provided vertical circulation. By 1934 more than 70,000 labourers from all over the Soviet Union worked in the tunnels, digging them largely by hand. Their labour was represented in the paintings of Aleksandr Samokhvalov and illustrated magazines and described in literary anthologies. The injuries and fatalities entailed by this dangerous work, however, remained confidential. Samuil Kravets, the chief architect of the Metro's architectural bureau, led a study tour of the urban rail systems of Berlin, Paris, London and New York in preparation for Moscow's new system, ensuring that it would become 'the most beautiful metro in the world'.[54] The first line was followed by a second in 1938, which added seven more stations to the city's network.

Whereas most metros strive for systemwide coherence, each station in Moscow's system was to be unique. Street-level pavilions formed an archipelago of experimental designs. Some were integrated into existing structures, as in the Lenin Library and Theatre Stations, others were

D. Chechulin, Dinamo Metro Station, Moscow; opened in 1938.

freestanding. Nikolai Ladovskii's vestibule for the Krasnye vorota Station (1935) was one of his few realized projects. Its nested arches converge on the entry, drawing passengers underground in a dynamic, funnel-like movement and recalling his early experiments with abstract form. For the Kirov (now Chistye prudy) Station (1935) Nikolai Kolli created a modernized Roman tomb: pillars screen glazed entries on each side of a rectangular block; a deep cornice crowns the structure; circular windows on lateral walls provide additional illumination.[55] The interior is bathed in soft natural light, modulating the transition from the site's verdant boulevard to the subterranean labyrinth. Other architects made more overt classical references. Dmitrii Chechulin's vestibule for the Dinamo Station (1938) incorporates Corinthian columns, sculptural reliefs and rich classical details.

The 'underground capital', according to André Lurçat, a French architect working in Moscow, was even more impressive. The efficiency and beauty of the underground stations conveyed more than comfort to millions of passengers; they also excited 'emotions that will enable the rapid rise of the spiritual level of the masses, who are so thirsty for culture and beauty'.[56] Architects turned the constraints of spatial extremes into monuments to transportation and collaborated with artists to create a new synthesis of the spatial and visual arts. Aleksei Dushkin was among the most talented and prolific architects of the Moscow Metro. He designed two stations for the first line, and one for the second. His Palace of the Soviets (now Kropokinskaia) Station (1935) is a monumental, column-filled space.

Aleksei Dushkin, Mayakovskaia Metro Station, Moscow; opened in 1938.

Dushkin found inspiration for an innovative structural solution in the architecture of ancient Egypt. He translated the flared forms of the columns of the temple of Amun at Karnak into reinforced concrete. Expanding as they rise, Dushkin's mushroom columns acquire the profile of five-pointed stars at ceiling height. Electric light springs upward from each column's capital, adding visual buoyancy to the hall and transforming each star into a pattern of light and shade. Dushkin's Mayakovskaia Station (1938) was the first station to be constructed in steel. Parallel arcades run the length of the platform. Transverse arches span the central corridor, creating a repetitive system of bays. The small footprint of the steel pillars opens up the station, allowing the central hall and side aisles to be perceived as a single space. Playing on the theme of the 'chassis', Dushkin embellished the frame with glimmering steel channels. Inspired by Mayakovsky's industrial lyricism, Dushkin and the painter Aleksandr Deineka sought to capture the image of the 'blue silk' of the sky that the poet described in 'Good!: A Poem of the October Revolution' (1927). The recessed ellipse of each structural bay contains a unique mosaic by Deineka. Softly illuminated from below, the panels present themes such as aviation and diving. Deep below ground, Mayakovskaia

Station conveys the sensation of ascent through a synthesis of structure and art.[57]

The opening of the Moscow–Volga Canal on 15 July 1937 was a triumph of contradictions. A parade of ships that had traversed the 128 km of the canal arrived at the banks of the Moscow River, becoming the centrepiece of a mass celebration. Party leaders assembled that evening in the Bolshoi Theatre to hear Matvei Berman, a commander of DmitLag, a labour camp whose prisoners had built the canal, describe the canal's correction of 'nature's mistake' of separating the Moscow and Volga Rivers. The previous day, 50,000 prisoners had been released from the camp, while two of the leaders of the construction project, Semen Firin and Sergei Puzhitskii, were arrested.[58] The chief architect of the canal, Iosif Fridliand, had been arrested in April and would soon be executed. His crime was a familial relationship to Genrikh Iagoda, former head of the NKVD, who had been arrested and charged with treason in the same month.[59] Achievement and punishment: these complementary elements of the opening celebration reflected the basic conditions of the canal's construction. Like the White Sea Canal, Stalin's first waterway, the Moscow–Volga Canal formed part of the GULAG archipelago. The city of Dmitrov, only 60 km from Moscow, was the centre of the new canal project. After 1932, when the decision to build the canal was reached, thousands of prisoners, engineers and bureaucrats descended upon Dmitrov, creating a prison camp with nearly 200,000 inhabitants. Living and working conditions were primitive: housing was provisional and improvised; most excavation was done by hand. Nevertheless, the dimensions of the canal were immense. It required hundreds of millions of tons of earth to be moved. It encompassed nearly 200 new buildings: dams, locks, pump stations, power stations and bridges.[60]

The elevation of the canal rises and falls along its course; at its highest, it is 38 m above the level of the Volga. The stoppage and redirection of water required to navigate this incline was given monumental form at locks and pump stations. Temple-like forms and hydroelectric dams punctuate large intervals of open landscape as the canal winds through once virgin land. Sergei Merkurov's enormous statues of Lenin and Stalin, as well as sculptures of ships and other nautical themes, adorn the canal's route. Like the Moscow Metro, the complex was composed of unique buildings by many architects. Fridliand oversaw the initial planning of the canal, but after his arrest his name was removed from the project.[61] Former members of ASNOVA made significant contributions to the architecture of the canal. Vladimir Krinskii designed the remarkable technical ensemble of Locks 7 and 8. Observation towers crowned by classical ornaments loom above the long horizontal basin of the lock. A reinforced

A. M. Rukhliadev, Karamyshevskaia Dam, Moscow Canal, 1937.

A. M. Rukhliadev, River Terminal, Khimki (Moscow), 1937.

concrete bridge that recalls the tense forms of Robert Maillart's work spans the waterway. Below, a tunnel for automobile traffic passes under the lock, emphasizing the technical mastery of vertical and horizontal dimensions. Aleksei Rukhliadev, also a former ASNOVA member, designed Lock 9, the Karamyshevskaia hydroelectric dam and the River Terminal in Khimki, the climax of the entire ensemble. Rukhliadev's dam combines the raw technical forms of concrete pylons with temple-like machine enclosures. Unlike the Dnepr dam complex, the Karamyshevskaia dam articulates the generation of power with the plasticity of what one critic called 'baroque motifs'.[62] The boat station links the canal's water to Moscow's territory. Composed of broad wings of balconies and a 75-m-tall tower, its form synthesizes the horizontal and vertical elements of the canal complex. The broad landscaped park in which it stands brings the sculptural and architectural language of the canal into Moscow's reach. Enclosed by galleries and arcades, its festive, maritime form resembles nothing more than a beached riverboat. The station's iconographic programme includes terracotta reliefs of the great buildings of socialism: the Palace of the Soviets, the Moscow Metro and the canal itself. Its celebration of socialist construction is so loud that it reduces the misery of Stalin's revolution to silence.

## Monuments to Bureaucracy

'Every regime has its monumental reflection in buildings and architecture', wrote Leon Trotsky in 1936. 'Characteristic of the present Soviet epoch are the numerous palaces and houses of the Soviets, genuine temples of the bureaucracy.'[63] The Soviet bureaucracy, from Party members to factory managers, constituted an elite class whose privileged status was given monumental architectural expression. Elites had access to both goods and spaces that were out of the public's reach. Elites received not 'living space' but spacious apartments; they rested not in parks but in first-rate recreational facilities; they worked not in shops but in grand administrative

I. V. Zholtovskii, apartment building, Mokhovaia Street, Moscow, 1934.

Andrei Kriachkov, apartment building for the Regional Party Committee, Novosibirsk, 1934–7.

structures. Loyalty to the regime and its vast networks of patronage conferred access to the new bastions of privilege and luxury.

When workers removed the scaffolding from Ivan Zholtovskii's building on Mokhovaia Street in 1934, Moscow recognized that it had acquired the most elegant residences built since the October Revolution. Though smaller than Boris Iofan's House on the Embankment, Zholtovskii's building was more monumental. The colossal Corinthian order on its facade reinterpreted Andrea Palladio's Loggia del Capitaniato in Vicenza (*c.* 1570). Zholtovskii was a lifelong student of Palladio, and he was translating the Italian master's *The Four Books on Architecture* as he designed the House on Mokhovaia Street. The building was controversial both for its fidelity to Palladian models and the grandiose dimensions of its apartments (some units are duplexes). Viktor Vesnin criticized the building's non-standard floor plan. Why, he wondered, would Zholtovskii give each dwelling a unique design when standardization was needed to solve the housing crisis? Others called the building the 'nail in the coffin of Constructivism', overstating its influence for polemical effect. Yet few Soviet citizens actually lived in the building: it became the seat of the Embassy of the United States, which formally recognized the USSR in 1933. It later became the central office of 'Intourist', the Soviet Union's foreign travel agency. Andrei Kriachkov and Vitalii Maslennikov's apartment building for the Regional Executive Committee of the Party in Novosibirsk (1934–7) was not as grandiose as Zholtovskii's building, but it did fulfil its intended purpose. Its four- and five-room apartments housed Siberia's political elite, and its refined decor, which Kriachkov called 'French neoclassicism', won its authors a grand prix at the International Exposition of 1937 in Paris.[64]

Soviet luxury had both urban and pastoral architectural forms: the hotel and the sanatorium. The grand hotels that were built throughout the USSR during the 1930s were not designed for Soviet tourists. Travel for ordinary citizens remained difficult throughout the decade. Instead, these buildings served travelling dignitaries with great style. The hotel of the Moscow Soviet (1932–8) was the largest and most sumptuous example of this extravagant building type. Initially conceived by a young pair of

A. V. Shchusev, L. N. Savelev, O. A. Stapran, Hotel Moscow, Moscow, 1932–8.

architects, L. Savelev and O. Stapran, Aleksei Shchusev was brought in late in the design process to give the building the classically inspired elegance that the Moscow Soviet desired. Standing at the centre of Okhotnyi Riad, on the site selected for the Palace of Labour in 1923, its great volume established a new dimension for the urban core. Towers flank an imposing row of pillars on its main facade.[65] The lavish heart of the project was the interior. White marble, granite, bronze and rare wood veneers lined the lobby, restaurant and guest-rooms. The hall of the restaurant was filled with colossal Corinthian columns and crowned by a grand mural on the ceiling. Luxury suites, located in the towers overlooking Manezh Square, have three rooms, a large bath and separate rooms for service personnel. The largest had nearly 100 square metres of living space – several orders of magnitude larger than the space available to the average Muscovite.

Like the Moscow Soviet Hotel, the sanatoria built during the 1930s were immense, monumental complexes. Kislovodsk, a city of thermal baths near the Black Sea coast, became a centre of elite leisure. The American journalist Louis Fischer visited the city in the 1930s, noting that 'of the sixteen new sanatoria going up at the resort, almost all are being built by government offices . . . All these [offices] also employ workers too, but my guess is that the officials have easier access to the baths and beds than the workers.'[66] Moisei Ginzburg's Ordzhonikidze Sanatorium for Narkomtiazhprom (1934–8) was among the most innovative resorts. Sprawling across a mountaintop site, the complex is composed of two residential blocks, a therapeutic block and a vast landscaped terrain. The centrepiece of the surrounding park is a lyrical, multi-terraced stair, one of Ivan Leonidov's few executed designs. Terraces anchor each building to the ground, while roof gardens allow visitors to experience broad vistas and healthy breezes. Throughout the complex Ginzburg employed pillars, string courses, pergolas and crisp cornices, recalling a broad range of precedents: Milanese architecture of the 1920s; classical design; and vernacular traditions of the Caucasus.[67] While some criticized alleged 'echoes of Constructivism' in the sanatorium's design, it was the richest and most complete articulation of Ginzburg's approach to architecture after asceticism.[68]

The largest monument to bureaucracy, the Palace of the Soviets, was never completed. Iofan and his collaborators, Vladimir Shchuko and Vladimir Gelfreikh, worked on the project continuously, producing ever-larger renderings and models. By the Soviet Union's entry into the Second World War, the foundations and lower registers of the Palace's steel frame were in place.[69] The conflict, however, interrupted its construction schedule. The unrealized project nevertheless served as a model for administrative buildings throughout the USSR. Ivan Fomin's final work was the House of the Soviet of Ministers of the Ukrainian SSR in Kiev, which replaced Kharkov as capital in 1934. It was begun in that year and finished with the help of Pavel Abrosimov in 1938, two years after Fomin's death. Encased in granite and bearing colossal Corinthian columns, the building looms above Kiev's central park. Leningrad's House of the Soviets (1936–41) was even more imposing. Noi Trotskii's building dominates the city's new administrative centre along Moskovskii

Moisei Ginzburg and others, Narkomtiazhprom Sanatorium, Kislovodsk, 1934–8.

Ivan Fomin, Government House of the Ukrainian SSR, Kiev, 1934–8.

Noi Trotskii, House of the Soviets, St Petersburg, 1936–41.

Prospect. Standing on a vast open square, the building is 200 m wide and maintains absolute symmetry. Heavy rusticated pylons mark the building's centre. Their unimpeded rise culminates in a sculptural frieze and a monumental emblem of the USSR. The heart of the building is a hall with a capacity of 3,000, where the ceremony and spectacle of Leningrad politics took place.

The architecture of bureaucracy acquired 'national forms' in 'non-European' Soviet republics. In the Caucasus and Central Asia, Soviet architects sought to synthesize modern institutions with local cultural traditions. Local traditions, however, were commonly subordinated to Moscow's centralized authority. This programme developed under the aegis of Soviet policy on national minorities: Soviet culture was to be 'national in form and socialist in content'.[70] In practice, this meant that

Aleksei Shchusev, Marx-Engels-Lenin Institute, Tbilisi, 1934–8.

contemporary architecture in national republics was to be enriched by regional architectural forms. Aleksei Shchusev designed the Marx-Engels-Lenin Institute in Tbilisi (1934–8) on the basis of this contradictory approach to regionalism. Originally dedicated to Stalin, the building housed the Georgian branch of the Union-wide scientific society devoted to the study of Marxism and the history of the Communist Party. Paired colossal columns adorn its principal facade, creating a shallow portico. Large relief panels by the Georgian sculptor Yakov Nikoladze flank the colonnade and depict Stalin as the 'leader and organizer of socialist victory' in Georgia. Although Shchusev employed local materials and local craftsmen in creating the building's decor, critics noted his heavy reliance on Italian Renaissance motifs.[71] Shchusev argued that in designing for national republics, architects needed to 'look to the future' and be guided by the 'development of the powers of production in each country'.[72] Modernization took precedence over local traditions in monuments to Soviet bureaucracy – a relationship embodied in the minor role assigned to Georgian forms in Shchusev's building and other projects for national republics.

Architects, too, were part of the bureaucratic elite. By the middle of the 1930s, leaders of the profession had become deputy members of the Moscow Soviet. Some were elected to the Supreme Soviet of the USSR, the Union's highest governmental body. The organization of the Union of Soviet Architects followed bureaucratic norms: its structure included a presidium, financial committees and many subcommittees devoted to everything from the study of housing to the facilitation of vacations for architects. Moscow's House of the Architect (1938–41) gave architectural form to the Union's structure. An expansion of a neo-Gothic urban villa of 1896, the new structure was the work of several architects. Aleksandr Vlasov designed the vestibule and hall; Miron Merzhanov designed the basement-level restaurant; and Andrei Burov designed the facade, the most prominent element of the project. Despite its modest size, Burov's facade achieves monumental scale. Arches divide the facade into three sections. Red ceramic bricks, gold inlay and marble trim articulate its forms. An emblem based on the plan for the reconstruction of Moscow hangs above the central portal. Above, a frieze proclaims the name of the Union of Soviet Architects, and a deep marble cornice crowns the structure.

Andrei Burov, House of the Architect, Moscow, 1938–41.

The facade asserts its independence from the existing structure, symbolizing Soviet architecture's alleged freedom from pre-revolutionary norms. Burov drew upon the painted architecture of Piero della Francesca's *Legend of the True Cross* fresco in Arezzo (begun after 1452), prompting many critics to interpret the facade as a symbolic statement of Soviet architecture's mission. Clear, logical and refined, the facade of the House of the Architect at once evokes and transforms historical models, creating what one critic called 'an image of the contemporary Soviet building'.[73]

## 'Life has become better, life has become more cheerful'

Reproduced on banners in factories, parks and labour camps, Stalin's slogan of 1935 on the improvement of life in the USSR inaugurated a spectacular celebration of Soviet abundance. Although Stalin's statement was initially addressed to the improvement of agriculture and the end of bread rationing, its meaning extended to all branches of Soviet life. It was part of a widespread campaign for what Soviet citizens called *kulturnost*, or 'culturedness'. A diffuse and dynamic concept, 'culturedness' stood for a belief that proper personal comportment contributed to the collective good.[74] Socialist civilization, according to cultural activists, required good manners, proper entertainment and a new ethic of consumption. While the Soviet elite remained the most privileged consumers, the masses could partake of the image of abundance in theatres, parks and exhibitions. Abundance also served as the symbol of Soviet achievement in the decade's international expositions, where the USSR sought to define its membership in a community of industrialized nations.

Cinemas, theatres and concert halls were key sites of the Soviet cultural system. Throughout the 1930s the number of films produced in the USSR increased as Mosfilm sought to imitate Hollywood's success. The number of movie theatres in the Soviet Union increased as well: by 1937 there were 31,000 state-run cinemas in the USSR.[75] Revolutionary narratives and musicals were by far the most popular genres. Georgii and Sergei Vasilev's *Chapaev* (1934), a story of the Soviet Civil War, and Grigorii Aleksandrov's light-hearted musicals *Jolly Fellows* (1934), *Circus* (1936) and *Radiant Path* (1940) were seen by audiences across the USSR. New multiplexes – monuments to cultured entertainment – accommodated the explosive growth of the film industry. V. P. Kalmykov's 'Star' Cinema in Tver (1935–7) epitomized the new building type. Standing on the manicured embankments of the Volga, Kalmykov's theatre originally contained two halls of 470 seats each. A recessed porch marks the entry to the large cubic volume. Cylindrical stairwells flank the central mass and provide access to a roof terrace. Like the musicals of the decade,

V. P. Kalmykov, 'Star' Cinema, Tver, 1935–7.

Kalmykov's building, which became a model for other cinemas throughout the country, conveys a lyrical monumentality.[76] Moscow's Red Army Theatre (1934–40), designed by Karo Alabian and Vasilii Simbirtsev, cast culture in an imposing, literal form. The plan of the building and the profile of its colossal order follow the outline of the five-pointed star, the symbol of the Red Army.

The USSR used the Paris World's Fair of 1937 as a stage for the proclamation of Soviet abundance. The USSR Pavilion, designed by Boris Iofan, showcased the country's achievements in agriculture, sports and aviation. A jewel-encrusted map described the extent of the Soviet Union's reach. The recently ratified Soviet Constitution was also put on display. Aleksandr Deineka, Aleksandr Samokhvalov and other painters contributed panels devoted to physical culture, Soviet dignitaries, life on the collective farm and other subjects. Nikolai Suetin, a former student of Kazimir Malevich, designed decorative pylons for the building's interior that recalled both his former teacher's architectural sculptures and crystalline skyscrapers. A 5-m-tall model of the Palace of the Soviets was the centrepiece of the

K. C. Alabian and V. N. Simbirtsev, Central Theatre of the Red Army, Moscow, 1934–40.

Boris Iofan, Soviet Pavilion, International Exposition, Paris, 1937.

architectural section. Iofan's pavilion, however, was the primary exponent. Designed in collaboration with the sculptor Vera Mukhina, the Soviet pavilion was one of the most memorable of the show. Mukhina's sculpture of a factory worker and collective farm labourer crowned the structure, broadcasting a heroic image of Soviet production to the world. The dynamic pair appeared to lunge at Albert Speer's Pavilion of the Third Reich, which stood directly opposite the Soviet structure. The proximity of these pavilions has often been seen as a dramatic face-off between the monumental architectures of Stalin's USSR and Hitler's Germany. Be that as it may, Iofan drew upon American skyscraper design in the creation of his pavilion. Its tower is composed of nested rectangular prisms and flanked by lower symmetrical structures – its massing and framing followed a pattern established by New York's Rockefeller Center, a complex Iofan knew and admired.[77] According to David Arkin, Iofan's pavilion represented a crystallization of Soviet architecture's development. He called it a model of the 'artistic method' of socialist realism, a method flexible enough to unite American precedents, monumental sculpture and the image of Soviet triumph in a dynamic architectural statement.[78]

Moscow's parks and exhibitions became landscapes of cultured leisure. Situated on the banks of the Moscow River, the Gorky Park of Culture and Recreation offered a dense schedule of activities. Aleksandr Vlasov directed the Park's construction from the mid-1930s onwards. It included facilities for concerts, lectures, games, popular amusements – such as the famous parachute drop – as well as broad ponds, granite embankments and lush grounds.[79] The All-Union Agricultural Exposition, which opened in Moscow in 1939, was according to Viacheslav Oltarzhevskii, the complex's initial architect, an 'exhibition of abundance'.[80] Continuing the tradition established at the 1923 exposition, the event showcased the products of Soviet agriculture and industry. But like other major undertakings of the 1930s, it would not proceed without difficulty. The exposition was scheduled to begin in 1937, but political intrigue and a series of construction problems delayed its opening by two years. In 1938 the People's Commissar of Agriculture, M. A. Chernov, was executed as an enemy of the people and Oltarzhevskii was arrested.[81] The plan of the exposition nevertheless followed Oltarzhevskii's initial layout: its primary axis led from a triumphal entry to the main pavilion, the square of collective farms and finally to the square of mechanization. The main pavilion, designed by Shchuko and Gelfreikh, was composed of a broad hall and a slender 'tower of the constitution'. Inside, dioramas depicted the cultural life of each Soviet republic. The national pavilions surrounding the square of collective farms expanded this image of the Soviet imperium. The distinctive design of each structure reinforced the ethnic particularism of each republic, and the entire ensemble gave architectural form to the ideology of the 'friendship among peoples'.[82] The Pavilion of the Uzbek SSR was among the most celebrated of the exposition. Designed by Stepan Polupanov, an Uzbek architect, its central feature was an elaborately carved arbour whose slender columns and latticework roof occupied a central court. Great heaps of cotton and images of Uzbek agriculture filled the interior. The building's ornamental carving, sculptural programme and ceramic tiles were executed by Uzbek artisans, lending an unprecedented degree of authenticity to the architecture of national forms.[83] An enormous statue of Stalin and the grand hangar of the mechanization pavilion, which displayed the newest models produced by the Chelyabinsk Tractor Factory, dominated the square of mechanization. Millions of people visited the exposition between its opening and the outbreak of the Second World War. But millions more saw the exposition in Aleksandrov's film *Radiant Path* of 1940. It depicts the life of the upwardly mobile peasant Tania Morozova (played by Liubov Orlova) as she transforms herself into a model factory worker. When rewarded for her achievement in Moscow, she becomes delirious and dreams of the future of Soviet production. She imagines a fantastic voyage over the USSR

V. A. Shchuko, V. G. Gelfreikh, A. V. Velikanov, Central Pavilion, All-Union Agricultural Exposition, Moscow, 1939.

S. Polupanov, Pavilion of the Uzbek SSR, All-Union Agricultural Exposition, Moscow, 1939–40.

in a flying car, which lands in the Agricultural Exposition – the image of the present as the realization of the Soviet future.[84]

But the reality of Soviet life in 1939 had little in common with Aleksandrov's *Radiant Path*. Within weeks of the Agricultural Exposition's opening, the USSR and Nazi Germany concluded the Molotov-Ribbentrop Pact – a non-aggression agreement that facilitated Hitler's invasion of Poland in that year. As Soviet and German diplomats divided Central Europe into spheres of influence, the Red Army moved into Western Ukraine, Belarus and the Baltic States. Diplomats and cultural emissaries tried to assure the international community of the USSR's peaceful intentions through the Union's participation in the New York World's Fair of 1939. The Soviet chargé d'affaires described Boris Iofan's building, one of the largest at the fair, as a manifestation of 'a will for peace and progress at a time when in various parts of the world forces of war and regression are unleashed'.[85] Yet the Soviet government could not maintain this rhetoric of peace for long. The Red Army's invasion of Finland during the 'Winter War' of late 1939 exposed the USSR's aggressive territorial ambitions. The USA and Europe were outraged; the Soviets demolished their New York Pavilion, refusing to participate in the Fair's second season; and images of the Soviet invasion were installed within the undulating walls of Alvar Aalto's Finnish Pavilion.[86] The Second World War had begun.

chapter six

# World War, Cold War, 1941–53

Surveying the ruins of Berlin on 2 May 1945, the day the city fell to the Red Army, the writer Vasily Grossman conflated the collapse of buildings with the fall of National Socialism: 'The new Reichschancellery. It's a monstrous crash of the regime, ideology, plans, everything, everything. Hitler kaput.'[1] That same day, Anna Nikulina, a Soviet political officer, climbed atop the remains of the building, which had been designed by Albert Speer to Hitler's colossal specifications, raised a red flag and laid claim to the capital of the Third Reich. A few blocks away, the photo correspondent Evgenii Khaldei invited a Red Army soldier to plant the Soviet Flag on top of the Reichstag, turning the symbolic possession of architecture into a photographic icon of victory. Soviet Flags would later serve as the dominant motif in the Memorial to Fallen Soviet Soldiers in Berlin's Treptow Park, designed by the sculptor Evgenii Vuchetich and the architect Iakov Belopolskii (1946–9), which commemorates those who fell during the storming of Berlin by rendering the symbols of the city's downfall in stone.[2]

The 'Great Patriotic War', as the conflict is known in Russia, ended in Europe with the occupation of Berlin. Wanting both revenge for the destruction of Soviet cities and a western outpost of Soviet influence, Stalin had pushed ahead of the allies in the drive to capture the city. His campaign, however, would not have been successful without the support of Britain and the United States, whose 'lend-lease' programme supplied critical materials and technologies to the USSR throughout the war. The subsequent division of the city into American, British, French and Soviet sectors represented a fleeting prospect of continued cooperation. But in 1949 the city would become the de facto capital of the newly founded German Democratic Republic, turning Berlin into the theatre of a new war – the Cold War. Architecture acquired great symbolic value in this conflict. The triumphant splendour of Berlin's Stalinallee (begun 1951), Warsaw's Marszałkowska Housing District (begun 1950) and other urban ensembles was the product of a new, anti-capitalist brand of architectural diplomacy. Using 'national traditions', classical precedents and monumental forms, architects transformed cities,

Iakov Belopolskii and Evgenii Vuchetich (sculptor), memorial to fallen Soviet soldiers, Treptow, Berlin, 1946–9.

erected vast memorial complexes and edified the expansion of the socialist bloc.

The Second World War had catastrophic effects for Russia and the territories on the Eastern Front. Although Soviet histories commonly take the Wehrmacht's invasion of the USSR on 22 June 1941 as the beginning of the conflict, violence had descended upon Central Europe in 1939. The first victims of the European war – primarily in Poland – fell soon after the conclusion of the non-aggression pact between Hitler and Stalin.[3] The attack of German forces precipitated widespread social upheaval. Industrial operations located in Russia's vulnerable western territory were relocated beyond the Urals and into Central Asia. The movement of peoples this entailed was enormous; some estimate that as many as 25 million workers and their families followed the migration of industry.[4] The German attack encircled Leningrad in the first weeks of the war, initiating the 900-day siege that would end with more than one million lives lost. Cities in the west and south fared far worse. When John Steinbeck visited Kiev in 1947, he found a scene of utter devastation: 'Every public building, every library, every theatre, even the permanent circus, destroyed, not with gunfire, not through fighting, but with fire and dynamite.'[5] Similarly, the battle of Stalingrad had levelled much of the city. Here, and in thousands of other cities, towns and villages, families lived in abandoned basements and earthen dugouts. Although statistical precision is difficult to obtain, nearly 25 million Soviet soldiers and citizens died as a result of the war and its ensuing civilian tragedies.[6]

Wartime destruction engendered a revival of national myths. In Russia, the war effort was undertaken not in the name of the USSR, but in defence of the 'fatherland'. The war transformed Bolshevik disdain for Tsarist traditions into reverence. The Red Army restored officers' epaulets and other symbols of Russian armed forces. The painter Pavel Korin created a monumental triptych devoted to Aleksandr Nevskii (1942–3), the mythical leader of ancient Rus. Evacuated to Alma-Ata, Sergei Eisenstein collaborated with Sergei Prokofiev on the historical film *Ivan the Terrible* (1944). Filled with symbols of Muscovy, the imperial dynasty and the Orthodox Church, the film presented Ivan as 'the commander who enhanced the military glory of Russia in the East and the West'. The war years also witnessed a rapprochement between church and state. In 1943 the government established the Council for Russian Orthodox Affairs, which sanctioned the opening of hundreds of houses of prayer.[7] Together, popular religiosity and the wartime destruction of religious monuments elevated the importance of architectural preservation and restoration, leading to the establishment of a special committee for the protection of monuments within the Union of Soviet Architects in 1942.

Architects decried the loss of historic structures. Upon hearing news of the damage inflicted upon Novgorod and the destruction of the New Jerusalem monastery in Istra, Aleksei Shchusev wrote that 'fascism is my personal enemy.'[8]

A symptom of the complementary relationship between nationalism and internationalism during the war years, Shchusev's elegy to Russian monuments appeared in the U.S.-based magazine *California Arts & Architecture*. The 'lend-lease' agreements that intensified the strategic relationship between the United States, Britain and the USSR fostered the cultivation of cultural contacts. *Life* magazine sought to introduce the Soviet Union to the American public with a special issue of March 1943. Its pages are filled with photographs of factories bound for Russia, Soviet paintings, profiles of Soviet leaders and images of Russian architecture. Joseph E. Davies, the former ambassador to the Soviet Union, answered readers' questions about the future of relations between the USA and the USSR. 'Without the cooperation of the Soviet Union', he wrote, 'there can be no permanent and durable peace projected.'[9] Through VOKS, the All-Union Organization of Cultural Ties with Foreign Countries, and organizations such as the New York-based National Council for American–Soviet Friendship, architects constructed a new network of exchange.[10] The U.S. and the USSR traded exhibitions, technical information and planning concepts. Soviet architects came to appreciate the vision of the United States described by the Soviet humorists Ilia Ilf and Evgenii Petrov in their 1937 travelogue *Odnoetazhnaia Amerika* (One-storey America).[11] According to Roman Khiger, who wrote no fewer than three books on American architecture during the war, the 'bold experimentation, organization, architectural merits and engineering methods employed in low-rise settlement construction have produced a worthy and able competitor to the skyscraper, which until quite recently had embodied the most advanced building practices and technologies in the USA'.[12] As American–Soviet friendship encouraged hope for post-war collaboration, Soviet architects made the small, detached house a basic element of the reconstruction effort.

But wartime alliances dissolved soon after the definitive victory of the Allies. Stalin, Churchill and Roosevelt had reached a preliminary agreement on European spheres of influence at the Yalta conference of February 1945, ceding much of Eastern Europe to the Soviet Union. The USSR ensured that Communist Parties would gain political control of the Eastern European states. In 1946 Churchill declared that 'from Stettin in the Baltic to Trieste in the Adriatic an iron curtain has descended across the Continent.' He noted that the countries along this line were subject to an 'increasing measure of control from Moscow'.[13] The USSR saw the

Marshall Plan, the American programme for European recovery, as a threat to its hegemony in the region and demanded that Eastern Europe reject the offer of assistance. In 1947, the diplomat George Kennan recommended a policy of 'vigilant containment of Russian expansive tendencies' to the U.S. government.[14] The same year, the Party ideologue Andrei Zhdanov articulated his theory that the world had been divided into two camps: the 'imperialist', led by the United States; and the 'anti-imperialist', led by the Soviet Union.[15] The Communist *coup d'état* in Czechoslovakia of 1948 ensured Soviet political influence throughout the region. That year, Soviet forces blockaded Berlin in response to U.S., British and French efforts at German currency reform. West Berlin survived through the heroic airlift of supplies from the non-Soviet sectors. By the time Soviet forces lifted the blockade in mid-1949, Berlin had become the centre of what George Orwell called a 'cold war', namely, 'a peace that is no peace'.[16]

Mounting international tension and the ossification of Soviet cultural policy went hand in hand. In late 1946, Zhdanov initiated a campaign against the journals *Leningrad* and *Zvezda*, which he claimed had published works characterized by 'cultural decadence' and 'formalist tendencies'.[17] The writers Anna Akhmatova and Mikhail Zoshchenko were Zhdanov's primary targets, but the campaign had far-reaching effects. In 1947, Viacheslav Molotov conflated 'cultural decadence' with anti-patriotic sentiments and called upon the Soviet people to 'launch unrelenting attacks on all manifestations of grovelling before and slavish imitation of the West and its capitalist culture'.[18] By 1949 these attacks acquired the banner of 'anti-cosmopolitanism' – a euphemism for the markedly anti-Semitic wave of repression that followed.[19] In the final years of Stalin's reign, intellectuals, artists and architects faced ever-greater restrictions on their work. As cultural policy tightened, Stalin's personality cult grew. He ultimately attained god-like status. The Soviet public was shocked when he died on 5 March 1953. Despite his brutality, his passing was mourned – both because the USSR had lost its leader of nearly 30 years and because Stalin's absence left a vacuum at the top of the Party hierarchy. Ilia Ehrenburg later recounted his experience of the event: 'I was not sorry for the god who had died . . . but I was afraid. What would happen now? I feared the worst.'[20]

## Home Fronts

The Second World War did not arrest architects' work; it reformulated architecture's tasks. When German forces attacked in June 1941, the Union of Soviet Architects reminded its members that 'the success of the war is decided not only on the front, but also in the rear.'[21] Both active participants in defence and managers of spaces of civilian life, architects occupied multiple home fronts. They built bunkers and stabilized damaged buildings; collaborated with visual artists and the air force on large-scale camouflage campaigns; measured endangered monuments; and, as the Red Army gained ground, completed vital construction projects. They followed the eastward migration of industry. In Central Asia architects experimented with local materials and vernacular traditions as they sought to provide housing for the millions of wartime refugees. In competitions for memorial complexes and prototypes for small, detached houses, Soviet architects imagined post-war life at both monumental and modest scales.

When German and Finnish forces surrounded Leningrad in September 1941, civil defence became a primary architectural concern. The destruction of Guernica in 1937 had given architects and engineers across Europe reason to develop ways to mitigate the destructiveness of aerial bombardment. For a dense and distinguished city like Leningrad, the Luftwaffe's incendiary bombs posed a lethal threat. During the first days of the siege architects undertook a variety of measures designed to protect the city and its monuments – camouflage was among the most important. Led by Nikolai Baranov, the city's chief architect, teams of architects sought to disrupt the ability of German pilots to identify landmarks by transforming the look of entire districts. Baranov had accompanied a Red Army pilot on a surveillance flight above Leningrad in 1940, viewing the city from the perspective of a dive bomber in preparation for its defensive needs. The first building to be disguised was the Smolny Institute, the seat of the Leningrad Soviet. Part of a large ensemble, which includes

Nikolai Baranov, project for the camouflage of the Smolny Institute, Leningrad, 1941.

Francesco Rastrelli's baroque Smolnyi Cathedral (1748–64), the Institute's broad, U-shaped plan stands out from its verdant surroundings. Baranov's task was to make it blend in. Working with decorators from Leningrad's theatres, he created a web of tarpaulin that could cover the building. Toned and patterned to resemble the canopies of surrounding trees, the net effectively obscured views of the institute from the air.[22] False landscapes and decoy buildings were erected in other parts of the city. A block of small structures was built within the municipal horse track, depriving the Luftwaffe of an important point of orientation. The roofs of factories were painted and covered with dummy buildings to diminish their easily identifiable expanse. False ruins of the Moscow and Vitebsk train stations were erected as decoys and tracks were covered. The camouflage effort hindered precision air attacks, forcing German planes to drop bombs indiscriminately.

The potential destruction of monuments redoubled the significance of architectural preservation. Although the registration and protection of historical structures had been codified in Soviet law in the 1920s, little had been done to save important buildings. Indeed, municipal authorities had overseen the destruction of key monuments such as Moscow's Kitai-gorod walls and the Sukharev Tower, as well as hundreds of churches. Baranov noted that he rarely thought of historical monuments during the 1930s, his first years as chief architect of Leningrad. 'Before the war all of my attention was concentrated on new construction . . . I naively assumed that fundamental documentation on architectural monuments was preserved in the archives.'[23] To his chagrin, it was not. Leningrad's office of architecture and planning did not even possess technical documentation on its wartime headquarters, which was located within Carlo Rossi's Alexandrine Theatre ensemble (1824–34). Hoping to collect sufficient information on endangered monuments, architects undertook emergency surveys throughout the Soviet Union. The Moscow House of the Architects held a large exhibition of Russian historical architecture on the occasion of the first Soviet conference on preservation in July 1942. Displays of monuments 'destroyed by German invaders' were also exhibited. Articles on the sacral architecture of Novgorod and other topics appeared regularly in the architectural press. Russian national traditions became embedded in the Soviet architectural consciousness like never before.

Housing the millions of wartime evacuees entailed the exploration of local building techniques. During the first years of the war, the Academy of Architecture was moved to Chimkent, Kazakhstan, where its members investigated the architectural potential of local, non-deficit materials such as plaster and adobe. According to the editors of *Arkhitektura SSSR*, the qualities of these improvised materials made low-rise residential

G. Zakharov and Z. Chernisheva, two-room house for Central Asia, 1942–3.

construction 'the most important architectural problem of our time'.[24] The organic unity of form, function and structure found in the vernacular building traditions of Central Asia led some architects to criticize the weight of Moscow's influence on the rest of the Soviet Union. Working in Tashkent, G. Zakharov and Z. Chernisheva noted that in the 'substantial architectural production of Uzbekistan – from its civic buildings to its residences – provincial copies of "capital tastes" abound, and these copies are usually limited to the reproduction of forms that are meant for the central regions of Russia'.[25] Regional climatic conditions and traditional ways of building were often overlooked in Central Asian republics. For Tashkent and nearby industrial settlements, Zakharov and Chernisheva created low, horizontal structures that seem to hug the earth. Thick mud brick walls and small apertures were to regulate climate within their buildings, while open terraces created secluded courts. Sergei Vasilkovskii and Aleksandr Arefev's design for a settlement for oil workers in Gurev, Kazakhstan (1943), displayed a similar concern for vernacular forms.[26] In their design for the 14th district of Magnitogorsk (1943), Andrei Ol and Evgenii Levinson used fieldstone and other rustic materials to create a human-scale residential quarter.[27] An anti-monumental impulse guided residential design throughout the Soviet Union during the war years.

Together, a growing awareness of regional traditions and the speed of construction required in refugee settlements gave architects reason to evaluate the state of their profession. At wartime meetings of the Union of Soviet Architects and the Academy of Architecture, Soviet architects

A. Ol, E. Levinson, G. Simonov, District 14, Magnitogorsk, 1943.

expressed a desire for change, for new standards of design and construction. Moisei Ginzburg asked, if Soviet architects could design beautiful buildings, why it was so difficult to identify an authentic 'humanism' in the production of the previous years. He noted that the reconstruction of Moscow succeeded in creating 'well-dressed, pompous' streets, but claimed that it had failed to solve the 'simple, human problem of the common, comfortable dwelling that is fit for all generations of a family'.[28] Andrei Burov was more critical of Soviet architectural conventions. He mocked the routine mediocrity of his colleagues and concluded that, 'overburdened with historical deposits', Soviet architecture had lost contact with the potential of contemporary technology. In America, however, Burov found 'the first sprouts of new, organic architectural forms'.[29] To Burov and many of his colleagues, the small American house – and the building industry that supported it – represented a promising model of architectural development.

After the USA and the USSR reached the lend-lease agreement in late 1941, American architecture's prominence on the Soviet scene steadily grew. *Arkhitektura SSSR* regularly published reports on American developments in wartime construction. Karo Alabian chaired a committee within the Academy of Architecture devoted entirely to the study of architecture and planning in the USA. 'Soviet-American friendship, which is increasingly strengthened on the battlefields and in the arena of cultural cooperation', Alabian wrote, 'will become even closer and more fruitful after the war's end.'[30] During the war, Soviet architects visited American building sites, while American architects supplied their colleagues in the USSR with a steady flow of information. The Building Committee of the National Council for American–Soviet Friendship (NCASF), a New York-based non-governmental organization, was the most active participant in this exchange. In 1944 the NCASF succeeded in sending an exhibition on 'Rapid Construction in the USA' to Moscow. Composed of material compiled by the Museum of Modern Art, the exhibition was greeted with great enthusiasm. In May 1945 the organization hosted an 'American-Soviet Building Conference' at which Soviet representatives investigated the possibility of purchasing machinery and equipment for the rapid fabrication of small houses. Most important, Alabian led a comparative investigation of the building industries of the USA and the USSR. The Soviet Union lagged far behind, the commission concluded. Alabian later noted that the commission's recommendations for the construction of a network of woodworking plants and a laboratory for experimental construction technologies were incorporated into the first post-war Five-year Plan (1946–50).[31] By 1948 plants around the Soviet Union were producing thousands of houses based on prototypes such as Boris Barkhin's TsV-1a model.[32]

B. Barkhin, prefabricated house, Type TsV–1a, Moscow, 1948.

## The Rebirth of Cities

Reconstruction began before the war was over. In 1943 Mikhail Kalinin, chairman of the Supreme Soviet of the USSR, issued an open letter that called upon architects to seize the tragic opportunity presented by the destruction of Soviet cities. 'Soviet architects are facing an unprecedented situation: architectural plans of unusually grand scale will become real construction', he wrote.[33] Reconstruction offered the distinct possibility of creating truly Soviet cities, cities characterized by great artistic ensembles, rational residential districts and efficient planning. Although the Soviet Union had experienced terrible devastation throughout the first decades of its existence (civil war, famine, the Great Terror), never before had its built environment suffered so greatly. After conducting a tour of Orel, Kaluga and other cities, Boris Pasternak described a 'monstrous impression of a whole small world in fragments'. The numbers issued from the front – 500 stone houses, 2,500 wooden houses destroyed – failed to convey the horror of the shapeless masses of stone and cement that so many Russian cities had become. 'Your head spins, your eyes dim, you break into sobs of pity and pain.'[34] Architects compensated for this dramatic sense of loss with memorials and urban plans; in the midst of ongoing destruction, they reconceived the Soviet city as a total work of art.

Planning for the future began with the design of monuments. Beginning in 1942, Soviet architects conducted a series of competitions for victory monuments and memorial ensembles. The projects that emerged were unprecedented. After the October Revolution, Soviet architects had brief encounters with funerary architecture, but, with the notable exception of Lenin's mausoleum, the topic received little attention in the following years. In 1943, G. Zakharov, Z. Chernisheva and the sculptor I. Rabinovich

G. Zakharov, Z. Chernisheva, Pantheon for the Heroes of the Great Patriotic War, Moscow, 1942–3 (competition project).

V. G. Gelfreikh, I. E. Rozhin, Elektrozavodskaia Metro Station, Moscow; opened in 1944.

won the first Union-wide competition for a 'monument to the heroes of the Great Patriotic War'. Their project consisted of a broad mound of earth crowned by a monumental Red Army soldier. Inside, a vast, crypt-like space was carved out of the earthworks. Although they called their entry a 'pantheon', its form departed from Roman tradition, recalling instead the kurgans erected by the Scythian tribes that roamed the steppes of southern Russia in antiquity. The kurgan was one of many archetypes that Soviet architects drew upon as they sought to edify fallen heroes with the forms of a mythic past. Andrei Burov revived religious imagery in his project for a 'Temple of Glory' in Stalingrad (1944). Its thin, parabolic concrete vaults represented an innovative structural solution, while its centralized massing evoked the monumental volumes of Russian Orthodox churches. Smaller monuments were incorporated into the ongoing construction of the Moscow Metro. Opened in 1943, Aleksei Dushkin's 'Stalin Factory' Station (now Avtozavodskaia) incorporated a large mosaic by V. F. Bordichenko and B. V. Pokrovskii depicting a battalion of tanks and a spirit-like Russian warrior against the backdrop of the Moscow Kremlin. Vladimir Gelfreikh and Igor Rozhin's Elektrozavodskaia Station (1944) was among the most spectacular spaces completed during the war. Georgii Motovilov's reliefs of 'work of the rear for the front' adorn the station's pylons, commemorating wartime production under the glow of electric lights.

Initially, urban reconstruction was seen as a problem of art. At a plenary meeting in 1944, Arkadii Mordvinov reminded fellow members of the Academy of Architecture of Alberti's claim that 'nature is the best artist'.[35] Reconstruction plans would have to accentuate natural topography. The post-war city was envisioned as a complete organism composed of a system of squares, arteries and secondary streets. But a city's beauty would only be as great as its centre. Civic buildings – government offices, train stations, universities and other public institutions – were to become the primary elements of artistic urban plans. 'They underscore the city's form and the character of its style, mark the city's most important points and determine a city's spatial structure and its silhouette.'[36] Concern for urban silhouettes and vertical dominants had been important to Soviet planning since the Palace of the Soviets competition and the subsequent plan for the reconstruction of Moscow. But the workshops established during the war years gave architects an unprecedented degree of control over urban form and structure. Whereas the planning and architectural offices of the Moscow Soviet established a formidable bureaucracy of urban administration, in the wartime studios responsibility for the design of cities passed to the singular figure of the chief architect. The visions that emerged from the wartime ateliers combined monumental and quotidian forms as architects reimagined the city's relationship to urban traditions, architectural heritage and the natural landscape.

Nikolai Kolli's plan for the reconstruction of Tver, then known as Kalinin, and Shchusev's plan for Novgorod each sought to restore and develop historical urban forms. Situated on the Volga River and occupying a strategic point between Moscow and St Petersburg, Tver had become a rich city by the mid-eighteenth century. After fires devastated the city's largely wooden urban fabric, an urban plan was established in 1767. A system of squares and diagonal axes defined the urban core. Its radiating streets recall the 'trident' at the heart of St Petersburg's urban plan, while its regular grid echoes the severity and uniformity of Russia's northern capital. Kolli restored and expanded this system after the city was badly damaged in the Second World War. His plan preserved Tver's network of streets but added a new transverse axis across the Volga, where he planned a new administrative centre.[37] Kolli argued that the 'identification of Russian urban traditions is necessary', even for cities without the rich historical forms that Tver possessed. 'The city', he wrote, 'should find its individuality.'[38] Like Kolli's design for Tver, Shchusev's project for the reconstruction of Novgorod emphasized the city's unique characteristics.

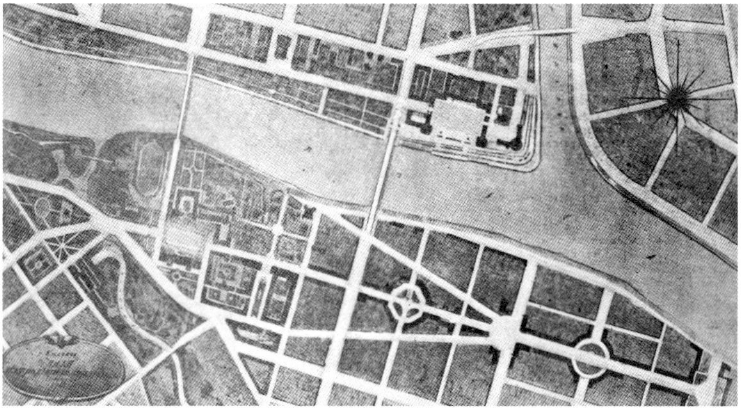

Nikolai Kolli, project for the reconstruction of Tver, 1946.

Aleksei Shchusev, project for the reconstruction of Novgorod, 1946.

An ancient Russian city, Novgorod possesses some of the oldest examples of sacred architecture in the country. Shchusev's task was to reconcile the richness of Novgorod's architectural heritage with the demands of urban development. His solution was to turn the city's kremlin into a monumental museum. This was to be the focal point of a radial-concentric street system. Framed by a broad garden, the kremlin's walls and churches dominated the urban core. Their austere, asymmetrical style also provided the formal vocabulary for new construction. Shchusev recommended that new buildings, when constructed in the vicinity of ancient monuments, adopt the forms of the surrounding ensemble. In this way, an aesthetic unity between old and new might be created. Although Shchusev's recommendations would not be carried out to the extent he envisioned, they motivated the neo-Russian forms of I. G. Iavein's design for the city's new train station (1950–53).[39]

Georgii Golts, Boris Iofan and Andrei Burov explored the vertical dimension of urban planning in their designs for the reconstruction of cities. Golts's plan for Smolensk, like the work of Kolli and Shchusev, reinforced the city's historical character but subordinated Old-Russian monuments to Soviet institutions through an innovative approach to the urban silhouette. Seen in elevation, Smolensk's churches and monasteries figure as prominent objects in the informal topography of the city's many hills. Golts placed a large administrative building on the highest point in the city. The building's outline both mimics the towers of surrounding churches and, through its verticality, marks the dominance of Soviet administration over the institutions of the past. Both Iofan and Burov explored the relationship between the urban silhouette and the sea. For Novorossiisk, Iofan reimagined the centre of the city as a series of terraces that would descend to the banks of the Black Sea. The tower of the municipal Soviet marks the pinnacle of the ensemble of terraces and the heart of the city's system of squares. He planned other verticals – at the train station and the theatre – throughout the city, creating a picturesque urban silhouette that broadcast the location of civic institutions in its outlines. Burov's project for the reconstruction of Yalta was among the most innovative proposals for urban reform from the war years. Located

Boris Iofan, project for the reconstruction of Novorossiisk, 1944–6.

on the Black Sea coast, Yalta's natural topography is among its primary assets, and Burov sought to reinforce them. He buried the primary highway, which runs along the coast, in a tunnel, creating a new freedom of movement between the city and the sea. High-rise hotels, placed at regular intervals, were to occupy the beach front, while low-rise housing was to cover the city's hills. Burov's project for Yalta benefited from the wartime alliance between the USA and the USSR. In his wartime diaries, he recorded his enthusiasm for a report on Miami Beach published in the American magazine *Architectural Forum*, which became Burov's model for evenly spaced, high-rise hotel towers.[40] Burov's project was criticized for being technically unfeasible at the time, but the exploration of the urban silhouette that he and others undertook would have broad implications for post-war urban planning in the Soviet Union.

Verticality and monumentality came together in projects for Stalingrad's and Kiev's urban centres. The site of the turning point in the Red Army's battle against Nazi forces, Stalingrad suffered enormous damage and became a symbol of the war effort. In 1943, soon after the capitulation of the Nazi General Paulus, a competition was held for the design of the city. While no project won outright, most proposals sought to define a new monumental centre for the city. The team of architects led by Karo Alabian was awarded the opportunity to further develop its proposal. Their plan reimagined the relationship between the Volga River and the urban core. A grand stair climbs the steep embankment to a broad terrace. This axis leads away from the river towards a monumental arch that opens onto the central square. Trapezoidal in plan, this vast open space is surrounded by multi-storey buildings. The tower of an administrative building rises above the square and marks a cross-axis that leads to a memorial complex for the fallen of the Battle of Stalingrad. The precise form of Stalingrad's centre would remain a contested issue among Soviet architects, but the elements of its ensemble – monumental axis, square and tower – would become defining themes of the post-war Soviet city. Similarly, competitions for Kiev's central avenue, the Kreshchatik, reflected a growing importance of the administrative centre as the monumental heart of the Soviet city. The proposals submitted to a competition of 1944 envisioned the city centre as a complex composed of a monumental avenue, a broad central square and a towering administrative building. In the words of one commentator, architects envisioned the Kreshchatik as 'an official, representative street of grand architectural scale – a street of ceremonial processions'.[41] In plans for Kiev and Stalingrad, Soviet architects made the administrative centre the monumental heart of the Soviet city, and the projects they created would have a lasting influence on Soviet design.

The composition of Soviet residential districts was also debated at the end of the war. In late 1945 a competition for experimental housing districts made the concept of the *mikroraion* – or micro-district – an object of public scrutiny.[42] The term had first been used in the USSR during the 1930s as a rough translation of the concept of the 'neighbourhood unit', which the American planner Clarence Perry had popularized in the 1920s. A *mikroraion* was an urban element composed of residences, pedestrian streets, parks and a community centre that was bounded by highways and arterial streets. The reappraisal of this concept in 1945 reflected a desire among some architects and planners for an alternative to the strictly monumental city. Instead, Soviet architects proposed

Dmitriii Chechulin, Residential District for Officers, Khoroshevskoe Chausee, Moscow, 1945–6.

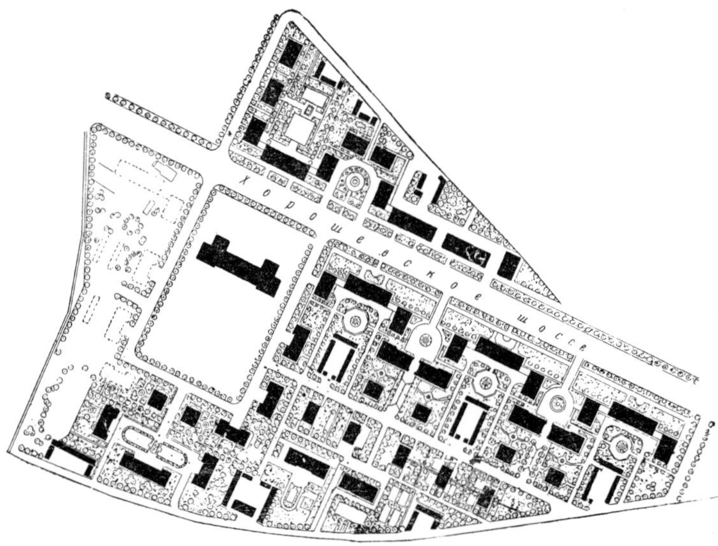


Residential District for Officers, Khoroshevskoe Chausee, general plan.

settlements that would both isolate residences from major traffic arteries and create networks of pedestrian streets among groups of houses, which were typically set amid green parkland. Entries to a 1945 competition projected *mikroraiony* for a number of cities: Moscow, Dnepropetrovsk, Kharkov, Stalingrad and others. None of these projects, however, were realized. Dmitrii Chechulin's residential settlement for officers along Khoroshevskoe Chausee in Moscow (1945–6) came closest to the ideal of the *mikroraion*.[43] Two-storey, semi-detached houses occupy large parcels along the Chausee. Footpaths integrate the territory, connecting apartment houses to a bathhouse, a laundry, a kindergarten, a nursery and a playground. By clearly distinguishing pedestrian zones from the traffic of the Chausee, the settlement achieves an intimate, human scale. Soon after Chechulin's project was completed, the concept of the *mikroraion* dropped rather suddenly out of favour. Its association with American and British planning concepts made it the target of increasingly vehement attacks as the broader cultural climate in the Soviet Union became more antagonistic to the West. Discussion of the theory of the *mikroraion* would be suppressed until the second half of the 1950s, when it re-emerged as the fundamental paradigm of Soviet urban planning.

## 'Anti-imperialist' Grandeur

The dawn of the Cold War transformed the geopolitics of Soviet architectural culture. Although Soviet architects had admired the technological and architectural achievements of the West for decades, they always insisted that socialism surpassed capitalism in its ability to manage the development of the built environment in a rational manner. As the wartime alliance between the USA and the USSR faltered in the early post-war years, Soviet architects followed the lead of cultural commissars in denouncing all products of the West. Soon after Zhdanov announced his 'two camp' theory of international relations, Soviet architects struggled to define a new, 'anti-imperialist' position. Architects' first response was to emphasize that the lack of private development in the Soviet Union enabled architecture and urbanization to be integrated. 'Among the most important qualities that differentiates Soviet architecture from the architecture of the past and from the architecture of the contemporary West', read an editorial in *Arkhitektura SSSR*, 'is . . . the urbanist basis in all fields of architectural activity.'[44] In accord with this new orientation, Western theories of urban planning – including the work of Frank Lloyd Wright, Eliel Saarinen and José Luis Sert, one of the leading representatives of the Congrès internationaux d'architecture moderne (CIAM) – were subjected to harsh ideological criticism.[45] As the USSR's anti-Western campaign escalated into a campaign against 'cosmopolitanism', architects who had looked favourably upon American architectural models during the war became targets in a series of public denunciations. In 1948 this culminated in what the American critic Peter Blake called the 'Soviet Architecture Purge', in which the Communist Party censured the Academy of Architecture for the alleged 'pro-Western, pro-American and general cosmopolitan outlook of its members'.[46] Several prominent architects and intellectuals – notably Andrei Burov and David Arkin – suffered slanderous public denunciations as the Academy and the Union of Soviet Architects sought to bring the profession into line with the Party's new position on culture.

Mikhail Tsapenko articulated the new Party line in a series of publications on 'socialist realism' in architecture. His important essay of 1949, which was expanded into a book in 1952, placed architecture at the centre of intense ideological confrontation. 'In both its symbolic and artistic qualities', Tsapenko wrote, 'Soviet architecture immeasurably surpasses contemporary bourgeois architecture, which lacks both authenticity and, most important, future prospects.'[47] This polarization of capitalist and socialist architecture drew upon and enhanced the logic of cultural affiliations that Zhdanov postulated with this 'two-camp' theory of global affairs. Although Tsapenko elevated the polemical tone of Soviet architectural discourse, he did little to clarify the meaning of 'socialist realism' in architecture. Following a circular logic, he argued that 'socialist realism distinguishes itself, above all, by revealing and ennobling national characteristics in their highest – socialist – expression and enabling the creation of realistic works of architecture . . . which embody the Stalinist concern for the person.'[48] Tsapenko's book went further than his initial essay in revising the history of Soviet architecture of the interwar period. His text cast the work of the rationalists and constructivists alike as deviations from the Party's official line on 'socialist realism'. He buried the contributions of Ladovskii, Ginzburg, Melnikov, the Vesnin brothers and many others under a mountain of grandiose rhetoric. It would take a generation for the work of these architects to be rediscovered.

As the volume of architectural propaganda rose, the scale and grandeur of built work increased. During the final years of Stalin's reign, apartment buildings grew ever larger, administrative buildings rose ever taller, and Soviet architectural influence expanded its geographical range. The forms and projects of the late 1940s and early 1950s differed from those of the 1930s by degree, not essence. Architecture's ideological dimension, however, underwent a qualitative shift. In the pages of journals, in the halls of the Kremlin and in international exhibitions, Soviet buildings were reimagined as representations of the USSR's absolute superiority over the West. The image of the Soviet state shifted as well:

N. Petrov, K. Ivanov, 'Glory to the Great Stalin – the Architect of Communism', poster, 1952.

in a conflation of the construction of Moscow with the construction of socialism, popular posters of the period presented Stalin himself as an architect.

Moscow's ensemble of high-rise buildings was Stalin's crowning achievement as a builder. The Soviet of Ministers of the USSR initiated plans for eight multi-storey buildings in January 1947. The decree that set the projects in motion bears Stalin's signature but, as Vladimir Sedov has pointed out, several architects advanced concepts for a series of tall buildings independent of the committee.[49] Vertical aspirations saturated Soviet thinking about Moscow's post-war form. The absent centre of the group was the Palace of the Soviets, which was slated to remain the tallest structure in the city. Together, the group of buildings would create an integrated and hierarchical urban silhouette. This desire for a harmonious skyline expressed the ideological paradox at the heart of the project: these structures were to be *vysotnye zdaniia*, tall buildings, not *neboskreby*, skyscrapers. The revival of anti-American sentiments in the early Cold War era made the enforcement of this distinction a necessity. Maksim Gorky's 1906 screed against New York City, 'The City of the Yellow Devil', supplied ideologues with anti-skyscraper rhetoric. In each of New York's

'silent, dark, "scrapers of the sky"', Gorky wrote, 'one feels the haughty arrogance of their height, their monstrosity'.[50] The 1947 decree called for the tall buildings to 'harmonize with the historical architecture of the city' and asserted that they 'must not repeat the forms of well-known multi-storey buildings abroad'.[51] Mikhail Posokhin, an architect of the high-rise on Vosstanie Square, later recalled that the consultation of foreign journals and magazines was strictly forbidden during the design stages.[52] Despite their nationalist intentions, the seven tall buildings that were ultimately realized depended upon the experience of Viacheslav Oltarzhevskii, the initial architect of the All-Union Agricultural Exposition, who had gained first-hand knowledge of skyscraper design and construction in New York City, where he worked from 1924 to 1935.[53] The anti-American rhetoric that surrounded the tall-building campaign obscured the strong continuities that linked pre-war and post-war enthusiasm for this American building type among Soviet architects.

The construction of the seven sisters, as the tall buildings came to be known, became a salient feature of Soviet public relations. Images of the steel frame of the Ministry of Foreign Affairs buildings, designed by Vladimir Gelfreikh and Mikhail Minkus (1948–53), circulated around the globe on the cover of the Soviet propaganda magazine *USSR in Construction*. Models, materials and plans figured prominently at building exhibitions in Moscow and other cities. The structures received their greatest exposure in the 1954 film *Vernye druzia* (True Friends). In Mikhail Kalatozov's comedy, one of the protagonists plays the architect-academician who designed Moscow's tall buildings. Scenes in his office feature models and renderings of the structures that were drawn from real architectural design bureaus. Montage sequences take the viewer on a tour of the buildings that gave Moscow an entirely new scale.

Although all seven of Moscow's tall buildings share a formal emphasis on verticality, symmetry and elaborate pinnacles, they serve a variety of distinct functions. The Ministry of Foreign Affairs on Smolensk Square and the office building at Lermontov Square, the latter designed by Aleksei Dushkin and Boris Mezentsev (1948–53), are vast temples of administration. The buildings on Kotelnicheskaia Embankment, designed by Dmitrii Chechulin and A. Rostokovskii (1948–53), and on Vosstanie Square, by Mikhail Posokhin and Ashot Mndoiants (1950–54), contain elite housing. The Hotel Leningrad by Leonid Poliakov and A. Boretskii (1947–53) and the Hotel Ukraine by Mordvinov and Oltarzhevskii (1950–55) offer stately accommodation for foreign visitors and the political elite. The centrepiece of the tall-building campaign, however, was the new home for Moscow State University (MGU) on the Sparrow Hills. The site was initially slated for another hotel, but the future rector of the university

V. G. Gelfreikh, M. A. Minkus, Ministry of Foreign Affairs, Moscow, 1948–53.

was able to convince Stalin of the need for more laboratory and research space. Boris Iofan, as director of the Council for the Construction of the Palace of the Soviets, received the commission for the new university. A sketch of his initial project survives. It shows a broad structure that expands outwards from a central tower. Secondary towers punctuate the wings. The building's height is emphasized by the grouping of windows and piers into uninterrupted vertical strips. Iofan defined the massing and general plan of the building, but he was removed from the project in 1948, when the commission was transferred to Lev Rudnev.

MGU's importance is indicated by the conditions of its construction. The project required enormous amounts of labour power to keep it on schedule. In addition to construction workers, soldiers and prisoners participated in the building's construction. Construction was managed by the General Directorate for the Construction of Camps for Industrial Construction (Glavpromstroi), a branch of the GULAG that was responsible for the construction of heavy industrial sites and facilities for atomic research. Glavpromstroi organized camps for prisoners on the construction site. Some of the most skilled labourers were housed in an improvised camp within the uncompleted building. The use of forced labour was a state secret. Only after the fall of the regime would confidential files reveal that at the height of the construction campaign in 1952, of the 24,400 people working on the building, 14,700 were soldiers and the rest were prisoners.[54] Elements of the building's design would also be kept secret: in 1950 the Council of Ministers of the USSR commissioned Metrostroi to design two underground silos beneath the MGU complex for use as secret laboratories for the physics faculty.[55]

When MGU was completed in 1954, it was, according to Soviet boosters, 'the largest educational institution in the world'. Its complex of 37 buildings reportedly contained fifteen times more usable space than Columbia University's campus in New York.[56] The central block is cruciform in plan and has a tower that rises 32 stories to a height of 239 m. A students' club, cafeterias, a cloakroom and other secondary spaces occupy the tower's lower floors. Banks of elevators provide access to the classrooms situated throughout the tower. Physics, the leading science of the atomic age, received more research and teaching space than any other faculty. The U-shaped arms of the residential quarters extend laterally from the central block. These wings contain nearly 6,000 student rooms and over 180 apartments for professors. Sculptures from the studio of Vera Mukhina and ceramic tile cladding lend texture and contrast to the building's exterior. Up close the building offers vertiginous vertical perspectives; from afar its placid triangular composition bespeaks order and rigorous hierarchy. The observation deck near the top of the central

L. V. Rudnev and others, Lomonosov Moscow State University, Moscow, 1949–53.

Rudnev and others, Moscow State University, ground-floor plan.

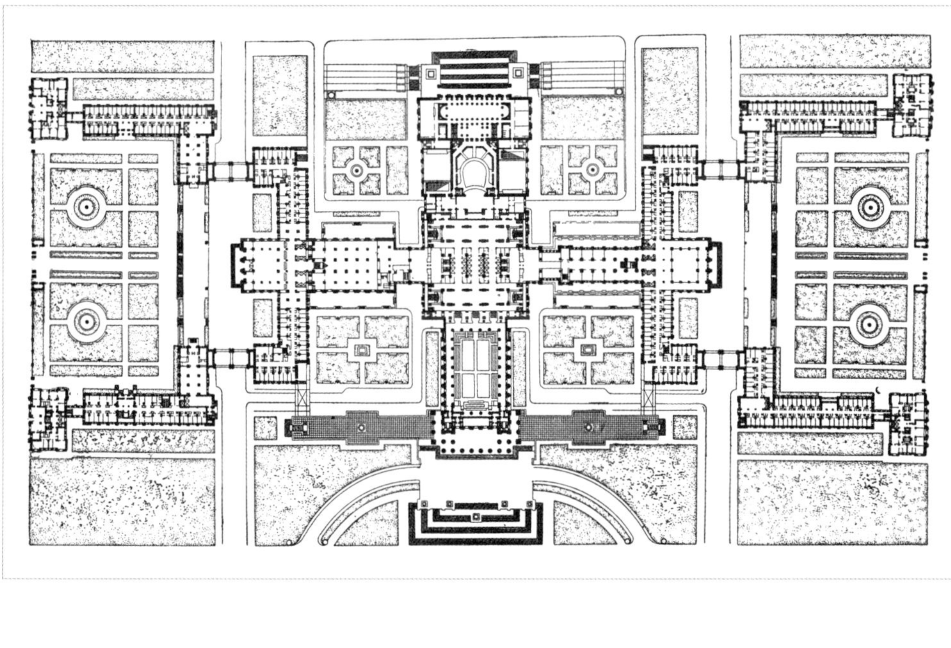

Central House of Culture, Warsaw, project of 1950; drawing by Kazimierz Marczewski.

block offers a panoramic view of Moscow in which each of the other tall buildings is visible.

Even before they were completed, the tall buildings of Moscow became models for the development and reconstruction of other cities in the USSR and the wider sphere of Soviet influence. From Berlin to Tashkent, architects sought to adapt the high-rise form to a variety of programmes: mass media in Bucharest's Casa Scânteii (1950–56); hospitality in Prague's Hotel International (completed in 1956); government offices in Berlin (unrealized). The influence of these projects extended as far as Beijing, where the architect Liang Sicheng, who had been trained in the Beaux-Arts tradition at the University of Pennsylvania, produced a series of projects for tall buildings after a visit to Moscow in 1953.[57] All of these projects shared a commitment to balance, symmetry and verticality, but they were distinguished by their ornamental forms. In this they represented a continuation of the logic of national particularism that had developed during the 1930s.

As in the Soviet republics, architecture in the satellite states of the socialist camp was to be 'national in form, socialist in content'. Warsaw's Palace of Culture and Science brought the contradictions of this slogan to new heights. After the city's near-complete destruction during the Second World War, the socialist government initiated a Six-year Plan for its reconstruction. The plan included speculative renderings of the city in 1955. Its central building was to be a palace of culture in the shape of a stepped high-rise. In 1952 the Soviet government offered to construct such a building as a gift to the People's Republic of Poland. The USSR supplied both the building materials and the designers: Lev Rudnev, the architect of MGU, Aleksandr Khriakov and the engineer Vsevolod Nasonov were awarded the commission. Rudnev and his team visited historical sites in Poland in the early stages of the design process, ultimately settling on a so-called 'Polish parapet' as a principal motif. The elaborate consoles and urns of these parapets enliven the profile of Warsaw's Palace of Culture, but the massing and organization of the building were derived from its Moscow prototype. Occupying a broad square in the centre of the city, the Palace of Culture and Science was Warsaw's most prominent vertical feature when it was completed in 1955. Its presence, however, would remain a contested symbol of the difficult relationship between Poland and the USSR.[58]

Vast horizontal developments complemented the vertical dominants of the post-war socialist city. Monumental streets gave urban centres new, monumental dimensions. Moscow's Gorky Street continued its pre-war development and served as the prototype for projects throughout the Soviet Union and in its satellite states. Following the reconstruction and elevation of the Moscow Soviet building on Sovetskaia Square, new administrative and apartment buildings along the southwestern side of the street gave the thoroughfare a new, larger scale. Aleksandr Zhukov's apartment building at the intersection of Gazetnyi Lane, built in 1949, achieves a baroque effect with paired columns and plastic bays of windows. The reconstruction of Kiev's Kreshchatik, the district along the central boulevard that was severely damaged during the war, was among the highest profile reconstruction projects of the Soviet Union. After a long competition and planning phase, construction began in 1949 with Aleksandr Vlasov as the director of a large team of architects, planners and engineers. A. Dobrovolskii and A. Zavarov, architects who worked on the project, argued that while the pre-revolutionary Kreshchatik was an example of 'unplanned,

Aleksandr Zhukov, apartment building, Gazetnyi Lane, Moscow, 1949.

chaotic development', the new Kreshchatik would 'respond to all the requirements of the Soviet science of planning'.[59] Vlasov and his team expanded the street from 44 m, its pre-war maximum, to 74 m, 24 of which were for the road, while the rest were given over to pavements and pedestrian zones. The street runs north–south along the base of a hill. Apartment buildings occupy the elevated eastern side, administrative buildings stand to the west. A mix of tall and mid-rise buildings gives the street a varied silhouette, while ceramic cladding and folk motifs unite the complex.

Both Gorky Street and the Kreshchatik served as models for a delegation of architects and politicians from the newly formed German Democratic Republic who toured the Soviet Union in 1950.[60] In consultation with the ministry of urban planning and Arkadii Mordvinov, the president of the Academy of Architecture of the USSR, the German delegation drafted the 'Sixteen Principles of Urban Planning', which would become a binding document for the reconstruction of cities in the GDR. The principles offered an implicit critique of the concepts contained

A. Vlasov and others, apartment buildings, Kreshchatik Street, Kiev, 1950–51.

Hermann Henselmann, Strausberger Platz, Stalinallee, Berlin, 1952–4.

in the Athens Charter, the document that elaborated CIAM's vision of urbanism. The Charter imagined the city as a combination of four distinct functions: habitation, leisure, work and traffic/circulation. The Sixteen Principles substituted 'culture' for traffic, noting that 'traffic should serve the city and its populace, not divide and encumber it'. It also noted that 'the city's appearance, its individual artistic form, is determined by plazas, major streets and significant buildings in its centre (in large cities, by high-rises)'.[61] Cities in the GDR were to be compact and defined by monuments; buildings and streets were to be integrated; CIAM's alleged utilitarianism was to be subordinated to a concern for urban beauty. The most significant product of the ideas contained in the Sixteen Principles was Berlin's Stalinallee (from 1961 known as Karl-Marx-Allee), the so-called 'first socialist street of the capital of Germany'. A team of six lead architects, including Richard Paulick and Hermann Henselmann, designed the nearly 2 km-long ensemble. Mixed-use residential buildings step back from the street, creating broad, manicured pavements. Loggias and triumphal arches mark transitions between blocks, while lyrical ceramic tiles, like those applied to the facades along the Kreshchatik, lend the structures a historically informed texture. Crucial parts of the complex were altered at the advice of Vlasov and Sergei Chernyshev, a co-author of the MGU building. At the First German Architectural Congress of 1951, the Soviet advisors recommended increasing the scale of the structures as they approach the city centre. This led Henselmann to redesign the buildings surrounding Strausberger Platz, giving the corner towers greater height and emphasis while recalling the curvilinear plan of Moscow's Leninskaia Gate (today's Gagarin Square). The first tenants moved into Stalinallee in early 1953. At the time, architects and propagandists promoted these

Fountain of the Friendship of Nations, VSSKhV, Moscow, 1954.

dwellings as the image of proletarian abundance, countering the 'rental barracks of capitalism' with 'residential palaces in socialism'.[62]

The renovation of the All-Union Agricultural Exposition in Moscow during Stalin's final years exaggerated both the image and geography of socialist abundance. Younger architects added a number of new pavilions to the Exposition, enriching the already theatrical grounds. The new centrepiece of the complex was an elaborate fountain devoted to the friendship of nations. The architects K. Topuridze and G. Konstantinovskii and the sculptors I. Chaikov, Z. Bazhenova, A. Taneta and N. Nyleeva created a red granite basin in which pillars support sixteen gilded female figures. Each of the women bears a national costume of one of the Soviet Republics. A gigantic, gilded bushel of wheat stands at the centre of the basin, symbolizing the importance of this staple crop to a population for which famine and starvation were recent memories.[63] Iurii Shchuko and E. A. Stoliarov's design for a new main pavilion recalls the stepped vertical forms of Moscow's tall buildings. The pavilion's curved colonnade supports a frieze that bears the insignias of the sixteen Soviet republics.

Beijing Exhibition Complex, Soviet Pavilion, 1952–4.

A bronze sculpture of the Soviet coat of arms rests above the architrave. Above, a star-topped spire rises 97 m high. The halls inside the pavilion are devoted to great moments in the history of the USSR; the central, circular hall contains an exhibition on the Soviet Constitution. A variety of new pavilions were constructed throughout the complex, notably the Lithuanian, Latvian and Estonian ones. These Baltic countries had been annexed to the USSR in 1940, and the assimilation of their 'national architectural forms' in their respective pavilions at the Agricultural Exposition symbolized their national subordination to Moscow's political geography.

But Moscow's Agricultural Exposition could both import national forms and serve as a model for export. Following the socialist revolution in China of 1949 and the signing of an agreement of Sino-Soviet friendship the following year, Moscow sent both technical experts and architectural conventions to the new member of the socialist camp. Among the many architectural manifestations of this relationship, the Beijing Exhibition Centre of the USSR, designed by Viktor Andreev, K. D. Kislova and Tai Nianshi, and built between 1952 and 1954, bears the closest relationship to its model. Its stepped, vertical

A. V. Shchusev, Komsomolskaia Metro Station (Circle Line), Moscow; opened in 1952.

massing and vertical spire produce a strong echo of the main pavilion of the Moscow Agricultural Exposition. The All-Chinese Agricultural Exposition of Beijing would open in 1959, following Moscow's lead, but using a distinctly Chinese vocabulary of forms to create a new image of socialist abundance.[64]

Architectural grandeur touched everyday life in subway stations in Moscow and Leningrad. New stations along Moscow's ring line opened in early 1952. Aleksei Shchusev's design for Komsomolskaia Station was the largest along the new line. One of his final projects, it was completed by Shchusev's collaborators A. Zabolotnaia and V. Varvanin after his death in 1949. The central hall of this deep station is nearly 150 m long. Stout pillars support a soaring barrel vault. Scrolls and acanthus leaves frame mosaics that punctuate the vault's surface. These images by the artist Pavel Korin celebrate the victory of the Soviet Union in the Second World War.[65] Evgenii Levinson proposed an ambitious decorative programme for the Avtovo Metro Station in Leningrad. He received the commission in 1948 with a proposal for a 'crystal station'. Working with the architect A. A. Grushko, Levinson sought to create a Metro station with columns

Evgenii Levinson, Avtovo Metro Station, Leningrad, 1948–55.

and cladding made entirely of glass. His task was to give the columns structural integrity while maintaining the transparency of glass. Years of model making and collaboration with the well-known specialist in glass production F. S. Entelis produced a grandiose solution. Levinson discovered that glass panels wrapped around a solid core would maintain the optical effect of transparency if given the correct profile. The station occupies a site that was on the line of defence during the Leningrad blockade, and Levinson commemorated the defence by giving each column the spiral form of Trajan's column. But before Avtovo station was completed, Levinson's project was sharply criticized for its 'decorative excess'. Only sixteen of the 46 columns were ultimately encased in Levinson's sumptuous glass forms by the time it opened in 1955.

Levinson's design was one of many casualties of a paradigmatic shift that was taking place in Soviet architectural politics in the early 1950s. As this process unfolded, the concept of socialist abundance would be redefined. Elaborate ornamentation, triumphal monumentality and historical forms came to be measured against the economic return on building activity. In this equation cornices and columns – crystal or otherwise – represented expenses that were pushing building costs into the red. But, most important, after Stalin died in 1953, the Soviet government came to understand that Soviet citizens could not survive on the image of grandeur alone. They needed relief from the rampant overcrowding of houses and apartments that characterized Soviet cities. They needed not 'residential palaces' but single-family apartments. They needed schools, shops, playgrounds and the entire infrastructure of everyday life to be modernized. They needed a new concept of socialist abundance, one that valued the communal provision of the many over the monumental desires of the few.

МОСКОВСКИЙ АРХИТЕКТОР
ВЕСНИНЫ
ВЕСНИН
ВОРОНИХИН
КАЗАКОВ
МАРШ „МОСПРОЕКТ" ДЛЯ ОСМЕРА С ОРКЕСТРО
КОМПОЗИТОР АПУ ОБРАБОТКА А. ЗАСЛАВСКОГО
РЕСТОРАН-ПОПЛАВОК
МЕНЮ:
ОСНОВНЫЕ БЛЮДА:
ЧТО ТАКОЕ АРХИТЕКТУРА" нет
ОСНОВЫ ТИПОВОГО ПРОЕКТИРОВАНИЯ"
ПРОБЛЕМЫ ИНДУСТРИАЛЬНОГО СТР-ВА"
ТЕОРИЯ АРХИТЕКТУРНОЙ КОМПОЗИЦИИ"
ИСТОРИЯ СОВЕТСКОЙ АРХИТЕКТУРЫ"
ДЕЖУРНЫЕ БЛЮДА:
РЕЦЕНЗИИ ПО-ПРИЯТЕЛЬСКИ
ПРЕДЪЯВЛЯЙТЕ БИЛЕТЫ
НА ПОСАДКУ

chapter seven

# Architecture without Excess, 1954–68

In late 1955, the journal *Arkhitektura SSSR* published an unusual cartoon showing Soviet architects boarding a ship destined for a new shore. The accompanying text described the bustling scene: 'After a long and costly stay on the island of excess, the leader of the architectural fleet is finally ready to set sail for the long-awaited shores of the typification and industrialization of construction.'[1] At the lower right, Dmitrii Chechulin, Leonid Poliakov and Arkadii Mordvinov, with tears in their eyes, kneel before a pile of capitals, rosettes and urns. At the top of the pile lies a tombstone bearing the word *izlishestva*, Russian for 'excesses' or 'luxuries'. To the left, the 'vessel of architectural theory', which had been turned into a floating restaurant, is being bailed out. Pavel Abrosimov, the newly appointed secretary of the Union of Soviet Architects, steers the departing ship, while the 'Mosproekt Orchestra' produces 'dissonant sounds' at the stern. Ivan Zholtovskii, dressed in a toga, reluctantly steps towards the gangway. At the centre of the image, Georgii Gradov sits behind a large bureaucrat's desk, checking tickets with a frown and directing traffic with a police officer's baton. Ready to abandon the heap of architectural excess, Soviet architects prepare to set sail for the factories, cranes and mass-produced housing on the horizon.

This cartoon was not a joke. Early in 1954, Gradov had addressed a lengthy letter to Nikita Khrushchev, First Secretary of the Communist Party, which outlined the reasons for Soviet architecture's alleged backwardness.[2] According to Gradov, Soviet architects had been satisfied with the creation of 'Potemkin villages' throughout the previous twenty years. He complained of overpopulated apartments in cities across the USSR; of the slums that had appeared in war-torn cities; of the disastrous state of hospitals and schools. Gradov accused the Academy of Architecture and a 'monopolistic group' of architects of retarding the growth of Soviet architecture. These architects allegedly distorted the Communist Party's stance on architecture and remained tied to 'the vestiges of nineteenth-century' architectural culture. He called upon the new Soviet leader and the Party to 'eliminate bourgeois perversions' in architecture; adopt measures to eliminate the backwardness of Soviet architecture and construction;

'On to new shores' (report from Moscow's architectural harbour), G. Shchukin and I. Kadina, *Arkhitektura SSSR* (November 1955).

convene a second Congress of Soviet Architects; and transform the venerable Academy of Architecture by making building construction a new priority.

Khrushchev, in an early and important attempt to distance himself from Stalin's legacy, obliged. In late 1954 he convened a meeting of 'builders, architects and workers in the building materials industry', at which he upbraided architects for having squandered state funds on architectural excesses.[3] Khrushchev attacked both individuals and organizations. As both the president of the Academy of Architecture and a co-author of Moscow's Hotel Ukraine (1950–55), one of the city's tall buildings, Mordvinov was a primary target. How, Khrushchev wondered, was it possible for Mordvinov's hotel to cost 175 per cent more per square metre than the Hotel Moscow (1932–8)? Only artistic self-indulgence and a lack of concern for building costs could explain such a situation. Certain architects justified the formal richness of their designs in the name of a battle with Constructivism, and Khrushchev sought cautiously to undermine this basic tenet of Stalin-era architectural theory. Citing the 1953 edition of the *Bolshaia sovetskaia entsiklopediia* (Great Soviet Encyclopaedia), Khrushchev defined Constructivism as a tendency to substitute technical aspects for design and an 'aesthetic admiration of form divorced from content'.[4] But he argued that those who applied 'sham detail' to their projects in order to avoid being labelled Constructivists were guilty of the same charge: they also divorced form from content, but fetishized classical forms instead of technical forms. 'We are not against beauty, but against excesses' – excess ornament and excess simplification. Khrushchev's speech was not an endorsement of Constructivist principles but an argument for the priority of economy in architecture and construction. 'Architects', Khrushchev maintained, 'must learn to count the people's money.'[5]

Khrushchev's intervention into architectural affairs had epochal consequences for both the USSR and the People's Republics. Although he was careful to avoid mentioning Stalin's name, it was clear to everyone that the theories, traditions and values developed during the recently deceased leader's reign were subject to attack. In the course of de-Stalinization, the focus of the architectural profession and the building industry would shift from the quality of singular monuments to the quantity of standardized constructions. Mass production, standardization and advanced building materials would become the guiding themes of architectural work. Khrushchev's policies made mass housing a national priority. Architects and designers would reinvent the domestic interior, while an increased availability of furniture and household appliances would reflect the Party's new interest in an expanded consumer sector. In the fifteen years after Stalin's death, an ideology of 'scientific and technical progress' would transform the fabric of everyday life in the Soviet Union.

Khrushchev's challenge to Stalin-era architectural dogma was among the first symbols of the general alleviation of cultural restrictions that came to be known as 'the Thaw'. Both the name and the metaphor for these years come from the title of Ilia Ehrenburg's novella that was published in the journal *Znamia* in 1954.[6] The story challenged the Soviet Union's rigid literary conventions by addressing topics that had previously been taboo: official anti-Semitism, mass arrests and the uncertainty of personal happiness.[7] But Ehrenburg's metaphor had strong political dimensions as well. He captured the blend of cautious optimism and collective anxiety that characterized the early post-Stalin years.

Although signs of change were widespread, Khrushchev waited until the Twentieth Congress of the Communist Party, held in February 1956, to confront the legacy of Stalinism directly. In his now infamous 'secret speech' on the 'Cult of the Individual and its Consequences', Khrushchev detailed Stalin's abuses to an audience of select Communist Party officials. He described Lenin's anxiety over Stalin's coarseness; the purges, repressions and deportations of the 1930s; Stalin's grave abuse of power; his use of torture; his propensity for self-adulation; and his orders to murder innocent Communists.[8] The speech represented a significant turn in Soviet political life. It dealt a decisive blow to the cult of Stalin among Communist Party members, which initiated a public re-evaluation of the deceased leader's alleged infallibility. More importantly, Khrushchev sought to demonstrate that recognizing Stalin's errors would not topple the entire Soviet system. As many scholars have noted, Khrushchev preserved the Soviet system by placing blame for structural abuses on Stalin alone and through the selective revelation of Party errors. Khrushchev mentioned neither his own role in organizing mass repression in the Ukraine during the 1930s, nor the devastation wrought on Soviet society by civil war, famine and the GULAG system. Thus Khrushchev secured his leadership within the Soviet Communist Party with denunciations and half-truths – political tactics he had learned from Stalin.

The social, cultural and technological achievements of Khrushchev's new course were myriad. His virgin lands campaign, which developed new agricultural areas in Kazakhstan and elsewhere, produced record grain harvests in the late 1950s. Despite the heavy losses Russia experienced during the Second World War, the population grew from nearly 108 million in 1939 to 117 million twenty years later.[9] In the same period Moscow's population grew by nearly a million people to just over 5 million; by 1959 Leningrad had nearly recovered from the devastation of the Blockade. But the conquest of space was the true achievement of Khrushchev's day. The launch of *Sputnik*, the world's first satellite, in 1957 pushed the USSR into a decisive lead in the space race. Yuri Gagarin's orbit of Earth in 1961 convinced many observers that the future of the 'scientific-technical revolution' lay in the Soviet Union. Taken by the technological optimism of the moment, in 1961 Khrushchev predicted a rapid and complete transformation of the Soviet Union's socialist society in his report on the new programme of the Communist Party: 'We base ourselves on strictly scientific estimates, which indicate that we shall, in the main, have built a communist society within 20 years.'[10]

The widespread belief in scientific progress through rationalization presented architects with new challenges. The industrialization of construction made the articulation of building systems a priority. This process required architects, engineers, building material manufacturers and onsite labour to coordinate their efforts to an unprecedented degree. Although the construction industry's production figures rose exponentially in the decade after Khrushchev's rise to power, the industry's products generated a pervasive monotony in housing districts and city centres throughout the USSR. This was due in large measure to the rapid expansion of design and construction bureaucracies. By the end of the 1960s, Glavapu, Moscow's Main Administration of Architecture and Town Planning, employed 10,000 people. The capital's administration of construction, Glavmosstroi, employed 250,000 people.[11] There was little room for individual architectural expression, and the interests of the architect were often subordinated to the interests of the building industry. 'Today', Feliks Novikov wrote in 1966, 'the architect has the voice of a consultant.'[12]

The Twentieth Congress of the Communist Party initiated both de-Stalinization and a policy of 'peaceful coexistence' with the capitalist world. Khrushchev understood the potential danger of competing nuclear superpowers and moved towards a practical policy of accommodation with the United States. The efforts at mutual understanding were strongest in the cultural sphere. In marked contrast to the official anti-Americanism of the late Stalin era, Khrushchev's policies fostered the growth of contacts between the USSR and the USA. He shocked the American audience of the television show *Face the Nation* in mid-1957. Khrushchev called openly for 'more contacts between our peoples, between businessmen'. In a surprising turn of phrase, he called upon the United States to 'do away with your Iron Curtain'.[13] By 1958, the two superpowers would sign an agreement on cultural, technical and educational exchange. The two countries exchanged exhibitions in 1959: images and artefacts of the American way of life were put on display in a geodesic dome in Moscow's Sokolniki Park; models of *Sputnik* and heroic realist paintings filled New York's Coliseum exhibition centre. It was now apparent that the curtain dividing the socialist and capitalist camps was not made of iron but, as György Péteri has suggested, of nylon: it was transparent and enabled international exchanges of culture, services and material goods.[14]

Soviet architects benefited greatly from this new openness to the capitalist world. They visited cities in Europe and America and established global relationships through their strong participation in the International Union of Architects. The amount of information about Western architecture, design and engineering that was published in the Soviet Union was unprecedented. A series of volumes on 'Construction and Architecture Abroad' appeared in Russian from 1956 to 1960. The Parisian journal *L'Architecture d'aujourd'hui* was published in an unauthorized Russian language edition, *Sovremennaia arkhitektura*, from 1961 to 1973. Although architecture and the Soviet cultural imagination in general were transformed by the new velocity of exchange, both Khrushchev and the Party apparatus remained committed to the specificity of the socialist cultural project. Khrushchev made this clear during the long denouement of the 'Manège affair' of 1962–3, when he charged Soviet painters with 'abstractionism' – his derogatory term for overreliance on Western formal models.[15] He brought his discussion of 'abstractionism' to architecture with a pointed attack on Konstantin Melnikov's Rusakov club, which he described as 'ugly as sin'.[16] The message was clear: despite its opposition to 'excess', the Party would not support a direct return to the formal vocabulary and spatial programmes of the 1920s.

Khrushchev's combative approach to Soviet culture was a symptom of other, deeper difficulties of his tenure as leader. In 1956 Hungary erupted in revolt as citizens pushed for a fundamental change to the Soviet-imposed system. The Red Army used tanks to pacify the rebels, while NATO countries refused to intervene on Hungary's behalf. Soviet–American rapprochement angered Mao Zedong and precipitated the collapse of Sino–Soviet relations after 1960. Khrushchev's approval of the construction of the Berlin Wall in 1961, and the near disaster of the Cuban Missile Crisis the following year, further strained Soviet relations with the capitalist world. More important, the presidium of the Communist Party had come to regard Khrushchev's willingness to entertain sweeping reforms to the Soviet system in agricultural, economic and cultural spheres with great scepticism.

In late 1964, a group of Party apparatchiks removed Khrushchev from his post as First Secretary of the Central Committee of the Communist Party. Leonid Brezhnev and Mikhail Suslov led the plot. Suslov criticized Khrushchev's allegedly arbitrary policies, which he thought had damaged both the Party and the USSR. As planned, Brezhnev was installed as the new Soviet premier, a post he would occupy until his death in 1982. Stabilization of economic, social and cultural life became a priority under Brezhnev.

The relative cultural freedoms of the Thaw era were reined in almost immediately. In 1965, two writers of satirical stories about the Soviet state, Andrei Siniavskii and Iulii Daniel, were arrested and later tried for circulating 'anti-Soviet propaganda'. Citizens protested the crackdown, thereby giving birth to the underground dissident movement. Brezhnev's authoritarian stabilization took on a frightening form during the 'Prague Spring' of 1968. Alexander Dubček attempted to create 'Socialism with a human face' in Czechoslovakia by liberalizing the press, allowing trade unions to push for workers' rights and instituting modest market reforms. Moscow saw this as a potential deviation from the Communist Party line. In August 1968, tanks of the Warsaw Pact countries rolled into Czechoslovakia, demonstrating that Moscow's policies would be carried out with an iron fist.

## Living Spaces

Housing was the centrepiece of Khrushchev's new line on architecture. In 1957, the Party issued a resolution on the improvement of housing in the USSR that called for a solution to the housing problem within ten to twelve years.[17] The Second World War had had devastating effects on the housing stock of occupied cities, but dwelling space had always been in short supply. Official Soviet sources measured this scarce resource in square metres of living space, defined as the combined area of living rooms and bedrooms. In 1956 the norm was 9 square metres per person, but the true amount of space available to urban dwellers was much lower: 4.75 square metres in Moscow; 5.18 square metres in Leningrad; 4.33 square metres in Stalingrad.[18] These low figures were due in large part to the prevalence of communal apartments in which the relative lack of utilities exacerbated the housing problem. The programme initiated by Khrushchev aspired to provide each family with a small but individual apartment by expanding the building materials industry. The 1957 resolution called for the construction of millions of square metres of living space in the span of a few years. These production figures were soon manifested in the innumerable four- and five-storey apartment blocks that populate the mid-century districts of cities across the Soviet Union.

Although Soviet builders had experimented with prefabrication prior to Khrushchev's programme, the political climate of the Thaw gave Soviet architects access to the international field of prefabrication techniques and practices that had been closed to them during the final years of Stalin's reign. Western models helped Soviet builders jump-start the process of industrialization. Reports on housing design in France, Czechoslovakia, Sweden, Switzerland and other countries flooded the architectural press. In 1955 alone, three Soviet delegations visited manufacturers and construction sites in Western Europe.[19] In the same year, a team of Soviet experts toured the United States and purchased furnishings and unassembled components of a suburban home from a developer in California.[20] In 1958, the USSR commissioned the French firm Raymond Camus et Cie, a major producer of prefabricated housing, to construct factories in Tashkent and Baku.[21] These exchanges not only accelerated the modernization and de-Stalinization of Soviet architecture; they brought the tensions of the cultural Cold War into the domestic sphere.

Moscow, Grimau Street, Novye Cheremushki District, late 1950s.

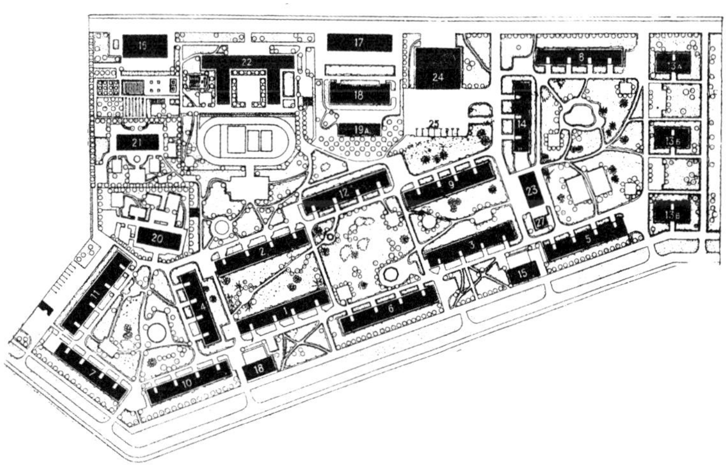

N. Osterman and others, Block 9, Novye Cheremushki, Moscow, 1956–8.

Block 9 of Moscow's Novye Cheremushki district was the first large-scale experiment in the industrialization of construction to be completed under Khrushchev's new initiatives. Designed by Natan Osterman, G. Pavlov, V. Svirskii and S. Liashchenko of the Special Bureau of Architecture and Construction (SAKB) and constructed between 1956 and 1958, Block 9 set a new standard for residential design in the USSR. The block is composed of thirteen four-storey buildings, three eight-storey buildings, a kindergarten, a school, a movie theatre, a cafeteria and two stores. Together, these units formed a *mikroraion*, or micro-district. After a brief appearance on the Soviet architectural scene in the immediate post-war years, the *mikroraion* became a central element of urban planning in the USSR from the 1950s onwards.[22] It was defined as the smallest unit of planning practice, typically encompassing 5,000–15,000 inhabitants. When combined, micro-districts created residential districts, which in turn created urban districts, which formed the largest units of the city as a whole. Block 9 is smaller than the standard *mikroraion*; it can accommodate nearly 3,000 residents. Simplicity of design unifies the complex. Architectural 'excess' is expressly avoided; balconies and flowerpots – not columns and pilasters – articulate the facades of the residential blocks. The apartment houses contain flats of one, two and three rooms. The norm of 9 square metres of living space per person was strictly followed in the design of the apartments. New materials such as linoleum and plastic were used in apartment interiors. New, economical counters, cupboards, built-in closets and appliances – some imported from Finland – were installed in each apartment. SAKB collaborated with state manufacturers to produce a line of furniture that had both clean lines and reduced dimensions. Block 9 was designed as a complete environment: its kitchen sinks, progressive construction and picturesque landscape express the ideal of a contemporary, economical way of life.

Public enthusiasm for Block 9 was tremendous. One report claimed that nearly 40,000 people visited the site before 1959. Among those visitors were the participants of the Fifth Congress of the International Union of Architects, which took place in Moscow in 1958. Robert Matthew, a prominent member of the Union and former architect of the London County Council, told a Soviet reporter that he saw 'great opportunities for the application of this healthy architectural experiment in other cities around the Soviet Union'.[23] Seeing the same opportunities, municipalities across the USSR drew on the experiment of Block 9 in the construction of new *mikroraiony*. New developments and the housewarming parties that took place in them were featured in popular magazines that offered readers a 'voyage into the world of the new settlers'.[24] But the rapid construction of apartment buildings came at a cost. Because the work was often shoddy and materials sub-par, these blocks were popularly called 'khrushcheby', a pun on the name of the Soviet leader and the Russian word for slum. Moreover, the proliferation of nearly identical buildings created monotonous living environments. But, as the painter Iurii Pimenov later recalled, this monotony was still an improvement over pre-existing conditions: 'I grew up in a city in which all of my conscious life was choked by overcrowding, by the foul atmosphere of shared apartments and communal kitchens where fumes, heat and irritation weighed upon people, and for this reason I look upon these bright, monotonous buildings with good feelings.'[25] Attitudes such as his made the new, single-family apartment a pervasive symbol of cultural aspiration. The 1962 film *Cheremushki*, directed by Gerbert Rappaport to a score by Dmitrii Shostakovich, dramatized this desire with a scene in which the actors dance on a prefabricated concrete panel as a crane hoists it above a new construction site.

Iurii Pimenov, *Wedding on the Street of Tomorrow*, 1962.

Soviet bedroom at the New York Exhibition of Soviet Culture, 1959.

The domestic interior became the subject of international competition in 1959, when the exchange of national exhibitions between the USA and the USSR transformed consumer goods and appliances into the elements of Cold War struggle. The Soviet fair opened in the New York Coliseum Building in late June. In addition to models of the *Sputnik* satellite, the exhibition included models of housing developments in various Soviet cities and a full-size, three-bedroom apartment interior. The apartment was outfitted with built-in cupboards, low-slung armchairs and sectional wall units. Olga Baiar, an interior design specialist, told the press that the apartment on display was a reality in the Soviet Union and that it would be duplicated many thousands of times in the following years. An incredulous *New York Times* reporter noted that 'by American standards, the apartment – though small – had at least upper-middle-class equipment, although the refrigerator and beds seemed to be for smaller-sized folk.'[26] This condescension was a prelude to the consumer chauvinism of the American National Exhibition of 1959. Situated on the grounds of Moscow's Sokolniki Park, the event displayed everything from architecture to fashion in a geodesic dome designed by Welton Becket and Associates and other, smaller venues. Charles and Ray Eames assembled a multi-screen film called *Glimpses of the USA*, a kaleidoscopic portrait of American urban culture that mesmerized Soviet audiences. A 'typical' American house, dubbed the 'splitnik' because it was divided in two for display purposes, was the stage for the dramatic climax of the exhibition. Here, within the 'Trojan horse' of American domestic culture, Khrushchev and Richard Nixon, then vice-president, squared off in the infamous 'kitchen debate'. In this highly orchestrated event, Khrushchev described how the USSR would overtake the USA in social and economic terms. Nixon told

Khrushchev that the Soviet Union was ahead in the exploration of space, 'but there may be some instances in which we are ahead of you – in colour television, for instance'. The Soviet leader dismissed the display of household appliances as mere gadgetry and retorted that 'you think the Russian people will be dumbfounded to see these things.'[27] Some Soviet women were impressed with the menagerie of appliances on display. But others, as Susan E. Reid has shown, approached the American kitchen with scepticism, seeing it as a form of isolation and bondage. The writer Marietta Shaginian warned of the danger of eternalizing the isolated role of the housewife through the mass production of technologically advanced kitchen appliances. She welcomed, on the other hand, 'innovations that actually emancipate women – new types of houses with public canteens for everyone living in the house'.[28]

In the 1960s the domestic interior became a site of aesthetic and social reform. Part of the impetus for experimentation in this arena came from above, from a decree of the Council of Ministries that promoted the improvement of consumer goods. This led to the establishment of the All-Union Scientific Research Institute for Technical Aesthetics (VNIITE) in 1962. VNIITE and other design institutes contributed to the 'decisive battle against tastelessness' that Khrushchev had declared at the Twenty-second Congress of the Communist Party in 1961.[29] Architects and designers sought to create a unity of comfort, economy and simplicity through the use of natural materials, harmonious colours and the integration of furniture with architectural space. Reformers promoted flexible planning: they sought to transform the family table from the apartment's gravitational centre into one of several functional zones. Furniture and movable dividers were to differentiate interior space according to use: a sofa in front of the television; a rug and a bookshelf to distinguish a living room; a curtain to enclose a sleeping nook. The Baltic republics – Estonia, Latvia and Lithuania – were major sources of innovative furniture design. Their proximity to Finland and the Scandinavian countries was evident in the shared commitment to natural materials, colourful textiles and organic forms. Moscow-based organizations such as Glavstandartdom produced impressive

Children's room designed by the Experimental Construction Studio of the Lithuanian SSR; from *Dekorativnoe Iskusstvo*, no. 1 (1962).

ensembles composed of multifunctional wall units, sheer curtains and low, ovoid armchairs – stage sets for a modern way of life.

But Soviet architects and designers sought to ensure that new dwellings would be collective as well as modern. The programme that the Communist Party put forward at its Twenty-second Congress contained provisions for a social and economic transition from socialism to communism through the accelerated development of socialized services. A key element of this programme required 'complete elimination of the unequal status of the woman in everyday life'.[30] To architects, designers and social theorists, the solution to this problem was to be found in the home, an arena of potential conflict among women's roles as workers, mothers, caregivers and citizens. *Byt*, or everyday life, became a site of spatial and social intervention. As they imagined new frames for everyday life, the models of collectivized housing advanced by Soviet architects during the 1920s and early 1930s acquired new practical relevance. Authors including Mikhail Ilin, Selim Khan-Magomedov and Aleksandr Riabushin began publishing some of the first positive studies of Constructivist architecture since the 1930s, and although the legacy of Constructivism remained a sensitive political issue, it soon became an important touchstone for architects interested in social reform.[31] Projects for 'residential complexes' with socialized services began to pour out of design and planning institutes. Georgii Gradov was among the first to articulate a revised version of the *dom-kommuna*. Gradov and other architects drew on both the housing concepts of the 1920s and contemporary models of collective housing. Václav Hilský and Evžen Linhart's collective house in Litvínov, Czechoslovakia (1946–57), was a particularly important model for Soviet architects.[32] Gradov's theoretical project was based on a primary residential unit for 1,440 inhabitants. The unit had three sectors: a housing block with one-, two- and three-room apartments, a service block with cafeteria and a nursery/kindergarten attached to the housing block by a heated, elevated corridor. Apartments did not have kitchens but small hotplates for 'episodic cooking'. Children could live in the nursery full-time or part-time. The aggregation of cooking and child-rearing into larger units, Gradov postulated, would 'further the realization of the Leninist idea of the transformation of small-scale housework into large-scale socialist industry'.[33]

Among the many projects for residential complexes with collective services of the 1960s, Natan Osterman's *Dom novogo byta* (DNB), or 'house of the new way of life', demonstrated the most architectural and scientific ambition. Continuing the work he initiated in Block 9 of the Novye Cheremushki district, Osterman led a team of architects, designers, economists and sociologists in a prognostic investigation of the future of

Natan Osterman and others, House of the New Way of Life, Moscow, 1961–9.

House of the New Way of Life, Moscow; ground-floor plan.

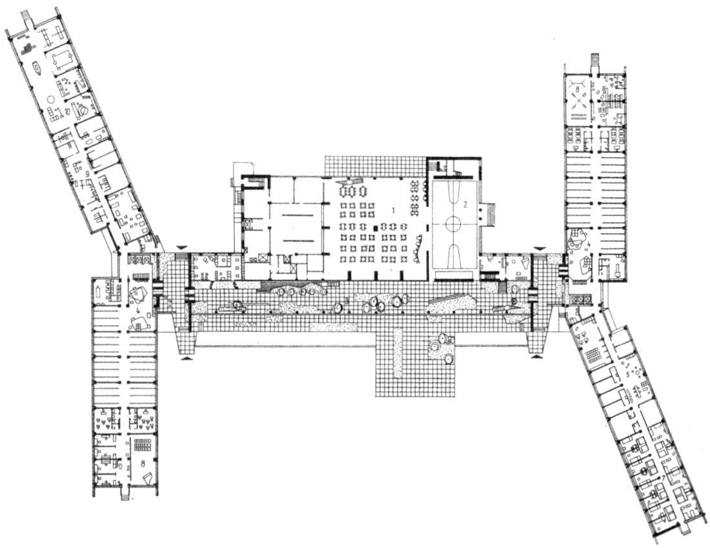

daily life in the USSR.[34] The building's form follows Hilský and Linhart's building closely: two bent housing slabs flank a lower service block. As in Gradov's projects and the communal house designs of the 1920s, apartments in the DNB reduced private amenities for the sake of collective services. Cooking nooks replaced private kitchens, but residents had access to a cafeteria in the service block and shared kitchens on each floor of the residential wings. The complex included a nursery, a gymnasium, a cinema, a clinic, study rooms and even a barber. The roof decks of the housing blocks were given over to gardens, clothes lines, a summer theatre and a solarium; the sculptural service towers clearly recall the facilities atop Le Corbusier's Unité d'habitation in Marseille (1946–52). Dwellings in the DNB were small, but the apartments had open, flexible plans. Conceived for a population of 2,200 people, the DNB was an attempt to create a microcosm of self-regulating communal life. Both the building and the concepts behind it elicited great enthusiasm. In 1968, as construction was nearly complete, the economist Stanislav Strumilin wrote that the building 'creates optimal conditions for the successful formation of the norms and regulations of a communist way of life'.[35] But before it was completed, amid the tightening of cultural restrictions in the aftermath of the Prague Spring, the Moscow Soviet decided that this sort of social experiment was no longer productive and gave the DNB to Moscow State University for use as a dormitory.[36]

## Consumption, Culture and Leisure

The Khrushchev-era reforms that elevated domestic life to a primary architectural concern also had wide-ranging effects on the spaces and material qualities of everyday life. The boom in residential construction of the 1950s and '60s was accompanied by a corresponding growth of the network of spaces for consumption, culture and leisure. With new building types and new interpretations of existing typologies, architects sought to manifest the reorientation of Soviet society towards consumption and cultured relaxation in built form. These years witnessed the construction of new kinds of shops, entertainment facilities, educational institutions and holiday resorts. Buildings for shopping, eating, swimming, spectator sports and other activities complemented the improvement of living standards at home with an array of newly accessible services in public.

The provision of space for consumer services within newly developed residential districts became standard practice. Block 9 of the Novye Cheremushki district had already included shops for meat, fish and vegetables in its first phase of construction. These modest buildings featured broad glazed shopfronts, open plans, a split-level internal layout and distinct customer and service entrances. The bright interiors and gleaming display windows of these buildings set the standard for shops built in housing districts across the Soviet Union. Like apartment buildings, most of these commercial enterprises were built according to type-projects. Giprotorg, the state institute for the design of commercial structures, was responsible for many of these projects. Some of the institute's designs, such as the Cheremushkinskii market in Moscow, constructed in 1963,

Covered market, Chelyabinsk, 1960–75, designed by Giprotorg; project leader F. Seletskii.

used thin concrete shell structures to enclose the sales area, thus using advanced structural techniques to enhance everyday life.[37] Giprotorg would also design the much larger central market in Chelyabinsk (1960–75) using a similar structural system.

The image of a new, socialist and consumer-orientated society underpinned the most ambitious urban project undertaken in the Khrushchev years: Kalinin Prospect, now known as New Arbat Street. The expansion of this radial artery to the west of the city centre had been foreseen by the 1935 Plan for Moscow, but it was not transformed until the 1960s. From the very beginning, Kalinin Prospect was presented as a symbol of the social and material progress Khrushchev hoped to achieve with his reforms. The construction of the complex would, however, outlast Khrushchev's tenure as the head of the Soviet State: construction began in

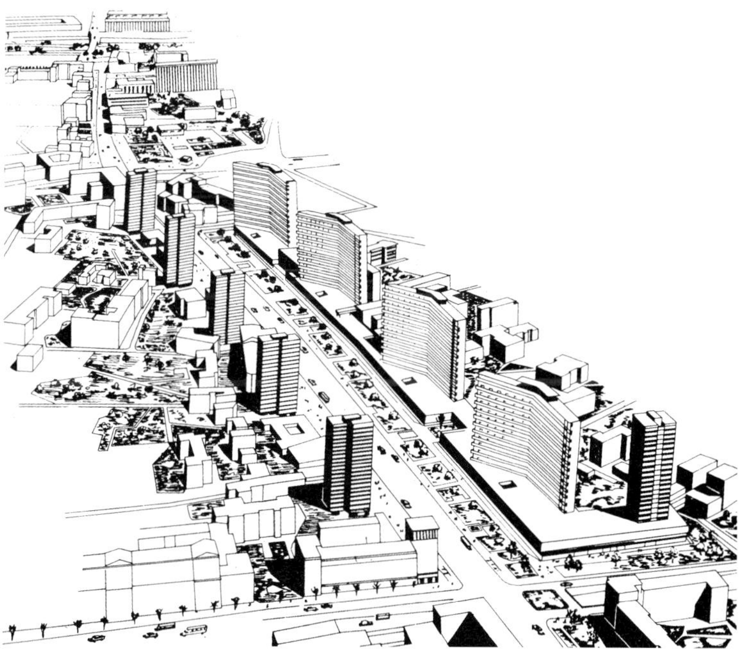

M. V. Posokhin and others, Kalinin Prospect (New Arbat Street), Moscow, 1962–9.

Palace of the Pioneers, Moscow, 1958–62; main entry.

Palace of the Pioneers, winter garden.

1964 and was completed four years later. Designed by a team of architects led by Mikhail Posokhin, Kalinin Prospect extends for 800 m on the north and south sides of the street. The complex houses a mix of residential, administrative, commercial and cultural functions. Five 25-storey housing towers on the north side of the street offer a counterpoint to the four 26-storey office buildings on the south side. The office buildings are bent slabs, and their form recalls an open book. While the House of Books and the 'October' cinema – each the largest of its kind in Moscow – stand on the north side of the street, a unified retail space extends along the entire length of the south side. Walking along a broad pavement, one could browse at a clothing store, visit a hair salon, plan a trip at a travel agency, purchase a bouquet at a florist and meet friends at a café or restaurant. 'Arbat', the largest restaurant in the complex, could seat 2,000 guests. At night, the street was transformed by illuminated signs and brightly lit shop windows. Although some observers lamented the destruction of the many structures torn down to make way for the new street, the integration of a range of spaces for consumption and display earned Kalinin Prospect the popular designation of 'our Broadway'.

As the image and form of consumption was redefined in urban centres, a new commitment to culture, education and leisure became evident in the construction of new complexes intended specifically for youth. The Moscow Palace of the Pioneers, designed and built between 1958 and 1962, was among the most significant architectural projects of the Khrushchev era. Situated in the city's southwestern district, it lies in the shadow of Moscow State University, countering the University's highly orchestrated verticality with an emphatic horizontal disposition. The striking contrast between the buildings seems to manifest the markedly different cultural tone in the Soviet Union in the wake of de-Stalinization. It was no accident that the hopeful outlook of Khrushchev's 'Thaw' was manifest so clearly in this building, as it served primarily as a space of after-school education and recreation for the Communist Party's children's organization, the Pioneers.[38] The forward-looking building was intended to serve as an incubator for future Communist leaders. The architects, Viktor Egerev, Vladimir Kubasov, Feliks Novikov, Igor Pokrovskii and Boris Khazhakian, adopted an asymmetrical, L-shaped scheme for the main building. A theatre with a capacity of 1,000 stands at the southern end of the site and is connected to the main building through an elevated, heated walkway. The main entrance is marked by a broad projecting awning and monumental mosaic panels featuring an image of Lenin and pioneers engaged in a variety of activities. The open space between the theatre and the main entry serves as a field for demonstrations. Inside, the Palace unfolds in a long glass-enclosed gallery from which pavilions for a variety of activities project to the rear of the site. A light-filled winter garden greets the visitor upon entry. Its double-height ceiling, organically curved reflecting pools, lush vegetation and geodesic skylights made it one of the most striking public interiors of its time. The quality of the Palace was evident to Soviet architects as soon as it was completed. One critic wrote that 'the complex has a human scale, lightness and an intimacy and poetry appropriate to its function, that is, everything that opposes the ostentation of many public buildings of the recent past.'[39]

The precedent established by the Moscow Palace of the Pioneers was quickly adopted by architects designing leisure facilities throughout the USSR. In his expansion of the Artek Pioneer Camp in Crimea, begun in 1959, Anatolii Polianskii used a variety of pre-cast concrete elements to merge buildings seamlessly with the landscape on the coast of the Black Sea. The sleeping pavilions of the 'Morskoi' section of the camp are perched on an embankment directly above the beach. Slender concrete supports descend to the boardwalk below. The open-plan structures offer sweeping views of the sea from within and access to the coastal atmosphere from covered roof decks. Though identical in form, the five pavilions of the 'Morskoi' section were differentiated by colour, which enlivened the complex. Elsewhere on the Black Sea, the architectural qualities of the Artek camp were adapted to adult facilities. For Pitsunda Beach, in the Georgian province of Abkhazia, Mikhail Posokhin, Ashot Mndoiants and others designed a resort that responded to the natural beauty of the site. Built between 1962 and 1967, the Pitsunda Resort remains a popular destination.

A. Polianskii, Artek Pioneer Camp, Morskoi Section, 1959–65.

A. Zhuk and others 'Oktiabrskii' Concert Hall, Leningrad, 1966–7.

Leisure was an important architectural theme within cities as well. This is evident in the range of new buildings for entertainment that brought new venues for cultural life into Russian and Soviet cities in the late 1950s and '60s. In Leningrad, Aleksandr Zhuk led the design of both the Theatre of the Young Viewer (1955–62) and the 'Oktiabrskii' Concert Hall (1966–7). The latter, with a capacity of 4,000, was the largest of its kind in the city, and its taut, cubic forms stood in stark contrast to earlier Soviet theatres. Likewise, the 'Rossiia' cinema in the centre of Moscow offered a new interpretation of this building type. Built in 1961 and designed by Iurii Sheverdiaev, D. Solopov and E. Gadzhinskaia, the building was said to represent the 'spirit of the new direction' in architecture.[40] The project freely interpreted a design for a cinema completed by Leonid Pavlov in 1959, which would serve as the prototype for countless cinemas built in the following years throughout the Soviet Union.

The effort devoted to buildings for theatre and cinema was matched by an equally strong interest in facilities for athletics. In this period stadiums that had been damaged during the Second World War were rebuilt and new arenas were raised in cities across the USSR. In Moscow, Aleksandr Vlasov led the design team for the Lenin Central Stadium, which was built between 1954 and 1956. Part of the 'Luzhniki' sports complex in the southwest of Moscow, the central stadium was among the largest in the USSR with a capacity of over 100,000. The cavities below the tribunes

Leonid Pavlov, project for a cinema with 4,000 seats, 1959.

Aleksandr Vlasov and others, Lenin Central Stadium, Moscow, 1954–6.

contain spaces for many kinds of athletic training as well as a cinema and restaurants. The colossal pillars that support the tribune are capped with stylized geometric capitals. This, combined with the stadium's alignment with the axis of Moscow State University, was testament to a lingering adherence to the monumental 'excesses' that Khrushchev so vigorously opposed. Nikolai Baranov's reconstruction of Lenin Stadium (now Petrovskii Stadium) in Leningrad between 1957 and 1961 also showed signs of architectural 'excess', though here the Corinthian capitals that crown the exterior pillars make more explicit reference to historical forms. Such historical references were absent from the stadium that Soviet architects designed and built for the Asian Games in Jakarta in 1962.[41] But the true breakthrough in Soviet stadium design was made by Vitalii Orekhov with his Central Stadium in the Siberian city Krasnoyarsk (1965–8). Orekhov's design emerged from his diploma project for the Leningrad Institute of Engineering and Construction, and the completed building retains much of the freshness of his student work.[42] Constructed of roughcast reinforced concrete, the tribunes of the stadium are supported by inclined pylons. Elevated ramps allow rapid access to the upper levels of the stands. In Orekhov's stadium, monumentality cedes to a new interest in the sculptural qualities of architectural form and an expressive use of material.

## 'Scientific-technical Progress' and its Image

The idea that humanity was at the threshold of an unprecedented 'scientific-technical revolution' was inscribed in the optimistic Third Programme of the Communist Party of 1961. Rapid advances in the exploration of space and the diffusion of atomic technology seemed to presage a new era in which the 'material foundations for Communism' could be established. Science itself was to become a 'direct productive force'.[43] The broad cultural, political and ideological drive to accelerate 'scientific-technical progress' in the Soviet Union had far-reaching effects on architecture and the built environment. During the 1960s new universities, institutes and

Vitalii Orekhov, Krasnoyarsk Central Stadium, 1965–8.

I. Adamov, A. Polianskii, A. Bortskii and V. Dubov, Soviet Pavilion, Brussels World's Fair, 1958.

even entire cities were founded to promote the development of socialist science. But this drive for progress was equally important in the symbolic realm. For while Soviet institutions supported the advancement of science and technology, they also wanted to project new, technologically advanced images of themselves to the world. The task for architects was thus twofold: to create spaces for the administration of progress and to generate forms that would render progress visible.

The Soviet pavilion at the Brussels World's Fair of 1958 was among the first attempts to cast the Soviet image of scientific progress in architectural form. The building differed markedly from the previous two pavilions that the USSR had presented at world's fairs. Unlike Boris Iofan's monumental buildings in New York and Paris, the Brussels Pavilion was light and open in both its form and structure. Anatolii Polianskii, the pavilion's principal designer, adopted an innovative method of construction to convey these spatial effects. The roof is supported by lightweight pylons that carry the central span through a system of guy-wires.[44] The exterior of the 150 × 72 m structure is enclosed by vertical sheets of glass set at 45 degree angles to enliven the facade. This system lent the building an almost translucent quality. Inside, the central object of display was no longer a model of the Palace of the Soviets, which had been shown in

New York and Paris, but rather a model of *Sputnik*, the first satellite to orbit the earth. Outer space also supplied the theme and much of the imagery for the failed Soviet bid to hold the 1967 World's Fair in Moscow.[45] 'Progress and Peace' was to be the theme of the exposition that would have transformed an enormous territory of Moscow had it taken place, for the Moscow fair was intended to be the largest in history. Dmitrii Chechulin was named chief architect of the event, and two spectacular competitions were held in 1961 and 1962 for a variety of sites around Moscow. For reasons that remain unclear, interest in holding the fair in Moscow declined after the second round of competition, and the event ultimately took place in Montreal. The USSR was represented at that event with a pavilion designed by Mikhail Posokhin, which offered a sweeping, dynamic reprise of the architectural themes raised by the Brussels pavilion.

Soviet leaders were interested in projecting an image of progress at home as well as abroad. The decision to launch a new round of competition for the Palace of the Soviets in 1957 was part of this effort. The central site on the Moscow River, which had already been excavated before the Second World War, was abandoned, and a new site was selected in the city's southwest district. With a formal stop to building activity, which had not in fact advanced since the war, the foundation pit in the city centre was transformed into an enormous, open-air swimming pool.[46] The new site for the Palace was set on axis with the Luzhniki Stadium and Moscow State University; it effectively continued the line of monuments that had the original site as its origin. This displacement of the Palace from the centre to the periphery was accompanied by a decisive shift in the architectural form of the building. 'Noble simplicity' was to be the formal aim of architects submitting projects to the competition.[47] Most submissions to the first and second rounds of competition were emphatically horizontal, in contrast to the strong verticality of Iofan, Shchuko and Gelfreikh's tower. Leonid Pavlov's project was one of many that used a screen of pillars to lend the building a forward-looking monumentality. Only 'prizes of encouragement' were given in the first round of competition, though Aleksandr Vlasov's project was clearly a favourite. His project would emerge victorious, albeit with only a second prize, in the 1959 round of competition. Vlasov's design enclosed three elliptical auditoria in a glass box. All four walls

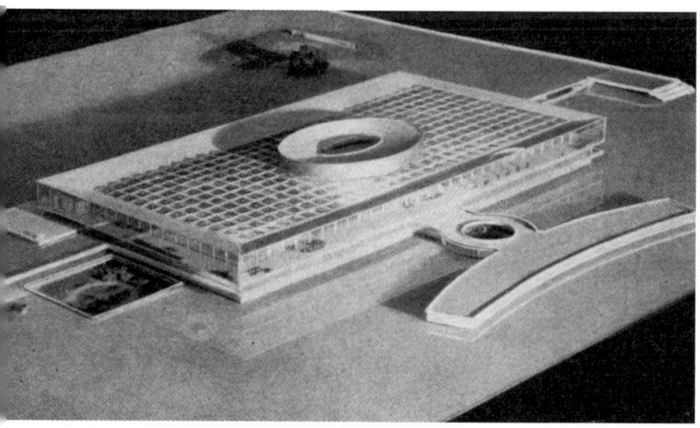

Aleksandr Vlasov, V. P. Davidenko, A. D. Meerson, Palace of the Soviets, Second Round Project, 1959.

were to be glazed from plinth to cornice, and the roof was conceived as a glass surface broken only by the elliptical volume of the central auditorium. The building's interior unfolds as an open, unified space in which the principal meeting rooms seem to float freely among the lush vegetation of the extensive interior landscape. The project cast the Palace of the Soviets as a winter garden. For this Vlasov was named chair of the directorate of the construction of the Palace of the Soviets, though this Palace, like its earlier version, would ultimately remain unbuilt.

The competition for the Palace of the Soviets of 1957–9 was not, however, without architectural consequences. This event established a new iconography for the Soviet governmental building, and the principles of horizontality, 'noble simplicity' and restrained monumentality that were distilled during the competition would inform the design of the most prestigious building of the Khrushchev era: the Palace of Congresses (1959–61). Designed by a team of architects led by Mikhail Posokhin, the Palace of Congresses was a major intervention into the fabric of Moscow's historic Kremlin. In order to ensure that it would be a world-class structure, Posokhin, the director of the State Construction Agency, and a large delegation of architects and engineers undertook an international study tour in 1960. They visited Italy, the United Kingdom, Germany (West, not East) – where they met with representatives of the Siemens Corporation, who provided lighting and sound for the Palace – and the United States.[48] In the U.S., they met with Edward Durrell Stone, Wallace Harrison, Max Abramovitz, Mies van der Rohe and others. The preparations and resources poured into this building indicate its supreme importance. The finished building synthesizes monumentality and openness. The pylons that form a pseudo-peristyle have a trapezoidal profile, which causes the building's appearance to oscillate between opacity and transparency as a visitor approaches. Plate glass spandrels offer views into and out of the building. Entering the Palace, one passes between banks of escalators into the main foyer, a double-height space opened up by lateral views outside and ornamented with mosaic emblems of each of the Soviet republics. The heart of the complex is the conference hall. With a capacity of 6,000, it was said to be the largest auditorium of its kind in the world when it was completed.[49] The interior is lined with lathes of wood, recalling the interior treatment of the United Nations General Assembly Hall in New York.[50] The curtain featured an image of Lenin against a variegated background. This hall, used for events ranging from congresses of the Communist Party to operatic performances, quickly became the central ceremonial space of the Soviet Union.

M. V. Posokhin and A. Mndoiants, Palace of Congresses, Kremlin, Moscow, 1959–61.

Palace of Congresses, main hall.

The drive to accelerate 'scientific-technical progress' generated new kinds of cities as well. Science, education and research had come to be

House of Scientists, Akademgorodok, 1962–8.

F. Novikov, I. Pokrovskii, V. Larionova and E. Lichtenberg, Scientific Centre of Microelectronics, Zelenograd, 1962–9.

seen as activities that would benefit from having urban forms and infrastructural systems that closely matched their needs. Akademgorodok ('Academy Town') was among the most important scientific cities constructed under Khrushchev's leadership. Located outside Novosibirsk, the city was intended to offer the Soviet Union a centre of scientific learning and research that might counterbalance the concentration of scientific institutions in Moscow and Leningrad.[51] Akademgorodok was begun in 1957, and by 1963 it already had a population of over 10,000.[52] The city was home to a new branch of the Novosibirsk State University and a number of institutes serving a variety of specializations: atomic physics, hydrodynamics, mathematics, chemistry, geology, among others. While the first phase of construction departed little from the pattern of settlements that were being deployed in Moscow's newer districts, Akademgorodok offered a close integration between developed areas and the countryside. By contrast, the form of Zelenograd, a new city begun in 1962 outside Moscow, was highly innovative. Designed to support research in electronics, Zelenograd was home to some of the most innovative buildings of the 1960s in Russia. The bent curtain-wall slabs of the Scientific Centre of Microelectronics (1962–9) by Feliks Novikov, Igor Pokrovskii and others display a degree of elegance on a par with international standards. The cultural and commercial centre of Zelenograd was composed of a 27-storey hotel, a building for political administration, a palace of culture and a range of commercial facilities. The number of unique buildings

NER Group, project for a settlement, 1968.

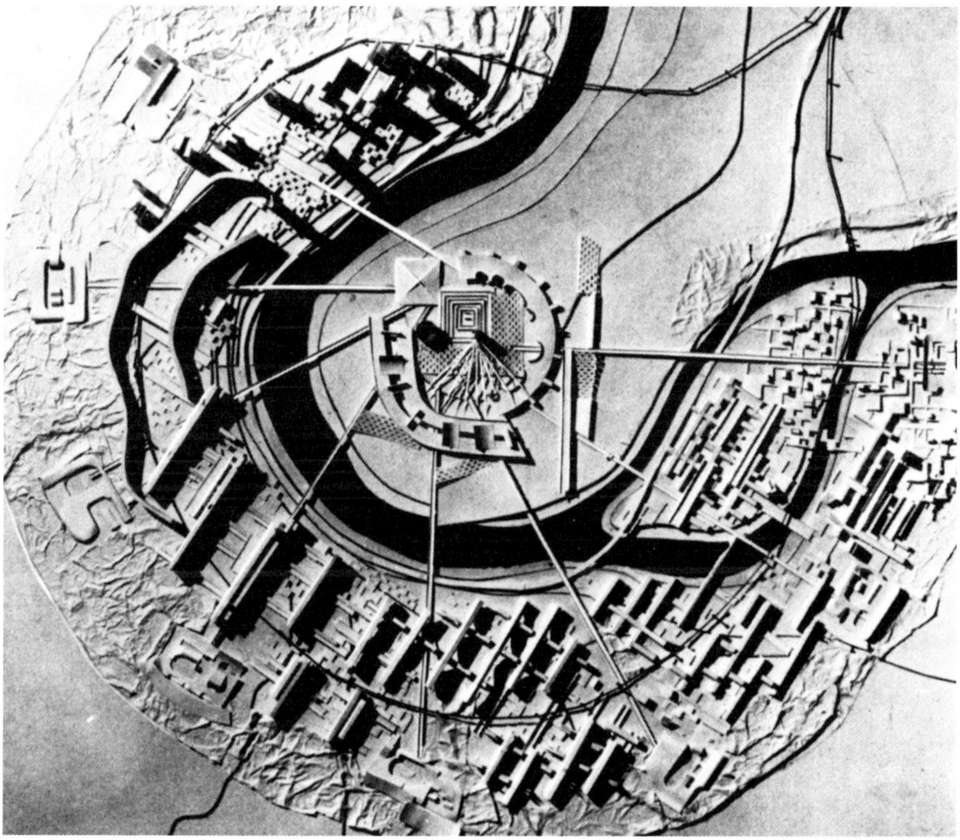

constructed in Zelenograd made it one of the most interesting, though least typical, new towns of the 1960s.

In addition to the construction of scientific and research centres, some architects sought to enlist progressive scientific methods in the development of new urban forms. This was the aim of Aleksei Gutnov, Ilia Lezhava and a group of like-minded students who formulated the concept of a *Novyi element rasseleniia* (new element of settlement), or NER, in their diploma project at the Moscow Architecture Institute in 1960. For this work and its development over the next decade, this circle came to be known as the 'NER Group'.[53] They sought to combine a Marxist understanding of social relations with advances in 'cybernetics, information theory, human engineering and the aesthetics of technology' in order to understand human demography and shape and control social processes.[54] This knowledge derived from social sciences formed the background against which the NER Group articulated its proposals for a new type of urban settlement. Within this system, each city or 'element' was to maintain spatial autonomy while remaining connected to industrial and agricultural areas. These nuclei were to have approximately 100,000 inhabitants. Through the reproduction and linkage of these nuclei, the chaotic growth of cities was to be replaced by a dynamic system of urban settlement that could accommodate a diversity of productive needs within its form. The NER Group earned international acclaim for their work on urban structure. Some in the capitalist world, including Peter Cook of Archigram, recognized distinct similarities in the drawings and models produced by the NER Group and the megastructural fantasies of the 1960s.[55] Cook was happy to 'welcome the NER boys and girls to the fold'. With the sponsorship of Giancarlo de Carlo, the group was invited to exhibit its work at the Milan Triennale of 1968. While the projects devised by the NER Group remained largely on paper, the group's members would exert a powerful influence on Soviet architecture through teaching.

L. Batalov, engineer N. Nikitin and others, Ostankino television broadcast tower, Moscow, 1960–67.

The modernization of technical installations throughout the Soviet Union was an important aim of the push for 'scientific-technical progress' of the 1960s. Technical structures such as broadcast towers and hydroelectric dams created a new set of landmarks in urban centres and transformed vast territories. In Moscow, the Ostankino

Bratsk hydroelectric dam, 1954–67, G. Orlov, chief engineer.

Television Centre offered new broadcast facilities and established a new vertical dominant in the city's northern district. At 533 m tall, the broadcast tower designed by N. Nikitin and L. Batalov and built between 1960 and 1967 was the tallest of its kind when completed. From a perforated conic base, the shaft of the tower rises in several stages up to a restaurant 330 m above ground. The breadth of the panoramic view of Moscow from this height corresponds to the length of the broadcast radius (130 km) afforded by the new tower.[56] In the eastern interior of Russia, the Bratsk Hydroelectric Station (1954–67) harnessed the power of the Angara River to provide electricity to a new industrial complex. The station was designed by the Soviet Union's Institute of Hydrological Works, Gidroproekt, under the leadership of Georgii Orlov, who had worked on the Dnepr Dam with the Vesnin brothers early in his career. When it was completed, the station was praised for its laconic simplicity and sublime proportions: the central power plant alone is over 500 m long.[57] It served the USSR's largest aluminium works and became the generator of new urban settlements in Irkutsk Province throughout the 1960s.

The institutes that designed technical projects for the territories of the USSR were also involved in the export of technical assistance to foreign nations. These exports could range from schools to sports facilities and even to entire town plans. One example of this process is the general plan for Kabul, Afghanistan, that was devised by Moscow-based design

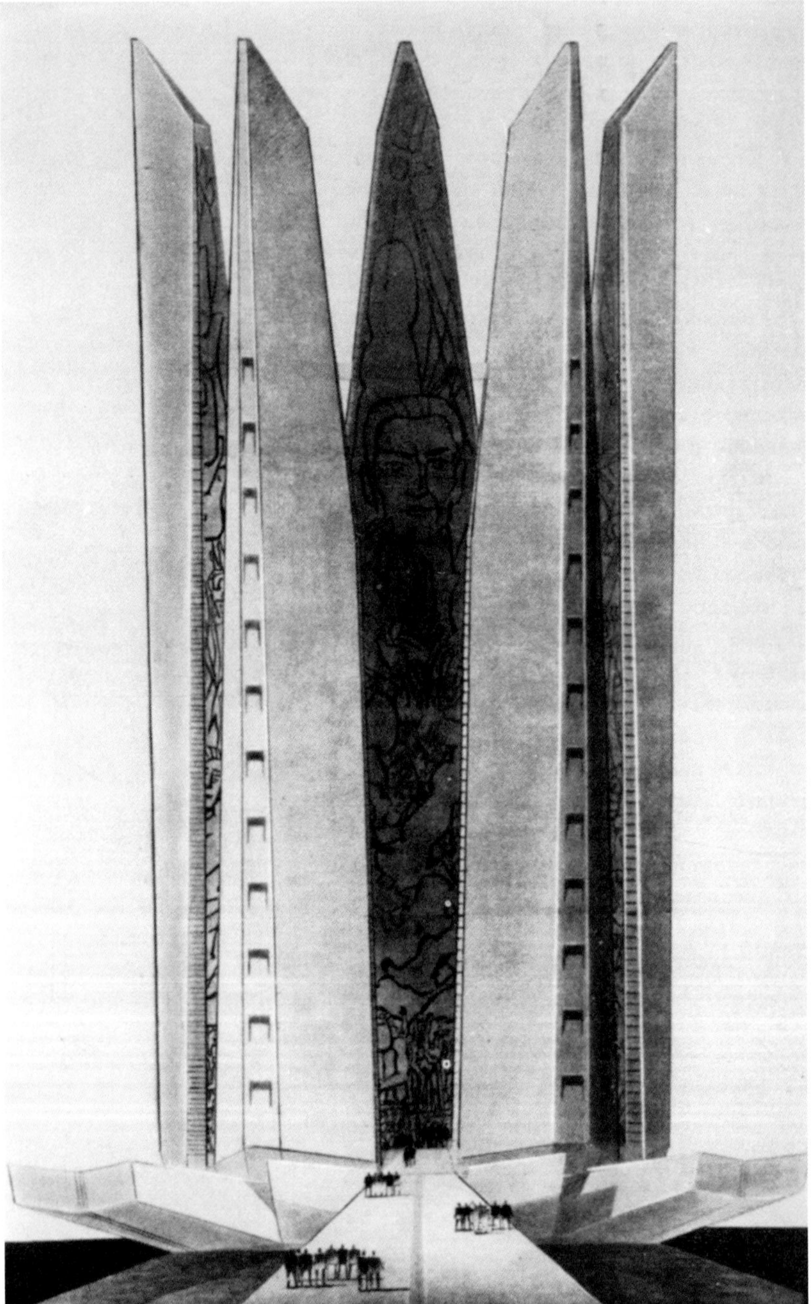

organizations beginning in 1962.[58] From the 1960s onwards, Gidroproekt provided hydroelectric stations to countries around the world. The institute's highest-profile project was the completion of the Aswan High Dam on the Nile River in Egypt. As a gift to the country, the dam complex was intended to secure Egypt's alliance with the USSR and, moreover, to present the Soviet Union as a competitor with the United States in the international field of technical assistance. The architectural project supplied by Gidroproekt in 1965 would be completed five years later.[59] At the crest of the dam stands the monument to 'Arab–Soviet Friendship' designed by Iurii Omelchenko and P. Pavlov as a flower in bloom. The Aswan High Dam and the many other buildings and installations designed by Soviet architects and engineers for foreign nations aimed to present the Soviet Union as a lender of resources and expertise. The export of Soviet architectural and technical knowledge was part of a bid to extend the Soviet Union's sphere of ideological influence by means of technological projects. Such efforts to disseminate the image of the 'scientific-technical progress' of Soviet socialism, however, would soon be hindered by the stricter regulation of Soviet culture and society in the aftermath of Brezhnev's military intervention in Prague in 1968.

Monument to Arab–Soviet Friendship, Aswan Dam Complex, begun 1966.

chapter eight

# Architecture in Developed Socialism, 1969–82

Eric Bulatov's painting *Krasikov Street* of 1977 depicts a typical urban landscape in Moscow's southwestern district. Rectangular apartment buildings tower above a broad motorway populated by buses and individual cars. In the foreground, several men and women walk along a dirt-strewn pavement. The women's fashionable dresses bear distinctive patterns, though their cut is nearly uniform. To their left, a sparsely planted and poorly maintained strip of grass betrays the relative youth of this section of Moscow, identifying it as a product of Khrushchev's housing campaign. At the centre of Bulatov's painting, a monumental billboard carrying an image of Lenin, captured in full stride, looms above the scene. With gazes directed away, Bulatov's men and women appear indifferent to the mythic Bolshevik leader. Indeed, their path into the background of the painting runs directly past Lenin's heroic, forward-looking image. In its representation of limited personal expression, Moscow's featureless industrial cityscape and an atmosphere of ideological and social alienation, Bulatov's painting effectively conveys both the cultural mood and spatial texture of the 1970s in the Soviet Union.

The period between the suppression of the Prague Spring in 1968 and the death of Leonid Brezhnev in 1982 was marked by the widespread stabilization of Soviet politics, society and culture. But the achievement of stability had contradictory outcomes. The ambitious social, economic and cultural reforms initiated by Khrushchev under the banner of de-Stalinization gave way to incremental adjustments to the system of 'developed socialism'. The term entered the official Soviet lexicon after Brezhnev used it in a speech to the Twenty-fourth Congress of the Communist Party in 1971. 'Developed socialism' lacked the optimism of Khrushchev's prediction of the immanent attainment of communist social relations, while signalling that a new stage in socialist society had been reached. One effect of the ideology of 'developed socialism' and its attendant political and economic programmes was a widespread sense that stasis had been substituted for progress as a governing principle of Soviet life.[1] The social and cultural alienation engendered by the stabilization of the long 1970s led many to retrospectively describe the period as one of 'stagnation'.

Eric Bulatov, *Krasikov Street*, 1977.

At the same time, this period witnessed an elevation of the Soviet Union's status on the world stage. The 'Peace Programme' that Brezhnev announced in 1969 was predicated on the notion that the USSR had achieved military parity with the USA, thus buttressing claims to equal superpower status.[2] The Soviet Union's new view of its geopolitical position paved the way for the series of policies that constituted the *détente*, or relaxation of relations, between the USSR and advanced capitalist countries. The arms-limitation treaties signed by Brezhnev and U.S. President Nixon in the early 1970s were significant outcomes of this new relationship. Meanwhile, Soviet interests were bolstered by events occurring elsewhere in the world. The revolution in Ethiopia in 1974 offered an opportunity for the USSR to support what it considered to be a young Marxist state. Likewise, the end of the Portuguese empire in Africa enabled the Soviet Union to intervene in civil wars in Angola and Mozambique as a protector nation. These actions were part of a broader strategy to exert Soviet influence in the world by advertising the USSR's readiness to support struggles of 'national liberation'.[3] As the Soviet Union forged new relationships with the developing world, the USA was demoralized by the extended conflict in Vietnam and the oil crisis of 1973. The aggregation of these events cast the stabilization of 'developed socialism' in an advantageous light.

Brezhnev's domestic policy in the aftermath of the 'Prague Spring' sought to reinforce the authority of the Communist Party. This was formalized with the addition of a new article to the Soviet Constitution in 1977 that defined the Party as the 'leading and guiding force of Soviet society and the nucleus of its political system'.[4] The formal primacy accorded to the Party during Brezhnev's tenure surpassed even the definition of the Party's role in Stalin's 1936 constitution. While the Party was led by a gerontocracy of members who had received promotion during the Stalin era, governance of the country passed largely to the *nomenklatura*, the key administrative officials appointed with the approval of Communist Party leaders. A cult of personality developed around Brezhnev himself, which has led some historians to describe the nearly two decades of his leadership as a 'soft Stalinism'. But representations of Brezhnev's capabilities as a leader belied the steady deterioration of his health. Even after he was virtually debilitated, he retained his leading post. It suited the system of Soviet governance to keep the failing leader in place until the very end.

The stability of this system depended on a sort of 'social contract' between the citizens and the state. A basic component of this relationship was the continued improvement of living standards. Brezhnev's policies would ultimately lead to significant increases in agricultural production during the 1970s. He also pursued a programme of increased consumer goods production. The Ninth Five-year Plan (1971–5) was the first plan that sought to produce more consumer goods than industrial capital goods.[5] While military spending continued to outweigh investment in other areas, basic commodities did become more widely available, particularly in large cities. Other elements of the social contract included job security, low prices for basic goods, toleration of an informal second economy, limited social mobility and the recognition of non-Russian cultural identities. Healthcare, transportation, education and housing were available at virtually no cost to most Soviet citizens. Such a broad provision of goods and services meant, however, that resources were often scarce or simply unavailable for long periods.[6] Queues for consumer products became a ubiquitous feature of the urban landscape. And with about 20 per cent of Moscow's apartments occupied by more than one family in 1979, the wait for a new flat became a common part of everyday life.[7]

Soviet architects served both the material and representational needs of developed socialism. Throughout the 1970s the design and construction complex expanded at a rapid pace. The design institutes that had been created under Khrushchev grew in staff numbers and produced countless projects for building types ranging from apartment houses to theatres. Architects, engineers and builders introduced a new generation of prefabricated building elements which enabled structures to rise higher and accommodate more variation than those implemented in the Khrushchev-era building campaigns. The decade offered architects and planners opportunities to design new cities and vast infrastructural complexes throughout the territory of Russia as capital was invested in the exploitation of natural resources and advantageous industrial locations. Characteristic of this strategy was the rapid development of Naberezhnye Chelny, one of the largest urban projects of the period, which followed the establishment of the Kama Automobile Factory, the largest producer of trucks in the USSR. Likewise, the construction of Brezhnev's signature project, the Baikal-Amur Railway, entailed the development of previously untouched territory and the design and construction of a network of new settlements. In both the capital and provincial cities, architecture and building industries were orientated to the production of grand ensembles – entire urban systems; residential districts for tens of thousands of inhabitants; and vast technological installations. The efforts of these years contributed to the modernization of the Russian built environment. But many observers noted a lack of character in newly built districts. The sea of new buildings – in residential areas in particular – provided a material basis for everyday life, but failed to offer the formal and spatial qualities that had enriched earlier urban forms. This condition solicited calls for a re-evaluation of the formal potential of mass construction.

The architectural profession acquired further differentiation during this period as it devolved into two principal spheres: those who worked primarily in the field of serialized construction and those who worked on unique buildings. The numbers of the former far outstripped the latter. Indeed, a handful of architects were responsible for many of the most prestigious buildings of the era. Mikhail Posokhin, chief architect of Moscow from 1960 to 1984, had his name attached to nearly every major project for the city – from the General Plan of 1971 to the organization of the 1980 Olympic Games.[8] Likewise, the architects of the Central Scientific Research Institute for the Experimental Design of Cultural, Athletic and Administrative Buildings (TSNIIEP zdanii kultury, sporta i upravleniia), which was based in Moscow, produced singular designs for theatres, museums, memorials and other cultural structures throughout the USSR and abroad. Boris Mezentsev, the founding director of the Institute, and Evgenii Rozanov, who directed it from 1970 to 1984, exerted a profound influence on Soviet architectural design.[9] The handful of architects charged with directing the design of major governmental and cultural building projects constituted an elite circle within the Soviet architectural profession. For most members of the Union of Soviet Architects, which had a membership of over 13,000 in 1976, the opportunity to design a singular project remained decidedly out of reach.[10] The tension between serialized and unique design had been a long-standing feature of Soviet architectural production, but it was exacerbated during these years. Such an asymmetrical distribution of labour would produce a sense of professional alienation by the early 1980s, when younger architects sought out alternative modes of practice.

Although the organization of architectural production in the USSR was unique to socialist countries, the concerns of Soviet architects resonated with global architectural practice. Soviet architects monitored the work of advanced capitalist countries with particular sensitivity. During the 1970s discussions of architecture in Western Europe and the United States became more frequent in the pages of *Arkhitektura SSSR*.[11] The Central Scientific Research Institute of the Theory and History of Architecture (TSNII teorii i istorii arkhitektury) published a series of volumes entitled *Arkhitektura zapada* (Architecture of the West) beginning in 1972.[12] These books collected critical essays by Soviet specialists on key architects and architectural themes of the West. The USA, seen as the USSR's counterpart in global politics, received special attention. Andrei Ikonnikov's *Arkhitektura SShA* (Architecture of the USA) of 1979 offered a survey of American architecture from the seventeenth century to the

1970s.[13] Likewise, the Institute of the Theory and History of Architecture devoted significant effort to understanding the architecture of the USA, which was considered representative of the social and economic processes of the 'intensification of the general crisis of capitalism'.[14] This sustained critical engagement with architecture of the West was accompanied by foreign study tours by Soviet architects and building professionals. As a result, Soviet architects were well prepared to respond critically to such key topics of Western architectural theory as contextualism, postmodernism and urban conservation. Architecture also continued to bolster the Soviet Union's image abroad. 'Gifts' of memorial complexes, hydroelectric dams and cultural buildings to countries in East Asia and Africa, in addition to a new generation of embassy buildings, ensured the architectural presence of the USSR over a global geopolitical territory.

## Grand Ensembles

The ratification of the new General Plan for Moscow in 1971 was heralded as a landmark event for Soviet Urbanism. Like the 1935 plan, the document was intended to make Moscow a model socialist city. The plan would become the matrix within which some of the largest projects of the 1970s and early '80s were conceived; it manifested the importance of large-scale architectural and urban thinking characteristic of this period. Mikhail Posokhin and a team of planners had begun work on the new plan nearly a decade earlier, when the municipal boundaries of Moscow were extended to the first ring road. As of 1961, the population of Moscow within the new borders was 6.2 million. The plan of 1971 established a target population of 8 million inhabitants by about 1990, the end of the period it was intended to cover.[15] Moscow was to reach beyond its borders to Moscow Region – including the ring of smaller cities that orbit the capital – to establish a more effective unity of the larger economic zone. Conversely, Moscow was divided into eight planning zones. Whereas the city's urban structure of radial-concentric streets had developed a monocentric core, the new planning document sought to distribute productive, residential and cultural resources in a more balanced fashion. The central planning zone encompassed the historical city within the Garden Ring. This zone was also the heart of the 'general city centre' (*obshchegorodskoi tsentr*) – a structure devised to link the historical centre with the peripheral planning zones through the controlled development of social centres along radial axes. New building within the centre was to adapt to its historical structure; the seven peripheral zones offered greater room for experiment. According to Posokhin, the aim of the plan was to create an ensemble, 'an architectural unity in

Moscow, general plan of 1971; schema of the development of the urban centre.

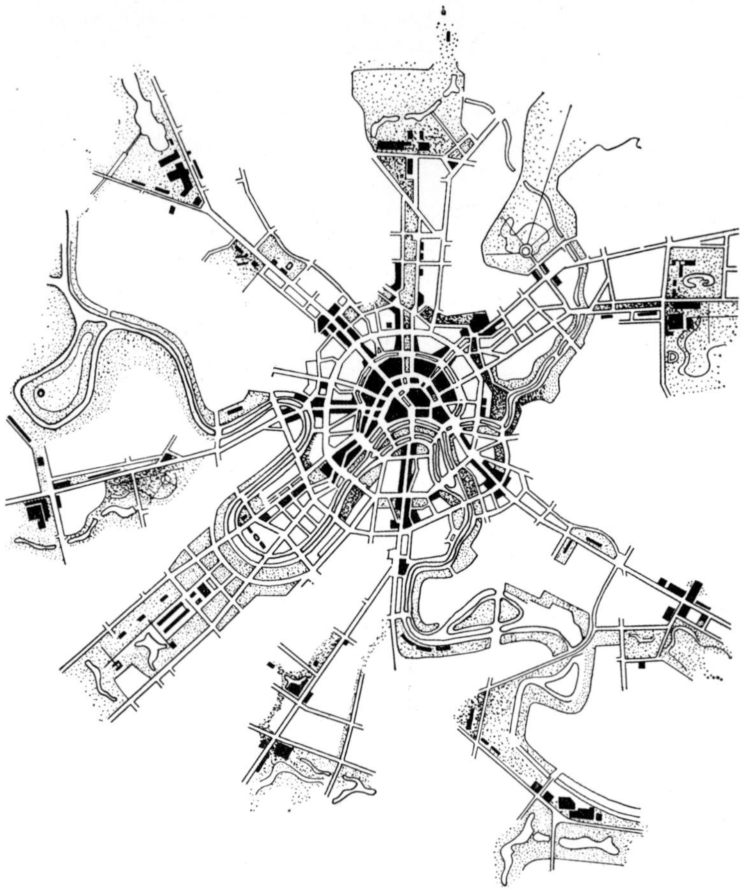

the construction of districts, streets and squares according to a single urban concept'.[16]

The approval of the general plan paved the way for the detailed planning of Moscow's districts. The proposed shift from a monocentric to a polycentric urban structure required the design of new social and cultural centres for the peripheral planning zones. These centres in turn provided the opportunity for large-scale formal experiment. It was recognized that each centre should in some way characterize its respective district, while establishing functional links with publicly accessible green space. Moscow's design institutes held a competition in 1972 to explore how these districts might be organized. The plan foresaw the construction of 40–60-storey buildings in zonal centres, and most participants proposed multifunctional high-rises. Commentators described these as universal structures that could incorporate administrative and scientific spaces with theatres, concert halls, museums, restaurants and transport infrastructures. Such buildings were intended to provide a 'high density of information exchange and a multiplicity of social contacts'.[17] Although not named as such, this competition displayed a clear, albeit belated, engagement with the concept of the megastructure that had developed in advanced capitalist countries.[18] The project by A. Bekker's team for the southeastern district represents a typical entry. An elevated roadway establishes a spine of development around which curvilinear structures are disposed. These buildings house a theatre, a library, a palace of culture, a hotel and other facilities, thus constituting a cultural centre in what had previously been Moscow's periphery. A vast urban park complements the dense structure of the centre. The ensemble's plastic silhouette and complex volumetric modelling offer a glimpse of the innovative urban forms developed within the framework of the 1971 plan.

A. Bekker and others, project for residential centre in the southeast district, Moscow, 1972.

Residential districts remained the fundamental units of the new plan. Each of the eight planning zones was intended to have a population of between 600,000 and one million inhabitants. Zones were subdivided into three or four planning districts of 250,000–400,000 residents; these were in turn subdivided into smaller residential units.[19] Although the figures for residential construction between 1961 and 1970 were staggering – about 36 million square metres of living space had been built during this time – there remained a serious housing shortage in Moscow. The plan prescribed an increase of the existing housing stock by 150 per cent and established new standards for the allocation of space within apartments. By the end of the period covered by the plan, every family was to have its own apartment and every adult was to have his or her own room. Thirteen and a half square metres of living space – as opposed to total space – per inhabitant became the target norm.[20]

The programme of residential construction proposed by the plan was a response to the 1969 decree from the Communist Party 'On the means of improving the quality of residential civil construction'. This document noted that the typified projects for apartment buildings that had served as a basis for mass construction did not fully meet the living standards of their inhabitants. Moreover, the document recognized that type-projects developed for Moscow were unsuitable for use in the Soviet Union's variety of extreme climatic zones. The decree called on architects to produce nearly 1,500 new type-projects for residential buildings in the period 1969–71. It also projected a shift in residential construction to a 'flexible technology for the machine production of the elements of apartment buildings'.[21] The decree can be understood as part of Brezhnev's effort to differentiate his housing initiatives from Khrushchev's without deviating from the established programme of industrialized construction.

Yet the response offered by architects and engineers to the 1969 decree amounted to a fundamental reconceptualization of the process of industrialized construction. The type-projects of the 1950s and early 1960s offered details for the complete residential building, from staircases to kitchens. Each type or 'series' required the production of a unique assortment of building components, which could be mass produced but were not interchangeable between types. This led to the unnecessary duplication of elements – wall units, floor plates and so on – from series to series, even when dimensions differed by as little as 10–20 cm. Between 1969 and 1972 the Moscow Scientific Research Institute of Experimental Design, directed by Lev Diubek, developed a system of 'open typification' in which building elements, not entire buildings, would be produced as an interchangeable set of components. Codified in the 'Unified Catalogue of Standardized Prefabricated Building Elements', this system was first introduced in Moscow's building industry. It was based on a module of 60 cm and offered a set of components that enabled the construction of buildings between nine and 25 storeys tall.[22] The implementation of this system marked a dramatic shift away from the five-storey apartment blocks characteristic of the first generation of industrialized housing towards a more flexible and varied set of types.

The new approach to construction was manifested in the residential districts designated for development in the 1971 plan of Moscow. Troparevo, in the city's southwestern district, was one of the first residential districts to be constructed according to the new system. Begun in 1970, the district was designed by A. Bergelson, G. Gavrilov, V. Korkina and M. Posokhin. Here, a series of sixteen-storey apartment buildings were constructed to the designs of A. B. Samsonov and V.I. Korkina in 1971–2 using the Unified Catalogue. The rhythm created by alternating

Sixteen-storey apartment buildings, based on the Unified Building Catalogue, Troparevo, 1971–2.

Ivanovskoe (model), Moscow, begun 1973.

groups of balconies and loggias lent variety to the broad facades, while effective interior planning made the project a prototype for many buildings in Moscow of the decade.[23] Elsewhere in Moscow, new districts were planned at an unprecedented scale. To the east, just inside the ring road, the Ivanovskoe residential district began construction in 1973. Designed by V. Lebedev and others, the estate occupied 117 hectares and had a population of 60,000. The primary elements of the district are extremely long nine-storey apartment blocks that curve to enclose interior courts 200 m wide. Iasenevo, one of the city's largest residential districts, began construction in 1975. Set amid a picturesque landscape just within the southwestern stretch of the ring road, Iasenevo occupies 700 hectares and houses 220,000 people. Buildings varying from nine to 25 storeys in height are disposed symmetrically in subgroups on either side of a central park space. The design by Iakov Belopolskii's team demonstrated the potential of industrialized construction to create a rich and varied urban landscape on a sublime scale.[24]

While most of the residential districts constructed within the framework of the 1971 plan were intended to serve immediate needs for housing on the basis of contemporary technology, another class of projects sought to explore future living conditions. The 'experimental residential district' of Severnoe Chertanovo, begun in 1972, served as a laboratory for testing building technologies and spatial arrangements in advance of widespread implementation. The complex was designed by a team of architects led by Mikhail Posokhin and Lev Diubek. The aim of the experiment was to create a model of a communist residential district as it might appear in 1990, the expiration date of the 1971 plan. It was to be a complete functional and aesthetic urban unit that incorporated progressive service systems and expanded spatial norms. Severnoe Chertanovo was relatively small compared to contemporary projects for Moscow, with a target population of 20,000–22,000 people. Residential buildings are grouped around a platform with public services and amenities – schools, athletics facilities, a shopping centre, a cultural centre and other facilities. A system of underground roads and parking spaces ensures the removal of vehicles from the green space above. At 'service centres' within the enlarged vestibules of each building, one could order groceries, everyday items and even prepared meals. The planning of individual apartments was innovative as well. Adopting the norm of 13.5 square metres of living space per person, Posokhin and Diubek developed a series of plans for apartments of one to five rooms. The largest apartments were split over two levels.[25] Outside, the reinforced concrete construction of the buildings is clearly visible – its hypertrophic details recall a range of precedents in advanced capitalist countries. The meandering plans of the buildings

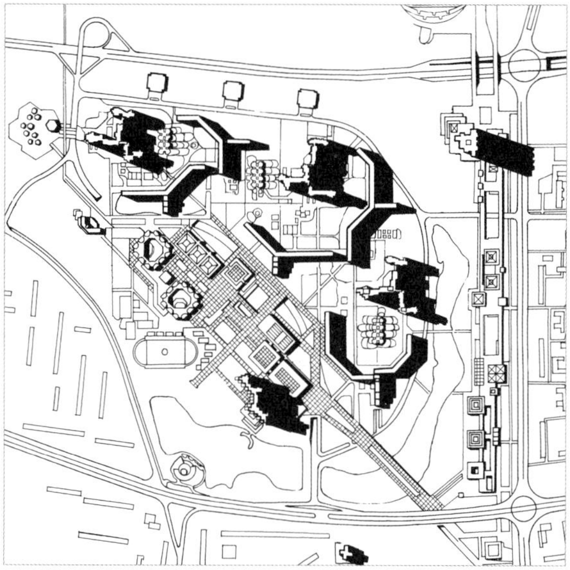

M. Posokhin and others, Severnoe Chertanovo, Moscow, begun 1972; general plan.

Severnoe Chertanovo, Moscow.

give the complex a picturesque character, while the elevated passages between blocks lend dynamic unity to the ensemble.

Although Severnoe Chertanovo was not completed until about 1990, it came to serve as a model for experimental residential design by the second half of the 1970s. By this time, experimental design had become an area of collaboration between the USSR and the German Democratic Republic. An agreement of cooperation between the two countries was approved in 1976, leading to a productive exchange of research and design expertise between the Soviet Central Institute for Experimental Residential Design (TSNIIEP zhilishcha) and the Academy of Construction of the GDR.[26] The most important product of this initiative was the decision to conduct collaborative research at specific building sites in the GDR and the USSR. In mutual consultation, teams of Soviet and East German designers developed two new experimental districts for 25,000 inhabitants each in Magdeburg and Gorky (Nizhniy Novgorod).[27] The residential complexes Neu Olvenstedt and Meshcherskoe Ozero, in Magdeburg and Gorky respectively, grew out of this collaboration.[28] They remain a testament to architectural cooperation within the socialist bloc.

In addition to the expansion of existing cities, the 1970s also witnessed the creation of new towns, often in remote regions of Soviet territory. Promoted as the 'largest urban complex of the Tenth Five-year plan (1976–80)', Naberezhnye Chelny grew from a city of 55,000 in 1971 to a city of 375,000 a decade later. This rapid growth was driven by the construction of the Kama Automobile factory, which became an engine of economic development in Tatarstan in the early 1970s. Directed by Boris Rubanenko of TSNIIEP zhilishcha, Naberezhnye Chelny was designed and constructed in an extraordinarily short period of time.[29] The general plan for the city was approved in 1973, and three years later the first residential districts had already been completed. The city centre manifested novel

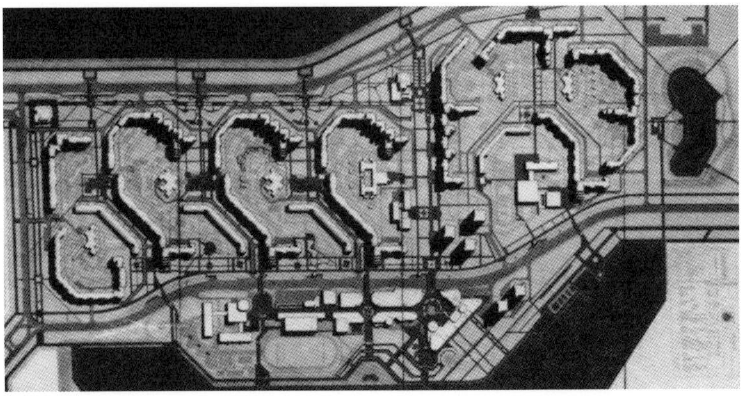

Experimental residential complex 'Meshcherskoe Ozero', Nizhniy Novgorod, begun 1975.

Naberezhnye Chelny, central esplanade; planning directed by B. R. Rubanenko and V. A. Shkvarikov; plan approved 1973.

planning concepts. Public buildings, parks and demonstration spaces occupied the surface of a raised platform. Automobiles were directed around and below this central esplanade, leaving it free for pedestrian use. This expansive public space was to be linked to cultural, commercial and residential structures through a continuous pedestrian zone.

The largest ensemble of the 1970s was not a single city, but rather a network of cities linked by a new infrastructural artery – the Baikal-Amur Mainline Railway (BAM). This railway was intended to stimulate the development of industry in Siberia and the Russian Far East. Passing north of Lake Baikal, the line extends more than 3,500 km, from Taishet in the west, where it branches north from the Trans-Siberian Railway, to Sovetskaia Gavan, on the Pacific Ocean. The chief architect of BAM, Vladimir Butuzov, compared the length of the line to the distance between Moscow and Lisbon.[30] When BAM was initiated by Brezhnev in 1974, it was promoted as 'the project of the era of developed socialism'.[31] Completion of the line required the creation of 60 new cities and settlements along the route. Tynda, the so-called capital of BAM, became a major centre of architectural and urban development over the course of the construction of the mainline. It grew from a small village to a city of 35,000 in only three years. The smaller cities along the route supported the construction of the railway and engaged in the extraction of various natural resources: oil, gas, asbestos and nickel, among other materials. The geographic and climatic variety along the line would inevitably lend each of these settlements a distinct character. However, as chief architect, Butuzov considered it his task to ensure that each element of this system would be recognizable as part of the larger whole so that 'anyone arriving would feel that he is in the region of BAM and nowhere else'.[32] Conceived as a unitary project, BAM constituted the largest ensemble of developed socialism.

## 'Individual Constructions'

In contrast to the mass production characteristic of the USSR's grand ensembles of the 1970s, the so-called 'individual constructions' and 'unique buildings' of the period manifested a wide range of architectural expression. Unlike type-projects, individual constructions were singular buildings. Their features were adjusted to a specific place, tailored to a specific institution and given a unique form. Although they were the products of distinct approaches to architectural design, individual and typical projects were understood to be complementary elements of Soviet architectural production. Because they demanded more labour and resources, this mode of production was typically reserved for public and cultural buildings: museums, memorials, resorts, theatres and other prestigious typologies. Likewise, the opportunity to design individual buildings was given only to the elite members of the profession.

The individual constructions that emerged from the design institutes during the 1970s did not represent a single stylistic trend. The architect Mikhail Barkhin attributed this to the lack of a strong architectural 'school' in the decade. Le Corbusier had been a model during the 1920s; Ivan Zholtovskii and Georgii Golts were models from the 1930s to the '50s. 'The "role models" of our day have been Mies van der Rohe, Paul Rudolph, Louis Kahn and others', Barkhin wrote.[33] While images of 'scientific-technical progress' had been fashionable during the 1960s, the formal research of those years appeared unable to sustain further investigation. As Barkhin noted, the impact of foreign architectural production on Soviet architectural design is readily apparent in many

Boris Mezentsev and others, Lenin Memorial, Ulyanovsk, 1969–74.

E. Rozanov, V. Shestopalov and others, Lenin Museum, Tashkent, 1967–70.

projects of the decade. This was due in part to a broader engagement with global architectural culture. It also reflected a set of architectural concerns shared by Soviet architects and their colleagues in the advanced capitalist world.

The centenary of Lenin's birth in 1970 was commemorated in a variety of architectural forms. The most important monument to the Bolshevik leader was the Lenin Memorial in Ulyanovsk (1969–74), the city of Lenin's birth, designed by the Central Institute for Cultural Buildings and its director, Boris Mezentsev.[34] Mezentsev had previously designed mausoleums for the Mongolian revolutionary Damdin Sükhbaatar in Ulaanbaatar (1952) and Ho Chi Minh in Hanoi (completed in 1970). While these earlier memorials drew explicitly on iconography established by Aleksei Shchusev's design for Lenin's tomb in Moscow, the Ulyanovsk memorial spoke a language of international modernism. Including a museum, an auditorium, a screening room and a ceremonial hall, the primary mass of the building is square in plan and elevated on a forest of pillars, leaving much of the ground plane open. This solution would be unthinkable without reference to Le Corbusier's work, both to his Villa Savoye and his later museums for Tokyo and Ahmedabad. Small structures in which Lenin lived as a child stand in the courtyard of the Ulyanovsk memorial, while a sculpture in white Ural marble occupies the ceremonial hall. As the Ulyanovsk Memorial was being designed and built, Evgenii Rozanov and Vladimir Shestopalov, who worked in the institute Mezentsev directed, were overseeing the completion of a branch of the Lenin Museum in Tashkent (1967–70).[35] This structure, like the Ulyanovsk building, took the form of an elevated box containing a ceremonial space

Central Museum of Lenin, Moscow, 1970; competition project, Mezentsev Institute.

devoted to Lenin. But the authors of the Tashkent museum sought to adapt the structure to its context by drawing on Uzbek folk motifs in the design of the *brise soleil* that encloses the upper portion of the museum.

The typology of the Lenin Museum was further developed in a series of competitions for a Central Museum of Lenin in Moscow between 1969 and 1972.[36] Most projects submitted to these competitions adopted the solution of the elevated, horizontal box seen at Ulyanovsk and Tashkent. In the third round of the competition, architects from Mezentsev's institute explored the possibility of locating the museum on the site intended for the Palace of the Soviets in the city centre, which had subsequently been transformed into a pool. This project included a monumental sculpture of Lenin standing atop a podium, recalling a monumental verticality not witnessed in Soviet architectural competitions since the Stalin era.[37]

The early 1970s brought Soviet architecture to an international stage when a Soviet project was given a special mention by the jury of the competition for a centre of contemporary art in the Beaubourg quarter of Paris. While Richard Rogers and Renzo Piano would ultimately design the Centre Pompidou, the competition of 1971 was the first occasion on which a Soviet architectural project was recognized in an international arena. The design submitted by Iurii Platonov and his team from the design bureau of the Academy of Sciences (GIPRONII) was one of 29

Iurii Platonov and others, competition project for a contemporary art centre, Paris, 1971.

submissions from the USSR out of a total of nearly 700 submissions.[38] Platonov had previously been a lead designer on Moscow's Museum of Palaeontology (1969–83), which is composed of solid brick pierced by square windows and sculptural circulation towers. The project for Paris marked a distinct departure: twelve semi-autonomous cubes support interior platforms, the outlines of which change from floor to floor, while the surfaces of the cubes themselves are opened up by gaping, circular apertures. The monumental scale implied by the project and the powerful interplay between positive and negative volumes respond directly to Louis Kahn's work in Dhaka and Ahmedabad. The Soviet press made little mention of Platonov's relationship to Kahn and hailed the project as a success, despite the fact that it would not be realized. Only 42 years old when he entered the competition, Platonov would create a number of unique buildings in the ensuing years. The Presidium of the Academy of Sciences of the USSR (1973–90) in Moscow was his most important realization. Traces of his project for Paris can be found in the decision to organize the Presidium according to a square module.[39]

Sanatoria and hotels – building types for escaping the rhythm of the ordinary – were favoured sites for the display of formal innovation during the 1970s. Ilia Cherniavskii, director of a design office of the Central Institute of Resort and Tourist Complexes (TSNIIEP kurortno-turisticheskikh kompleksov) from 1966, produced a ground-breaking series of pensions just outside Moscow.[40] His 'Voronovo' Pension for the State

Ilia Cherniavskii, 'Voronovo' Pension, near Moscow, 1966–74.

Planning agency (1966–74), his finest work, occupies the park-like territory of a former country estate to the southwest of Moscow. Composed of a communal block and a serrated residential wing, the building both adapts elegantly to its site and demonstrates the extent to which the forms and strategies associated with 'brutalism' had been absorbed.[41] Cherniavskii's building is complex in plan, section and elevation. The main block houses a pool and a variety of public spaces situated on several levels. The building's exterior details – enlarged water spouts, emphatic trabeation – recall elements drawn from an international field of sources. As a whole, the complex makes a powerful impression; the critic Andrei Gozak compared it to a train that had come to halt, but which still appeared to move.[42] 'Voronovo' was one of many innovative resorts constructed in natural reserves and coastal regions during the 1970s.

V. Kuzmin, E. Gorkin, I. Nikova, E. Zorina, Central House of the Tourist and Hotel Center, Moscow, 1970–80.

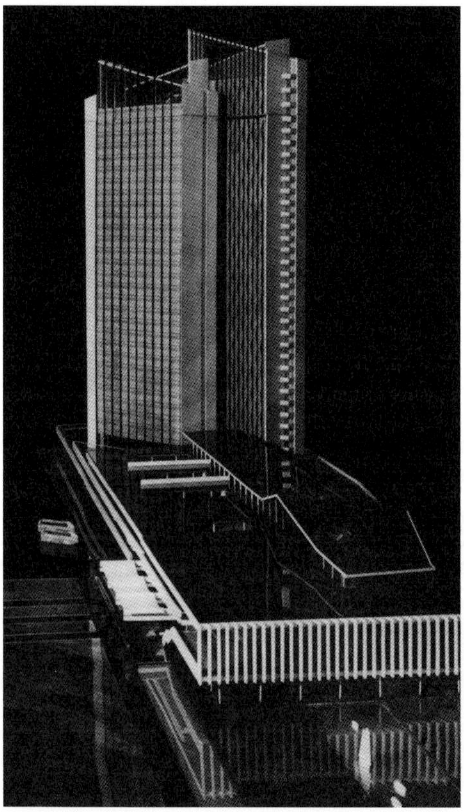

The individual treatment of leisure architecture also affected the production of hotels. Like the Intourist Hotel in Moscow (1960–69), hotels of the 1960s were typically located in city centres and often resembled administrative office blocks.[43] A new, sculptural class of hotels emerged in the 1970s. The dynamic interplay of the towers and elongated base of the Central House of the Tourist in Moscow (1970–80), by Viktor Kuzmin and others, establishes a strong visual landmark on the southwestern reaches of Leninskii Prospect. In Leningrad, the Pribaltiskaia Hotel (1969–78) became the centrepiece of the city's 'sea facade'. Designed by Nikolai Baranov, Sergei Evdokimov and others, and built by a Swedish construction firm, the hotel overlooks the Gulf of Finland from a new residential district on Vasilevskii Island. The monumental canted wings of its H-shaped plan open up to embrace the sea.[44]

Despite the general emphasis on the serial production of housing, some apartment buildings were built according to individual designs. Among this group, Vsevolod Voskresenskii's so-called Apartment Building for 1,000 Flats (1972–8) in Moscow is perhaps the largest. Close to 400 m long and fifteen storeys high, the building creates an urban wall. The design of the larger flats in the upper levels as maisonettes recalls earlier prototypes such as

N. N. Baranov, S. I. Evdokimov and V. I. Kovaleva, Pribaltiskaia Hotel, St Petersburg, 1969–78.

the Narkomfin Building (1928–30). Voskresenskii conceived the building as a self-contained residential complex complete with internal residential services. In this, and its elevation on colossal pillars, the structure is related to Le Corbusier's Unité d'Habitation (1947–52) in Marseille. Le Corbusier's Unité also served as a model for the most controversial apartment building of the 1970s in Moscow: the apartment building on Begovaia Street (1967–78) by A. Meerson, E. Podolskaia and others. The building is popularly known as the 'house on knives' for the shape of the supports on which the apartment block rests. In addition to Le Corbusier, the building's tough concrete forms owe something to the work of Kunio Maekawa and Basil Spence.[45] Heavily articulated balconies run in vertical tracts across the facade, while cast-in-place concrete stairwells add a sculptural dimension to the structure. The building on Begovaia Street looked radically different from the type-projects that had become ubiquitous features of Moscow's cityscape. And even before it was completed the building was criticized as a mere 'pursuit for originality', indicating a scepticism among some in the building industry about the value of individual projects for residential construction.[46]

The cultural significance of the theatre was reflected in the individual attention devoted to this building type in Russian and Soviet cities. In 1973 the new building of the Moscow Artistic Theatre (MKhAT) opened on Tverskoi Boulevard. Begun in 1965 and designed by Vladimir Kubasov, A. Morgulis and V. Uliashov, the theatre served as a satellite venue for the building Feodor Shekhtel had designed in 1902 for the same

A. Meerson, E. Podolskaia, M. Mostovoi and G. Klimenko, residential complex, Moscow, 1967–78.

V. Kubasov, A. Morgulis and V. Uliashov, MKhAT, Moscow, 1972–3.

D. Lure, N. Stuzhin, N. Belousova, Musical Theatre, Omsk, 1970–81.

institution a short distance away. Widely considered Russia's most important theatre, the building demanded corresponding architectural treatment. Kubasov and his team conceived their project as a 'temple of art' and imbued the structure with a monumental character, despite its difficult site and building conditions.[47] The exterior is clad in tufa, lending the structure a strong presence on the street. The texture of the cladding is amplified in the rustication of the podium on which it stands. Tufa is also used in the interior spaces, where it contrasts with the rough plaster finish of the walls. The irregular channels of these surfaces recall both the modern lines of Shekhtel's building and the bush-hammered concrete surfaces popular the world over during the 1960s and '70s. While few theatres could compete with the MKhAT in the capital, theatre buildings were important in regional centres as well. The Musical Theatre in Omsk (1970–81), designed by D. Lure and others in the Central Institute of Cultural Buildings, broke with the conventional organization of theatre buildings. By placing a painting studio above the theatre fly tower, they were able to unite all the functions of a working theatre under a single, sweeping roof. The combination of volumetric clarity and dynamic form in the Omsk theatre was a singular achievement in the design of cultural buildings.

Moscow's successful bid to host the 1980 Summer Olympic Games required the construction of a wide range of new buildings. This included both athletic facilities and new tourist infrastructure. Moscow commissioned the German architectural firm von Gerkan Marg und Partner to design a new international airport for the city – today's Sheremetevo-2 (1974–80). The firm had completed Berlin's Tegel Airport in 1975, and they applied the hexagonal geometry of the German building to their Moscow project. Although von Gerkan Marg und Partner's design would

Olympic Athletic Complex, Moscow, 1977–80.

be altered during construction, the terminal served as a primary 'aerial gate' to the games.[48] In order to accommodate the visitors to the games, Moscow constructed a series of new hotels with an aggregate capacity for approximately 25,000 guests. The 'Izmailovo' Hotel Complex (1977–80), designed by a team led by D. Burdin, could house 10,000 people. Most athletics venues were distributed throughout Moscow and its immediate surroundings.[49] Each site was given distinctive architectural treatment. The Central Olympic Complex (1977–80), designed by Mikhail Posokhin and others, is a monumental ellipse with a capacity of 35,000. The Football and Athletic Complex of the Red Army (1976–9) was among the most striking venues of the games. As Andrei Ikonnikov has pointed out, its detailing reflected the strong interest in post-Second World War Japanese architecture among Soviet architects.[50] Together with the many other buildings constructed for the games, these structures established an archipelago of buildings for sport and tourism that remains an active part of everyday life in Moscow. The diversity of form in the individual designs created for the Olympic Games also reflects the range of architectural expression found in new buildings throughout the USSR.

## Modernism, Postmodernism and Tradition

Despite the variety of unique projects built in Russian and Soviet cities in the 1970s, by the end of the decade large parts of the architectural profession became dissatisfied with the conventions of Soviet architectural design. Increasing numbers of architects came to regard the urban landscape and its sparse population of individual constructions as a monotonous field of urban infrastructure. The uniformity of the built environment had been a concern since the full-scale industrialization of construction, but at the end of the 1970s this condition had become critical. This concern was expressed both by practitioners and theorists. Aleksandr Riabushin, Secretary of the Union of Architects and one of the most perceptive critics of his generation, addressed this problem with a call for the reform of the 'administrative machine' that considered only the 'narrow utilitarian and technical' aspect of architecture. At a conference on architecture and ideology in 1982, he stated that Soviet architects 'must critically evaluate the current state and new tendencies of our creative practice, giving attention to the real expectations of Soviet people, their desire for varied, rich architecture that is nationally and historically inflected'.[51] This call for change conveyed the widely felt sentiment that Soviet architecture should be more than a branch of the building industry – that it had a fundamental role to play in the definition and communication of cultural values.

Efforts to redefine Soviet architecture's relationship to history, nationality and communication coincided with the emergence of the range of positions that collectively gave rise to postmodernism in the architecture of the capitalist West. Soviet architects were keenly aware of this convergence of interests, and they engaged directly with the work of their western counterparts. As early as 1972, portions of Robert Venturi's book *Complexity and Contradiction in Architecture* (1966), which initiated a sweeping re-evaluation of architectural practice, were included in one of the most widely read compilations of 'Western' architectural theory.[52] Critical debate on the concept of postmodernism unfolded in the pages of the USSR's leading architecture and design publications. Charles Jencks's book *The Language of Postmodern Architecture* (1977) was widely discussed; it would appear in Russian translation in 1985.[53] While Soviet critics generally applauded the critique of 'functionalism' offered by Western postmodernism, there remained a general anxiety about the ideological stakes of postmodernism for Soviet practice. Some dismissed postmodernism as an expression of capitalism's dominant ideology. Others sought to learn from the new ideas and projects coming out of the West. Riabushin and the critic Vladimir Khait were among these

A. Larin and E. Asse, Pharmacy No. 375, Orekhovo-Borisovo, Moscow, 1973–5.

enthusiasts. In 1979, in one of the first assessments of postmodernism to appear in the Soviet press, they proposed that it would be possible to 'cleanse' the newly developed professional methods of the bourgeois ideology out of which they had been born. Recalling the revival of interest in historical forms among Soviet architects in the 1930s, Riabushin and Khait argued for the 'critical assimilation' of the principles developed by Western postmodernists.[54] But this was not an invitation to Soviet architects to imitate their Western colleagues; on the contrary, it signalled the recognition that a set of architectural values had obtained global significance in the industrialized world, in both capitalist and socialist societies. Projects proposed and executed by Soviet architects from the mid-1970s onwards manifested these values.

Communication was a pressing concern for architects who were dissatisfied with the monotonous built environment characteristic of developed socialism. Architects sought to enrich their work by using conventional signs as architectural forms and by deploying standardized elements in new syntactical arrangements. Aleksandr Larin and Evgenii Asse developed the concept of the 'building-sign' (*zdanie znak*) in their Pharmacy No. 375 (1973–5) in the Orekhovo-Borisovo district of Moscow. The building combines a low, box-like building, and an entry facade in the shape of a cross.[55] Painted bright red, the cross stands out from the white ground of the rest of the building and offers a stark contrast to the surrounding residential towers. While some have compared the cross on this building to the Suprematist forms of Kazimir Malevich's paintings, it conjures immediate associations with medical practice and the care of the self. Viktor Lebedev also pursued this search for a speaking architecture in a project for a 'monument-sign' to the snipers of the Great Patriotic War (1978) in the shape of a circular target. Other architects created communicative buildings by assembling architectural components in unusual combinations. This was the approach adopted by Sergei Shmakov and V. V. Meliakovaia for their kindergarten on Dzhambul Lane in Leningrad (1980–83). Here, the unconventional use of standard building elements – drainpipes, heating elements and other technical details – lent the building a festive variety appropriate to the character of a kindergarten. When the building was completed, one critic compared its communicative forms to 'masonic symbols'.[56]

Soviet architects participated in the broad revision of architecture's relationship to history and historical context that unfolded in many parts

S. Shmakov and V. Meliakovaia, kindergarten, Leningrad, 1980–83.

Leonid Pavlov, V. I. Lenin Museum, Gorky Leninskie, 1975–87.

of the globe during the 1970s and '80s. The Soviet interest in historical forms is evident in both individual buildings and urban development programmes. Leonid Pavlov's Lenin Museum in Gorky Leninskie (1975–87), where Lenin's dacha was located just south of Moscow, combined minimalist volumes and ancient architectural forms to create an austere and monumental museum. While the main block of the building is composed of hollow cubic volumes that enclose a central exposition space, the entry is marked by a freestanding portico. The cylindrical shafts of the columns terminate in cubic pseudo-capitals, recalling the form and scale of structures from ancient Egypt. Other architects looked to the more recent past for inspiration. The apartment building on Gorky Street (now Tverskaia) by Zinovii Rozenfeld and others (1976–7) responds not to forms of the distant past but to the conventions established in the reconstruction of Gorky Street between the 1930s and 1950s – during the Stalin era. Indeed, the rhythmic articulation of the facade with projecting bay windows recalls Rozenfeld's apartment building on Sadovaia-Triumfalnaia Street (1949), located a short distance from the 1970s building. One of the largest projects to integrate new construction with historical forms was the reconstruction of Arbat Street in Moscow (1974–86). 'Old Arbat', as the reconstructed pedestrian zone came to be known, offered a vision of urbanity radically opposed to the automobile-oriented 'New Arbat' only a short distance away. The lead designers of Old Arbat, Mikhail Posokhin, Aleksei Gutnov and Z. Kharitonova, sought to modernize the street while retaining its historical character and

Z. Rozenfeld, V. Orlov, D. Alekseev, apartment building on Gorky St, Moscow, 1976–7.

M. V. Posokhin and others, Arbat pedestrian zone, project, 1974–86.

the specificity of its morphology. As they noted, the historical value of the district derived from the spatial structure of the small streets and alleys that date to the reconstruction of Moscow after the routing of Napoleon's forces and the fire that devastated the city in 1812.[57] The reconstruction of the street entailed the renovation of existing theatres and restaurants, as well as the construction of new shops, cafés and sites for entertainment. Old Arbat remains one of the most popular tourist destinations in the city to this day.

In addition to drawing on ancient architectural forms and contextual clues, some Soviet architects attempted to incorporate forms and motifs derived from vernacular building traditions into projects of the 1970s and early '80s. Typically, such projects were constructed at sites outside Russia, and at times beyond the borders of the USSR. Felix Novikov and G. Saevich sought to give the USSR Embassy to Mauritania (1973–7), in Nouakchott, a form appropriate to the climate and artistic traditions of the small Islamic republic. The embassy buildings are composed of blind, white walls with chamfered corners. Novikov did not visit Mauritania – or anywhere in Africa – before the design was complete, and he has described how impressions from Uzbekistan informed his understanding of the traditions characteristic of Mauritania.[58] Novikov would later apply a similar approach to unrealized projects for tourist centres in Samarkand and Bukhara (both 1980–83). Andrei Kosinskii, a Moscow-trained architect who worked in Tashkent from 1966 to 1980, took a different approach to national forms in his work. His first buildings in Uzbekistan focused on creating industrialized building components for sun protection in the hot, arid climate of Central Asia. But in his National Bathhouse in Tashkent (1973–7), Kosinskii assimilated and reworked the

Felix Novikov, G. Saevich, USSR Embassy in Nouakchott, Mauritania, 1973–7.

Andrei Kosinskii, Georgii Grigoriants, National Bathhouse (hammam), Tashkent, 1973–7.

E. Rozanov and others, Palace of the Friendship of Peoples, Tashkent, 1970–81.

vaulted structures of traditional Uzbek architecture. He also employed Uzbek craftsmen in the construction of the building. Its rich colour palette of blues and earth tones recalled vernacular building traditions, but its unusual massing and composition would be described by critics as characteristic elements of Kosinskii's 'strange architecture'.[59] While Kosinskii's work was considered idiosyncratic, other attempts to integrate national traditions into contemporary design were lauded as landmarks in Soviet architectural practice; Evgenii Rozanov's Palace of the Friendship of Peoples in Tashkent (1970–81) was among the most significant. The

D. Chechulin and others, Government House of the Soviets of the RSFSR, Moscow, completed 1981.

Nikolari Baranov (with Shestopalov and others), Regional Headquarters of the KPSS, Yaroslavl, 1981.

building's cubic volume is wrapped in an envelope of abstract geometric forms that suggest affinities with the decorative muqarnas vaults of the religious monuments of Samarkand and Bukhara. The synthesis achieved by Rozanov was a paradigmatic response to the search for a nationally and historically inflected architecture that occupied Soviet architects in the second half of the 1970s. It was also an indication that the motto 'national in form, socialist in content', which was coined in the 1930s, was still operative.

Within the territory of Russia, the search for a historically informed architecture gave birth to a generation of large, usually administrative, buildings that adopted monumental, pseudo-classical forms. It was in the context of this search that Dmitrii Chechulin designed the House of the Soviets of the Russian Soviet Federative Socialist Republics (completed 1981). Known today as the Government House of the Russian Federation, or simply the 'White House', the design was a loose reinterpretation of Chechulin's project of 1934 for the headquarters of the Aeroflot National Airline. The completed building is faced in white marble, and its broad forecourt opens towards the Moskva River. The vertical lines of the main office block are emphasized by projecting piers. While explicit references to classical forms are rare, the building nonetheless conveys a sense of immensity appropriate for the seat of a national bureaucracy. The regional headquarters of the Communist Party in Yaroslavl (completed 1981), by Nikolai Baranov and others, displays the features shared by a range of administrative buildings of the late 1970s and early '80s. Encased in colossal piers, the building boasts a monumental entry that consists of faux-arches at ground level and a bulky sculptural frieze above. The building, and others like it, appears as an imposing grey mass, not unlike the Party officials who occupied it.

While the search for an expressive architectural language initiated in the 1970s would continue well into the following decade, one event of 1982 brought the unresolved tensions within Soviet architectural culture into sharp focus: the competition for a new home for the Academy of Fine Arts of the USSR in Moscow. Despite the small number of entries – only eight were submitted – the jury and other commentators understood the event as an important moment in Soviet architectural design. Riabushin wrote that the discussion of the competition projects was in fact a discussion of the 'future path of development of our architecture as a whole'.[60] But the entries did not indicate a clear path forward at all. They ranged from Grigorii Zakharov's project, which seemed to many to be a direct return to the principles of the Stalinist 1940s and '50s, to Evgenii Rozanov's and Iakov Belopolskii's projects, each of which reinterpreted pre-Renaissance Russian forms. Mikhail Posokhin's project, which was

Mikhail Posokhin, N. I. Pyshkin, S. I. Nekrasov, S. I. Kulev, Academy of Fine Arts of the USSR, Competition Project, 1982.

awarded first prize, combined a portico in the shape of a triumphal arch and a centralized plan. It was described as a 'combination of contemporary interpretations of Roman-baroque classicism'.[61] In the published discussions of the projects, it emerged that many participants and commentators felt the works submitted raised serious problems for Soviet architectural design. Anatolii Polianskii identified the most pressing of these as the 'retro problem'. The formal tendencies visible in projects for the Academy of Fine Arts induced an anxiety about the possible re-emergence of the 'decorativism' of a bygone era.[62] This shift in the direction of Soviet architectural practice was one aspect of a broad dialogue with postmodernist approaches hailing from the West, but it also suggested that Soviet architects were tentatively engaging in the kind of formal excess that had been denounced less than 30 years earlier. Although this issue would remain unresolved, the competition made visible a more acute problem of Soviet architectural culture: with only eight entries, the event was characteristic of the widening gap of professional opportunity between the circle of architectural elites and the majority of practising architects. This problem would be exacerbated in the following years, leading a younger generation of architects to seek out a mode of practice beyond the Soviet design bureaucracy – a mode of practice that might offer conceptual and formal freedom to the individual designer.

ISSN 0004—19

# АРХ

АРХИТЕКТУРА СССР

март-апрель 1989

chapter nine

# From *Perestroika* to 'Capitalist Realism', 1983 to the Present

Tanks rolled into Moscow on the morning of 19 August 1991, occupying key sites throughout the city: television stations, newspaper offices, Lenin Hills and Moscow City Hall. They converged on the 'White House', the colloquial name for the Government House of the Russian Soviet Federative Republic (RSFSR), located on the embankment of the Moscow River in the city centre. Completed only a decade earlier to designs by Dmitrii Chechulin, the building became a stage for political theatre in the early 1990s. The tanks were called in by the so-called State Executive Committee, which had been organized to oppose the impending dissolution of the USSR. While Mikhail Gorbachev, still general secretary of the Communist Party, was on holiday in Crimea, the members of the Committee seized state power, declaring on national television that 'the policy of reforms, launched at Mikhail Gorbachev's initiative and designed as a means to ensure the country's dynamic development and the democratization of social life, have entered for several reasons into a blind alley.'[1] The social and economic policies Gorbachev had introduced – summarized in the concepts of *glasnost* (openness) and *perestroika* (reconstruction) – had allegedly led the country 'into the quagmire of violence and lawlessness'. By this time Communist authority in Eastern Europe had collapsed: the anti-Communist Solidarity party had formed a coalition government in Poland; Hungary had relaxed border controls; and in November 1989 the Berlin Wall had fallen. In 1990 the parliaments of the Soviet republics of Lithuania, Estonia and Latvia had voted to secede from the Soviet Union. Even Russia had asserted its 'sovereignty' in relation to the Union. Other republics followed, prompting Gorbachev to attempt to save the integrity of the USSR and the central authority of Moscow through the promotion of a new 'Union Treaty'. Gorbachev's hopes were pinned on successful negotiations with the leaders of the republics, most importantly Boris Yeltsin.

A former Communist Party boss, Yeltsin pushed for greater sovereignty of the RSFSR and would become its president in 1991. Gorbachev appeared to have agreement on a treaty that would preserve a voluntary union before he went on holiday in early August. But upon seeing that

Iksander Galimov, *Arkhitektura SSSR* (March–April 1989).

the draft treaty meant an almost certain end to the unitary state of the USSR, the State Executive Committee confined Gorbachev to his Crimean dacha and initiated plans for a coup that would defend the Union from claims of separatist autonomy. When the Committee called the tanks into Moscow, it hoped for a rapid reinstatement of the geopolitical primacy of the Union. Instead it was met with three days of popular protest, symbolically ignited when Yeltsin climbed on top of a tank and appealed to 'the citizens of Russia', who had gathered by the thousands in front of the White House, to stop the reactionary coup. Soviet military personnel 'defected' to the Russian side and directed their tank guns away from the building, signalling a symbolic victory for Yeltsin for having prevented an attack on the seat of Russia's government.

Amid the dwindling prospects for salvaging a formalized union of the Soviet republics, Yeltsin sought to secure the inheritance of Soviet institutions for Russia. Gorbachev had lost the support of the military and agreed to step down. On 25 December 1991 the Soviet flag was lowered at the Kremlin and the red, white and blue flag of Russia was raised in its place. The end of the year marked the end of the Soviet Union. The disintegration of the world's first experiment in socialist modernity entailed a sweeping and tumultuous revaluation of values. Characteristic of the uncertainty and rapid pace of change in the first years of the Russian Federation was the attack, orchestrated by none other than Yeltsin, to quash another attempted coup on the White House in 1993. This time the building was bombarded, transforming it from a symbol of liberation into an index of the cultural, economic and political realities of post-Soviet Russia.

The collapse of the Soviet Union began long before its ultimate dissolution. The Soviet economy had been in a dismal state since the 1970s. It was largely dependent on heavy industry, which accounted for the majority of the economy by the mid-1980s. The factories and mines that drove Soviet industry had been largely built in the 1930s (or rebuilt to original specifications after the Second World War), and four decades later they were becoming increasingly inefficient, if not obsolete. The Soviet economy was spared painful restructuring by its most valuable resource: oil. Tapping the petroleum reserves of Western Siberia, the USSR became a net oil exporter by the early 1970s – at the same time that the Arab-Israeli war and the embargo it entailed made oil prices soar throughout the world. Oil exports brought much-needed infusions of hard currency into the Soviet budget; and high oil prices increased the buying power of oil-exporting countries who were interested in purchasing Soviet arms. Together, the sale of energy and weapons enabled the Soviet Union to build up the Soviet military, sustain an ageing elite, purchase feed for livestock, import consumer goods and mitigate the protracted invasion of Afghanistan, which had put pressure on the Soviet economy since it began in 1979.[2]

The income generated by resource extraction also ensured that political stability could be maintained well into the 1980s. When Leonid Brezhnev died in 1982, he was succeeded by two long-time members of the gerontocracy of the Communist Party. When Iurii Andropov became general secretary of the Central Committee he instituted moderate reforms that sought to modernize industrial operations by giving them more autonomy. When he passed away in 1984, leadership of the Party was conferred on Konstantin Chernenko, a conservative who only served thirteen months before he, too, passed away.

Gorbachev's ascendance in 1985 paved the way for systemic reform. He signalled his appetite for change by initiating a campaign to combat alcoholism, freeing the dissident scientist Andrei Sakharov from internal exile and adopting *glasnost* as a guiding principle. *Glasnost*, roughly translated as 'openness', was not, however, a programme of political transparency or freedom of information, although it did entail the relaxation of censorship laws and led to the invigoration of the Soviet press. *Perestroika* brought far-reaching economic reforms. Gorbachev discussed the need for *perestroika*, or reconstruction, as early as 1985, and he would adopt the term for the title of his best-selling book published two years later. Reconstruction began with the Law on the State Enterprise, which was passed in 1987. This legislation allowed factory workers to elect their own directors, gave producers relative autonomy in setting prices and, importantly, endorsed the creation of a private sector for services and small industry. The introduction of market elements into the Soviet planned economy represented the most significant reform since Lenin's New Economic Policy. Although new 'cooperatives' – that is, private enterprises – sprang up in cities, Gorbachev's economic reforms failed to stabilize the Soviet economy, which was still heavily dependent on weapons and energy exports. What is more, when Gorbachev sought to turn the Communist Party into an object of *perestroika* by demanding the introduction of competitive elections and reorganizing its administrative structure, he weakened its monopoly on state power and exposed it to political challenges which it had never before faced.

By the late 1980s, economic difficulty, a weakened Party and an emboldened national government combined to create the conditions for the failed coup attempt by conservative Party members of 1991 and Yeltsin's subsequent rise to power. Following the disintegration of the USSR, Yeltsin became president of the new Russian Federation. He presided over the difficult 'transition' to a market economy. In the process, formerly state-owned enterprises passed into private hands, creating enormous personal wealth and exacerbating economic disparities within the Russian population. The social and economic structure of new Russia had little room for the Soviet welfare programmes which had guaranteed essential services and resources to everyone. The decades following the Soviet collapse were beset with crisis – notably the sovereign debt default of 1998 – and political uncertainty. Yeltsin, an erratic personality, remained at the summit of Russian politics until he surprised the country by announcing his retirement in December 1999. Vladimir Putin, as prime minister, immediately became president. He has remained the key political force in Russia, as either president or prime minister, since this time. Unlike Yeltsin, Putin has maintained an authoritarian control of the country and has sought to restore to Russia some of the international prestige that was lost with the Soviet Union's collapse.

In the period from the early 1980s to the first decade of the twenty-first century, the architectural profession experienced profound changes, the most important of which was the shift from an exclusive dependence on state commissions to a mixed economy of public and private clients. Some commentators have called this shift a 'fourth revolution' in Russian architecture, following the revolutions of 1917, the Stalin era and Khrushchev's reforms.[3] Private clients, particularly the well-heeled 'new Russians', demanded architectural services that had been largely neglected during the Soviet era. Interior design became a new sphere of architectural activity as clients sought to create individualized dwellings. Likewise, the private house or dacha re-emerged as a focal point of an architect's work as wealthy individuals sought to secure their own identities by recalling the patron-client relationships of pre-revolutionary Russia. By the end of the 1990s, a new class of residential, commercial and cultural buildings would transform city centres across the country.

But the 'fourth revolution' in Russian architecture should not be understood as an absolute break with the Soviet architecture and building complex. On the contrary, many of the state design institutes survived the Soviet collapse and continued to operate in new market conditions. Some, like Gidroproekt, are now competitive corporations. In Moscow, the municipal design bureau Mosproekt-2 now bears the name of its founding director, Mikhail Vasilevich Posokhin, and is directed by his son, Mikhail Mikhailovich. This institute has been responsible for some of the most ambitious transformations of post-Soviet Moscow. There are continuities across the divide of 1991 for independent firms as well. Many of the architects who made names for themselves in the 1980s, either as experimental 'paper architects' or as directors of *perestroika*-era design cooperatives, are now leading members of the Russian architectural profession.

A significant vector of continuity between late-Soviet and new-Russian architectural culture is the increasing engagement with international architectural culture. In the 1980s, Soviet architects participated with great success in international conceptual competitions sponsored by magazines such as *Japan Architect* (*Shinkenchiku*). Soviet architects also competed in several high-profile international competitions in these years, notably the competitions for two of François Mitterrand's *grand projets*, the Parc de la Villette and the Tête-Défense in Paris (1982–3).[4] While few Russian firms can claim unqualified success in contemporary architectural competitions, it is commonplace to find foreign architectural firms competing for commissions in Russia. There is also a strong internationalism in architectural education. In the years of *perestroika*, the Moscow Architecture Institute (MARKhI) introduced collaborative architectural studios with the Columbia University School of Architecture in New York.[5] The two institutions have recently resumed collaboration, and MARKhI maintains working relationships with institutions around the world. The independent institutes for architectural and design education that have emerged in recent years, including the Strelka Institute and the Moscow Architectural School, continue to integrate Russian architectural culture with global concerns.

Russian architects are nevertheless confronted by the specificity of their professional inheritance. The urban landscape generated by socialism presents serious challenges. Housing stock is in need of repair and replacement. Semi-permanent kiosks are a ubiquitous testament to the relatively underdeveloped permanent infrastructure for consumer services. The increasing number of vehicles in Moscow threatens permanent gridlock in its radial-concentric street system. The loosely regulated suburban settlements around major cities encroach on open wilderness and blur municipal boundaries. The current generation of architects must also address the neglect suffered by landmarks of Russian and Soviet modern architecture. The preservation of such structures as Moisei Ginzburg and Ignatii Milinis's Narkomfin Building (1928–30), Konstantin Melnikov's house and studio (1927–9) and Vladimir Shukhov's Shabolovka Radio Tower (1919–22) depends on the successful mediation of private interests, public concern and government protection. The growing support for preservation within the Russian architectural community represents a conscientious opposition to the dangers of unchecked urban development; at the same time, it manifests the value ascribed to the history of Russia's modern architecture for the present.

## Children of Stagnation

The architectural phenomenon that would propel Soviet and Russian architecture forward during the years of *perestroika* began in the final years of Brezhnev's reign. Variously described as 'paper architecture', 'conceptual architecture' or 'easel architecture', this new approach to design both offered a creative outlet for a younger generation of architects that was reluctant to enter the unrewarding world of the large design institutes and brought Soviet architecture to world prominence. A characteristic feature of many of the projects associated with this approach was a rejection of functional demands as irrelevant and an embrace of narrative and expressive means from disciplines ranging from literature to poetry and cinema. The work produced by the 'paper architects' in the early and mid-1980s demonstrated the emergence of a vital, unique and Soviet perspective, the existence of which seems to have taken outside observers by surprise. Indeed, while introducing an exhibition devoted to paper architecture held at the German Architectural Museum in 1989, Heinrich Klotz noted that 'the sharp contrast between official architecture and these "paper castles" urged us to abandon the usual attitude of a certain condescension with which we normally react to the large scale state architecture of the Soviet Union.'[6] Soviet architects had not received such a positive international reception since the 1920s.

The representatives of this phenomenon, many of whom are today leaders in contemporary Russian practice, date its origins to 1981, the year that the young architects Mikhail Belov and Max Kharitonov won first prize in a conceptual competition for an exhibition house sponsored by the magazine *Japan Architect*. While this was certainly a genre-defining success, the creative impetus behind this and other projects appeared much earlier. Belov himself has described these works as 'children of the stagnation', suggesting that they grew out of a dissatisfaction with the opportunities for creativity offered to young architects in the Brezhnev era.[7] The teaching of Ilia Lezhava had an enormous impact on students of MARKhI, including Belov, in the late 1970s. It was under his guidance that some of them first entered the world of international architectural competitions.[8] The projects that Lezhava and his colleagues had devised for a 'New Element of Settlement' (NER) in the 1960s and '70s established the foundations and provided inspiration for the paper projects of the 1980s.[9]

Mikhail Belov, M. Kharitonov, exhibition house, 1981.

Belov and Kharitonov's project for an exhibition house of 1981 in many ways set the tone for the paper projects that followed. The project was presented in two etched sheets, each 70 × 50 cm. In addition to plans,

shinkenchiku
1981

Crystal Palace is a beautiful but unrealizable
dream a Mirage which calls you always seen
at the edge of visible. But as each dream, in
close examination it will prove the other thing
than it seemed afar. A person who wants to
visit it will make a long way through the town
borderland, blocks of slums and dumps but co-
ming at last to the Palace find neither roof nor
walls only the huge glass plates stuck into the
huge box with sand. A Mirage remains simply
a Mirage, though it can be touched. Passing
from one glass chink to another a visitor will
walk the Palace through and find himself at
the border of a small square, where the Landscape
commences... Did he learn the very essence of the Crys-
tal Palace, will he have a desire to visit it once more?
Nobody knows ...
Crystal Palace
Sea-weed swarms with
Transparent fins Catch them-
They shall thaw without a trace
Basho
The Landscape
DUMPS
TO WN BORDERLAND
SECTION SCALE 1:666
PLAN SCALE 1:1000

sections and elevations, each sheet contains a number of narrative frames, recalling the format of a comic strip. Belov and Kharitonov also included two texts, which do not describe the project per se, but rather convey the different experiences of the 'visitor' and the 'host'. Situated on the grounds of a modern art museum, the house is approached from a tree-lined avenue, which terminates at a sculpture of a woman's head. Behind this, stairs lead through a portal. The 'visitor' describes this sequence as follows: 'I entered the house through the frame, but it turned out I had left it. I was standing in an empty street, at the end of which was the house I had just entered.'[10] Through a series of theatrical distortions, Belov and Kharitonov orchestrate a surreal journey for the 'visitor' through the structure that ends right where it started. For the 'host', however, the house is just a house with 'many cosy corners' that friends visit on weekends. The uncanny relationship between space, display and domestic life that Belov and Kharitonov conveyed with this project manifested an urge to the surreal and fantastical shared by many other paper architects. That Fumihiko Maki, the judge of the competition, awarded Belov and Kharitonov first prize was an unprecedented success for Soviet architects, not least because censors and postal restrictions made the very shipment of the drawings to Japan quite difficult.

In 1982 Soviet architects prevailed in another of *Japan Architect*'s conceptual competitions, this time sponsored by the Central Glass Co. on the theme of a crystal palace. Out of the 386 competition entries, seventeen of which were sent from the USSR, Alexander Brodsky and Ilia Utkin's project was judged the best. Like Belov and Kharitonov, Brodsky and Utkin combined architectural graphics with lyrical imagery and poetic text on a single sheet measuring approximately 86 × 60 cm. The haunting vignettes of the crystal palace are enhanced by the rich and expressive textural qualities of the lines. The etched images betray intense manual dexterity and incredible skill in printmaking, perhaps inherited from Brodsky's father, Savva, a well-known book illustrator. The accompanying text describes the crystal palace as an 'unrealizable dream', a 'mirage which calls you always, seen on the edge of the visible'.[11] The palace itself looms over the city on the outskirts. The structure has neither roof nor walls; it is composed of glass plates of various profiles that stand on a low base. Motifs of Joseph Paxton's Crystal Palace of 1851 are discernible within Brodsky and Utkin's work, though their references to this monument are not celebratory but melancholic. It is difficult not to interpret this project as a meditation on the poetic potential of architecture to convey hopes, aspirations and dreams.

A. Brodsky and I. Utkin, Crystal Palace, 1982.

Seeing the great success of young Soviet architects in the international arena, *Arkhitektura SSSR* initiated its own series of conceptual competitions.

The first, announced in 1983, sought new concepts for a social and recreational centre for a residential complex.[12] More than 350 entries were submitted to the competition, and A. Asadov and M. Asadova won first prize. The Union of Architects, however, refused to offer space for an exhibition of the projects submitted to this competition and other prize-winning work. This indicated the reluctance with which 'conceptual' architecture was greeted by the leaders of the Soviet profession. The work would ultimately be shown in the cramped quarters of the youth magazine *Iunost* in summer 1984. This was a landmark event for the young architects who participated. It was here that the term 'paper architecture', with its connotations of challenge and irony, first entered common parlance. The event also allowed its participants to construct a genealogy of their work. Belov, who was instrumental in staging the exhibition, counted Piranesi, Boullée, Sant'Elia, Leonidov, Zholtovskii, Golts and others among the precedents for his work. He noted that architecture 'had become an appendage of construction', and presented the competition projects as a way to 'renew architectural reality' through 'social intensification'.[13]

Other commentators drew more consequential conclusions from the exhibition. The poet Andrei Voznesenskii, himself a former architecture student, described the work as a 'sublimation of despair'. Mikhail Tumarkin, a young architect and critic, described the paper projects as 'a form of escape from architectural reality', and noted that the authors of these works 'feel excommunicated from genuine architecture as it is handled by the building industry, and see these competitions as a parallel mode of quasi-architectural existence alongside the profession'.[14] While the professional alienation that Tumarkin described was certainly a significant factor in pushing architects towards conceptual work, this may not have applied equally to all 'paper architects'. No doubt some architects viewed conceptual work as an escape from a practical profession that they sought to renew and ultimately join; for others conceptual work was their calling. Responding to the latter, Aleksei Tarkhanov identified the new figure of the architect-artist (*arkhitektor-stankovist*), who worked more like a fine artist than an architect and was able to 'express the most subtle emotions' with architectural and urban forms.[15] Brodsky, Iurii Avvakumov and others were responsible for articulating the position that Tarkhanov described. But regardless of whether 'paper architecture' was viewed as a practice in itself or as preparation for practical work, the phenomenon would ultimately be embraced by a broad spectrum of Soviet architects. The remarkable covers designed by Iksandr Galimov for *Arkhitektura SSSR* in 1989 and 1990 are testament to this.

## Reform and the Building Complex

The 'paper architecture' phenomenon brought the problems facing young architects into sharp focus at a critical moment. In the new atmosphere of public debate ushered in by *glasnost* and *perestroika* – terms which entered Soviet architectural discourse as early as 1985 – the alternative practices of the 'paper architects' gave pause for reflection on the state of Soviet architecture and thus provided an opportunity to advocate for reform. Calls for change in the structure of the architecture and building complex – which encompassed design institutes and construction organizations – were not only issued by those who had allegedly escaped into a world of conceptual projects; calls for reform came from the Union of Architects as well. A survey conducted by *Arkhitektura SSSR* in 1985 – this form of communication itself was a manifestation of *glasnost* – found that most young architects working in design institutes were dissatisfied with the lack of responsibility entrusted to them and objected to the bureaucratic administration of design.[16] Iurii Gnedovskii, Secretary of the Union of Architects, admitted that the byzantine administrative structure of the building industry had robbed architects of the 'right to responsibility' for projects, which were often modified to unrecognizability through many levels of approval.[17] The despondence of young professionals and the decreasing number of students choosing to become architects presented the Union of Architects with serious problems. The concerns of the younger generation were aired at a conference of young architects held in Kiev in April 1986. Here representatives called for the 'acceleration of *perestroika*' in society and the profession, demanding that the problems of the architectural youth be given full attention at the upcoming Congress of Soviet Architects, which was scheduled for June 1987.[18]

Assembled 50 years after the First Congress of Soviet Architects, the Eighth Congress opened at a moment of crisis. Only days before the event a so-called 'initiative group', which included both young architects, such as Belov and Avvakumov, and experienced practitioners like Aleksandr Larin and Andrei Kosinskii, published a 'Programme of *perestroika*' in the newspaper *Arkhitektura*.[19] The authors published the programme before the Congress because they feared the event would simply rehearse the 'habitual model' of organizational procedures characteristic of the 'period of stagnation'. In contrast, the programme outlined provisions for a new model of architectural work based on independent design teams and studios. They called for a unit of architectural research independent of state design and construction interests. Likewise, the 'initiative group' sought the integration of architectural education with practical experience in a design office. Tension and a desire for change animated the proceedings

Akant Cooperative, Interquadro Offices, Moscow, 1989–90.

of the Congress once it opened. The young architect Leonid Seitkhalilov openly criticized the work of the Board of the Union and its president, Anatolii Polianskii. Kosinskii declared that 'today is the first day of a new era, and from today we must start to work in an entirely new way'.[20] The delegates of the Congress agreed. Polianskii was voted out as union president, and Iurii Platonov, with a mandate for reform, replaced him. Later that year, the Communist Party issued a decree 'On the Further Development of Soviet Architecture and Urban Planning' that accepted nearly all the points raised by the 'initiative group' prior to the Congress.[21]

This decree and the Law on State Enterprise, which was adopted in June 1987 and went into effect in the following January, created conditions for the reestablishment of a feature of architectural work that had long been absent from Soviet practice: the independent design studio. Even during the Congress, Andrei Bokov had called for the creation of independent design workshops within the Union of Architects in order to 'deprive the large design institutes of their monopoly'.[22] Such studios were independent insofar as they were not subject to the control of state design institutes or building trusts. This opportunity was not lost on Soviet architects, for design cooperatives appeared as soon as they could be legally registered. One of the first was established by Oleg Gridasov, who registered the Akant Cooperative in 1987. Among the group's first realized projects was the redesign of an office for Interquadro, an electronics company established by a Soviet, French and Italian partnership.[23] The

Boris Shabunin, residential district for Naberezhnye Chelny, 1990.

renovation was modest, but the experience of working with a private client was, according to Gridasov, an important lesson. The client imported Italian lights, German kitchen appliances and French wallpaper, but nevertheless described the project as 'Russian modern' in style. The combination of imported building elements with a loose interpretation of historical styles would become a common feature of architectural work in ensuing years. Other cooperatives of the late 1980s had larger ambitions. Boris Shabunin, who organized an independent studio in 1989, designed a housing complex for Naberezhnye Chelny that rivalled the scale of work undertaken by state design bureaus.[24] After setting up a studio in the same year, Aleksandr Asadov experimented with building types not commonly associated with Soviet practice, as seen in his design for a Yacht Club in Ulyanovsk (1990).[25]

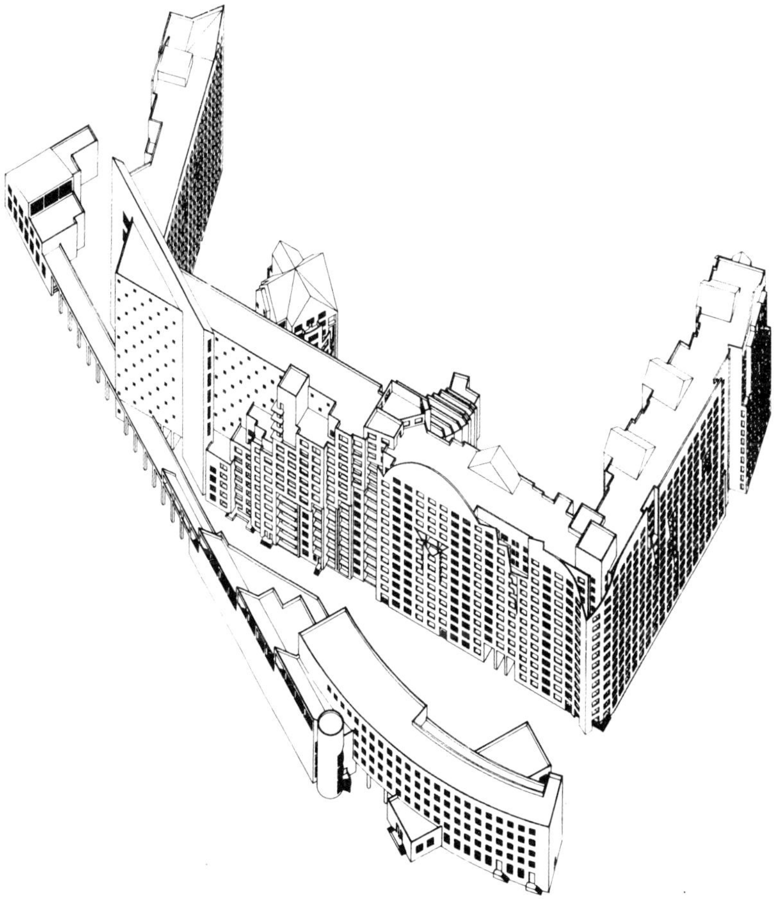

Former 'paper architects' also established design cooperatives. The group 'Brigada A', founded in 1988, was comprised of Mikhail Belov, Mikhail Filippov (two leaders of the 'paper architecture' phenomenon), the graphic artist Sergei Barkhin and the architects Mikhail and David Krikheli and Oleg Eremin.[26] The work of 'Brigada A' ranged from hypothetical projects such as Filippov's conceptual reconstruction of Moscow's Kremlin embankment (1990), to the executed 'Rodnik' café in Sukhumi (1990) by the Krikhelis and Eremin. Brodsky and Utkin also executed a 'real project' in the wake of their great success with conceptual work. Their interior for the 'Atrium' cooperative café (1987–9) is the surprising result of a translation of the expressive qualities of Brodsky and Utkin's conceptual work into built form. Entirely conceived and executed by the architects themselves, the interior is composed of hypertrophic classical elements that were intended to lend an antique hue to evening leisure. The exaggerated forms and fine classical details were executed in the spirit of humour, a sensibility rarely found in Soviet practice.[27]

Aleksandr Asadov, Yacht Club, Ulyanovsk, 1990.

Alexander Brodsky and Ilia Utkin, Café 'Atrium', Moscow, 1987–9.

In addition to stimulating new forms of creative practice, the reforms ushered in after the Congress of 1987 affected the large design institutes as well. The 'right to responsibility' for architectural design and execution was incorporated into the brief for a competition, held in 1987, for a new hotel on Lenin Square, next to Paveletskaia Train Station in Moscow. Glavapu, Moscow's architecture and planning authority, wrote that 'The author (or leader of a collective) of the winning project will be accorded the right to further develop the project for a hotel on Lenin Square in the role of the author in one of the design institutes of Glavapu, Moscow.'[28] That this opportunity was welcomed by the architectural youth is indicated by the fact that 130 entries were submitted before the competition's very short deadline. Boris Uborevich-Borovskii's winning

Boris Uborevich-Borovskii, project for an international hotel, Moscow, 1988.

design consisted of an asymmetrical stepped-back tower of 30 storeys, and two wings of eight and nine storeys each. One critic described the hotel, which was to be built and run by a Japanese firm, as part of a 'new generation of tall buildings' that would harmonize with the high-rises built in the final years of Stalin's reign.[29] For his part, Uborevich-Borovskii was thrilled to have won the competition. He offered the following report in 1989: 'Now I am doing the working drawings. I consider myself lucky. Something like this would not have been possible before the *perestroika* . . . My own personal experience leads me to believe that the times have really changed.'[30]

As reforms opened up new opportunities and methods of work in the capital, regional centres began to cultivate and promote local architectural identities. In Kuibyshev (Samara) on the Volga, architects displayed new interest in the city's particularly strong heritage of *stil modern* buildings. Iurii Khromov's new Philharmonic Hall (1988) incorporates motifs from the 'Olympic' Theatre (1907) that previously stood on the site. This is particularly evident in the organic curves that define the corner portals of Khromov's building. A. Panin and Leonid Kuderov developed this line of research even further. Kuderov's 'Fly' House (1991–5) exaggerates the formal devices of the *stil modern*, demonstrating what he called a 'new artistic quality' that was intended to surpass the usual standards of design and construction in Russia.[31] Architects in Gorky (Nizhniy Novgorod) were also interested in developing a new locally inflected architecture in the late 1980s. The work of Aleksandr Kharitonov, Evgenii Pestov and others would lay the foundations for the emergence of the 'Nizhniy Novgorod' school in the early 1990s.

By 1991 it was clear that the structures and conventions of Soviet architectural culture had been radically altered. The Union of Architects' journal, *Arkhitektura SSSR*, both registered and promoted these changes. In its March–April issue it introduced a recurring feature on the 'ABCs of the market', which featured decidedly anti-Leninist advice from advisors from MENATEP, an international holding company founded by Mikhail Khodorkovsky. In the first instalment of business advice the key terms of the day were introduced: 'the market, privatization, de-nationalization'.[32] In following issues MENATEP advisors discussed 'prices and risks' for architects, the functions of banks and a range of other topics in market-driven architectural development. Well before the climactic events of August 1991, the Union of Architects was busy preparing its members, in at least a rudimentary fashion, for a transition to market relations. The editorials of 1991, which began to be published with English translations from the March–April issue, made this clear. In the penultimate issue of *Arkhitektura SSSR*, Andrei Bokov published a scathing critique of the

Leonid Kuderov, 'Fly' House, Samara, 1991–5.

'dictatorship of mediocrity' that had been sustained by the bureaucratic design and building complex throughout the years of stagnation. He professed faith in the 'market's laws' and the 'equal in rights principles' on which they are allegedly based. The way forward depended on a new, non-state client and the introduction of the institution of private property. Bokov described the 'future owner' who builds private houses as 'the main hope for architecture' and concluded that 'Post-Totalitarian, or say Post-Soviet Architecture, is not an invention, but a reality which is inevitable as a result of wholesome forces and professional potentiality'.[33]

## 'Capitalist Realism'

Much of Russia's architectural production in the decades following the collapse of the Soviet Union has been described as 'capitalist realism'. Clearly an allusion to the theory of 'socialist realism', capitalist realism has a diffuse meaning, referring as much to the proliferation of stylistic trends in the 1990s and 2000s as to a mode of architectural practice in new social and economic conditions. Bart Goldhoorn, the founding editor of the country's leading architectural journal, *Project Russia*, has done much to popularize the term. He writes that 'capitalist realism is an architecture that is wanted by the population in contrast to an elitist *architecture pour l'architecture*'.[34] It is 'realist' insofar as it is populist, and it characterizes an approach to architecture that draws on a variety of historical styles and references, from neo-Russian to *stil modern* and even forms derived from the Stalin era. Indeed, the eclectic group of buildings commonly subsumed under the term 'capitalist realism' flirt with just about every phase of Russia's architectural history – except the technocratic forms of the late-Soviet period. The churches, banks, apartment buildings, shopping centres and office buildings that emerged after the Soviet collapse manifest a widespread desire for variety, local identity and 'authenticity' in the post-Soviet city. Nevertheless, capitalist realism should not be understood as an expression of the free play of market forces; on the contrary, it is a phenomenon produced by the institutional legacies – or survivals – of the Soviet Union and their activation by a dynamic and volatile economy.

Nowhere are the ambiguities of capitalist realism more visible than in Moscow. It is now commonplace to associate a new 'Moscow Style', a sub-genre of capitalist realism, with the grand projects undertaken by Mayor Iurii Luzhkov, who ran the city from 1992 to 2010.[35] Yet these works – and the 'Moscow Style' itself – are deeply indebted to a late-Soviet project that Luzhkov helped to completion soon after coming to office: the Museum of the Great Patriotic War (1982–93). The museum, which opened to the public in 1995, is the central monument of the Park of

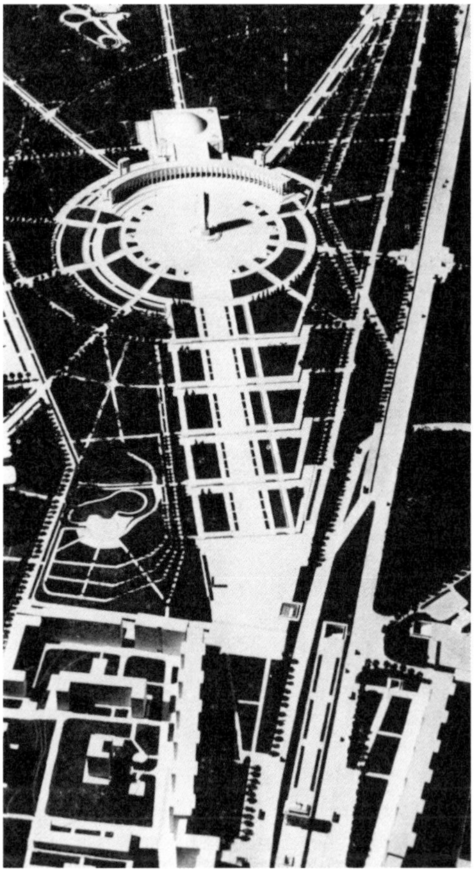

Memorial complex devoted to the Victory of the Soviet People in the Great Patriotic War, 1941–5, Moscow, 1982–93.

Victory in Moscow's southwestern district. Iakov Belopolskii, who had designed the Memorial to the Fallen Soviet Soldiers in Treptow Park in Berlin (1946–9), and the sculptor Nikolai Tomskii led the initial design team. In 1984 Anatolii Polianskii was called in to oversee the project as head of a special design studio within Mosproekt-2, the institute responsible for public buildings.[36] Periodic work stoppages delayed the completion of the museum until the early 1990s, when Luzhkov was able to push the project forward in order to have the museum and its surrounding complex complete by the 60th anniversary of the end of the war. Luzhkov enlisted the artist Zurab Tsereteli, who would play a pivotal role in defining the new 'Moscow Style' in his work on Luzhkov's other projects, to oversee the museum's completion. The executed design remained remarkably faithful to the version proposed in 1982. It bears strong nationalist overtones (particularly in the 'hall of glory'), combines vaguely historical forms, which seem to refer to Stalin-era models rather than classical precedents, and conveys a strong sense of monumentality, despite its predominant horizontality. These stylistic traits would mark the projects sponsored by Luzhkov in the 1990s. These traits are equally characteristic of works associated with the term 'capitalist realism', a fact that complicates attempts to correlate post-Soviet architectural design directly with the emergence of capitalist market conditions.

The centrepiece of Luzhkov's grand projects is undoubtedly the reconstructed Cathedral of Christ the Saviour (1994–2000). The original building by Konstantin Ton had been demolished in 1931 to make way for the unrealized Palace of the Soviets. Supported by President Yeltsin, the reconstruction of the cathedral was at once an effort to repudiate the destruction of Russian monuments by the Soviet regime and to symbolize the resurgence of public religiosity, which had been largely suppressed in the seven decades of Soviet rule. The cathedral mimics the neo-Byzantine forms of Ton's building, but it is an entirely modern structure. The most significant departure from the original building is the two-

Cathedral of Christ the Saviour, Moscow, 1994–2000.

storey car park on which the new Cathedral stands. The building was designed in Mosproekt-2 by Mikhail Posokhin (the younger) and Aleksei Denisov; its sculptural decor was overseen by Tsereteli, whose decision to apply relief sculptures in bronze, not marble like the original, to the exterior caused a public scandal. While the cathedral was seen as a controversial project by many of Moscow's architects, it was immediately embraced by the public as a symbol of the city.

The prominence of Mosproekt-2 in the reconstruction of Moscow is remarkable. The institute is responsible for a wide range of projects in the Russian capital. These include the subterranean shopping mall at Okhotnyi Riad (1995–7), the reconstruction of the Gostinyi dvor (1998–2000), the high-rise office complex at Paveletskaia Train Station

(2003), the reconstruction of Hotel Moscow (2005–13) and many others. The continued work of this institute demonstrates the strong institutional continuities within the design and building complex that extend across the divide of 1991. In this sense, capitalist realism as developed by Luzhkov is an heir to Soviet-era practices of centralized design administration.

Although the city administration played a major role in defining the new style, some of the most provocative representatives of capitalist realism were funded and designed by private parties. Sergei Tkachenko's 'Patriarch' apartment building (1997–2002) has sharply divided professional opinion. It stands in a quiet corner of central Moscow, overlooking the Patriarch Ponds, but its form seems to undermine the tranquil character of its context. Its thirteen storeys tower above the surrounding buildings, and its bright yellow render and profuse pseudo-classical ornamentation loudly proclaim its presence in the cityscape. The paradoxical climax of the building appears on the roof, where a loose interpretation of Vladimir Tatlin's *Monument to the Third International* stands. In the words of one critic, the building is 'the true symbol of everything associated with the new Russian'.[37] Like Tkachenko's building, the 'Triumph Palace' (2001–6) constructed by the development company Donstroi has generated significant controversy. The building's lead architect, Andrei Trofimov, describes it as part of 'the traditional monumental style of the seven tall buildings

Mosproekt-2, Paveletskaia Plaza, Moscow, 2003.

Sergei Tkachenko, 'Patriarch' apartment building, Moscow, 1997–2002.

of the capital'.[38] Its explicit references to the architecture of the Stalin era and its evident popularity in the market for elite housing have given many architects cause to reflect on the legacy of this approach to design in the present. While the 'Triumph Palace' lived up to the ambitions of its predecessors in being recognized as the tallest residential building in Europe (264 m) upon completion, it also demonstrates the inability of this type of building to fully integrate with its urban context in the absence of the tight urban regulations that governed the siting of the Stalin-era high-rises.

Among the spectrum of practices associated with capitalist realism, the works of Mikhail Filippov and Mikhail Belov are distinguished by a commitment to classical design. Filippov, perhaps more than any of his contemporaries, has sought to translate the historical worlds of his drawing of the 1980s into built form. His so-called 'Roman House' in Moscow (2002–5) embodies his staunch opposition to modern architecture, which he has called 'cultural barbarism'.[39] The building incorporates a circular courtyard, appearing as a small urban square, into its rectangular footprint. The galleries of the upper floors of the building make explicit reference to the Palazzo Davanzati in Florence (fourteenth century). Filippov's

Donstroi, Triumph Palace, Moscow, 2001–6.

Mikhail Filippov, Roman House, Moscow, 2002–5.

A. Kharitonov, E. Pestov, 'Loudspeaker' office building, Nizhniy Novgorod, 1995.

'Italian Quarter' in Moscow (2003–13) is even richer in historical allusions. Belov's interest in classical design is evident in his 'Pompeii House' in Moscow (2002–6). His overt reference to the architecture of ancient Roman wall paintings in this building recalls the early success of his graphic projects in conceptual architectural competitions as well as the work of such Soviet-era predecessors as Andrei Burov and Georgii Golts.

Outside Moscow, the city with the strongest interest in reconnecting with past architectural traditions is Nizhniy Novgorod. In the early and mid-1990s, Aleksandr Kharitonov, the city's chief architect, supported a resurgence of architectural modes that originated in the early twentieth century. His 'Loudspeaker' office building (1995), designed with Evgenii Pestov, drew explicitly on the formal vocabulary of the neo-Russian structures built in the city in the 1910s. Its varied profile, bright white render and richly sculpted volumes appear to give the elements of a bygone style new life. Kharitonov and Pestov displayed a similar approach in their 'Guarantee' bank of the same year. The work of the 'Nizhniy Novgorod School', as it came to be known, remains extremely popular, and highlights the diversity of architectural approaches encompassed by the concept of capitalist realism.

## Between the USSR and the West

While capitalist realism describes an important aspect of architecture unique to Russia (but perhaps shared by other post-Soviet states), it in no way captures all of the developments in the country in the decades following the collapse. Many architects in both independent practices and in design institutes objected to the widespread reversion to historical styles. Instead, these architects sought to calibrate their work to the standards set by international clients and international architectural firms. Some critics have labelled the work of this diverse group the 'International Style in Russia' or 'Post-Soviet Modernism'.[40] Alternatively, this work could simply be described as contemporary architecture, suggesting that certain Russian architects might be part of the global architectural community that this term presupposes.

A sign that Russia has become an active participant in the world of international architecture is the growing number of foreign architects who contribute to Russian competitions. Many members of the Russian architectural community take pride in this, for it indicates that distant architectural stars are now colleagues competing for the same commissions and (nominally) under the same conditions. This had not been the case in Russian competitions since the 1930s.[41] The competition for a new city hall for Moscow of 2002 was the first event in which large numbers of foreign architects competed and were awarded prizes. From the 147 projects from nineteen countries submitted, Mikhail Khazanov's was awarded first prize. Will Alsop took fifth place.[42] Although Moscow's city hall would not be realized according to Khazanov's design, the event set the stage for the landmark competition for a new Mariinskii Theatre in St Petersburg, which took place the following year. The French architect Dominique Perrault won with a design that enclosed the new theatre building in a delicate geometric mesh, offering a distinct counterpoint to the city's restrained urban landscape.[43] This was a first indication that international firms might be invited to build in Russia. Nevertheless, after years of work, Perrault's office was removed from the project in 2008, leaving the building to be completed by the Canadian firm Diamond Schmitt Architects.

The combination of elevated expectations and disappointing results in the Mariinskii competition would become typical features of major competitions in ensuing years. The competition for a new headquarters for Gazprom, Russia's largest energy company, in 2006 solicited innovative projects by Rem Koolhaas/OMA, Daniel Libeskind and others. The British firm RMJM won with a project for the tallest skyscraper in Europe. It was initially to be located in the centre of the city, but amid protests by both local residents and the international community the project site was moved to a location on the periphery. Despite these difficulties, RMJM plans to bring the building to completion by 2018.[44] The outcomes of other recent competitions have been less clear. First prizes were awarded to the Swiss architect Valerio Olgiati and the Russian architect Boris Bernaskoni in the competition for a museum of contemporary art in Perm of 2008, but neither project appears to be moving towards construction.[45] Likewise, it remains to be seen if Diller Scofidio + Renfro's winning project for a park in Zariade (2013) in the centre of Moscow will be implemented.

Despite the complications of international competitions in Russia, there are many foreign firms practising in the country. The Dutch architect Erick van Egeraat has been particularly active in the Moscow housing market. Nicholas Grimshaw Architects has designed St Petersburg's new Pulkovo airport (2014). Just outside Moscow, in the Skolkovo 'innovation centre', David Adjaye Associates completed the Moscow School of Management (2005–10). Zaha Hadid, who has drawn inspiration from the Constructivists and Suprematists throughout her career, is also building in Russia. Her first finished structure in the country is the 'Dominion' office complex in Moscow (2005–14). Foreign architects also participated in the design of the facilities for the 2014 Winter Olympic Games in Sochi. The international firm Populous Architects designed the 'Fisht' Olympic Stadium and the Canadian firm Cannon Design was responsible for the Adler Skating Center. Many of the buildings for the games, however, were the work of the design institutes Mosproekt-4 and Mostovik. The body charged with managing the construction of the buildings and infrastructure of the games was Olimpstroi, a name and organization that recalls the great projects of the Soviet era, in particular Dneprostroi.

In the decades since the collapse of the USSR, Russian firms that work to international standards of professionalism and quality have become leaders on the architectural scene. Aleksandr Skokan's firm Ostozhenka has made valuable contributions to the Moscow cityscape since the mid-1990s. Guided by what he describes as 'contextual modernism', his firm's work brings new structures into dialogue with historical morphologies. This is evident in virtually all of their projects, from the Moscow International Bank (1995) to the Millennium House Office Building (1999, with Alsop Architects) and the high-rise Penguin Office Building (2004). Sergei Skuratov's work in the first decades of the twenty-first century – particularly his Copper House (2002) and his Business Centre on Novodanilovskaia Embankment (2005–9) – is of consistently high quality. Project Meganom, a firm of younger practitioners led by Iurii

Ostozhenka, Moscow International Bank, Moscow, 1995.

Grigorian, has designed some of the most striking and sensitive new buildings in Moscow. Their residential complex on Molochnyi Lane in Moscow (2002) set a new residential standard. Likewise, their 'Ether' Office Building (2008) situated on an adjacent plot is at once contextual and highly inventive. The subtle use of glass louvres on the building's main office block causes its appearance to shift from opaque to transparent as one moves around the building. Alexander Brodsky occupies a special place on the Russian scene. After his paper projects of the 1980s and his work with Utkin at the Atrium Café, his practice developed in many directions at once. His sculptural installations are just as strong and evocative as his architectural projects. Among other works, his 'Ice Bar' (2002), a small pavilion enclosed by sheets of ice and erected on a frozen reservoir, and his interior for Café Apshu in Moscow (2003) convey his continued interest in conceptually challenging work and the potential of architecture to express an atmosphere of nostalgia.

Grigorii Revzin, one the most articulate critics in contemporary Russia, has described the state of the country's architecture as somewhere 'between the USSR and the West'.[46] This apt characterization conveys the ambiguity of the current situation. On the one hand, contemporary Russian architecture cannot be understood without acknowledging the crucial importance of Soviet legacies. As we have seen, the centralized design apparatus remains a significant element of architectural culture, particularly in Moscow. Likewise, the cityscape produced by seven decades of socialist modernization forms the basic context for contemporary work. The problems posed by this ageing urban infrastructure

View of Moscow from Sparrow Hills with Moscow City in background, 2010s.

have not been solved in the decades since the collapse of the USSR. But this Soviet legacy also provides some of the tools to respond to issues confronting Russian cities today. In the field of residential construction, many of the factories that produced mass housing in the Soviet era continue to do so today. The continued use and development of such resources is a necessity. The legacy that is perhaps strongest and most difficult to shake is the centralization of architectural life in the capital. Moscow remains an absolute centre of Russian architectural culture, though it is hoped that the regional schools that began to emerge in the 1980s will continue to flourish. On the other hand, there are definite signs of an increasing openness of Russian architectural culture to the wider world. The educational initiatives of institutions like MARKhI, the Moscow Architectural School and the Strelka Institute promise to include a new generation of architects and designers in a global set of architectural concerns. At the same time, the growing visibility of Russian architecture on the international stage has demonstrated that Russian architects have matured and adapted to the new social and economic environment in which they practise. This was the lesson that Revzin wanted to convey at the Eleventh Venice Biennale in 2008 when he described the identity of Russian architecture as a mix 'between the USSR and the West'. Russian architects are right to be proud of the conceptual projects that brought them international fame in the 1980s, but they can now present their built work with confidence as well. The best work acknowledges the complexity of working in a post-Soviet built environment, where the

Project Meganom, 'Ether' office building, Moscow, 2008.

Alexander Brodsky, Ice Bar, near Moscow, 2002.

competing demands of real-estate development, architectural conservation and public interest have yet to be resolved. A reconciliation of these demands will only be achieved by confronting the specific legacy of the Soviet built environment – with its myriad problems and advantages – in a meaningful and productive way.

# References

## A note on transliteration and translation

In the references, a simplified version of the Library of Congress conventions for transliteration has been used. In the main text, diacritics for hard and soft signs have been omitted, and common Anglicized variants of names (Ulyanovsk, not Ul'ianovsk) have been adopted. Unless otherwise noted, all translations are my own.

### Introduction


1 On Vertov's film see Oksana Sarkisova, 'Across One Sixth of the World: Dziga Vertov, Travel Cinema, and Soviet Patriotism', *October*, CXXI (2007), pp. 19–40.
2 See William Craft Brumfield, ed., *Reshaping Russian Architecture: Western Technology, Utopian Dreams* (Cambridge, 1990); D. O. Shvidkovskii, *Russian Architecture and the West* (New Haven, 2007).
3 Recently, Russian authors have begun using the terms *avangard* (avant-garde) and *konstruktivizm* (Constructivism) as labels applicable to all the innovative work of the 1920s and early '30s. In the interest of specificity, this usage is avoided here.
4 See, for example, A. V. Riabushin and A. Shukurova, 'Tvorcheskie protivorechiia v noveishei arkhitekture Zapada', *Arkhitektura SSSR* (October 1982), pp. 54–9.
5 Hergé, *The Adventures of Tintin in the Land of the Soviets*, trans. Leslie Lonsdale-Cooper and Michael Turner (New York, 2007), p. 78.
6 See in particular Jean-Louis Cohen's *The Future of Architecture Since 1889* (London, 2012), which incorporates Russian and Soviet contributions throughout the twentieth century.
7 See, for example, Alessandro De Magistris, *URSS, anni '30–'50: Paesaggi dell'utopia staliniana*, exh. cat., Accademia Albertina delle Belle Arti, Turin (Milan, 1997); Danilo Udovički-Selb, 'Between Modernism and Socialist Realism: Soviet Architectural Culture under Stalin's Revolution from Above, 1928–1938', *Journal of the Society of Architectural Historians*, LXVIII/4 (2009), pp. 466–95.


### chapter one: National Forms, Rational Techniques


1 A.I.U. Polunov, *Russia in the Nineteenth Century: Autocracy, Reform and Social Change, 1814–1914* (Armonk, NY, 2005).
2 F. M. Dostoevskii, 'Dnevnik pisatelia', in *Polnoe sobranie sochinenii v tridtsati tomakh* (Leningrad, 1980), vol. XXI, p. 107.
3 L. Dal', 'Istoricheskoe issledovanie russkogo zodchestva', *Zodchii*, I/2 (1872), p. 3.
4 Apollinarii Krasovskii, *Grazhdanskaia arkhitektura: Chasti zdaniia* (St Petersburg, 1851), p. 29.
5 See V. V. Eval'd, *Konstruktivnye osobennosti Amerikanskikh zdanii i estestvennye kamni, primeniaemye v sooruzheniiakh v soedinennykh shtatakh* (St Petersburg, 1895).

6 Cited in Soiuz arkhitektorov SSSR, *Sto let obshchestvennykh arkhitekturnykh organizatsii v SSSR, 1867–1967: Istoricheskaia spravka* (Moscow, 1967), pp. 9–10.
7 R. A. Gedike, 'Rech' predsedatelia I-go otdela', in *Trudy I s"ezda russkikh zodchikh v Sankt-Peterburge: 1892 god* (St Petersburg, 1894), p. 2.
8 M. D. Bykovskii, *O neosnovatel'nosti mneniia, chto arkhitektura grecheskaia, ili greko-rimskaia, mozhet byt' vseobshcheiu i chto krasota arkhitektury osnovyvaetsia na piati izvestnykh chinopolozheniiakh* (Moscow, 1834), p. 4.
9 V. G. Lisovskii, *Leontii Benua i peterburgskaia shkola khudozhnikov-arkhitektorov* (St Petersburg, 2006), p. 37.
10 Cited in T. A. Slavina, *Konstantin Ton* (Leningrad, 1989), p. 91.
11 Cited in Lisovskii, *Leontii Benua*, p. 42.
12 Dostoevskii, 'Dnevnik pisatelia', p. 106.
13 See Ivan Zabelin, *Opyty izucheniia russkikh drevnostei i istorii* (Moscow, 1872). On Zabelin see Ivan Zabelin, V. B. Muraveva and Elena Tonchu, *Cherty moskovskoi samobytnosti* (Moscow, 2007).
14 Cited in T. A. Slavina, *Issledovateli russkogo zodchestva: russkaia istoriko-arkhitekturnaia nauka XVIII–nachala XX veka* (Leningrad, 1983), p. 83.
15 On these exhibitions see E. I. Kirichenko, 'K voprosu o poreformennykh vystavkakh Rossii kak vyrazhenii istoricheskogo svoeobraziia arkhitektury vtoroi poloviny XIX v.', in *Khudozhestvennye protsessy v russkoi kul'ture vtoroi poloviny XIX veka*, ed. G. Iu. Sternin (Moscow, 1984), pp. 83–136.
16 V. V. Stasov, 'Khudozhestvennye zametki o politekhnicheskoi vystavke v Moskve (1872)', in *Sobranie sochinenii V. V. Stasova, 1847–1886* (St Petersburg, 1894), vol. II, p. 373.
17 See Viktor Ivanovich Butovskii, *Istoriia russkogo ornamenta s X po XVI stoletie po drevnim rukopisam*, 2 vols (Paris, 1870–73); V. V. Stasov, *L'ornement national russe. 1ère livraison: Broderies, tissus, dentelles* (St Petersburg, 1872).
18 On Ropet see E. I. Kirichenko, 'Arkhitektor I. P. Ropet', *Arkhitekturnoe nasledstvo*, XX (1972), pp. 85–93.
19 Ivan Zabelin, 'Cherty samobytnosti v drevne-russkom zodchestve', *Drevniaia i novaia Rossiia*, IV/3 (1878), p. 197.
20 Cited in V. G. Lisovskii, *'Natsional'nyi stil'' v arkhitekture Rossii* (Moscow, 2000), p. 140.
21 Cited in E. I. Kirichenko, 'Arkhitektor V. O. Shervud i ego teoreticheskie vozzreniia', *Arkhitekturnoe nasledstvo*, XXII (1974), p. 5.
22 See E. V. Paston, *Abramtsevo: iskusstvo i zhizn'* (Moscow, 2003); G. Iu. Sternin, ed., *Abramtsevo: khudozhestvennyi kruzhok, zhivopis', grafika, skul'ptura, teatr, masterskie* (Leningrad, 1988).
23 See E. A. Borisova, 'Arkhitektura v tvorchestve khudozhnikov abramtsevskogo kruzhka (U istokov "neorusskogo stilia")', in *Khudozhestvennye protsessy v russkoi kul'ture vtoroi poloviny XIX veka*, ed. G. Iu. Sternin (Moscow, 1984), pp. 137–82.
24 I. Kitner, in *Trudy I s"ezda russkikh zodchikh v Sankt-Peterburge: 1892 god* (St Petersburg, 1894), p. 10.
25 See N. A. Smurova, 'Arkhitekturnaia shkola instituta grazhdanskikh inzhenerov', in *Problemy istorii sovetskoi arkhitektury: istoricheskie predposylki i nachal'nyi etap razvitiia: sbornik nauchnykh trudov*, ed. A. A. Strigalev (Moscow, 1985), pp. 31–41.
26 Krasovskii, *Grazhdanskaia arkhitektura*. On Krasovskii see A. Punin, 'Idei ratsionalizma v russkoi arkhitekture vtoroi poloviny XIX veka', *Arkhitektura SSSR* (November 1962), pp. 55–8.
27 Krasovskii, *Grazhdanskaia arkhitektura*, p. 4.
28 Ibid., p. 5.
29 Ibid., p. 27.
30 Ibid., p. 28.
31 Eugène-Emmanuel Viollet-le-Duc, *L'Art russe: ses origines, ses éléments constitutifs, son apogée, son avenir* (Paris, 1877). Two years later the book was translated into Russian.

See Eugène-Emmanuel Viollet-le-Duc, *Russkoe iskusstvo, ego istochniki, ego sostavnye elementy, ego vyschee razvitie, ego budushchnost'*, trans. N. V. Sultanov (Moscow, 1879). Significantly, Viollet-le-Duc neither knew Russian nor travelled to Russia. Instead, his son-in-law, Maurice Ouradou, visited Russia and supplied him with information on Russian architecture and design that he obtained from Viktor Butovskii, director of the Moscow Museum of Art and Industry and its associated Stroganov School of Industrial Arts. On this and Viollet-le-Duc's relationship to Russia see Lauren O'Connell, 'A Rational, National Architecture: Viollet-le-Duc's Modest Proposal for Russia', *Journal of the Society of Architectural Historians*, LII/4 (1993), pp. 436–52; Robin Middleton, 'Viollet-le-Ducsky?', *Architectural Design* (February 1970), pp. 67–8.

32 Viollet-le-Duc, *L'Art russe*, p. 192.

33 N. V. Sultanov, 'Odna iz zadach stroitel'nogo uchilishcha', *Zodchii*, XI/5 (1882), p. 71.

34 Ibid., p. 72.

35 Z. Zosimovskii, 'Po povodu rechi grazhdanskago inzhenera Sultanova "Odna iz zadach Stroitel'nogo uchilishcha"', *Zodchii*, XI/6 (1882), p. 86.

36 I. Kitner, 'Kirpichnaia arkhitektura', *Zodchii*, I/6 (1872), pp. 84–5.

37 Ibid., p. 85.

38 See Iu. S. Lebedev, *Konstruktsii i arkhitekturnaia forma v russkom zodchestve XIX - nachala XX vv.* (Moscow, 1977).

39 See M. S. Shtiglits, *Promyshlennaia arkhitektura Peterburga v sfere 'industrialnoi arkheologii'* (St Petersburg, 2003).

40 T. I. Nikolaeva, *Viktor Shreter, Ieronim Kitner* (St Petersburg, 2007), p. 251.

41 On Kitner's travels abroad see Iu. I. Kitner, 'Arkhitektor I. S. Kitner', *Arkhitekturnoe nasledstvo*, XXV (1976), pp. 154–75.

42 Murat Gappoev, 'Bogenkonstruktionen mit einem System aus biegweichen Zuggliedern', in *Vladimir G. Šuchov, 1853–1939: Kunst der Konstruktion*, ed. Rainer Graefe (Stuttgart, 1990), pp. 54–9.

43 K. M. Bykovskii, 'Zadachi arkhitektury XIX veka', in *Trudy II s"ezda russkikh zodchikh v Moskve*, ed. I. P. Mashkov (Moscow, 1899), p. 18.

44 Ibid.

45 Ibid.

## chapter two: Style, Innovation and Tradition

1 Anton Chekhov, *The Sea Gull* (1896), in *The Major Plays* (New York, 1964), p. 109.

2 Cited in E. I. Kirichenko, *Russkaia arkhitektura 1830–1910-kh godov*, 2nd edn (Moscow, 1986), p. 183.

3 Richard Wortman, *Scenarios of Power: Myth and Ceremony in Russian Monarchy* (Princeton, 1995), p. 344.

4 Maksim Gorky, 'S vserossiiskoi vystavki', http://gorkiy.lit-info.ru (accessed 3 December 2014).

5 See James H. Bater, *St Petersburg: Industrialization and Change* (London, 1976).

6 Alexander Blok, 'Vozmezdie', in *Sobrannye sochinenii*, ed. V. N. Orlova, A. A. Surkov and K. I. Chukovskii (Moscow, 1960), vol. III, p. 298.

7 Velimir Khlebnikov, 'My i doma', in *Sobrannye sochinennii*, ed. R. V. Duganov (Moscow, 2005), vol. VI, pp. 229–38.

8 P. M., 'Novyi stil' i "dekadentstvo"', *Zodchii*, XXXI/6 (1902), p. 66.

9 Ibid.

10 M. Syrkin, 'Novyi stil'', *Arkhitekturnyi muzei*, II/2 (1903), p. 26.

11 Ibid., p. 27.

12 See M., 'Novyi stil' i "dekadentstvo"', pp. 65–70; V. Apyshkov, *Ratsional'noe v noveishei arkhitekture* (St Petersburg, 1905).

13 Otto Wagner, *Modern Architecture: A Guidebook for his Students to this Field of Art*, trans. Harry Francis Mallgrave (Santa Monica, CA, 1988).
14 Cited in Apyshkov, *Ratsional'noe v noveishei arkhitekture*, p. 38. Translation from Wagner, *Modern Architecture*, p. 60.
15 B. M. Kirikov, 'Otto Wagner i stanovlenie peterburgskogo moderna', in *Arkhitektura Peterburga kontsa XIX-nachala XX veka: Eklektika, Modern, Neoklassitsizm* (St Petersburg, 2006), pp. 229–42.
16 On 'retrospectivism' see Katerina Clark, *Petersburg, Crucible of Cultural Revolution* (Cambridge, MA, 1995), pp. 58–65.
17 Alexandre Benois, 'Zhivopisnyi Peterburg', *Mir iskusstva*, VII/1 (1902), pp. 1–5.
18 See I. Fomin, 'Moskovskii klassitsizm', *Mir iskusstva*, XII/7 (1904), pp. 187–98; I. Fomin, 'Istoricheskaia vystavka arkhitektury v S.-Peterburge', *Starye gody* (July–September 1908), pp. 576–9.
19 G. K. Lukomskii, *Staryi Peterburg: progulki po starinnym kvartalam stolitsy*, ed. B. M. Kirikov [1917] (St Petersburg, 2002), p. 32.
20 See Paul Mebes, *Um 1800: Architektur und Handwerk im letzten Jahrhundert ihrer traditionellen Entwicklung* (Munich, 1918). The first edition was published in 1908.
21 On the Russian revival of arts and crafts see Wendy R. Salmond, *Arts and Crafts in Late Imperial Russia* (New York, 1996).
22 *Talashkino: Izdelie masterskikh Kn. M. Kl. Tenishevoi* (St Petersburg, 1905), p. 28.
23 Ibid., p. 29.
24 Maliutin would bring this approach to architecture to Moscow in his Pertsov Apartment Building (1905–7), designed with Nikolai Zhukov.
25 See V. G. Lisovskii, *Ivan Fomin i metamorfozy russkoi neoklassiki* (St Petersburg, 2007).
26 V. S. Karpovich, 'Arkhitekturnaia i khudozhestvenno-promyshlennaia vystavka v Moskve', *Arkhitekturnyi muzei*, II/2 (1903), p. 31.
27 F. Shekhtel', 'Skazka o trekh sestrakh: zhivopisi, arkhitekture, skul'pture. 1919 g.', in *Mastera sovetskoi arkhitektury ob arkhitekture*, ed. M. G. Barkhin (Moscow, 1975), vol. II, p. 21.
28 V. Apyshkov, 'Dom osobniak S. N. Chaeva v Peterburge', *Zodchii*, XXXVII/48 (1908), pp. 440–41.
29 Apyshkov, *Ratsional'noe v noveishei arkhitekture*, p. 59.
30 Apyshkov, 'Dom osobniak S. N. Chaeva v Peterburge', p. 440.
31 See Clark, *Petersburg*, pp. 58–61.
32 *Istoricheskaia vystavka arkhitektury*, exh. cat., Academy of Fine Arts, St Petersburg (St Petersburg, 1911), p. 4.
33 Lisovskii, *Ivan Fomin*, p. 193.
34 At the time, Fomin and many others considered the building to be a work of M. F. Kazakov.
35 See in particular Viktor Vesnin's design for the Dynamo joint-stock company of 1916–17.
36 P. L., 'Dom gvardeiskogo ekonomicheskogo obshchestva', *Zodchii*, XXXIX/48 (1910), pp. 471–3.
37 'K rabote arkh. S. B. Zaslavskogo', *Zodchii*, XLV/19 (1916), pp. 182–4.
38 V. G. Lisovskii, *Sankt-Peterburg: Ocherki arkhitekturnoi istorii goroda*, 2 vols (St Petersburg, 2009), vol. II, pp. 242–5.
39 See V. Bass, *Peterburgskaia neoklassika 1900–1910-kh gg. Arkhitekturnye konkursy: zodchii, tsekh, gorod* (St Petersburg, 2005).
40 See *Maisons du peuple: Belgique, Allemagne, Autriche, France, Grande-Bretagne, Italie, Pays-Bas, Suisse* (Brussels, 1984).
41 L. Armand et al., *Narodnye doma* (Moscow, 1915), p. 1.
42 B. M. Kirikov, *Arkhitektura peterburgskogo moderna: osobniaki i dokhodnye doma* (St Petersburg, 2003), pp. 263–5.
43 See the designs by A. Zelenko and I. I. Kondakov in Armand et al., *Narodnye doma*.

44 Ibid., p. 8.
45 On Gaideburov's work after the revolution see Clark, *Petersburg*, pp. 100–121. On Panina's fate after the October Revolution see Adele Lindenmeyer, 'The First Soviet Political Trial: Countess Sof'ia Panina before the Petrograd Revolutionary Tribunal', *Russian Review*, LX/4 (2001), pp. 505–25.
46 On the industrialization of Moscow and St Petersburg see Bater, *St Petersburg*; Joseph Bradley, *Muzhik and Muscovite: Urbanization in Late Imperial Russia* (Berkeley, 1985).
47 V. N. Semenov, *Blagoustroistvo gorodov* (Moscow, 1912), pp. 172–3.
48 See E. I. Kirichenko, 'O nekotorykh osobennostiakh evoliutsii gorodskikh mnogokvartirnykh domov vtoroi poloviny XIX-nachala XX vv (Ot otdel'nogo doma k kompleksu)', *Arkhitekturnoe nasledstvo*, XV (1963), pp. 154–70.
49 On the Lidval building see Kirikov, *Arkhitektura peterburgskogo moderna*, pp. 212–33.
50 Zazerskii quoted ibid., p. 539.
51 Timothy J. Colton, *Moscow: Governing the Socialist Metropolis* (Cambridge, MA, 1995), p. 57.
52 See N. Dmitriev, 'Tovarishchestvo ustroistva i uluchsheniia zhilishch dlia trudiashchegosia nuzhdaiushchegosia naseleniia', *Stroitel'*, IX (1903), pp. 721–38.
53 See M. G. Dikanskii, *Kvartirnyi vopros i sotsial'nye opyty ego resheniia* (St Petersburg, 1908).
54 See Stephen Kotkin and David Wolff, eds, *Rediscovering Russia in Asia: Siberia and the Russian Far East* (Armonk, NY, 1995).
55 See K. G. Skolimovskii, 'O proektirovanii plana goroda Dal'niago', *Zodchii*, XXXIII/12 (1904), pp. 113–14.
56 See Josef Stübben, *Der Städtebau* (Darmstadt, 1890).
57 See T. I. Shevtsova, 'Russkaia arkhitektura za rubezhom: Kharbin dalekii i blizkii', *Sankt-Peterburgskaia panorama* (September 1993), pp. 32–4; N. P. Kradin, *Kharbin: Russkaia Atlantida* (Khabarovsk, 2001).
58 Cited in V. G. Lisovskii, *Leontii Benua i peterburgskaia shkola khudozhnikov-arkhitektorov* (St Petersburg, 2006), p. 281.
59 F. E. Enakiev, *Zadachi preobrazovaniia S.-Peterburga* (St Petersburg, 1912). See also S. Frederick Starr, 'The Revival and Schism of Russian Planning in Twentieth-century Russia', in *The City in Russian History*, ed. Michael F. Hamm (Lexington, 1976), pp. 222–42.
60 Cited in S. F. Fedorov, '"Novyi Peterburg" - zabytaia mechta Rikardo Gualino', in *Nevskii arkhiv*, ed. A. I. Dobkin and A. V. Kobak (Moscow, 1993), p. 268.
61 Ebenezer Howard, *To-Morrow: A Peaceful Path to Real Reform* (London, 1898).
62 Catherine Cooke, 'Le mouvement pour la cité-jardin en Russie', in *URSS, 1917–1978: la ville, l'architecture*, ed. Jean-Louis Cohen, Marco De Michelis and Manfredo Tafuri (Paris, 1979), pp. 200–233.
63 Dikanskii, *Kvartirnyi vopros i sotsial'nye opyty ego resheniia.*
64 See V. Dadonov, *Sotsializm bez politiki: goroda-sady budushago v nastoiashchem* (Moscow, 1913).
65 On dacha settlements see Stephen Lovell, *Summerfolk: A History of the Dacha, 1710–2000* (Ithaca, NY, 2003).
66 See Mod., 'V Imperatorskom Spb. Obshchestve Arkhitektorov', *Zodchii*, XLII/47 (1913), pp. 483–7; V. N. Belousov and O. V. Smirnova, *V. N. Semenov* (Moscow, 1980), pp. 25–35.
67 Cited in Kirichenko, *Russkaia arkhitektura 1830–1910-kh godov*, pp. 257–8.
68 G. K. Kosmachevskii, 'Novaia zhizn'', *Zodchii*, XLVI/10–13 (1917), p. 77.
69 'Vserossiiskii soiuz zodchikh', *Zodchii*, XLVI/19–20 (1917), p. 139.

## chapter three: Laboratories of Soviet Architecture

1 H. G. Wells, *Russia in the Shadows* (New York, 1921), p. 17.
2 Ibid., p. 28.
3 Ibid., pp. 158–9.
4 V. I. Lenin, 'Communism and Electrification (1920)', in *The Lenin Anthology*, ed. Robert C. Tucker (New York, 1975), p. 494.
5 On the social utopianism of pre-Revolutionary Russia, see Richard Stites, *Revolutionary Dreams: Utopian Vision and Experimental Life in the Russian Revolution* (New York, 1989), pp. 13–36.
6 See Sheila Fitzpatrick, *The Russian Revolution*, 2nd edn (Oxford, 1994).
7 See ibid., p. 68.
8 These characterizations and the following statistics are drawn from Moshe Lewin, *The Soviet Century* (London, 2005), pp. 296–7.
9 For information on the Cheka see Richard Pipes, *A Concise History of the Russian Revolution* (New York, 1995), pp. 217–30. On Soviet 'concentration camps' see Anne Applebaum, *Gulag: A History* (New York, 2003). Information on the camps in and around Moscow is drawn from Timothy J. Colton, *Moscow: Governing the Socialist Metropolis* (Cambridge, MA, 1995), p. 90.
10 On the Russian interest in German wartime planning see Silvana Malle, *The Economic Organization of War Communism, 1918–1921* (Cambridge, 1985), pp. 299–300.
11 On the utopian aspect of planning and War Communism see Stites, *Revolutionary Dreams*, pp. 46–52.
12 Cited ibid., p. 48.
13 Cited ibid. On the *Proletkult* see Maria Zalambani, *L'arte nella produzione: avanguardia e rivoluzione nella Russia sovietica degli anni '20* (Ravenna, 1998).
14 Kendall E. Bailes, 'Alexei Gastev and the Soviet Controversy over Taylorism, 1918–24', *Soviet Studies*, XXIX/3 (1977), pp. 373–94.
15 See K. N. Afanas'ev and V. E. Khazanova, eds, *Iz istorii sovetskoi arkhitektury, 1917–1925 gg.: dokumenty i materialy* (Moscow, 1963), pp. 13–14.
16 See ibid., pp. 202–3.
17 See Alessandro De Magistris, *La città di transizione: politiche urbane e ricerche tipologiche nell'URSS degli anni venti* (Turin, 1988), pp. 17–21.
18 S. Gurevich, 'O domakh-kommunakh', *Kommunal'noe khoziaistvo*, II/1 (1922), p. 10.
19 The most succinct account of these movements remains Camilla Gray's pioneering text. See Camilla Gray, *The Russian Experiment in Art, 1863–1922*, rev. and enl. edn (New York, 1986).
20 See Charlotte Douglas, *Swans of Other Worlds: Kazimir Malevich and the Origins of Abstraction in Russia* (Ann Arbor, 1980).
21 John E. Bowlt, *Russian Art of the Avant-Garde: Theory and Criticism, 1902–1934*, rev. and enl. edn (London, 1988), p. 119.
22 N. N. Punin, *O Tatline*, ed. V. Rakitin (Moscow, 1994), p. 33. See also Maria Gough, 'Faktura: The Making of the Russian Avant-garde', *Res*, XXXVI (1999), pp. 32–59.
23 Wassily Kandinsky, *Concerning the Spiritual in Art* (New York, 1977).
24 Wassily Kandinsky, 'Content and Form', in *Kandinsky, Complete Writings on Art*, ed. Kenneth Clement Lindsay and Peter Vergo (Boston, 1982), p. 88. On the Wagnerian origins of this idea see Juliet Koss, *Modernism after Wagner* (Minneapolis, 2010).
25 On Lunacharskii and Narkompros see Sheila Fitzpatrick, *The Commissariat of Enlightenment: Soviet Organization of Education and the Arts under Lunacharsky, October 1917–1921* (Cambridge, 1970).
26 Christina Lodder, *Russian Constructivism* (New Haven, 1983), p. 48.
27 See, for example Osip Brik, 'Into Production!', in *The Tradition of Constructivism*, ed. Steven Bann (New York, 1974), pp. 83–5; Christina Kiaer, *Imagine no Possessions: The Socialist Objects of Russian Constructivism* (Cambridge, MA, 2005).

28 See L. I. Ivanova-Veen, 'Prostranstvo VKhUTEMASa. Arkhitekturnye shkoly Moskvy 1920–1930-kh godov i ikh tvorcheskoe nasledie', in *Ot VKhUTEMASa k MARKhI. 1920–1936: Arkhitekturnye proekty iz sobraniia Muzeia MARKhI*, ed. L. I. Ivanova-Veen (Moscow, 2005), pp. 9–17.
29 Cited from Lodder, *Russian Constructivism*, p. 118.
30 See Fitzpatrick, *The Russian Revolution*, pp. 95–6.
31 El Lissitzky and Il'ia Ehrenburg, 'Blokada Rossii konchaetsia', *Veshch'/Objet/Gegenstand*, I/1–2 (1922), p. 1.
32 Ibid., p. 4.
33 Vladimir Mayakovsky, 'Prikaz po armii iskusstv', *Iskusstvo kommuny* (7 December 1918), p. 1.
34 On these festivals and celebrations see Vladimir Pavlovich Tolstoi, I. M. Bibikova and Catherine Cooke, eds, *Street Art of the Revolution: Festivals and Celebrations in Russia, 1918–33* (London, 1990).
35 On the plan for monumental propaganda see A. A. Strigalev, 'K istorii vozniknoveniia leninskogo plana monumental'noi propagandy (mart-aprel' 1918 goda)', in *Voprosy sovetskogo izobratel'nogo iskusstva i arkhitektury* (1976), pp. 213–50; Lodder, *Russian Constructivism*, pp. 53–5.
36 Lenin, 'On Proletarian Culture (1920)', p. 676.
37 On the Monument to the Victims of the Revolution see Afanas'ev and Khazanova, *Iz istorii sovetskoi arkhitektury, 1917–1925 gg.*, pp. 205–9; V. G. Lisovskii, *Ivan Fomin i metamorfozy russkoi neoklassiki* (St Petersburg, 2007), pp. 364–8.
38 R. Khiger, *Puti arkhitekturnoi mysli, 1917–1932* (Moscow, 1933), pp. 7–29.
39 On Fomin's project see Lisovskii, *Ivan Fomin*, pp. 341–5.
40 On these competitions see Afanas'ev and Khazanova, *Iz istorii sovetskoi arkhitektury, 1917–1925 gg.*, pp. 214–17.
41 See S. O. Khan-Magomedov, *Il'ia Golosov* (Moscow, 1988).
42 Cited in L. Zhadova, ed. *Tatlin* (New York, 1988), p. 185.
43 N. N. Punin, 'O pamiatnikakh', in *O Tatline*, ed. V. Rakitin (Moscow, 1994), pp. 14–17.
44 Lodder, *Russian Constructivism*, p. 61; Il'ia Ehrenburg, *A vse-taki ona vertitsia* (Berlin, 1922), p. 18.
45 On the later impact of Tatlin's *Monument*, see Richard Anderson, 'Vladimir Tatlin's *Monument to the Third International*', in *Wiley-Blackwell Companion to Architecture*, ed. David Leatherbarrow and Alexander Eisenschmidt (Chichester, forthcoming).
46 On Shukhov's tower see Rainer Graefe, ed. *Vladimir G. Šuchov, 1853–1939: Kunst der Konstruktion* (Stuttgart, 1990).
47 See I. Gel'man, 'Garden Cities for Russia', *Garden Cities and Town Planning*, XIII/2 (1923), pp. 21–4; Catherine Cooke, 'Le mouvement pour la cité-jardin en Russie', in *URSS, 1917–1978: la ville, l'architecture*, ed. Jean-Louis Cohen, Marco De Michelis and Manfredo Tafuri (Paris, 1979), pp. 200–233.
48 V. N. Semenov, 'O gorode-sade', *Kommunal'noe khoziaistvo*, II/8–9 (1922), p. 10.
49 'Tsentrosoiuz i Zhilishchnaia Kooperatsiia', *Kommunal'noe khoziaistvo*, II/13 (1922), pp. 17–18.
50 'Stroitel'no-poselkovoe Tovarishchestvo "Sokol"', *Kommunal'noe khoziaistvo*, II/13 (1922), p. 17.
51 See I. N. Khlebnikov, 'Plan GOELRO – Pervyi gosudarstvennyi zakaz sovetskoi arkhitektury', in *Problemy istorii sovetskoi arkhitektury: istoricheskie predposylki i nachal'nyi etap razvitiia: sbornik nauchnykh trudov*, ed. A. A. Strigalev (Moscow, 1985), pp. 52–61.
52 Cited ibid., p. 54.
53 On Klutsis see Margarita Tupitsyn, *Gustav Klutsis and Valentina Kulagina: Photography and Montage After Constructivism* (New York, 2004).
54 On these plans see V. E. Khazanova, *Sovetskaia arkhitektura pervykh let Oktiabria. 1917–1925 gg.* (Moscow, 1970).

55 On Fomin's projects for the redesign of Petrograd see Lisovskii, *Ivan Fomin*, pp. 355–69.

56 On the competition see Afanas'ev and Khazanova, *Iz istorii sovetskoi arkhitektury, 1917–1925 gg.*, pp. 51–2.

57 On the relationship between Melnikov's project and the *phalanstère* see S. Frederick Starr, *Melnikov: Solo Architect in a Mass Society* (Princeton, 1978), pp. 47–51.

58 After setting the tone of discussions within SINSKULPTARKh and contributing graphic material to the group's output, Istselenov vanished from the Soviet scene. Istselenov appeared a short time later with an essay on new architecture in Russia that Bruno Taut published in his journal *Frühlicht*. See N. I. Istselenov, 'Die Architektur in Russland', *Frühlicht*, III (1922), pp. 88–91.

59 On Taut's conception of the non-utilitarian building and the *Stadtkrone* see Bruno Taut, 'A Necessity (1914)', in *Expressionist Utopias: Paradise, Metropolis, Architectural Fantasy*, ed. Timothy O. Benson and Edward Dimendberg (Berkeley, 2001), pp. 298–9; Bruno Taut, *Die Stadtkrone* (Jena, 1919). Istselenov's text is reproduced in S. O. Khan-Magomedov, *Ratsionalizm: ratsio-arkhitektura: 'formalizm'* (Moscow, 2007), pp. 59–62.

60 N. A. Ladovskii, 'Iz protokolov zasedaniia Komissii Zhivopisno-skul'pturno-arkhitekturnogo sinteza', in *Mastera sovetskoi arkhitektury ob arkhitekture*, ed. M. G. Barkhin (Moscow, 1975), vol. I, p. 44.

61 Cited in Khan-Magomedov, *Ratsionalizm*, p. 103.

62 Wassily Kandinsky, 'The Great Utopia', in *Kandinsky, Complete Writings on Art*, ed. Kenneth Clement Lindsay and Peter Vergo (Boston, 1982), vol. II, p. 448.

63 On the General Working Group of Objective Analysis see Lodder, *Russian Constructivism*, pp. 81–3.

64 Cited ibid., p. 89.

65 'Programa rabochei gruppy konstruktivistov INKhUKA', in S. O. Khan-Magomedov, *INKHUK i rannii konstruktivizm* (Moscow, 1994), p. 94.

66 Aleksei Gan, *Konstruktivizm* (Tver, 1922).

67 See Kiaer, *Imagine no Possessions*.

68 A. A. Vesnin, 'KREDO (1922)', in *Mastera sovetskoi arkhitektury ob arkhitekture*, ed. M. G. Barkhin (Moscow, 1975), vol. II, p. 14.

69 See Khan-Magomedov, *Ratsionalizm*, p. 110. For a compelling interpretation of the work of Ladovskii and the 'rationalists', see Margarete Vöhringer, *Avantgarde und Psychotechnik: Wissenschaft, Kunst und Technik der Wahrnehmungsexperimente in der frühen Sowjetunion* (Göttingen, 2007).

70 N. A. Ladovskii, 'Osnovy postroeniia teorii arkhitektury', *Izvestiia ASNOVA*, I (1926), p. 3.

71 Khan-Magomedov, *Ratsionalizm*, pp. 142–4.

72 El Lissitzky, 'The Film of El's Life', in *El Lissitzky: Life, Letters, Texts*, ed. Sophie Lissitzky-Küppers (London, 1980), p. 329.

73 Cited in Sophie Lissitzky-Küppers, ed., *El Lissitzky: Life, Letters, Texts* (London, 1980), p. 21.

74 On Lissitzky's transmission of this trend see Christina Lodder, 'El Lissitzky and the Export of Constructivism', in *Situating El Lissitzky: Vitebsk, Berlin, Moscow*, ed. Nancy Lynn Perloff and Brian Reed (Los Angeles, 2003), pp. 27–46.

75 Gan, *Konstruktivizm*, pp. 69–70.

76 Cited in M. Astaf'eva-Dlugach, 'Die erste Allrussiche Landwirtschaftsausstellung', in *Avantgarde I 1900–1923: Russisch-sowjetische Architektur* (Stuttgart, 1991), p. 117.

77 See A. V. Shchusev, 'Stroitel'stvo vystavki', *Stroitel'naia promyshlennost'*, 1/2 (1923), pp. 5–7.

78 Cited in Afanas'ev and Khazanova, *Iz istorii sovetskoi arkhitektury, 1917–1925 gg.*, p. 148.

79 Ibid., p. 146–7.

80 Cited in Igor' A. Kazus', 'Allrussischer Wettbewerb zum Projekt "Palast der Arbeit"

in Moskau (1922–1923)', in *Avantgarde I 1900–1923: Russisch-sowjetische Architektur* (Stuttgart, 1991), p. 120.

81 A. Vesnin, B. Vesnin and V. Vesnin, 'Konkursnyi proekt "Dvortsa Truda"', *Lef*, II/4 (1924), p. 59. On the Vesnin brothers' project see also K. Paul Zygas, *Form follows Form: Source Imagery of Constructivist Architecture, 1917–1925* (Ann Arbor, 1981); Catherine Cooke, 'The Vesnins' Palace of Labour: The Role of Practice in Materializing the Revolutionary Architecture', in *Architecture and Revolution: Contemporary Perspectives on Central and Eastern Europe*, ed. Neil Leach (London, 1999), pp. 38–52.

82 M. Ia. Ginzburg, 'Itogi i perspektivy SA', *Sovremennaia arkhitektura*, II/4–5 (1927), p. 112.

83 V. F. Krinskii, 'Iz doklada v INKhUKE "Put' architektury" (1921)', in *Mastera sovetskoi arkhitektury ob arkhitekture*, ed. M. G. Barkhin (Moscow, 1975), vol. II, pp. 116–17.

84 K. Zelinskii, 'Stil' i stal'', *Pravda*, 13 June 1923.

85 A. V. Shchusev, 'O printsipakh arkhitekturnogo stroitel'stva', *Stroitel'naia promyshlennost'*, II/12 (1924), p. 761.

## chapter four: Socialist Construction

1 Erich Mendelsohn, *Russland, Europa, Amerika, ein architektonischer Querschnitt* (Berlin, 1929), p. 112. Translation modified.

2 See Richard Pipes, *A Concise History of the Russian Revolution* (New York, 1995), p. 377.

3 Walter Benjamin, 'Moscow', in *Reflections: Essays, Aphorisms, Autobiographical Writing* (New York, 1986), p. 106.

4 Aleksandr Rodchenko, 'Against the synthetic portrait, for the snapshot', in *Photography in the Modern Era: European Documents and Critical Writings, 1913–1940*, ed. Christopher Phillips (New York, 1989), pp. 238–42.

5 See Devin Fore, 'The Operative Word in Soviet Factography', *October*, CXVIII (2006), pp. 95–131.

6 Statistics from Timothy J. Colton, *Moscow: Governing the Socialist Metropolis* (Cambridge, MA, 1995), p. 155.

7 Walter Benjamin, 'Moscow Diary', *October*, XXXV (1985), p. 18.

8 Moshe Lewin, 'Society, State, and Ideology during the First Five-Year Plan', in *Cultural Revolution in Russia, 1928–1931*, ed. Sheila Fitzpatrick (Bloomington, IN, 1978), p. 52.

9 Margaret Bourke-White, *Eyes on Russia* (New York, 1931), p. 23.

10 See I. V. Nevzgodin, *Arkhitektura Novosibirska* (Novosibirsk, 2005), p. 12.

11 On 'cultural revolution' see Sheila Fitzpatrick, *The Cultural Front: Power and Culture in Revolutionary Russia* (Ithaca, NY, 1992); Michael David-Fox, 'What is Cultural Revolution?', *Russian Review*, LVIII/2 (1999), pp. 181–201.

12 On Larin see Anatole Kopp, *Changer la vie, changer la ville: de la vie nouvelle aux problèmes urbains, U.R.S.S. 1917–1932* (Paris, 1975).

13 M. Ia. Ginzburg, 'Itogi i perspektivy SA', *Sovremennaia arkhitektura*, II/4–5 (1927), p. 116.

14 Cited in A. A. Strigalev and I. V. Kokkinaki, eds, *Konstantin Stepanovich Mel'nikov: arkhitektura moei zhizni, tvorcheskaia kontseptsiia: tvorcheskaia praktika* (Moscow, 1985), p. 174.

15 See Jean-Louis Cohen, *Le Corbusier and the Mystique of the USSR: Theories and Projects for Moscow, 1928–1936* (Princeton, 1992).

16 Excerpts from Behne's book *Der Moderne Zweckbau* (Munich, 1926) appeared in Russian translation *before* it was published in its original German. See 'Sovremennaia tselesoobraznaia arkhitektura', *Stroitel'naia promyshlennost'*, III/12 (1925), pp. 871–3. See also the Russian translation of Neutra's *Wie baut Amerika?* (Stuttgart, 1927); Richard Neutra, *Kak stroit Amerika?* (Moscow, 1929).

17 'New Architecture Develops in Russia', *New York Times* (29 May 1927), p. E1.
18 M. Ia. Ginzburg, 'Mezhdunarodnyi front sovremennoi arkhitektury', *Sovremennaia arkhitektura*, I/2 (1926), pp. 41–6.
19 On VOKS and its role in architectural life see 'Sobesedovanie v VOKS'e', *Sovremennaia arkhitektura*, I/2 (1926), pp. 60–62; Michael David-Fox, 'From Illusory "Society" to Intellectual "Public": VOKS, International Travel and Party-Intelligentsia Relations in the Interwar Period', *Contempoary European History*, XI/1 (2002), pp. 7–32.
20 Cited in Cohen, *Le Corbusier and the Mystique of the USSR*, p. 90.
21 Christian Borngräber, 'Die Mitarbeit antifaschistischer Architekten am sozialistischen Aufbau während der ersten beiden Fünfjahrpläne', in *Exil in der UdSSR*, ed. Klaus Jarmatz, Simone Barck and Peter Diezel (Frankfurt, 1979), pp. 326–47.
22 See Thomas Flierl, ed., *Standardstädte: Ernst May in der Sowjetunion 1930–1933: Texte und Dokumente* (Berlin, 2012).
23 See Eric Mumford, *The CIAM Discourse on Urbanism, 1928–1960* (Cambridge, MA, 2000), p. 66.
24 Karel Teige, 'Architektura a třídní boj', *ReD*, III/10 (1929–31), pp. 297–310. Cited in Otakar Máčel, 'Paradise Lost: Teige and Soviet Russia', *Rassegna*, XV/53 (1993), p. 73.
25 'Arbeitsgemeinschaft proletarischer Architekten', *Bauwelt*, XXX/4 (1931), p. 128.
26 Kollektiv für sozialistisches Bauen, *Proletarische Bauausstellung* (Berlin, 1931); Kurt Junghanns, 'Vor 50 Jahren: Erste Proletarische Bauausstellung in Berlin 1931', *Architektur der DDR* (May 1981), pp. 305–7.
27 Alexander von Senger, *Die Brandfackel Moskaus* (Zurzach-Schweiz, 1931).
28 El Lissitzky, 'SSSR's Architektur', *Das Kunstblatt*, IX (1925), p. 49.
29 El Lissitzky, *Rußland: Die Rekonstruktion der Architektur in der Sowjetunion*, ed. Joseph Ganther (Vienna, 1930).
30 N. A. Ladovskii, 'Psikho-tekhnicheskaia laboratoriia arkhitektury (V poriadke postanovki voprosa)', *Izvestiia ASNOVA*, I (1926), p. 7. Münsterberg's key work *Grundzüge der Psychotechnik* (Leipzig, 1914) was published in Russian translation in 1924–5.
31 N. Dokuchaev, 'Sovremennaia russkaia arkhitektura i zapadnye paralleli', *Sovetskoe iskusstvo*, III/2 (1927), p. 10.
32 See J. Christoph Bürkle, ed., *El Lissitzky: der Traum vom Wolkenbügel: El Lissitzky – Emil Roth – Mart Stam* (Zurich, 1991).
33 M. Ia. Ginzburg, *Stil' i epokha* (Moscow, 1924); M. Ia. Ginzburg, *Style and Epoch*, trans. Anatole Senkevitch (Cambridge, MA, 1982).
34 Ginzburg, *Style and Epoch*, pp. 100–101.
35 The book drew on Le Corbusier's *Vers une architecture* (1923). On the resonance of American industrial architecture in the European context see Reyner Banham, *A Concrete Atlantis: U.S. Industrial Building and European Modern Architecture, 1900–1925* (Cambridge, MA, 1986).
36 See Kristin Romberg, 'From *Veshch'* to SA: Journal as Object', in *Architecture in Print: Design and Debate in the Soviet Union, 1919–1935* (New York, 2005), pp. 15–24.
37 'ASNOVA', *Sovremennaia arkhitektura*, I/2 (1926), p. 59.
38 I. V. Kokkinaki, 'The First Exhibition of Modern Architecture in Moscow', *Architectural Design Profile*, XLVII (1983), pp. 50–59.
39 K. Melnikov, 'Arkhitektura moei zhizni', in *Konstantin Stepanovich Mel'nikov*, ed. A. A. Strigalev and I. V. Kokkinaki (Moscow, 1985), p. 81.
40 See Fitzpatrick, *The Cultural Front*.
41 VOPRA, 'Deklaratsiia ob"edineniia proletarskikh arkhitektorov', *Pechat' i revoliutsiia*, VI/6 (1929), p. 127.
42 On the competition see Catherine Cooke and I. A. Kazus', *Soviet Architectural Competitions, 1924–1936* (London, 1992), pp. 468–72; Danilo Udovički-Selb, 'Between Modernism and Socialist Realism: Soviet Architectural Culture under Stalin's

Revolution from Above, 1928–1938', *Journal of the Society of Architectural Historians*, LXVIII/4 (2009).
43 'Protest', *Sovremennaia arkhitektura*, IV/3 (1929), p. i; 'Moskovskie arkhitekturnye organizatsii po povodu konkursa na zdanie Leninskoi biblioteki', *Stroitel'stvo Moskvy*, VI/7 (1929), p. 22.
44 'Deklaratsiia VANO', *Sovremennaia arkhitektura*, VI/3 (1930), p. i.
45 See V. E. Khazanova, 'Rabota arkhitektora A. Burov v kino', in *Voprosy sovetskogo izobrazitel'nogo iskusstva i arkhitektura*, ed. V. E. Khazanova (Moscow, 1973), pp. 466–71.
46 See Iakov Georgievich Chernikhov, *Konstruktsiia arkhitekturnykh i mashinnykh form* (Leningrad, 1931).
47 Henri Barbusse, *One Looks at Russia*, trans. Warre B. Wells (London, 1931).
48 M. Ia. Ginzburg, 'Dom pravitel'stva v Alma-Ata', *Sovremennaia arkhitektura*, III/3 (1928), pp. 75–6.
49 M. Ia. Ginzburg, 'Natsional'naia arkhitektura narodov SSSR', *Sovremennaia arkhitektura*, I/5–6 (1926), p. 114.
50 A. V. Shchusev, 'Proekt vremennogo mavzoleia na mogile Vladimira Il'icha Lenina', *Stroitel'naia promyshlennost'*, II/4 (1924), p. 235. On the construction history of Lenin's Mausoleum see A. N. Kotyrev, *Mavzolei V. I. Lenina: Proektirovanie i stroitel'stvo* (Moscow, 1971).
51 On Mendelsohn's factory see M. S. Shtiglits, 'Erich Mendelsohn's Red Banner Factory and Saint Petersburg's Industrial Architecture', *Future Anterior*, V/1 (2008), pp. 28–37.
52 See 'Problema "zagranitsy"', *Stroitel'naia promyshlennost'*, III/12 (1925), pp. 819–20.
53 Cited in Cohen, *Le Corbusier and the Mystique of the USSR*, p. 79.
54 See Le Corbusier, *Precisions* (Cambridge, MA, 1991).
55 M. Merzhanov, 'Sanatorii-gigant', *Arkhitektura SSSR* (August 1934), pp. 28–31.
56 See Boris M. Shpotov, 'Ford in Russia, from 1909 to World War II', in *Ford, 1903–2003: The European History*, ed. Hubert Bonin, Yannick Lung and Steven Tolliday (Paris, 2003), pp. 509–29.
57 See Richard Cartwright Austin, *Building Utopia: Erecting Russia's First Modern City, 1930* (Kent, OH, 2004).
58 Anatole Senkevitch, 'Albert Kahn in Russland', *Bauwelt*, LXXXVI/48 (1995), pp. 2808–17.
59 Anne Dickason Rassweiler, *The Generation of Power: The History of Dneprostroi* (New York, 1988).
60 On *byt* and its meaning see Victor Buchli, *An Archaeology of Socialism* (Oxford, 1999).
61 See A. Lunacharskii, *O byte* (Moscow, 1927).
62 El Lissitzky, 'Kul'tura zhil'ia', *Stroitel'naia promyshlennost'*, IV/12 (1926), p. 877.
63 See A. Karra and V. V. Smirnov, 'Besprintsipnyi eksperiment', *Stroitel'stvo Moskvy*, VI/10 (1929), p. 20.
64 See Iurii Trifonov, *Another Life; and, The House on the Embankment* (New York, 1983).
65 M. Ia. Ginzburg, 'Slushali: problemy tipizatsii zhil'ia RSFSR', *Sovremennaia arkhitektura*, IV/1 (1929), p. 4.
66 Benjamin, 'Moscow', p. 108.
67 On the Narkomfin project see Victor Buchli, 'Moisei Ginzburg's Narkomfin Communal House in Moscow: Contesting the Social and Material World', *Journal of the Society of Architectural Historians*, LVII/2 (1998), pp. 160–81.
68 See Karel Teige, *The Minimum Dwelling* (Cambridge, MA, 2002).
69 Jean-Louis Cohen discovered the blueprints of the Narkomfin building that Le Corbusier brought back to Paris, in 1929, in the collection of the Fondation Le Corbusier. See Cohen, *Le Corbusier and the Mystique of the USSR*, pp. 122–4.
70 John Robert Mullin, 'City Planning in Frankfurt, Germany, 1925–1932: A Study in Practical Utopianism', *Journal of Urban History*, IV/1 (1977), pp. 3–28.
71 On May's activities in the USSR see Flierl, *Standardstädte: Ernst May in der Sowjetunion 1930–1933: Texte und Dokumente*, pp. 33–164.

72 See N. A. Miliutin, *Sotsgorod: Problema stroitelstva sotsialisticheskikh gorodov: osnovnye voprosy ratsionalnoi planirovki i stroitelstva naselennykh mest SSSR* (Moscow, 1930).
73 See L. M. Sabsovich, *Sotsialisticheskie goroda* (Moscow, 1930).
74 See M. Okhitovich, 'K probleme goroda: o sposobakh vospriiatiia arkhitekturnogo opyta', *Sovremennaia arkhitektura*, IV/4 (1929), p. 133.
75 TSK VKP(b), 'Concerning the work of reconstructing our way of life; Resolution of the TSK VKP(b) 16 May 1930', in *Sotsgorod: The Problem of Building Socialist Cities* (Cambridge, MA, 1974), p. 124.
76 Beatrice King, *Changing Man: The Education System of the USSR* (London, 1936).
77 Cited in Gail Warshofsky Lapidus, 'Educational Strategies and Cultural Revolution: The Politics of Soviet Development', in *Cultural Revolution in Russia, 1928–1931*, ed. Sheila Fitzpatrick (Bloomington, IN, 1978), p. 82.
78 See Cohen, *Le Corbusier and the Mystique of the USSR*, pp. 205–9.
79 El Lissitzky, *Russland: Architektur für eine Weltrevolution* (Braunschweig, 1989), p. 28.
80 V. Shcherbakov, 'Kul'turnyi Dneprostroi: vtoroi konkurs proektov dvortsa kul'tury v leninskoi slobode', *Stroitel'stvo Moskvy*, VIII/1 (1931), pp. 29–34.
81 Ivan Leonidov, 'Dvorets kul'tury', *Sovremennaia arkhitektura*, V/5 (1930).
82 Aleksandr Karra and Vasilii Simbirtsev, 'Forpost proletarskoi kul'tury (Konkurs na proekt Dvortsa kul'tury Proletarskogo raiona)', *Stroitel'stvo Moskvy*, VII/8-9 (1930), pp. 20–24.
83 A. G. Mordvinov, 'Leonidovshchina i ee vred', *Iskusstvo v massy* (December 1930), pp. 12–15.
84 See K. N. Afanas'ev and V. E. Khazanova, eds, *Iz istorii sovetskoi arkhitektury, 1926–1932 gg.: dokumenty i materialy: tvorcheskie ob'edineniia* (Moscow, 1970), p. 142.

## chapter five: Architecture and Stalin's Revolution

1 Aleksei Tolstoi, 'Poiski monumental'nosti', *Izvestiia* (27 February 1932), p. 3.
2 N. P. Zapletin, 'Perelomnyi etap proletarskoi arkhitektury', *Stroitel'stvo Moskvy*, IX/3 (1932), p. 28.
3 Hans Schmidt, 'Die Sowjetunion und das neue Bauen', *Die neue Stadt*, VII/6–7 (1932), p. 146. See also Max Raphael's critique of the project: Max Raphael, 'Das Sowjetpalais: Eine marxistische Kritik an einer reaktionären Architektur', in *Für eine demokratische Architektur* (Frankfurt am Main, 1976), pp. 53–131.
4 Cited in Jean-Louis Cohen, *Le Corbusier and the Mystique of the USSR: Theories and Projects for Moscow, 1928–1936* (Princeton, 1992), pp. 193–4.
5 See 'Protokol zasedaniia Soveta Stroitel'stva Dvortsa Sovetov,' March–April 1931, TSAGM, f. 694, op. 1, d. 3, l. 65–6.
6 Cited from José Manuel Prieto, 'Reading Mandelstam on Stalin', *New York Review of Books* (10 June 2010). Translation from Prieto's Spanish by Esther Allen.
7 R. W. Davies et al., eds, *The Stalin-Kaganovich Correspondence, 1931–1936* (New Haven, 2003), pp. 177–8.
8 See N. Atarov, *Dvorets Sovetov* (Moscow, 1940).
9 On 'Ever Higher' see Katerina Clark, *The Soviet Novel: History as Ritual*, 3rd edn (Bloomington, IN, 2000), pp. 136–41.
10 Stephen Kotkin, *Magnetic Mountain: Stalinism as a Civilization* (Berkeley, 1995), p. 2.
11 Leon Trotsky, *The Revolution Betrayed: What is the Soviet Union and Where is it Going?*, 1st edn (Garden City, NY, 1937), p. 105.
12 See Sheila Fitzpatrick, *The Cultural Front: Power and Culture in Revolutionary Russia* (Ithaca, NY, 1992), pp. 91–114.
13 See Stephen Wheatcroft, 'The Scale and Nature of German and Soviet Repression and Mass Killings, 1930–45', *Europe-Asia Studies*, XLVIII/8 (1996), pp. 1319–53.

14 See Catherine Merridale, 'The 1937 Census and the Limits of Stalinist Rule', *Historical Journal*, XXXIX/1 (1996), pp. 225–40; Karl Schlögel, *Terror und Traum: Moskau 1937* (Munich, 2008).
15 Timothy J. Colton, *Moscow: Governing the Socialist Metropolis* (Cambridge, MA, 1995), pp. 757–8.
16 See Sheila Fitzpatrick, *Everyday Stalinism: Ordinary Life in Extraordinary Times: Soviet Russia in the 1930s* (New York, 1999), pp. 41–2. See also Alessandro De Magistris, 'Culture architecturale et projet urbain dans les années 30', *Cahiers du Monde russe et soviétique*, XXXII/4 (1991), pp. 609–26.
17 André Gide, *Afterthoughts: A Sequel to Back from the U.S.S.R.*, trans. Dorothy Bussy (London, 1937), p. 18.
18 Alec Nove, *An Economic History of the U.S.S.R: 1917–1991*, 3rd edn (London, 1992), pp. 259–72.
19 See J. Arch Getty and Oleg V. Naumov, *The Road to Terror: Stalin and the Self-Destruction of the Bolsheviks, 1932–1939* (New Haven, 1999), pp. 247–99.
20 See Anne Applebaum, *Gulag: A History* (New York, 2003).
21 Mikhail Bulgakov, *The Master and Margarita*, trans. Richard Pevear and Larissa Volokhonsky (New York, 1997), p. 76.
22 TSK VKP(b), 'O perestroike literaturno-khudozhestvennykh organizatsii', in *Iz istorii sovetskoi arkhitektury 1926–1932 gg.: dokumenty i materialy: tvorcheskie ob'edineniia*, ed. K. N. Afanas'ev and V. E. Khazanova (Moscow, 1970), p. 163.
23 Cited in Fitzpatrick, *Everyday Stalinism*, p. 68.
24 See Francine Hirsch, *Empire of Nations: Ethnographic Knowledge and the Making of the Soviet Union* (Ithaca, NY, 2005).
25 See Yuri Slezkine, 'The USSR as a Communal Apartment, or How a Socialist State Promoted Ethnic Particularism', *Slavic Review*, LIII/2 (1994), pp. 414–52.
26 Cited in Fitzpatrick, *Everyday Stalinism*, p. 69.
27 See Hugh D. Hudson, *Blueprints and Blood: The Stalinization of Soviet Architecture, 1917–1937* (Princeton, 1993), pp. 136–46.
28 'Tvorcheskaia diskussiia Soiuza Sovetskikh Arkhitektorov', *Arkhitektura SSSR* (September–October 1933), p. 6.
29 D. Arkin, 'Vmesto zakliuchitel'nogo slova', *Arkhitektura SSSR* (September–October 1933), p. 25.
30 'Ob arkhitekturnom obrazovanii', *Sovetskaia arkhitektura* (November–December 1933), p. 1.
31 Harald Bodenschatz and Christiane Post, *Städtebau im Schatten Stalins: Die internationale Suche nach der sozialistischen Stadt in der Sowjetunion 1929–1935* (Berlin, 2003), p. 161.
32 See M. Kriukov, 'Proektno-planirovochnoe delo na vysshuiu stupen', *Stroitel'stvo Moskvy*, X/9 (1933), pp. 1–4.
33 M. Ia. Ginzburg, V. A. Vesnin and A. A. Vesnin, 'Problemy sovremennoi arkhitektury', *Arkhitektura SSSR* (February 1934), p. 69.
34 See Hugh D. Hudson, 'Terror in Soviet Architecture: The Murder of Mikhail Okhitovich', *Slavic Review*, LI/3 (1992), pp. 448–67.
35 'Sumbur vmesto muzyki: Ob opere *Ledi Makbet Mtsenskogo uezda*', *Pravda* (28 January 1936).
36 Arkhitektor, 'Kakofoniia v arkhitekture', *Pravda* (20 February 1936); 'Kakofoniia v arkhitekture', *Arkhitekturnaia gazeta* (23 February 1936), p. 2.
37 D. Arkin, 'Tvorcheskie uroki', *Arkhitektura SSSR* (July–August 1937), p. 51.
38 Cohen, *Le Corbusier and the Mystique of the USSR*, pp. 127–63.
39 Le Corbusier, *La ville radieuse, éléments d'une doctrine d'urbanisme pour l'équipement de la civilisation machiniste* (Boulogne, 1935).
40 On these schemes see Bodenschatz and Post, *Städtebau im Schatten Stalins*, pp. 137–53.

41 See L. M. Kaganovich, *Socialist Reconstruction of Moscow and Other Cities in the U.S.S.R.* (New York, 1931).
42 Bodenschatz and Post, *Städtebau im Schatten Stalins*, p. 155.
43 See A. V. Shchusev and L. E. Zagorskii, *Arkhitekturnaia organizatsiia goroda* (Moscow, 1934). On the Soviet interest in Ferriss see Jean-Louis Cohen, *Scenes of the World to Come: European Architecture and the American Challenge, 1893–1960* (Paris, 1995), pp. 151–6.
44 Schlögel, *Moskau 1937*, p. 69.
45 Lion Feuchtwanger, *Moskau 1937: Ein Reisebericht für meine Freunde* (Amsterdam, 1937), p. 32.
46 A. Ikonnikov, *Arkhitektura Moskvy: XX vek* (Moscow, 1984), p. 88; Greg Castillo, 'Gorki Street and the Design of the Stalin Revolution', in *Streets: Critical Perspectives on Public Space*, ed. Zeynep Çelik, Diane G. Favro and Richard Ingersoll (Berkeley, 1994), pp. 57–70.
47 See N. V. Baranov, 'General'nyi plan razvitiia Leningrada (Printsipy arkhitekturno-planirovochnoi kompozitsii)', *Arkhitektura Leningrada*, IV/3 (1939), pp. 7–20; V. G. Lisovskii, *Sankt-Peterburg: Ocherki arkhitekturnoi istorii goroda*, 2 vols (St Petersburg, 2009), vol. II, pp. 385–7.
48 Cited in G. A. Ol' and E. E. Levinson, *Evgenii Levinson* (Leningrad, 1976), p. 49.
49 V. M. Gal'perin cited ibid., pp. 49, 52.
50 G. I. Smirnov, 'Arkhitektura i stroitel'nye zadachi v tret'ei piatiletke', *Arkhitektura SSSR* (July–August 1937), pp. 11–13.
51 M. Ia. Ginzburg, 'Industrializatsiia zhilishchnogo stroitel'stva', *Arkhitekturnaia gazeta* (28 June 1937), p. 2.
52 Viollet-le-Duc is cited in B. N. Blokhin, *Arkhitektura krupnoblochnykh sooruzhenii* (Moscow, 1941), p. 122.
53 N. Bylinkin, 'Podlinnoe novatorstvo: O novoi rabote A. K. Burova i B. N. Blokhina', *Stroitel'naia gazeta* (10 June 1940), p. 2.
54 S. M. Kravets, 'Metro na zapade', *Arkhitektura SSSR* (April 1934).
55 Kolli's vestibule is modelled in part on the Tomb of Eurysaces (*c.* 30 BC) in Rome.
56 André Lurçat, 'Podzemnaia stolitsa', *Sovetskoe iskusstvo* (5 February 1935), p. 1.
57 On Dushkin's work on the Moscow Metro see N. O. Dushkina, ed., *Aleksei Nikolaevich Dushkin: Arkhitektura 1930–1950-kh godov* (Moscow, 2004).
58 I have drawn on Karl Schlögel's description of the canal's opening. See Schlögel, *Moskau 1937*, pp. 361–3.
59 On Fridliand's role in the construction of the canal, see I. S. Fridliand, 'Arkhitektura kanala Moskva-Volga', *Stroitel'stvo Moskvy*, XII/7 (1936), pp. 2–17.
60 I. G. Sushkevich, ed., *Arkhitektura kanala Moskva-Volga* (Moscow, 1939), p. 12.
61 His name does not appear in the official publication, *Arkhitektura kanala Moskva-Volga* (Moscow, 1939).
62 A. I. Mikhailov, 'Znachenie kanala Moskva-Volga v razvitii sovetskoi arkhitektury', in *Arkhitektura kanala Moskva-Volga*, ed. I. G. Sushkevich (Moscow, 1939), p. 87.
63 Trotsky, *The Revolution Betrayed*, pp. 116–17.
64 I. V. Nevzgodin, *Arkhitektura Novosibirska* (Novosibirsk, 2005), pp. 138–42.
65 Though symmetrical, the towers are not identical. Legend has it that when Shchusev sought Stalin's approval for one of two schemes, Stalin approved both, and the architects executed an incoherent design instead of contradicting Stalin's recommendation.
66 Louis Fischer, *Soviet Journey* (New York, 1935), p. 217.
67 Ginzburg had studied in Milan before the October Revolution. On references to the Milanese Novecento see Danilo Udovički-Selb, 'Between Modernism and Socialist Realism: Soviet Architectural Culture under Stalin's Revolution from Above, 1928–1938', *Journal of the Society of Architectural Historians*, LXVIII/4 (2009), pp. 466–95.
68 See M. Ia. Ginzburg, *Arkhitektura sanatoriia NKTP v Kislovodske* (Moscow, 1940).

69 See, for example, 'Betonirovanie fundamentov vysotnoi chasti Dvortsa Sovetov', *Arkhitekturnaia gazeta* (3 February 1938), p. 1.
70 See 'Problemy natsional'noi arkhitektury sovetskogo vostoka', *Arkhitektura SSSR* (August 1934), pp. 1–3.
71 M. Chkhikvadze, 'Zdanie filiala instituta Marksa-Engel'sa-Lenina v Tbilisi', *Arkhitektura SSSR* (April 1938), pp. 44–55.
72 A. V. Shchusev, 'Natsional'naia forma v arkhitekture', *Arkhitektura SSSR* (December 1940), pp. 55–6.
73 'Dom soiuza sovetskikh arkhitektorov', *Arkhitektura SSSR* (April 1941), p. 7.
74 See the contributions of Julie Hessler and Vadim Volkov in Sheila Fitzpatrick, ed., *Stalinism: New Directions* (London, 2000), pp. 182–230.
75 Schlögel, *Moskau 1937*, p. 478.
76 See V. P. Kalmykov, *Arkhitektura i proektirovanie kino-teatrov* (Moscow, 1941).
77 Iofan visited New York with a delegation of Soviet architects in the mid-1930s. See, for example: B. M. Iofan, 'Ob arkhitekture SShA', *Arkhitekturnaia gazeta* (12 March 1935).
78 See D. Arkin, 'Arkhitekturnyi obraz strany sovetov', in *Pavil'on SSSR na mezhdunarodnoi vstavke v Parizhe: Arkhitektura i skul'ptura* (Moscow, 1938), p. 4.
79 On Gorky Park see Katharina Kucher, *Der Gorki-Park: Freizeitkultur im Stalinismus 1928–1941* (Cologne, 2007).
80 V. K. Oltarzhevskii, 'Vystavka izobiliia', *Arkhitekturnaia gazeta* (8 April 1938), p. 3.
81 Vladimir Paperny, *Culture Two: Architecture in the Age of Stalin* (Cambridge, 2002), pp. 150–51.
82 See Slezkine, 'The USSR as a Communal Apartment', pp. 447–8; Greg Castillo, 'Peoples at an Exhibition: Soviet Architecture and the National Question', in *Socialist Realism without Shores*, ed. Thomas Lahusen and E. A. Dobrenko (Durham, NC, 1997), pp. 91–119.
83 See A. Ershov, 'Dva pavil'ona', *Arkhitektura SSSR* (February 1939), pp. 12–16.
84 See Jamey Gambrell, 'The Wonder of the Soviet World', *New York Review of Books* (22 December 1994), pp. 30–35.
85 'Russia Lays Stone for Fair Building', *New York Times* (7 November 1938), p. 21.
86 See 'Russia Quits Fair; Finns to Stay; Reds to Raze $4,000,000 Pavilion', *New York Times* (2 December 1939), p. 1; Anthony Swift, 'The Soviet World of Tomorrow at the New York World's Fair, 1939', *Russian Review*, LVII (July 1998), pp. 364–79.

## chapter six: World War, Cold War

1 Vasily Grossman, *A Writer at War: Vasily Grossman with the Red Army 1941–1945*, ed. Antony Beevor (New York, 2005), p. 342.
2 See 'Pamiatnik sovetskim voinam, pavshim pri shturme Berlina', *Arkhitektura i stroitel'stvo*, IV/7 (1949), pp. 9–13.
3 See Timothy Snyder, *Bloodlands: Europe between Hitler and Stalin* (New York, 2010).
4 See R. J. Overy, *Russia's War* (New York, 1998), p. 170; Lydia V. Pozdeeva, 'The Soviet Union: Phoenix', in *Allies at War: The Soviet, American, and British Experience, 1939–1945*, ed. David Reynolds, Warren F. Kimball and Aleksandr Oganovich Chubarian (New York, 1993), pp. 145–71.
5 John Steinbeck, *A Russian Journal* (New York, 1999), p. 51.
6 For a discussion of the demographic effects of the Second World War on Russian society see Overy, *Russia's War*, pp. 287–9.
7 Elena Zubkova, *Russia After the War: Hopes, Illusions, and Disappointments, 1945–1957* (Armonk, NY, 1998), p. 69.
8 A. V. Shchusev, 'Fascism is my Personal Enemy: A Russian Architect Looks upon Destruction', *California Arts & Architecture* (December 1942), p. 30.
9 Joseph E. Davies, 'The Soviets and the Post-War', *Life* (29 March 1943), p. 55.

10 See Richard Anderson, 'USA/USSR: Architecture and War', *Grey Room*, XXXIV (2009), pp. 80–103.
11 Il'ia Il'f and Evgenii Petrov, *Odnoetazhnaia Amerika: Pis'ma iz Ameriki* (Moscow, 2004); trans. as *Little Golden America* (New York, 2010).
12 R. Khiger, *Maloetazhnye doma v SShA*, ed. Karo Alabian (Moscow, 1944), p. 8.
13 Winston Churchill, *The Sinews of Peace: Post-war Speeches* (London, 1948), p. 100.
14 George Kennan, 'The Sources of Soviet Conduct', *Foreign Affairs*, XXV/4 (1947), p. 575.
15 Andrei Zhdanov, *O mezhdunarodnom polozhenii: doklad, sdelannoi na informatsionnom soveshschanii predstavitelei nekotorykh kompartii v Pol'she v kontse sentiabria 1947 g.* (Moscow, 1947).
16 George Orwell, 'You and the Atom Bomb', in *The Collected Essays, Journalism and Letters of George Orwell* (London, 1968), vol. IV, pp. 6–10.
17 See Andrei Artizov and Oleg Naumov, eds, *Vlast' i khudozhestvennaia intelligentsiia: Dokumenty TsK RKP(b)-VKP(b), VChK-OGPU-NKVD o kul'turnoi politike, 1917–1953 gg.* (Moscow, 1999), pp. 559–65.
18 Cited in Konstantin Azadovskii and Boris Egorov, 'From Anti-Westernism to Anti-Semitism: Stalin and the Impact of the "Anti-Cosmopolitan" Campaigns on Soviet Culture', *Journal of Cold War Studies*, IV/1 (2002), p. 68.
19 See Zubkova, *Russia After the War*, pp. 130–38; Snyder, *Bloodlands*, pp. 339–77.
20 Zubkova, *Russia After the War*, p. 152.
21 K. N. Afanas'ev, ed. *Iz istorii sovetskoi arkhitektury, 1941–1945 gg.: dokumenty i materialy: khronika voennykh let: arkhitekturnaia pechat'* (Moscow, 1978), p. 8.
22 See N. V. Baranov, *Siluety blokady* (Leningrad, 1982), pp. 16–18.
23 Ibid., pp. 20–21.
24 'Stroitel'stvo na vostoke', *Arkhitektura SSSR*, III (1943), p. 2.
25 G. Zakharov and Z. Chernysheva, 'Opyt proekirovania zhilishch dlia srednei azii', *Arkhitektura SSSR*, IV (1943), p. 16.
26 N. Bylinkin, 'Zhiloi poselok v gorode Gur'eve', *Arkhitektura i stroitel'stvo*, I/1 (1946), pp. 12–16.
27 Iu. Shass, 'Zhiloi kvartal v Magnitogorske', *Arkhitektura i stroitel'stvo*, III/2 (1948), pp. 17–22.
28 Ginzburg cited in Iu. L. Kosenkova, *Sovetskii gorod 1940-kh-pervoi poloviny 1950-kh godov: Ot tvorcheskikh poiskov k praktike stroitel'stva* (Moscow, 2009), p. 252.
29 A. Burov, 'Na putiakh k novoi russkoi arkhitekture', *Arkhitektura SSSR*, IV/4 (1943), p. 34.
30 K. S. Alabian, 'Predislovie', in *Maloetazhnye doma v SShA* (Moscow, 1944), p. 4.
31 On the NCASF and Alabian's study of American precedents see Anderson, 'USA/USSR: Architecture and War', pp. 80–103.
32 B. Barkhin, 'Sboryni dom tipa TSV-1a', *Arkhitektura i stroitel'stvo*, III/9 (1948), pp. 12–13.
33 M. I. Kalinin, 'Vosstanovitel'noe stroitel'stvo i zadachi arkhitektorov', *Arkhitektura SSSR*, VI (1944), p. 1.
34 Pasternak cited in Alexei Tarkhanov and Sergei Kavtaradze, *Architecture of the Stalin Era* (New York, 1992), p. 97.
35 See A. G. Mordvinov, *Khudozhestvennye problemy sovetskoi architektury* (Moscow, 1944), p. 23.
36 Ibid., p. 26.
37 See N. Ia. Kolli, 'O proekte planirovki goroda Kalinina', *Arkhitektura i stroitel'stvo*, I/9 (1946), pp. 3–6.
38 Cited in Kosenkova, *Sovetskii gorod*, p. 66.
39 See A. V. Shchusev and V. A. Lavrov, 'General'nyi plan Novgoroda', *Arkhitektura i stroitel'stvo*, I/5 (1946), pp. 3–5; A. N. Trifonova, *Velikii Novgorod v XX veke: k 1150-letiiu goroda* (Moscow, 2009).
40 O. I. Rzhekhina and R. G. Burova, eds, *Andrei Konstantinovich Burov: pis'ma, dnevniki, besedy s aspirantami, suzhdeniia sovremennikov* (Moscow, 1980), p. 102.
41 N. Bylinkin, 'Glavnaia magistral' Kieva', *Arkhitektura SSSR* XI (1945), p. 1.

42 See Iu. L. Kosenkova, 'Konkurs na sostavlenie eksperimental'nykh proektov zhilogo mikroraiona goroda. 1945–1946 gg.', *Arkhitekturnoe nasledstvo*, XL (1996), pp. 177–84.
43 K. I. Afanas'ev, 'Novaia zastroika na Khoroshevskom shosse v Moskve', *Arkhitektura i stroitel'stvo*, I/5 (1946), pp. 11–14.
44 'Gradostroitel'naia osnova sovetskoi arkhitektury', *Arkhitektura SSSR*, XV (1947), p. 1.
45 N. Bylinkin, 'Gradostroitel'nye utopii zapadnykh arkhitektorov', *Arkhitektura i stroitel'stvo*, II/1 (1947), pp. 14–16.
46 Peter Blake, 'The Soviet Architecture Purge', *Architectural Record*, CVI/9 (1949), p. 127.
47 M. P. Tsapenko, 'Sotsialisticheskii realizm – metod sovetskogo zodchestva', *Arkhitektura i stroitel'stvo*, IV/11 (1949), p. 11. See also M. P. Tsapenko, *O realisticheskikh osnovakh sovetskoi arkhitektury* (Moscow, 1952).
48 Tsapenko, 'Sotsialisticheskii realizm – metod sovetskogo zodchestva', p. 2.
49 See Vladimir Sedov, 'Vysotnye zdaniia pozdnego stalinizma', *Proekt klassika*, XVIII (2006), pp. 139–55; A. I. Kokurin and Iu. N. Morukov, '"Priniat' predlozhenie tovarishcha Stalina": Postanovleniia Soveta Ministrov SSSR o stroitel'stve novykh zdanii MGU na Leninskikh gorakh. 1947–1954 gg.', *Istoricheskii arkhiv*, XII/1 (2004), pp. 28–55.
50 Cited in Tsapenko, *O realisticheskikh osnovakh sovetskoi arkhitektury*, p. 355.
51 Kokurin and Morukov, '"Priniat' predlozhenie tovarishcha Stalina"', p. 33.
52 M. V. Posokhin, *Dorogi zhizni: iz zapisok arkhitektora* (Moscow, 1995), p. 49.
53 E. V. Markova et al., 'Sudby intelligentsii v Vorkutinskikh lageriakh. 1930–1950-e gody', *Novaia i noveishaia istoriia*, XLII/5 (1999), pp. 57–9. See also Oltarzhevskii's portfolio of skyscraper imagery and his authoritative book on Moscow's tall buildings: V. K. Oltarzhevskii, *Contemporary Babylon in pencil drawings* (New York, 1933); V. K. Oltarzhevskii, *Stroitel'stvo vysotnykh zdanii v Moskve* (Moscow, 1953).
54 Kokurin and Morukov, '"Priniat' predlozhenie tovarishcha Stalina"', p. 31. See also V. I. Pluzhnikov, 'Bezizvestnye stroiteli MGU na Leninskikh gorakh', in *Arkhiv naslediia* (2003), pp. 368–73.
55 A. I. Kokurin and Iu. N. Morukov, '"Priniat' predlozhenie tovarishcha Stalina' (prodolzhenie)', *Istoricheskii arkhiv*, XII/2 (2004), p. 41.
56 N. Kuleshov and A. Pozdnev, *Vysotnye zdaniia Moskvy* (Moscow, 1954), p. 32.
57 On Liang Sicheng and Soviet architectural influence in Beijing, see Jianfei Zhu, *Architecture of Modern China: A Historical Critique* (London, 2009), pp. 75–104.
58 On the Palace of Culture and Science see Anders Åman, *Architecture and Ideology in Eastern Europe during the Stalin Era: An Aspect of Cold War History* (New York, 1992), pp. 125–35; David Crowley, *Warsaw* (London, 2003), pp. 38–47.
59 A. Dobrovol'skii and A. Zavarov, 'Printsipy zastroiki Kreshchatika v Kieve', *Arkhitektura SSSR* (October 1952), p. 3.
60 The delegation included Kurt Junghans, Walter Pisternik, Kurt Liebknecht, Waldemar Adler, Edmund Collein and Kurt Leucht.
61 'Sixteen Principles for the Restructuring of Cities', in *Architecture Culture, 1943–1968: A Documentary Anthology*, ed. Joan Ockman and Edward Eigen (New York, 1993), pp. 127–8. Translation modified.
62 The literature on Stalinallee is enormous. See Johann Friedrich Geist and Klaus Kürvers, *Das Berliner Mietshaus, 1945–1989* (Munich, 1989), pp. 308–53; Werner Durth, Jörn Düwel and Niels Gutschow, *Architektur und Städtebau der DDR*, 2 vols (Frankfurt, 1998).
63 See Diana Kurkovsky, 'Monumentalizing Wheat: Soviet Dreams of Abundance', *Gastronomica*, VII/1 (2007), pp. 15–17.
64 On the relationship between Soviet and Chinese architects see Chzhou Tsziunian, 'Arkhitektura Kitaia v period c 1949 po 1959 god: tendentsii, napravleniia, stili', *Izvestiia Rossiiskogo gosudarstvennogo pedagogicheskogo universiteta im. A. I. Gertsena*, XXXV/76 (2008), pp. 381–7.
65 'Novye stantsii Moskovskogo metropolitena', *Arkhitektura SSSR* (February 1952), pp. 13–16.

1 G. Shchukin and I. Kadinaia, 'K novomu beregu (reportazh iz moskovskoi arkhitekturnoi gavani)', *Arkhitektura SSSR* (November 1955).

2 See Georgii Gradov to Nikita Khrushchev, 12 February 1954, RGANI, f. 5, op. 41, d. 6, l. 47–160. Natalia Solopova's research on this letter and Gradov's relationship to Khrushchev is indispensable. See Natalia Solopova, 'La préfabrication en URSS: Concept technique et dispositifs architecturaux' (PhD thesis, Paris VIII, 2001), pp. 118–76.

3 See N. S. Khrushchev, 'On Wide-scale Introduction of Industrial Methods, Improving the Quality and Reducing the Cost of Construction', in *Khrushchev Speaks: Selected Speeches, Articles, and Press Conferences, 1949–1961*, ed. Thomas P. Whitney (Ann Arbor, 1963), pp. 153–92.

4 See ibid., p. 171; 'Konstruktivism', in *Bol'shaia sovetskaia entsiklopediia*, ed. B. A. Vvedenskii (Moscow, 1953), vol. XXII, p. 437.

5 Khrushchev, 'On Wide-scale Introduction of Industrial Methods', p. 172.

6 See the collected volume that includes both *The Thaw* and its sequel, *The Spring*: Il'ia Ehrenburg, *A Change of Season* (New York, 1962).

7 I have relied on Stephen Bittner's interpretation of the thaw as both a metaphor and literary work: Stephen V. Bittner, *The Many Lives of Khrushchev's Thaw: Experience and Memory in Moscow's Arbat* (Ithaca, NY, 2008), pp. 1–18.

8 On the secret speech see Robert Service, *A History of Modern Russia: From Nicholas II to Putin*, 2nd edn (Cambridge, MA, 2003), pp. 338–41; William Taubman, *Khrushchev: The Man and his Era* (New York, 2003), pp. 270–75.

9 See E. M. Andreev, L. E. Darskii and T. L. Khar'kova, *Demograficheskaia istoriia Rossii: 1927–1959* (Moscow, 1998).

10 N. S. Khrushchev, *Report on the Program of the Communist Party of the Soviet Union: October 17, 1961* (New York, 1961), p. 37.

11 On Glavapu and Glavmosstroi see B. M. Frolic, 'Municipal Administrations, Departments, Commissions and Organizations', *Soviet Studies*, XXII/3 (1971), pp. 376–93.

12 F. Novikov, 'Vozrozhdenie arkhitektury', *Novyi mir*, XLII/3 (1966), p. 214.

13 Cited in J. D. Parks, *Culture, Conflict and Coexistence: American-Soviet Cultural Relations, 1917–1958* (Jefferson, NC, 1983), p. 166.

14 György Péteri, 'Nylon Curtain – Transnational and Transsystemic Tendencies in the Cultural Life of State-Socialist Russia and East-Central Europe', *Slavonica*, X/2 (2004), pp. 113–23. See also Greg Castillo, *Cold War on the Home Front: The Soft Power of Midcentury Design* (Minneapolis, 2010).

15 See Susan E. Reid, 'In the Name of the People: The Manège Affair Revisited', *Kritika*, VI/4 (2005), pp. 673–716.

16 N. S. Khrushchev, 'Khrushchev Speaks Again', in *Khrushchev and the Arts: The Politics of Soviet Culture, 1962–1964*, ed. Priscilla Johnson and Leopold Labedz (Cambridge, MA, 1965), p. 171.

17 'O razvitii zhilishchnogo stroitel'stva v SSSR', *Arkhitektura SSSR* (September 1957), pp. 1–6.

18 Timothy Sosnovy, 'The Soviet Housing Situation Today', *Soviet Studies*, XI/1 (1959), pp. 5–6.

19 See Solopova, 'La préfabrication en URSS', pp. 207–18.

20 See P. Spyshnov, 'Sanitarno-tekhnicheskoe oborudovanie zhilykh zdanii v SShA', *Arkhitektura i stroitel'stvo Moskvy* (June 1956), pp. 28–33; Castillo, *Cold War on the Home Front*, pp. 130–36.

21 See Solopova, 'La préfabrication en URSS', pp. 177–245; M. V. Posokhin, *Dorogi zhizni: iz zapisok arkhitektora* (Moscow, 1995), p. 146.

22 See Iu. L. Kosenkova, 'Konkurs na sostavlenie eksperimental'nykh proektov zhilogo mikroraiona goroda. 1945–1946 gg.', *Arkhitekturnoe nasledstvo*, XL (1996), pp. 177–84.

23 N. Svetlova, 'Tvoi dom', *Ogonek* (January 1959), p. 14.
24 See, for example, 'Puteshestvie v mire novoselov', *Ogonek* (August 1962), pp. 12–21.
25 Cited from D. Chechulin, *Zhizn' i zodchestvo* (Moscow, 1978), p. 111.
26 Peter Kihss, 'Soviet Fair Open; Kozlov and Nixon Stress Peace Aim', *New York Times* (30 June 1959), p. 16.
27 Quotes from the debate cited from 'The Two Worlds: a Day-Long Debate', *New York Times* (25 July 1959), pp. 1, 8.
28 Cited in Susan E. Reid, '"Our Kitchen is Just as Good": Soviet Responses to the American National Exhibition in Moscow, 1959', in *Cold War Modern: Design 1945–1970*, ed. David Crowley and Jane Pavitt (London, 2008), p. 160.
29 Khrushchev cited from N. Luppov, 'Sovremennyi inter'er dolzhen proektirovat'sia v komplekse s proektom zdaniia', *Arkhitektura SSSR* (October 1962), pp. 3–4. My discussion of the cultural politics of the Khrushchev-era interior is indebted to Victor Buchli's important work on the subject. See Victor Buchli, 'Khrushchev, Modernism, and the Fight against Petit-bourgeois Consciousness in the Soviet Home', *Journal of Design History*, X/2 (1997), pp. 161–76; Victor Buchli, *An Archaeology of Socialism* (Oxford, 1999).
30 Party programme cited in G. Gradov, *Gorod i byt (Perspektivy razvitiia sistemy i tipov obshchestvennykh zdanii)* (Moscow, 1968), p. 121.
31 See Mikhail Andreevich Il'in, *Vesniny* (Moscow, 1960); S. O. Khan-Magomedov, 'M. Ia. Ginzburg (K 70-letiiu so dnia rozhdeniia)', *Arkhitektura SSSR* (October 1962), pp. 33–46; A. V. Riabushin, 'Iz istorii sovetskogo zhilishcha', *Sovetskaia arkhitektura*, XVII (1965), pp. 175–86. On the contested nature of Constructivism in the early 1960s see Stephen V. Bittner, 'Remembering the Avant-Garde: Moscow Architects and the "Rehabilitation" of Constructivism, 1961–1964', *Kritika*, II/3 (2001), pp. 553–76.
32 On Hilský and Linhart's project see Rostislav Švácha, 'Funkcionalistická tvorba architekta Václava Hilského', *Umení*, XLIII/1–2 (1995), pp. 134–48.
33 Gradov, *Gorod i byt*, p. 157. See also G. Gradov, 'Etapy razvitiia sistemy kollektivnogo rasseleniia v gorodakh', *Arkhitektura SSSR* (June 1961), pp. 36–45.
34 Osterman's team included the architects A. Petrushkova, I. Kanaeva, G. Konstantinovskii, A. Guzeev and G. Karlsen.
35 S. G. Strumilin, 'Sozdaiutsia optimal'nye usloviia', *Literaturnaia gazeta* (6 November 1968), p. 10.
36 See Leonid Zhukhovitskii, 'Byt' li DNB?', *Literaturnaia gazeta* (14 January 1970), p. 12.
37 The Cheremushkinskii market was designed by F. Seletskii, V. Zhadovskaia, and the engineers B. Markov and L. Nikolaeva. See 'Krytyi rynok na iugo-zapade stolitsy', *Stroitel'stvo i arhitektura Moskvy* (December 1963), p. 21.
38 Susan E. Reid, 'Khrushchev's Children's Paradise: The Pioneer Palace, Moscow, 1958–1962', in *Socialist Spaces: Sites of Everyday Life in the Eastern Bloc*, ed. David Crowley and Susan E. Reid (Oxford, 2002), pp. 141–79.
39 N. A. Pekareva, 'Dvorets pionerov v Moskve', *Arkhitektura SSSR* (September 1962), p. 51.
40 A. V. Riabushin, 'V dukhe novoi napravlennosti: O kinoteatre "Rossiia" na pushkinskoi ploshchadi', *Stroitel'stvo i arhitektura Moskvy* (September 1961), pp. 11–14.
41 'Stadion v Dzhakarte', *Arkhitektura SSSR* (September 1960), pp. 14–17.
42 On Orekhov and his stadium see N. I. Smolina, 'Vitalii Orekhov', *Arkhitektura SSSR* (January 1988), pp. 46–52.
43 See *Programme of the Communist Party of the Soviet Union* (Moscow, 1961).
44 I. S. Nikolaev and N. P. Mel'nikov, *Vsemirnaia vystavka v Briussele, 1958: Arkhitektura, Konstruktivnye formy pavil'onov* (Moscow, 1963), pp. 98–102.
45 On this event, see Ol'ga Kazakova, 'Vsemirnaia vystavka 1967 goda v Moskve', *Proekt Rossiia*, LX (2011), pp. 191–200.
46 See D. Chechulin and N. Vishnevskii, 'Otkrytyi plavatel'nyi bassein "Moskva"', *Stroitel'stvo i arhitektura Moskvy*, IX/8 (1960), pp. 16–19.

47 L. I. Kirillova, ed., *Dvorets Sovetov: materialy konkursa 1957–1959 gg.* (Moscow, 1961), p. 12.

48 See Posokhin, *Dorogi zhizni*, pp. 151–2; 6–60; 65–76.

49 M. V. Posokhin, Ashot Ashotovich Mndoiants and N. A. Pekareva, *Kremlevskii dvorets s"ezdov* (Moscow, 1966), p. 94.

50 See A. Gozak, 'Sorok let spustia: Istoriia proektirovaniia i stroitel'stva Dvortsa S"ezdov', *Proekt Rossiia*, XXII (2002), p. 84.

51 Aleksandr Lozhkin, 'Akademgorodok: Sud'ba Utopii', *Proekt Rossiia*, XLVIII (2008), pp. 171–74.

52 See 'Gorod nauki', *Arkhitektura SSSR* (December 1963), pp. 3–19.

53 This circle also included A. V. Baburov, A. I. Zvezdin, S. A. Sadovskii, N. D. Kostrikin, E. P Sukhanova, Z. V. Kharitonova, I. Bel'man, G. Diumenton and N. B. Gladkova. On the NER group see Daria Bocharnikova, 'Inventing Socialist Modern: A History of the Architectural Profession in the USSR, 1932–1971', PhD thesis, European University Institute, Florence, 2014.

54 A. Gutnov et al., *The Ideal Communist City* (New York, 1971), p. 17. This English language book is a translation of the Russian first edition of 1966.

55 Peter Cook, 'The NER Group', *Architectural Design* (October 1968), pp. 481–2.

56 M. Rzianin, 'Moskovskie novostroiki: Ansambl' v Ostankine', *Arkhitekturnoe tvorchestvo SSSR*, II (1974), pp. 49–63.

57 B. Blokhin, 'Arkhitektura Bratskoi gidroelektrostantsii imeni 50-letiia Velikogo Oktiabria', *Arkhitektura SSSR* (November 1968), pp. 3–12.

58 See Elke Beyer, 'Competitive Coexistence: Soviet Town Planning and Housing Projects in Kabul in the 1960s', *Journal of Architecture*, XVII/3 (2012), pp. 309–32.

59 R. Iakubov, 'Gidroelektrostantsiia v Asuane', *Arkhitektura SSSR* (February 1965), pp. 33–42.

## chapter eight: Architecture in Developed Socialism

1 See Alexei Yurchak, *Everything Was Forever, Until It Was No More: The Last Soviet Generation* (Princeton, 2006).

2 Stephen E. Hanson, 'The Brezhnev Era', in *The Cambridge History of Russia*, ed. Ronald Grigor Suny (New York, 2006), vol. III, p. 306.

3 Robert Service, *A History of Modern Russia: From Nicholas II to Putin*, 2nd edn (Cambridge, MA, 2003), pp. 398–9. See also Odd Arne Westad, *The Global Cold War: Third World Interventions and the Making of Our Times* (Cambridge, 2005).

4 Service, *A History of Modern Russia*, p. 406.

5 Ibid., p. 407.

6 My analysis in this section draws on Hanson, 'The Brezhnev Era', pp. 300–305.

7 Ia. Dikhter, *Mnogoetazhnoe zhilishche stolitsy* (Moscow, 1979), pp. 46–7.

8 N. A. Pekareva, *M.V. Posokhin: narodnyi arkhitektor SSSR* (Moscow, 1985).

9 E. G. Rozanov, V. V. Lazarev and N. I. A. Matveeva, eds, *Arkhitektura obshchestvennykh zdanii* (Moscow, 1980).

10 See 'Soiuz arkhitektorov SSSR', in *Bol'shaia sovetskaia entsiklopediia*, ed. A. M. Prokhorov (Moscow, 1969–78), vol. XXIV, pp. 265–6.

11 See, for example, V. Khait, 'Arkhitektura zapada: konets 1960-kh – 1970-e gody', *Arkhitektura SSSR* (October 1975), pp. 49–57.

12 The series appeared in four volumes between 1972 and 1987.

13 A. Ikonnikov, *Arkhitektura SShA* (Moscow, 1979).

14 TSNII teorii i istorii arkhitektury, ed., *Sovremennaia arkhitektura SShA: kriticheskie ocherki* (Moscow, 1981), p. 1.

15 Timothy J. Colton, *Moscow: Governing the Socialist Metropolis* (Cambridge, MA, 1995), pp. 459–62. Colton has shown that the target population wavered between six and eight

million. Moscow's population would in fact rise to nearly nine million by 1990.

16 M. V. Posokhin, *Perspektivy razvitiia Moskvy* (Moscow, 1973), p. 20.

17 See M. V. Posokhin and L. Kulaga, 'Sozvezdie tsentrov planirovochnykh zon: Itogi konkursa proektov', *Stroitel'stvo i arhitektura Moskvy* (August 1972), p. 6.

18 See Reyner Banham, *Megastructure: Urban Futures of the Recent Past* (London, 1976).

19 Posokhin, *Perspektivy razvitiia Moskvy*, p. 13.

20 Ibid., p. 22.

21 'Na uroven' vozrosshikh trebovanii naroda', *Arkhitektura SSSR* (August 1969), p. 2.

22 See L. Diubek, 'V interesakh proektirovaniia i stroitel'stva', *Arkhitektura i stroitel'stvo Moskvy* (October 1970), pp. 2–7.

23 See L. Diubek, 'Na osnove edinogo kataloga', *Arkhitektura i stroitel'stvo Moskvy* (January 1969), pp. 4–11.

24 On Ivanovskoe and Iasenevo see A. Ikonnikov, *Arkhitektura Moskvy: XX vek* (Moscow, 1984), pp. 171–7.

25 M. V. Posokhin and L. Diubek, *Eksperimental'nyi zhiloi raion Chertanovo-Severnoe* (Moscow, 1976).

26 'Dlia sleduiushchego etapa zhilishchnogo stroitel'stva', *Arkhitektura SSSR* (June 1979), p. 13.

27 See B. Rubanenko and V. Kutuzov, 'Eksperimental'nyi zhiloi komkpleks v g. Gor'kom', *Arkhitektura SSSR* (June 1979), pp. 14–33; G. Kherkhol'd, 'Eksperimental'nyi zhiloi komkpleks v Magdeburge', *Arkhitektura SSSR* (June 1979), pp. 34–40.

28 See Hans Krause and Werner Rietdorf, eds, *Neue Wohnkomplexe in der DDR und der UdSSR* (Berlin, 1987).

29 B. Rubanenko and R. Patveev, 'Naberezhnye Chelny: Proektirovanie, stroitel'stvo', *Arkhitektura SSSR* (August 1976), pp. 4–22.

30 'Arkhitektory – BAMu', *Arkhitektura SSSR* (January 1977), p. 4.

31 On the promotion of the project see Christopher J. Ward, 'Selling the "Project of the Century": Perceptions of the Baikal-Amur Mainline Railway (BAM) in the Soviet Press, 1974–1984', *Canadian Slavonic Papers*, XLIII/1 (2001), pp. 75–95.

32 'Arkhitektory – BAMu', p. 7.

33 M. Barkhin, 'O novom etape sovetskoi arkhitektury', *Arkhitektura SSSR* (March 1975), p. 27. The work of these architects and many others was chronicled in the volumes of *Arkhitektura zapada*, published between 1972 and 1987.

34 Literature on this building is extensive. See Vitalii Samogorov et al., *Iubileinyi Ul'ianovsk* (Yekaterinburg, 2013).

35 'Zdanie muzea V. I. Lenina v Tashkente', *Arkhitektura SSSR* (December 1969), pp. 30–32.

36 See E. G. Rozanov and V. I. Reviakin, *Arkhitektura muzeev V.I. Lenina* (Moscow, 1986).

37 See the project by V. Shestopalov, Evgenii Rozanov and E. Shumov.

38 V. Lebedev, 'Premiia na mezhdunarodnom konkurse', *Arkhitektura SSSR* (February 1972), p. 51.

39 See Iu. Platonov, 'Tsentr sovetskoi nauki', *Stroitel'stvo i arhitektura Moskvy* (September 1973), pp. 2–7.

40 See A. Gozak and Viktoriia Krylova, eds, *Il'ia Cherniavskii* (Moscow, 2009).

41 Reyner Banham's *The New Brutalism* (1966) appeared in Russian translation in 1973, but the buildings and trends Banham discussed were well known to Soviet architects prior to the Russian edition. See Reyner Banham, *Novyi brutalizm: Etika ili estetika?*, trans. A. M. Khristani (Moscow, 1973).

42 Gozak and Krylova, *Il'ia Cherniavskii*, p. 10.

43 The 'Intourist' Hotel on Tverskaia Street was designed by V. Voskresenskii, A. Boltinov and Iu. Sheverdiaev, and constructed by the French firm Sefri Co. It was demolished in 2003.

44 Iu. Iaralov and Iu. Volchok, 'Fragment morskogo fasada goroda na Neve', *Arkhitektura SSSR* (December 1979), pp. 50–54.

45 See in particular Maekawa's Housing at Harumi (1957–8), Tokyo, and Spence's Hutchesontown C Flats (1958–65) in Glasgow.

46 V. Simbirtsev, 'V pogone za original'nost'iu: O dome na Begovoi ulitse', *Stroitel'stvo i arhitektura Moskvy* (November 1975), pp. 26–7.

47 The designers were obliged to incorporate the stage machinery of a different, uncompleted theatre into their design. See M. Rzianin, 'Novoe zdanie MKhATa, ego mesto i znachenie v zastroike Moskvy', *Arkhitektura SSSR* (August 1973), p. 9.

48 After von Gerkan, Marg und Partner's design was complete, the project was executed by Wilke Architects and Fa. Rütterbau, a subsidiary of the steel manufacturer Salzgitter AG. See V. Ivanov, 'Vozdushnye vorota Olimpiady', *Stroitel'stvo i arhitektura Moskvy* (December 1979), pp. 4–6.

49 Yachting competitions were held at the Olympic Yachting Centre (1975–80) in Tallinn, Estonia, designed by Avo-Himm Looveer, Henno Sepmann, Peep Jänes and Ants Raid.

50 See Ikonnikov, *Arkhitektura Moskvy*, p. 210.

51 A. V. Riabushin, 'Arkhitektura i ideologiia', *Arkhitektura SSSR* (May 1982), p. 17.

52 Robert Venturi, 'Iz knigi "Slozhnost' i protivorechiia v arkhitekture"', in *Mastera arkhitektury ob arkhitekture*, ed. A. Ikonnikov (Moscow, 1972), pp. 543–58. This volume, which had a print run of 20,000, made the writing of Venturi and other architects, albeit in excerpted form, widely available to Russian-language readers.

53 Charles Jencks, *Iazyk akhitektury postmodernizma*, ed. A. V. Riabushin and V. L. Khait (Moscow, 1985).

54 A. V. Riabushin and V. Khait, '"Postsovremennaia arkhitektura" – minusy i pliusy', *Dekorativnoe iskusstvo SSSR* (October 1979), p. 39.

55 According to Asse, the intention of the project was to 'combine constructivism with the work of Robert Venturi'. This aim accounts for the awareness of Venturi's concept of the 'decorated shed' that is evident in the building. Eugene Asse, interview with author, 18 July 2014, Moscow.

56 V. Glazychev, 'Dom v pereulke', *Arkhitektura* (3 June 1984).

57 See M. V. Posokhin, A. Gutnov and Z. Kharitonova, 'Arbat–peshekhodnaia ulitsa v zapovednoi zone', *Stroitel'stvo i arhitektura Moskvy* (September 1979), pp. 3–9.

58 See Vladimir Belogolovskii, *Felix Novikov: Architect of the Soviet Modernism* (Berlin, 2013), p. 79.

59 A. V. Riabushin, '"Strannaia arkhitektura" Andreia Kosinskogo', *Arkhitektura SSSR* (January–February 1990), pp. 67–75.

60 'Novoe zdanie Akademii khudozhestv SSSR', *Arkhitektura SSSR* (March–April 1983), p. 38.

61 A. V. Riabushin, *Gumanizm sovetskoi arkhitektury* (Moscow, 1986), p. 345.

62 See 'Novoe zdanie Akademii khudozhestv SSSR', p. 33. Many of the architects who participated in the competition had practised during the heyday of post-Second World War triumphalist excess.

## chapter nine: From *Perestroika* to 'Capitalist Realism'

1 Cited from David Remnick, *Lenin's Tomb* (New York, 1994), p. 461.

2 My analysis here draws on Stephen Kotkin's discussion of the Soviet collapse. See Stephen Kotkin, *Armageddon Averted: The Soviet Collapse, 1970–2000* (Oxford, 2001), pp. 15–19.

3 See Bart Goldhoorn, 'Architecture after Communism', in *Capitalist Realism: New Architecture in Russia* (Berlin, 2006), pp. 9–15.

4 See E. Asse, 'Sovetskie arkhitektory na mezhdunarodnom konkurse Tet-Defans', *Arkhitektura SSSR* (December 1983), pp. 34–42; 'Park XXI veka', *Arkhitektura SSSR* (March 1984), pp. 114–17.

5 'MARKhI – Kolumbia', *Arkhitektura SSSR* (March–April 1989), pp. 52–8.

6 Heinrich Klotz, *Paper Architecture: New Projects from the Soviet Union*, exh. cat., Deutsches Architekturmuseum, Frankfurt am Main (New York, 1990), p. 7.
7 See *Nostalgia of Culture: Contemporary Soviet Visionary Architecture*, exh. cat., Architectural Association, London (London, 1988), p. 6.
8 In particular, Lezhava directed a number of entries to the International Student Competition in 1978, sponsored by the International Union of Architects. See Vladimir Sedov and Sergei Khodnev, 'Ustnaia istoriia. K 20-letiiu bumazhnoi arkhitektury [Interview with Il'ia Lezhava and Mikhail Belov]', *Proekt klassika*, VI (2003), pp. 16–22.
9 Catherine Cooke has emphasized the relationship among Lezhava, the NER Group and the paper architects. See Catherine Cooke, 'A Picnic by the Roadside, or Work in Hand for the Future?', *AA Files*, XVIII (1989), pp. 15–24.
10 'Winners of the *Shinkenchiku* Residential Design Compeition', *Japan Architect* (February 1982), p. 12.
11 Lois Nesbitt, *Brodsky & Utkin: The Complete Works*, 2nd edn (New York, 2003), pl. 6.
12 'Konkurs zhurnala "*Arkhitektura SSSR*"', *Arkhitektura SSSR* (December 1983), p. 17.
13 Mikhail Belov, 'Zametki "bumazhnogo" arkhitektora', *Iunost'* (February 1986), pp. 107–9.
14 M. Tumarkin, 'Bumazhnaia arkhitektura: Piknik na obochine ili zadel' na budushchee?', *Arkhitektura* (13 January 1985), pp. 4–5; cited in Cooke, 'A Picnic by the Roadside', p. 19.
15 A. Tarkhanov, 'Stankovaia arkhitektura', *Arkhitektura i stroitel'stvo Moskvy* (January 1988), p. 6; see also A. Tarkhanov, 'Bumazhnaia arkhitektura po ee sostoianiu na 1986 g.', in *God arkhitektury*, ed. A. Polianskii and E. G. Rozanov (Moscow, 1987), pp. 77–9.
16 'Molodoi arkhitektor v proektnom protsesse', *Arkhitektura SSSR* (July–August 1985), p. 35.
17 Iurii Gnedovskii, 'Pravo na otvetsvennost'', *Arkhitektura SSSR* (November–December 1986), pp. 12–16.
18 'Vsesoiuznoe soveshchanie molodykh arkhitektorov v Kieve (aprel' 1986 g.)', *Arkhitektura SSSR* (November–December 1986), pp. 16–23.
19 'Zodchestvo: Programma perestroiki', *Arkhitektura* (13 June 1987), pp. 4–5; on this and the events leading up to the Congress see Cooke, 'A Picnic by the Roadside', pp. 21–3.
20 'Iz vystuplenii delegatov s"ezda', *Arkhitektura* (27 June 1987), p. 14.
21 'Postanovlenie TSK KPSS i Soveta Ministrov SSSR: O dal'neishem razvitii sovetskoi arkhitektury i gradostroitel'stva', *Arkhitektura* (24 October 1987), pp. 1, 4–5.
22 'VIII s"ezd arkhitektorov SSSR', *Arkhitektura SSSR* (January–February 1988), p. 16.
23 See '"Akant" dlia "Interkvadro"', *Arkhitektura SSSR* (July–August 1990), pp. 44–9.
24 Boris Shabunin, 'Pervaia stadiia svobody', *Arkhitektura SSSR* (January–February 1991), pp. 32–47.
25 Dmitrii Fesenko, 'Masterskaia Aleksandra Asadova: pervye itogi', *Arkhitektura SSSR* (July–August 1991), pp. 72–7.
26 'Brigada A', *Arkhitektura SSSR* (July–August 1991), pp. 64–71.
27 See 'Inter'ery kooperativnogo kafe "Atrium"', *Arkhitektura SSSR* (March–April 1989), pp. 6–7.
28 Iu. Grigor'ev, 'Vysotnaia gostinitsa na Leninskoi ploshchadi v Moskve', *Arkhitektura SSSR* (September–October 1988), p. 80.
29 M. Kubasova, 'Novoe pokolenie moskovskikh vysotok', *Arkhitektura i stroitel'stvo Moskvy* (November 1988), pp. 7–9.
30 'Six Monologues, or What Young Muscovite Architects Talk about in the Age of Perestroika', *Metamorfosi*, XI (1989), p. 44.
31 See 'Leonid Kuderov', *Arkhitektura SSSR* (July–August 1991), p. 43.
32 'Vizit v MENATEP', *Arkhitektura SSSR* (March–April 1991), p. 68.
33 A. Bokov, 'Tribuna', *Arkhitektura SSSR* (May–June 1991), pp. 2–3. Translation slightly modified.
34 Bart Goldhoorn, 'Editorial: Capitalist Realism', *Project Russia*, XXIV (2002), p. 5.

35 D. O. Shvidkovskii, 'Moscow Architecture in 1997: Trade, Power and the "New Russians"', *AA Files*, XXXIII (1997), pp. 3–12.
36 See O. A. Shvidkovskii, 'Glavnyi monument: Pamiatnik Pobedy sovetskogo naroda v Velikoi Otechestvennoi voine 1941–1945 godov', *Arkhitektura SSSR* (March–April 1984), pp. 81–3.
37 Irina Korob'ina, *Novaia Moskva 4: gid po arkhitekture Moskvy i Moskovskoi Oblasti 1987–2007* (Moscow, 2007), p. 44.
38 Andrei Trofimov on www.donstroy.com (accessed 20 May 2014).
39 Filippov cited in N. Malinin, *Arkhitektura Moskvy 1989–2009: putevoditel'* (Moscow, 2009), p. 301.
40 See Bart Goldhoorn and Philipp Meuser, *Capitalist Realism: New Architecture in Russia* (Berlin, 2006).
41 Many recent commentators have described the Palace of the Soviets competition of 1931–2 as the last time foreign architects had competed for a Russian commission. It appears, however, that the competition for the Academy of Sciences of the USSR (1934–5), in which the French architect André Lurçat participated, may have been the last event in which non-Russian/Soviet architects took part. See Jean-Louis Cohen, *André Lurçat, 1894–1970: L'Autocritique d'un Moderne* (Liège, 1995).
42 On this event see *Project Russia*, XXIX (2004), which is entirely devoted to international architectural competitions.
43 The competition was held after the director of the theatre, Valerii Gergiev, had unsuccessfully proposed awarding the commission to the American architect Eric Owen Moss in 1997. On the events surrounding the new Mariinskii Theatre, see Anastasiia Printseva, 'Kryshu sneslo', *Bol'shoi gorod* (10 December 2008), pp. 18–21.
44 See http://proektvlahte.ru (accessed 21 May 2014).
45 See Sergei Sitar, 'V preddverii i za porogom sakral'nogo', *Project Russia*, XLVIII (2008), pp. 30–36.
46 Grigorii Revzin, 'Mezhdu SSSR i Zapadom', *Proekt klassika*, XXV (2008), pp. 10–17.

# Select Bibliography


Afanas'ev, K. N., *Ideen, Projekte, Bauten: Sowjetische Architektur 1917 bis 1932*, trans. Helmut Barth (Dresden, 1973)

—, ed., *Iz istorii sovetskoi arkhitektury, 1941–1945 gg.: dokumenty i materialy: khronika voennykh let: arkhitekturnaia pechat'* (Moscow, 1978)

—, ed., *Iz istorii sovetskoi arkhitektury, 1926–1932 gg.: dokumenty i materialy: rabochie kluby i dvortsy kul'tury* (Moscow, 1984)

Afanas'ev, K. N., and V. E. Khazanova, eds, *Iz istorii sovetskoi arkhitektury, 1917–1925 gg.: dokumenty i materialy* (Moscow, 1963)

—, eds, *Iz istorii sovetskoi arkhitektury, 1926–1932 gg.: dokumenty i materialy: tvorcheskie ob'edineniia* (Moscow, 1970)

Åman, Anders, *Architecture and Ideology in Eastern Europe during the Stalin Era: An Aspect of Cold War History* (New York, 1992)

Anderson, Richard, 'USA/USSR: Architecture and War', *Grey Room*, XXXIV (2009), pp. 80–103

—, 'The International Fronts of Soviet Architecture, 1919–1939', in *In Search of a Forgotten Architect: Stefan Sebök 1901–1942* (London, 2012), pp. 192–206

—, 'A Screen that Receives Images by Radio', *AA Files*, LXVII (2013), pp. 3–15

Anderson, Richard, and Kristin Romberg, *Architecture in Print: Design and Debate in the Soviet Union, 1919–1935*, exh. cat., Miriam and Ira D. Wallach Art Gallery, Columbia University (New York, 2005)

Apyshkov, V., *Ratsional'noe v noveishei arkhitekture* (St Petersburg, 1905)

*Architectural Drawings of the Russian Avant-Garde*, exh. cat., Museum of Modern Art, New York (New York, 1990)

*Arkhitektura: raboty proektnykh i nauchnykh institutov Moskvy*, 5 vols (Moscow, 1970–91)

Arkin, D., ed., *10 rabochikh klubov Moskvy* (Moscow, 1932)

—, ed., *Arkhitektura sovremennogo zapada* (Moscow, 1932)

—, *Iskusstvo bytovoi veshchi: ocherki noveishei khudozhestvennoi promyshlennosti* (Moscow, 1932)

Astafeva-Dlugach, M. I., S. O. Khan-Magomedov and Christian Schädlich, *Avantgarde I 1900–1923: Russisch-sowjetische Architektur*, exh. cat., Kunsthalle Tübingen (Stuttgart, 1991)

Astafeva-Dlugach, M. I., Iu. P. Volchok and A. M. Zhuravlev, eds, *Zodchie Moskvy: XX vek* (Moscow, 1988)

Atarov, N., *Dvorets Sovetov* (Moscow, 1940)

Baiar, O. G., and R. N. Blashkevich, *Kvartira i ee ubranstvo* (Moscow, 1962)

Bann, Steven, ed., *The Tradition of Constructivism* (New York, 1974)

Barkhin, M. G., ed., *Mastera sovetskoi arkhitektury ob arkhitekture*, 2 vols (Moscow, 1975)

Bellat, Fabien, *Amériques-URSS: architectures du défi* (Paris, 2014)

Belousov, V. N., and O. V. Smirnova, *V. N. Semenov* (Moscow, 1980)

Bocharov, Iu. P., L. V. Baldin and N. F. Gulianitskii, eds, *Arkhitektura SSSR, 1917–1987* (Moscow, 1987)

Bodenschatz, Harald, and Christiane Post, *Städtebau im Schatten Stalins: Die internationale Suche nach der sozialistischen Stadt in der Sowjetunion 1929–1935* (Berlin, 2003)

Borisova, E. A., *Russkaia arkhitektura vtoroi poloviny XIX veka* (Moscow, 1979)
—, 'Arkhitektura v tvorchestve khudozhnikov abramtsevskogo kruzhka (U istokov "neorusskogo stilia")', in *Khudozhestvennye protsessy v russkoi kul'ture vtoroi poloviny XIX veka*, ed. G. Iu. Sternin (Moscow, 1984), pp. 137–82
Borisova, E. A., and T. P. Kazhdan, *Russkaia arkhitektura kontsa XIX–nachala XX veka* (Moscow, 1971)
Borisova, E. A., and G. Iu. Sternin, *Russkii neoklassitsizm* (Moscow, 2002)
Borngräber, Christian, 'Ausländische Architekten in der UdSSR: Bruno Taut, die Brigaden Ernst May, Hannes Meyer und Hans Schmidt', in *Wem gehört die Welt?: Kunst und Gesellschaft in der Weimarer Republik*, ed. Jürgen Kleindienst (Berlin, 1977), pp. 109–42
Bouvard, Josette, *Le Métro de Moscou: La construction d'un mythe soviétique* (Paris, 2005)
Brumfield, William Craft, ed., *Reshaping Russian Architecture: Western Technology, Utopian Dreams* (Cambridge, 1990)
—, *The Origins of Modernism in Russian Architecture* (Berkeley, 1991)
—, *A History of Russian Architecture* (Cambridge, 1993)
Buchli, Victor, 'Moisei Ginzburg's Narkomfin Communal House in Moscow: Contesting the Social and Material World', *Journal of the Society of Architectural Historians*, LVII/2 (1998), pp. 160–81
—, *An Archaeology of Socialism* (Oxford, 1999)
Burov, A. K., *Ob arkhitekture* (Moscow, 1960)
Bykov, Veniamin Evgenevich, and Mikhail Vladimirovich Alpatov, *Georgii Gol'ts* (Moscow, 1978)
Castillo, Greg, 'Gorki Street and the Design of the Stalin Revolution', in *Streets: Critical Perspectives on Public Space*, ed. Zeynep Çelik, Diane G. Favro and Richard Ingersoll (Berkeley, 1994), pp. 57–70
—, 'Peoples at an Exhibition: Soviet Architecture and the National Question', in *Socialist Realism without Shores*, ed. Thomas Lahusen and E. A. Dobrenko (Durham, NC, 1997), pp. 91–119
—, *Cold War on the Home Front: The Soft Power of Midcentury Design* (Minneapolis, 2010)
Chechulin, D., *Zhizn' i zodchestvo* (Moscow, 1978)
Chiniakov, A. G., *Brat'ia Vesniny* (Moscow, 1970)
Clark, Katerina, *Petersburg, Crucible of Cultural Revolution* (Cambridge, MA, 1995)
—, *Moscow, the Fourth Rome: Stalinism, Cosmopolitanism, and the Evolution of Soviet Culture, 1931–1941* (Cambridge, MA, 2011)
Cohen, Jean-Louis, 'America: A Soviet Ideal', *AA Files*, V (1984), pp. 32–40
—, 'Architecture and Modernity in the Soviet Union 1900–1937: Parts 1–4', *Architecture and Urbanism* (March, June, August, October 1991), pp. 46–67; 20–41; 3–19; 1–21
—, *Le Corbusier and the Mystique of the USSR: Theories and Projects for Moscow, 1928–1936* (Princeton, 1992)
—, *Scenes of the World to Come: European Architecture and the American Challenge, 1893–1960* (Paris, 1995)
—, *Architecture in Uniform: Designing and Building for the Second World War* (Montréal, 2011)
Cohen, Jean-Louis, Marco De Michelis and Manfredo Tafuri, eds, *URSS, 1917–1978: la ville, l'architecture* (Paris, 1979)
Colton, Timothy J., *Moscow: Governing the Socialist Metropolis* (Cambridge, MA, 1995)
Cooke, Catherine, 'Soviet Reaction to Post-Modernism', *Architectural Design News Supplement* (January 1982), pp. 18–21
—, 'Fedor Osipovich Shekhtel: An Architect and his Clients in Turn-of-the-century Moscow', *AA Files*, V (1984), pp. 3–29
—, 'A Picnic by the Roadside, or Work in Hand for the Future?', *AA Files*, XVIII (1989), pp. 15–24
—, *Russian Avant-Garde Theories of Art, Architecture and the City* (London, 1995)
—, 'Beauty as a Route to "the Radiant Future": Responses to Soviet Architecture', *Journal of Design History*, X/2 (1997), pp. 137–60

—, 'The Vesnins' Palace of Labour: The Role of Practice in Materializing the Revolutionary Architecture', in *Architecture and Revolution: Contemporary Perspectives on Central and Eastern Europe*, ed. Neil Leach (London, 1999), pp. 38–52

Cooke, Catherine, and I. A. Kazus', *Soviet Architectural Competitions, 1924–1936* (London, 1992)

Cooke, Catherine, and Susan E. Reid, 'Modernity and Realism: Architectural Relations in the Cold War', in *Russian Art and the West: A Century of Dialogue in Painting, Architecture, and the Decorative Arts*, ed. Rosalind P. Blakesley and Susan E. Reid (DeKalb, IL, 2007), pp. 172–94

Crowley, David, *Warsaw* (London, 2003)

Crowley, David, and Jane Pavitt, *Cold War Modern: Design 1945–1970*, exh. cat., Victoria and Albert Museum, London (London, 2008)

Crowley, David, and Susan E. Reid, eds, *Socialist Spaces: Sites of Everyday Life in the Eastern Bloc* (Oxford, 2002)

De Feo, Vittorio, *URSS architettura, 1917–1936* (Rome, 1963)

De Magistris, Alessandro, *La città di transizione: politiche urbane e ricerche tipologiche nell'URSS degli anni venti* (Turin, 1988)

—, *Mosca, 1900–1950: Nascita di una capitale* (Milan, 1994)

—, *La costruzione della città totalitaria: Il piano di mosca e il dibattito sulla città sovietica tra gli anni venti e cinquanta* (Milan, 1995)

—, *URSS, anni '30–'50: Paesaggi dell'utopia staliniana*, exh. cat., Accademia Albertina delle Belle Arti, Turin (Milan, 1997)

De Magistris, Alessandro, and Irina Korob'ina, eds, *Ivan Leonidov, 1902–1959* (Milan, 2009)

DeHaan, Heather D., *Stalinist City Planning: Professionals, Performance, and Power* (Toronto, 2013)

Dushkina, N. O., ed., *Aleksei Nikolaevich Dushkin: Arkhitektura 1930–1950-kh godov* (Moscow, 2004)

Egorov, V., 'Sovetskaia arkhitektura za rubezhom', *Arkhitektura SSSR* (June 1984), pp. 102–13

Eigel', I. Iu., *Boris Iofan* (Moscow, 1978)

Essaïan, Elisabeth, *Le prix de Rome: le grand tour des architectes soviétiques sous Mussolini* (Paris, 2012)

Eval'd, V. V., *Konstruktivnye osobennosti Amerikanskikh zdanii i estestvennye kamni, primeniaemye v sooruzheniiakh v soedinennykh shtatakh* (St Petersburg, 1895)

Fesenko, Dmitrii, *Fasad/Razrez: Rossiiskaia arkhitektura 1990-kh – 2000-kh gg. Po stranitsam zhurnala 'Arkhitekturnyi Vestnik'* (Moscow, 2008)

Feuchtwanger, Lion, *Moskau 1937: Ein Reisebericht für meine Freunde* (Amsterdam, 1937)

Ginzburg, M. Ia., *Ritm v arkhitekture* (Moscow, 1923)

—, *Zhilishche* (Moscow, 1934)

—, *Arkhitektura sanatoriia NKTP v Kislovodske* (Moscow, 1940)

—, *Style and Epoch*, trans. Anatole Senkevitch (Cambridge, MA, 1982)

Goldhoorn, Bart, and Philipp Meuser, *Capitalist Realism: New Architecture in Russia* (Berlin, 2006)

Gough, Maria, *The Artist as Producer: Russian Constructivism in Revolution* (Berkeley, 2005)

Gozak, A., *Ivan Leonidov* (Moscow, 2002)

Gozak, A., and Viktoriia Krylova, eds, *Il'ia Cherniavskii* (Moscow, 2009)

Gozak, A., Andrei Leonidov and Catherine Cooke, eds, *Ivan Leonidov: The Complete Works* (New York 1988)

Gradov, G., *Gorod i byt (Perspektivy razvitiia sistemy i tipov obshchestvennykh zdanii)* (Moscow, 1968)

Graefe, Rainer, ed., *Vladimir G. Šuchov, 1853–1939: Kunst der Konstruktion* (Stuttgart, 1990)

*The Great Utopia: The Russian and Soviet Avant-garde, 1915–1932*, exh. cat., Solomon R. Guggenheim Museum, New York (New York, 1992)

Gutnov, A., A. Baburov, G. Diumenton, Z. Kharitonova, I. Lezhava and S. Sadovskii, *The Ideal Communist City* (New York, 1971)

Hain, Simone, ed., *Reise nach Moskau: Quellenedition zur neueren Planungsgeschichte* (Berlin, 1995)
Hoisington, Sona Stephan, '"Ever Higher": The Evolution of the Project for the Palace of the Soviets', *Slavic Review*, LXII/1 (2003), pp. 41–68
Hudson, Hugh D., *Blueprints and Blood: The Stalinization of Soviet Architecture, 1917–1937* (Princeton, 1993)
Ikonnikov, A., *Arkhitektura Moskvy: xx vek* (Moscow, 1984)
—, *Russian Architecture of the Soviet Period* (Moscow, 1988)
Il'in, Mikhail Andreevich, *Vesniny* (Moscow, 1960)
Isachenko, V. G., ed., *Zodchie Sankt-Peterburga XIX-nachalo XX veka* (St Petersburg, 1998)
Isachenko, V. G., and I.U.V. Artem'eva, eds, *Zodchie Sankt-Peterburga, XX vek* (St Petersburg, 2000)
Kaganovich, L. M., *Socialist Reconstruction of Moscow and Other Cities in the U.S.S.R.* (New York, 1931)
Kazus', I. A., *Sovetskaia arkhitektura 1920-kh godov: organizatsiia proektirovaniia* (Moscow, 2009)
Khan-Magomedov, S. O., *M. Ia. Ginzburg* (Moscow, 1972)
—, *Alexandr Vesnin and Russian Constructivism* (New York, 1986)
—, *Pioneers of Soviet Architecture: The Search for New Solutions in the 1920s and 1930s* (New York, 1987)
—, *Il'ia Golosov* (Moscow, 1988)
—, *Konstantin Mel'nikov* (Moscow, 1990)
—, *VKhUTEMAS: Vysshie gosudarstvennye khudozhestvenno-tekhnicheskie masterskie: tekstil', skul'ptura, zhivopis', grafika, keramika, metal, derevo, arkhitektura, 1920–1930*, 2 vols (Moscow, 2000)
—, *Konstruktivizm: kontseptsiia, formoobrazovaniia* (Moscow, 2003)
—, *Nikolai Ladovskii* (Moscow, 2007)
—, *Ratsionalizm: ratsio-arkhitektura: 'formalizm'* (Moscow, 2007)
—, *Suprematizm i arkhitektura: problemy formoobrazovaniia* (Moscow, 2007)
—, *Ivan Nikolaev* (Moscow, 2008)
Khan-Magomedov, S. O., and Christian Schädlich, *Avantgarde II: 1924–1937: Sowjetische Architektur*, exh. cat., Kunsthalle Tübingen (Stuttgart, 1993)
Khazanova, V. E., *Sovetskaia arkhitektura pervykh let Oktiabria. 1917–1925 gg.* (Moscow, 1970)
—, *Sovetskaia arkhitektura pervoi piatiletki: problemy goroda budushchego* (Moscow, 1980)
—, *Klubnaia zhizn' i arkhitektura kluba, 1917–1941* (Moscow, 2000)
Khiger, R., *Puti arkhitekturnoi mysli, 1917–1932* (Moscow, 1933)
Khmel'nitskii, Dmitrii, *Arkhitektura Stalina: Psikhologiia i stil'* (Moscow, 2007)
—, *Zodchii Stalin* (Moscow, 2007)
Kiaer, Christina, *Imagine no Possessions: The Socialist Objects of Russian Constructivism* (Cambridge, MA, 2005)
Kirichenko, E. I., 'Arkhitektor I. P. Ropet', *Arkhitekturnoe nasledstvo*, XX (1972), pp. 85–93
—, *Feodor Shekhtel'* (Moscow, 1973)
—, 'Arkhitektor V. O. Shervud i ego teoreticheskie vozzreniia', *Arkhitekturnoe nasledstvo*, XXII (1974), pp. 3–18
—, *Arkhitekturnye teorii XIX veka v Rossii* (Moscow, 1986)
—, *Russkaia arkhitektura 1830–1910-kh godov*, 2nd edn (Moscow, 1986)
—, *Mikhail Bykovskii* (Moscow, 1988)
—, *Russkii stil': poiski vyrazheniia natsional'noi samobytnosti: narodnost i natsionalnost': traditsii drevnerusskogo i narodnogo iskusstva v russkom iskusstve XVIII–nachala XX veka* (Moscow, 1997)
—, *Gradostroitel'stvo Rossii serediny XIX–nachala XX veka*, 2 vols (Moscow, 2001)
Kirichenko, E. I., and G. A. Ivanova, *Khram Khrista Spasitelia v Moskve: istoriia proektirovaniia i sozdaniia: stranitsy zhizni i gibeli, 1813–1931* (Moscow, 1992)

Kirikov, B. M., *Arkhitektura peterburgskogo moderna: osobniaki i dokhodnye doma* (St Petersburg, 2003)
—, *Arkhitektura Peterburga kontsa XIX–nachala XX veka: Eklektika, Modern, Neoklassitsizm* (St Petersburg, 2006)
—, *Aleksandr Dmitriev: Arkhitektor pervoi poloviny XX veka* (St Petersburg, 2009)
Kirikov, B. M., and M. S. Shtiglits, *Arkhitektura leningradskogo avangarda: Putevoditel'* (St Petersburg, 2008)
Kirillova, L. I., ed., *Dvorets Sovetov: materialy konkursa 1957–1959 gg.* (Moscow, 1961)
Kitner, Iu. I., 'Arkhitektor I. S. Kitner', *Arkhitekturnoe nasledstvo*, XXV (1976), pp. 154–75
Klotz, Heinrich, *Paper Architecture: New Projects from the Soviet Union*, exh. cat., Deutsches Architekturmuseum, Frankfurt am Main (New York, 1990)
Kokkinaki, I. V., 'K voprosu o vzaimosviaziakh sovetskikh i zarubezhnykh arkhitektorov v 1920–1930-e gody: Kratkii obzor', *Voprosy sovetskogo izobratel'nogo iskusstva i arkhitektury* (1976), pp. 350–82
—, 'The First Exhibition of Modern Architecture in Moscow', *Architectural Design Profile*, XLVII (1983), pp. 50–59
Kopp, Anatole, *Town and Revolution: Soviet Architecture and City Planning, 1917–1935* (New York, 1970)
—, *Changer la vie, changer la ville: de la vie nouvelle aux problèmes urbains, U.R.S.S. 1917–1932* (Paris, 1975)
—, *L'Architecture de la période stalinienne* (Grenoble, 1978)
—, *Constructivist Architecture in the USSR* (London, 1985)
—, *Quand le Modern n'était pas un style mais une cause* (Paris, 1988)
Korob'ina, Irina, *Novaia Moskva 4: gid po arkhitekture Moskvy i Moskovskoi Oblasti 1987–2007* (Moscow, 2007)
Kosenkova, Iu. L., *Sovetskii gorod 1940-kh-pervoi poloviny 1950-kh godov: Ot tvorcheskikh poiskov k praktike stroitel'stva* (Moscow, 2009)
Kotkin, Stephen, *Magnetic Mountain: Stalinism as a Civilization* (Berkeley, 1995)
—, *Armageddon Averted: The Soviet Collapse, 1970–2000* (Oxford, 2001)
Kotyrev, A. N., *Mavzolei V. I. Lenina: Proektirovanie i stroitel'stvo* (Moscow, 1971)
Kradin, N. P., *Kharbin: Russkaia Atlantida* (Khabarovsk, 2001)
Krasheninnikov, A. F., and A. V. Rogachev, eds, *Zodchie Moskvy vremeni eklektiki, moderna i neoklassitsizma (1830-e–1917 gody): illiustrirovannyi i biograficheskii slovar'* (Moscow, 1998)
Krasovskii, Apollinarii, *Grazhdanskaia arkhitektura: Chasti zdaniia* (St Petersburg, 1851)
Krause, Hans, and Werner Rietdorf, eds, *Neue Wohnkomplexe in der DDR und der UdSSR* (Berlin, 1987)
Kreis, Barbara, *Moskau, 1917–35: vom Wohnungsbau zum Städtebau* (Düsseldorf, 1985)
Kruzhkov, Nikolai, *Vysotnye zdaniia v Moskve: fakty iz istorii proektirovaniia i stroitel'stva 1947–1956* (Samara, 2007)
*'Kunst in die Produktion!' Sowjetische Kunst während der Phase der Kollektivierung und Industrialisierung 1927–1933*, exh. cat., Akademie der Bildenden Künste, Berlin (West) (Berlin, 1977)
Latour, Alessandra, *Rozhdenie metropolii, Moskva 1930–1955: vospominaniia i obrazy* (Moscow, 2002)
—, *Moskva, 1890–2000: putevoditel' po sovremennoi arkhitekture* (Moscow, 2007)
Levoshko, S. S., ed., *Arkhitekturnoe nasledie russkogo zarubezh'ia: vtoraia polovina XIX–pervaia polovina XX v.* (St Petersburg, 2008)
Lisovskii, V. G., *'Natsional'nyi stil'' v arkhitekture Rossii* (Moscow, 2000)
—, *Leontii Benua i peterburgskaia shkola khudozhnikov-arkhitektorov* (St Petersburg, 2006)
—, *Ivan Fomin i metamorfozy russkoi neoklassiki* (St Petersburg, 2007)
—, *Sankt-Peterburg: Ocherki arkhitekturnoi istorii goroda*, 2 vols (St Petersburg, 2009)
Lissitzky, El, *Russia: An Architecture for World Revolution*, trans. Eric Dluhosch (Cambridge, 1970)
—, *Russland: Architektur für eine Weltrevolution* (Braunschweig, 1989)

Lissitzky-Küppers, Sophie, ed., *El Lissitzky: Life, Letters, Texts* (London, 1980)
Lissitzky-Küppers, Sophie, and Jen Lissitzky, eds, *Proun und Wolkenbügel: Schriften, Briefe, Dokumente* (Dresden, 1977)
Lodder, Christina, *Russian Constructivism* (New Haven, 1983)
Lovell, Stephen, *Summerfolk: A History of the Dacha, 1710–2000* (Ithaca, NY, 2003)
Lukhmanov, Nikolai, *Arkhitektura kluba* (Moscow, 1930)
Lukomskii, G. K., *Sovremennyi Peterburg: ocherk istorii vozniknoveniia i razvitiia klassicheskogo stroitel'stva (1900–1915 gg.)*, ed. B. M. Kirikov [1917] (St Petersburg, 2002)
—, *Staryi Peterburg: progulki po starinnym kvartalam stolitsy*, ed. B. M. Kirikov [1917] (St Petersburg, 2002)
Lynton, Norbert, *Tatlin's Tower: Monument to Revolution* (New Haven, 2009)
Macetti, Silvio, and Gert Gibbels, *Grosswohneinheiten* (Berlin, 1968)
Malinin, N., *Arkhitektura Moskvy 1989–2009: putevoditel'* (Moscow, 2009)
Masalina, N. V., 'Tserkov v Abramsteve (k istorii postroiki)', in *Iz istorii russkogo iskusstva vtoroi poloviny XIX – nachala XX veka* (Moscow, 1978), pp. 47–58
Meerovich, M. G., Evgeniia Konysheva, and Dmitrii Khmel'nitskii, *Kladbishche sotsgorodov: gradostroitel'naia politika v SSSR 1928–1932 gg.* (Moscow, 2011)
Miliutin, N. A., *Sotsgorod: The Problem of Building Socialist Cities*, trans. Arthur Sprague (Cambridge, MA, 1974)
Milner, John, *Vladimir Tatlin and the Russian Avant-garde* (New Haven, 1983)
Minkus, M., and N. A. Pekareva, *I. A. Fomin* (Moscow, 1953)
Nashchokina, M. V., *Sto arkhitektorov moskovskogo moderna: tvorcheskie portrety*, 2nd edn (Moscow, 2000)
—, *Moskovskii modern* (Moscow, 2003)
*Naum Gabo and the Competition for the Palace of Soviets, Moscow, 1931–1933*, exh. cat., Berlinische Galerie, Berlin (Berlin, 1993)
Neutatz, Dietmar, *Die Moskauer Metro: Von den ersten Plänen bis zur Grossbaustelle des Stalinismus (1897–1935)* (Cologne, 2001)
Nevzgodin, I. V., *Arkhitektura Novosibirska* (Novosibirsk, 2005)
Nikolaev, I. S., and N. P. Mel'nikov, *Vsemirnaia vystavka v Briussele, 1958: Arkhitektura, Konstruktivnye formy pavil'onov* (Moscow, 1963)
Nikolaeva, T. I., *Viktor Shreter, Ieronim Kitner* (St Petersburg, 2007)
Noever, Peter, *Tyrannei des Schönen: Architektur der Stalin-Zeit*, exh. cat., Österreichisches Museum für angewandte Kunst, Vienna (Munich, 1994)
*Nostalgia of Culture: Contemporary Soviet Visionary Architecture*, exh. cat., Architectural Association, London (London, 1988)
Novikov, Feliks, *Formula arkhitektury* (Moscow, 1984)
—, *Zodchie i zodchestva* (New York, 2002)
Novikov, Feliks, and Vladimir Belogolovskii, *Soviet Modernism, 1955–1985* (Yekaterinburg, 2010)
O'Connell, Lauren, 'A Rational, National Architecture: Viollet-le-Duc's Modest Proposal for Russia', *Journal of the Society of Architectural Historians*, LII/4 (1993), pp. 436–52
Olmo, Carlo Maria, and Alessandro De Magistris, eds, *Jakov Černichov: sowjetischer Architekt der Avantgarde* (Stuttgart, 1995)
Oltarzhevskii, V. K., *Stroitel'stvo vysotnykh zdanii v Moskve* (Moscow, 1953)
Opochinskaia, Anna, 'Iz istorii sovetskoi nauki ob arkhitekture (Vsesoiuznaia akademiia arkhitektury)', *Sovetskoe iskusstvoznanie*, XX (1986), pp. 270–300
Orel'skaia, Ol'ga, *Arkhitektura epokhi sovetskogo avangarda v Nizhnem Novgorode* (Nizhniy Novgorod, 2005)
Paperny, Vladimir, *Culture Two: Architecture in the Age of Stalin* (Cambridge, 2002)
Pare, Richard, and Jean-Louis Cohen, *The Lost Vanguard: Russian Modernist Architecture 1922–1932* (New York, 2007)
Paston, E. V., *Abramtsevo: iskusstvo i zhizn'* (Moscow, 2003)
Pekareva, N. A., *M.V. Posokhin: narodnyi arkhitektor SSSR* (Moscow, 1985)

Perloff, Nancy Lynn, and Brian Reed, eds, *Situating El Lissitzky: Vitebsk, Berlin, Moscow* (Los Angeles, 2003)
Posokhin, M. V., *Perspektivy razvitiia Moskvy* (Moscow, 1973)
—, *Towns for People* (Moscow, 1980)
—, *Dorogi zhizni: iz zapisok arkhitektora* (Moscow, 1995)
—, ed., *Mosproekt-2: arkhitektura, gradostroitel'stvo, restavratsiia* (Moscow, 1995)
Posokhin, M. V., and L. I. Kirillova, eds, *Sovetskaia arkhitektura za 50 let* (Moscow, 1968)
Post, Christiane, *Arbeiterklubs als neue Bauaufgabe der sowjetischen Avantgarde* (Berlin, 2004)
Punin, N. N., *O Tatline*, ed. V. Rakitin (Moscow, 1994)
Quilici, Vieri, *Architettura sovietica contemporanea* (Bologna, 1965)
—, *Il costruttivismo* (Rome, 1991)
Reid, Susan E., 'Destalinization and Taste, 1953–1963', *Journal of Design History*, x/2 (1997), pp. 177–201
—, 'Cold War in the Kitchen: Gender and the De-Stalinization of Consumer Taste in the Soviet Union under Khrushchev', *Slavic Review*, LXI/2 (2002), pp. 211–52
—, 'The Khrushchev Kitchen: Domesticating the Scientific-Technological Revolution', *Journal of Contemporary History*, XL/2 (2005), pp. 289–316
—, 'Who Will Beat Whom?: Soviet Popular Reception of the American National Exhibition in Moscow, 1959', *Kritika*, IX/4 (2008), pp. 855–904
Revzin, Grigorii, 'Mezhdu SSSR i Zapadom', *Proekt klassika*, XXV (2008), pp. 10–17
Riabushin, A. V., *Gumanizm sovetskoi arkhitektury* (Moscow, 1986)
—, 'Fenomen "bumazhnoi arkhitektury"', *Sovetskoe iskusstvoznanie*, XXV (1989), pp. 64–97
—, *Novye gorizonty arkhitekturnogo tvorchestva, 1970–1980-e gody* (Moscow, 1990)
Ritter, Katharina, Ekaterina Shapiro-Obermeir, Dietmar Steiner and Alexandra Wachter, *Soviet Modernism 1955–1991: Unknown History*, exh. cat., Architektur Zentrum Wien (Zurich, 2012)
Rozanov, E. G., V. V. Lazarev and N. I. A. Matveeva, eds, *Arkhitektura obshchestvennykh zdanii* (Moscow, 1980)
Rozanov, E. G., and V. I. Reviakin, *Arkhitektura muzeev V. I. Lenina* (Moscow, 1986)
Rüthers, Monica, *Moskau bauen von Lenin bis Chruščev: Öffentliche Räume zwischen Utopie, Terror und Alltag* (Vienna, 2007)
Rzhekhina, O. I., R. N. Blashkevich and R. G. Burova, *A. K. Burov* (Moscow, 1984)
Rzhekhina, O. I., and R. G. Burova, eds, *Andrei Konstantinovich Burov: pis'ma, dnevniki, besedy s aspirantami, suzhdeniia sovremennikov* (Moscow, 1980)
Salmond, Wendy R., *Arts and Crafts in Late Imperial Russia* (New York, 1996)
Samokhina, T., ed., *Iz istorii sozdania Soiuza sovetskikh arkhitektorov* (Moscow, 2007)
Schlögel, Karl, *Petersburg: Das Laboratorium der Moderne, 1909–1921* (Munich, 2002)
—, *Moscow* (London, 2005)
—, *Moscow, 1937* (Cambridge, 2012)
Semenov, V. N., *Blagoustroistvo gorodov* (Moscow, 1912)
Senkevitch, Anatole, 'Aspects of Spatial Form and Perceptual Psychology in the Doctrine of the Rationalist Movement in Soviet Architecture in the 1920s', *Via*, VI (1983), pp. 78–115
—, 'Albert Kahn's great Soviet venture as architect of the First Five Year Plan, 1929–1932', *Dimensions* (1996), pp. [34]–49
Shass, Iu., *Arkhitektura zhilogo doma. Poselkovoe stroitel'stvo 1918–1948 godov* (Moscow, 1951)
Shchusev, A. V., and L. E. Zagorskii, *Arkhitekturnaia organizatsiia goroda* (Moscow, 1934)
Shkvarikov, V. A., *Sovetskaia arkhitektura za XXX let RSFSR* (Moscow, 1950)
—, ed., *Moskva: Planirovka i zastroika goroda* (Moscow, 1958)
Shvidkovskii, D. O., 'Moscow Architecture in 1997: Trade, Power and the "New Russians"', *AA Files*, XXXIII (1997), pp. 3–12
—, *Russian Architecture and the West* (New Haven, 2007)
Soiuz arkhitektorov SSSR, *Sto let obshchestvennykh arkhitekturnykh organizatsii v SSSR, 1867–1967: Istoricheskaia spravka* (Moscow, 1967)

Sokolov, N. B., *A.V. Shchusev* (Moscow, 1952)
Starr, S. Frederick, 'The Revival and Schism of Russian Planning in Twentieth-century Russia', in *The City in Russian History*, ed. Michael F. Hamm (Lexington, KY, 1976), pp. 222–42
—, *Melnikov: Solo Architect in a Mass Society* (Princeton, 1978)
—, 'Visionary Town Planning during the Cultural Revolution', in *Cultural Revolution in Russia, 1928–1931*, ed. Sheila Fitzpatrick (Bloomington, IN, 1978), pp. 207–40
Strigalev, A. A., and I. V. Kokkinaki, eds, *Konstantin Stepanovich Mel'nikov: arkhitektura moei zhizni, tvorcheskaia kontseptsiia: tvorcheskaia praktika* (Moscow, 1985)
Sushkevich, I. G., ed., *Tvorcheskie voprosy sovetskoi arkhitektury* (Moscow, 1940)
Szech, Anna, ed., *Tatlin: New Art for a New World: International Symposium* (Ostfildern, 2013)
Tarkhanov, Alexei, and Sergei Kavtaradze, *Architecture of the Stalin Era* (New York, 1992)
*Tatlin: New Art for a New World*, exh. cat., Museum Tinguely, Basel (Basel, 2012)
Taut, Bruno, *Moskauer Briefe 1932–1933: Schönheit, Sachlichkeit und Sozialismus*, ed. Barbara Kreis (Berlin, 2006)
Teige, Karel, *Vyvoj sovetské architektury* (Prague, 1936)
Tolstoi, Vladimir Pavlovich, ed., *Vystavochnye ansambli SSSR, 1920–1930-e gody: materialy i dokumenty* (Moscow, 2006)
Tsapenko, M. P., *O realisticheskikh osnovakh sovetskoi arkhitektury* (Moscow, 1952)
Tupitsyn, Margarita, ed., *El Lissitzky: Beyond the 'Abstract Cabinet': Photography, Design, Collaboration* (New Haven, 1999)
Udovički-Selb, Danilo, 'Between Modernism and Socialist Realism: Soviet Architectural Culture under Stalin's Revolution from Above, 1928–1938', *Journal of the Society of Architectural Historians*, LXVIII/4 (2009), pp. 466–95
Velichenko, M. N., and G. A. Miroliubova, *Dvorets velikogo kniazia Vladimira Aleksandrovicha* (St Petersburg, 1997)
Viollet-le-Duc, Eugène-Emmanuel, *L'Art russe: ses origines, ses éléments constitutifs, son apogée, son avenir* (Paris, 1877)
*VKhUTEMAS: mysl' material'na*, exh. cat., A. V. Shchusev State Museum of Architecture, Moscow (Moscow, 2011)
Vöhringer, Margarete, *Avantgarde und Psychotechnik: Wissenschaft, Kunst und Technik der Wahrnehmungsexperimente in der frühen Sowjetunion* (Göttingen, 2007)
Volchok, Iu., ed., *Problemy izucheniia istorii sovetskoi arkhitektury* (Moscow, 1991)
Zhadova, L., ed., *Tatlin* (New York, 1988)
Zholtovskii, Ivan Vladislavovich, *Proekty i postroiki. Vstup. stat'ia i podbor illiustratsii G. D. Oshchepkova* (Moscow, 1955)
Ziuskevich, O. M., L. I. Ivanova-Veen, and T. V. Lysova, *Ot VKhUTEMASa k MARKhI, 1920–1936*, exh. cat., Muzei MARKhI (Moscow, 2005)
Zueva, P. P., and I. V. Shishkina, *Torgovye zdaniia Moskvy sovetskogo perioda 1920–1980* (Moscow, 2006)
Zygas, K. Paul, *Form follows Form: Source Imagery of Constructivist Architecture, 1917–1925* (Ann Arbor, 1981)

# Acknowledgements

This book has been a long time in the making. Vivian Constantinopoulos at Reaktion Books deserves first recognition for initiating the Modern Architectures in History series and patiently awaiting the completion of this volume. I thank Jean-Louis Cohen in particular for inspiring and supporting my interest in Russian and Soviet architecture, for his thoughtful comments on an early draft of this text and for suggesting that the challenge of writing this book would be a worthwhile undertaking.

Grants and fellowships from numerous organizations made research and writing possible. Through the generous support of Columbia University, I was able to make several trips to Russia to collect images and primary documents. A fellowship from the National Endowment for the Humanities allowed me to participate in a Summer Research Institute hosted by Edward Kasinec and Robert Davis at the Slavic and Baltic Division of the New York Public Library, where I was able to make use of the Library's unparalleled collection of Russian and Soviet visual resources. Likewise, a summer residency at the Canadian Centre for Architecture enriched my understanding of the production of Russian and Soviet architects. A postdoctoral fellowship from the American Council of Learned Societies facilitated the writing of major portions of this manuscript. The University of Edinburgh, my home institution, provided generous support for image research in Russia and assistance for illustrations. I also thank the Society of Architectural Historians of Great Britain for a publication award that subsidized image costs.

Many individuals deserve thanks for their help at various stages of this book's production. The staff of Columbia University's Media Center for Art History facilitated my work on this project. The late Caleb Smith provided key resources and equipment in the collection of visual documents. Gabriel Rodriguez and Emily Shaw provided timely technical assistance. This project benefited from conversations with many other colleagues at Columbia as well: Barry Bergdoll, Vittoria Di Palma and Gwendolyn Wright were generous and helpful in the early stages of this project. At the University of Edinburgh, my colleagues in architectural history, in particular Alex Bremner and Iain Boyd Whyte, have provided valuable support for the completion of this book.

I am also indebted to many colleagues who shared their time to discuss the long history of Russia's architecture. In Russia, many architects, historians and photographers opened doors for me, provided advice and supplied crucial visual material for this book: Olga Alexeyenko, Eugene Asse, Mikhail Belov, Alexander Brodsky, Anna Bronovitskaia, Natalia Dushkina, Alexander Ignatiev, Nikolai Malinin, Nadia Nilina, Yuri Palmin, Igor Palmin, Vladimir Sedov, Boris Uborevich-Borovsky. Colleagues outside of Russia have provided equally valuable conversations and assistance: Edward Denison, Juliet Koss, Michael Kunichika, Alessandra Latour, Branko Mitrović, Richard Pare, Susan E. Reid. James D. Graham and Daria Bocharnikova deserve special thanks for offering timely and insightful comments on an early version of this manuscript. I am also grateful to Laura Bowie for her assistance in editing the final version of this text.

This project could not have been completed without the support of my family. Patricia Anderson helped this project in many ways, not least though accompanying me to St Petersburg on my first trip to Russia and joining me on a journey through Ukraine. Patrick Anderson and the late Carla Anderson offered unending encouragement. Christine and

Michael Lynch have contributed in more ways than they know: from providing a home base in the U.S. from which much of the final research for this book was conducted, to hosting my family while I travelled to Russia. I am continually grateful for their generosity. Greta and Tara deserve to be thanked last because their contribution has been the greatest. This book is far older than Greta, but I can't imagine how it would have been completed without the joy she brings us. Finally, I thank Tara, whose support, trust and reassurance have been invaluable, and to whom this book is dedicated.

# Photo Acknowledgements

The author and publishers wish to express their thanks to the below sources of illustrative material and/or permission to reproduce it.

© Olga Alexeyenko: pp. 127, 128; © Richard Anderson: pp. 14, 18, 20, 22, 31, 35, 37, 40, 46, 50, 51, 53 (top), 68 (top), 86, 119 (top), 122 (top and bottom), 129, 130, 135, 139, 140, 141, 143, 144, 160, 161, 163, 164, 165, 172 (top and bottom), 176, 193, 202, 205 (top), 207, 208, 209, 210, 211 (bottom), 227 (top), 230 (top), 233, 240 (bottom), 242, 255 (top), 257 (bottom), 265, 266 (top and bottom), 268, 271, 272, 273 (top), 276 (top), 300, 301, 302, 303 (top), 304, 307, 308 (top), 309; courtesy Richard Anderson: pp. 6, 89, 100, 121, 123, 133, 137, 138, 146, 159, 167 (top), 167 (bottom), 168, 170, 177 (top), 179, 182, 205 (bottom), 211 (top), 221 (top), 227 (bottom), 229 (top), 229 (bottom), 234 (bottom), 235, 236, 239 (top), 239 (bottom), 241, 244, 252, 255 (bottom), 257 (top), 258, 259, 260, 262, 263 (top), 264, 267, 273 (bottom), 275 (bottom), 278, 280, 299; courtesy Eugene Asse: p. 270; courtesy Mikhail Belov/ © Mikhail Belov and Max Kharitonov: p. 287; courtesy Merrill C. Berman Collection: p. 74; © Edward Denison: p. 43 (top); courtesy Ronald Feldman Fine Arts/ © Alexander Brodsky and Ilia Utkin: p. 288; © Mikhail Filippov: p. 303 (bottom); courtesy Fondation Le Corbusier/ © FLC /ADAGP, Paris, and DACS, London, 2015: p. 148; courtesy gta Archiv/ ETH Zürich: p. 114; courtesy Museum of History of Architecture of Siberia: p. 169; courtesy the Museum of Moscow: pp. 21, 26, 38, 44, 82; courtesy the New York Public Library: pp. 43 (bottom), 53 (bottom), 54 (left); © Igor Palmin: pp. 48, 83, 111, 174, 295; © Yuri Palmin: p. 308 (bottom); © Richard Pare: p. 171; courtesy private collection: pp. 8, 23, 36, 57 (bottom), 60, 62, 65, 66, 68 (bottom), 72, 84 (top), 84 (bottom), 85, 88, 91, 93, 97, 98, 99, 101, 103, 104, 106, 109, 119 (bottom), 120, 124, 131 (bottom), 131 (top), 134, 136, 142, 173, 177 (bottom), 180, 187, 189, 191, 195 (top), 195 (bottom), 201, 206, 214,. 221 (bottom), 224, 237, 240 (top), 243, 253, 263 (bottom), 274, 275 (top), 276 (bottom), 292, 293, 294, 297; courtesy Russian State Library: pp. 11, 27, 29, 34, 49, 52, 54 (right), 57 (top), 59, 63, 69, 71, 116, 118, 157, 198 (top and bottom), 225, 234 (top); courtesy Schusev State Museum of Architecture: pp. 81, 90, 94, 126, 154, 190, 192, 196, 212, 230 (bottom), 232, 261; courtesy State Tretyakov Gallery: pp. 156, 223; courtesy Boris Uborevich-Borovskii: p. 296; courtesy Zimmerli Art Museum/ copyright Eric Bulatov: p. 246.

# Index

Page numbers in *italic* indicate illustrations